# English G 21

## D4

Grundausgabe
für differenzierende
Schulformen

Cornelsen

# English G 21 • Band D 4 • Grundausgabe


*Im Auftrag des Verlages herausgegeben von*
Prof. Hellmut Schwarz, Mannheim

*Erarbeitet von*
Susan Abbey, Nenagh, Irland
Barbara Derkow Disselbeck, Köln
Allen J. Woppert, Berlin
*sowie* Laurence Harger, Wellington, Neuseeland

*unter Mitarbeit von*
Wolfgang Biederstädt, Köln
Joachim Blombach, Herford
David Christie, Banbury, England
Helmut Dengler, Limbach
Claire Lamsdale, Bristol, England
Martina Schroeder, Stedtlingen
Jennifer Seidl, München
Udo Wagner, Voerde
Herbert Willms, Herford
*sowie* Ulrike Flach, Köln; Silke Lehmacher, Monheim

*in Zusammenarbeit mit der Englischredaktion*
Dr. Christiane Kallenbach (Projektleitung);
Dr. Eva Grabowski (verantwortliche Redakteurin);
Susanne Bennetreu (Bildredaktion); Stefanie Bayer;
Britta Bensmann; Dr. Philip Devlin; Gwendolyn Düwel;
Cornelia Frisse; Bonnie S. Glänzer; Mara Leibowitz;
Anne Linder; Nathalie Schwering; Kathrin Spiegelberg;
Uwe Tröger; Klaus G. Unger *sowie* Olivia Gruver

*Beratende Mitwirkung*
Walter Droste, Spenge; Manuela Feierabend-Vonhausen,
Rossfeld; Birgit Heinemann, Neu Wulmstorf;
Ivette Huxol, Wilkau-Haßlau; Bernd Jost, Salzbergen;
Heike Jurenz, Neukirch/Lausitz; Heike Meisner,
Bad Klosterlausnitz; Gabriele Rotter, Wiesbaden;
Karl Starkebaum, Diekholzen

*Illustrationen*
Silke Bachmann, Hamburg; Roland Beier, Berlin;
Stéphane Gamain/NB Illustration, London;
Jörn Hennig, Berlin

*Layoutkonzept*
Aksinia Raphael; Korinna Wilkes

*Technische Umsetzung*
Aksinia Raphael; Korinna Wilkes;
Stephan Hilleckenbach; Rainer Bachmaier

*Umschlaggestaltung*
Klein & Halm Grafikdesign, Berlin



**www.cornelsen.de**
**www.EnglishG.de**





Druck: Mohn Media Mohndruck, Gütersloh

1. Auflage, 5. Druck 2015
broschiert
978-3-06-031322-8

1. Auflage, 4. Druck 2016
gebunden
978-3-06-031374-7

PEFC zertifiziert
Dieses Produkt stammt aus nachhaltig bewirtschafteten Wäldern und kontrollierten Quellen.
www.pefc.de
PEFC/04-31-1033

## Dein Englischbuch enthält folgende Teile:

| | |
|---|---|
| **Introduction** | Hier lernst du die jungen Leute von Band 4 kennen. |
| **Units** | die fünf Kapitel des Buches |
| **Getting ready for a test** | Hier kannst du dich gezielt auf einen Test vorbereiten. |
| **EXTRA: Text File** | viele interessante Texte zum Lesen (passend zu den Units) |
| **Skills File (SF)** | Beschreibung wichtiger Lern- und Arbeitstechniken |
| **Grammar File (GF)** | Zusammenfassung der Grammatik jeder Unit |
| **Vocabulary** | Wörterverzeichnis zum Lernen der neuen Wörter jeder Unit |
| **Dictionary** | alphabetische Wörterverzeichnisse zum Nachschlagen |

### Die Units bestehen aus diesen Teilen:

| | |
|---|---|
| **Lead-in** | Einstieg in das neue Thema |
| **A-Section** | neuer Lernstoff mit vielen Aktivitäten und **Background File** |
| **Practice** | Übungen |
| **Text** | eine spannende oder lustige Geschichte |
| **How am I doing?** | Hier kannst du dein Wissen und Können überprüfen. |

### In den Units findest du diese Überschriften und Symbole:

| | |
|---|---|
| **Looking at language** | Hier sammelst du Beispiele und entdeckst Regeln. |
| **STUDY SKILLS** | Einführung in Lern- und Arbeitstechniken |
| **Dossier** | Schöne und wichtige Arbeiten kannst du in einer Mappe sammeln. |
| **All about ...** | Hier übst du Wortschatz zum Thema der Unit. |
| **READING COURSE** | Lesekurs in vier Kapiteln mit Hilfen zum Lesen von Texten |
| **EVERYDAY ENGLISH** | Übungen zum Bewältigen wichtiger Alltagssituationen |
| **MEDIATION** | Hier vermittelst du zwischen zwei Sprachen. |
| **LISTENING** | Aufgaben zu Hörtexten auf der CD |
| **Now you** | Hier sprichst und schreibst du über dich selbst. |
| **REVISION** | Übungen zur Wiederholung |
| **WORDS** | Übungen zu Wortfamilien, Wortfeldern und Wortverbindungen |
| **Extra** | Zusätzliche Aktivitäten und Übungen |
| | Partnerarbeit / Gruppenarbeit |
| | nur auf CD / auf CD und im Schülerbuch |
| > | Textaufgaben |
| ○ ● | leichtere Übungen / schwierigere Übungen |
| //○ //● | parallele Übungen auf zwei Niveaus |
| more help | Hier findest du zusätzliche Hilfen für das Lösen einer Aufgabe. |

# Inhalt

# Welcome to the United States of America

**1 The Grand Canyon**

**a)** *Imagine you are the girl in the photo. Describe what you can see.*

The view is amazing/beautiful/fantastic/...

It looks exciting/windy/dangerous/quiet/hot/... there.

**b)** **Extra** *Imagine what the girl is saying.*

I don't like this place. It's really scary!

...

This is so exciting!

**2 Where is it?**

**a)** *Where is the Grand Canyon? Look at the map of the US on the front inside cover and find out.*

It's in the east/west/...

It's in the state of ...

**b)** *What other places in the US do you know? What can you say about those places?*

► *WB 1 (p. 2)* • **Text File 1** *(pp. 116–117)*

## 1 Four summer holidays

*Four young people visited the Grand Canyon in their summer holidays. On pp. 8–11 you can read about their trips. Quickly scan the four pages and find the answers to these questions.*

*Tip: Look first at the headings, photos and maps.*

1. What are the names of the four people?
2. Where are they from? (Look at the maps.)
3. Who lives closest to the Grand Canyon?
4. Who camped at the Grand Canyon?
5. Who went by car/bus/plane?
6. Who wrote about their trip for school?

▸ *SF Scanning (p. 142)*

**Extra Americana ★ ★ ★**

**The Grand Canyon**
In Arizona there's a place where the Colorado River cuts deep into the rocks. This is the Grand Canyon. It's 446 km long, between 6 to 24 km wide and over 1 km deep. It became a national park in 1919.

## 2 It's awesome!

**Caitlin's blog**

About me

Name:
Caitlin

Birthday:
July 9

Hometown:
New York,
New York

**August 26**

Hi guys – I'm back from my summer vacation. My parents always go to a national park, and this year it was the Grand Canyon. We went by car. It's 2500 miles away from NYC. The drive took three and a half days and we were in three time zones!
The Grand Canyon is awesome! We camped at two different places and went on day trips in the car or hiked from there.

**Comments** ➔ *On 8/27 Ruth wrote*

Hi Cait, sounds like an awesome trip!
Good to have you back.
CU Ruth

▷ *How far is the Grand Canyon from Caitlin's home in kilometres? (1 mile = 1.6 kilometres)*

A *1000 km* B *2000 km* C *4000 km*

▸ *SF Learning new words (p. 136)*

▷ *Go to the map on the front inside cover. When it's 11.00 am in New York, what time is it in Arizona?*

## 3 A trip with a youth group

Shorecliffs Middle School
San Clemente, California

Student's name: *Luis Morales*

Grade: *8*

Date: *September 3*

*My summer vacation*

*This summer I was very lucky. I was able to go to Grand Canyon National Park with the youth group from my church. Before we went, we raised money for the trip. And we were very good at it. We washed cars, cut the grass, cleaned pools, and we had a bake sale.*

*The bus ride took about nine hours with a short lunch break. We sang songs in Spanish and English all the time – till the driver said that we had to stop!*

*We stayed at the canyon for three days. We went on long hikes. At night we slept in tents – that was new for me – and cooked our own meals. That was really great.*

*The park rangers told us a lot about the canyon. One of the rangers was a Native American. She told us about the Native Americans who still live in the canyon.*

> *How did Luis get the money for his trip? Why do you think the group sang songs in English and Spanish?*

## 4 Extra Now you

***a)*** *What kinds of things could kids at your school do to raise money?*

***b)*** *If your class had € 500, what would you do?*

**Extra Americana ★ ★ ★**

**Park Rangers**
US park rangers work in national parks and at famous monuments. In the Grand Canyon, it's their job to look after the park and the animals. They also tell visitors about the natural and human history of the area.

## 5 On the road with Dad

**Hermann High School,**
**Hermann, Missouri**

Name: Jake Kruger, 14

Grade: 9

MY ROAD DIARY

August 7 – Dad and I said goodbye to Mom at the farm and began our trip from Missouri to the Grand Canyon along Route 66. We traveled west – into Kansas and Oklahoma. Dad has always dreamed about this trip. He loves the old TV series and he sings the Route 66 song all the time. It's really sad!

He has already bought some souvenirs of Route 66 – a license plate for the car and a key ring. Tonight we're at a motel outside Tulsa.

August 8 – Another day in the car. Boring! Left Oklahoma and drove into Texas. Stopped in a small town in New Mexico. Dad has added a cap to his souvenirs.

August 9 – Went to Santa Rosa and the Route 66 Auto Museum. More cars! In Arizona now. It's very hot. Today was a very long day.

August 10 – Arrived at the Grand Canyon at last. We left the car at our motel and went to look across the canyon. It's really GRAND! When it got cooler, we walked down into the canyon. We saw a condor! What a bird – 9 feet from wing to wing – wow! I forgive Dad for all the hours in the car!

Today was a day I will never forget!

**Extra Americana ★ ★ ★**

**Route 66**

In the US, Route 66 is a modern legend. People often call it the Mother Road because it was one of the first roads that linked the Midwest (Chicago) to the west coast (Los Angeles). It opened in 1926 and was 3940 km long.

The original road closed in 1985. Parts of it, called Historic Route 66, still exist in Arizona and New Mexico.

1 *Which of these souvenirs did Jake's dad buy?*

2 *What states did the Krugers drive through? (Find the states on the map on the front inside cover.)*

3 *'9 feet from wing to wing' – what's that in metres? (1 foot = 0.3 m)*

## 6 What a fantastic trip!

*Look at the photos. What did Madison do in her summer holidays?*

### My summer vacation

**Presentation by:**

Madison Young (14),
Grade 9
Martin Luther King High School,
Atlanta, Georgia

**The journey**

Atlanta – Las Vegas = 2000 miles
Flight time = 4.5 hours
Drive Vegas – Canyon = 3.5 hours

### The Bellagio Hotel, Las Vegas

### Grand Canyon Skywalk

### Our mule train

## 7 Madison's trip

*Read the questions below. Listen to the CD and answer the questions.*

1. How long was Madison's vacation?
   A a week B 2 weeks C 3 weeks
2. What did Madison think was more exciting?
   A Las Vegas B the Grand Canyon
3. What was 'the big adventure'?
   A The Bellagio Hotel B the mule train
   C the skywalk

► SF Listening (p. 141)

## 8 Extra Now you

*Think of a place in the US that you would like to visit. (Look at the map on the front inside cover of this book for ideas. You can also go to www.EnglishG.de.)*
*Find out where it is, what you can see and do there.*
*Make a page about your place for your DOSSIER.*

► WB 2–8 (pp. 3–5) • Text File 2 (pp. 118–119)

# New York, New York

A The Manhattan skyline with the Empire State Building in the middle.

## 1 New York sights

***a)*** *Find the sights on the map of Manhattan.*
It's near ... / It's on an island.
It's on Fifth Avenue/Broadway/...

***b)*** *Which sight would you like to visit first?*

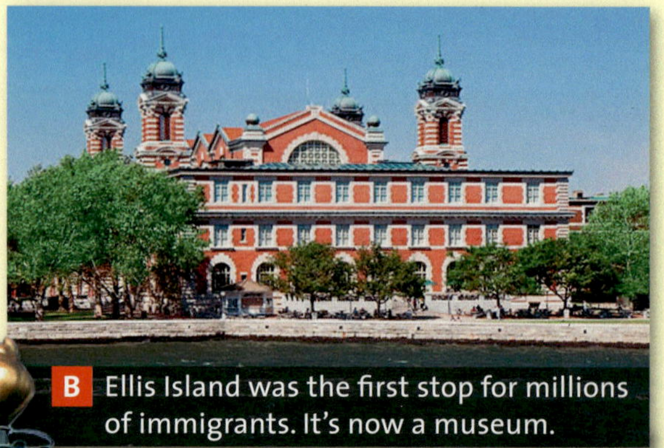

B Ellis Island was the first stop for millions of immigrants. It's now a museum.

## 2 Planning a sightseeing trip

***a)*** *Listen to Caitlin and Ruth. In what order do they talk about the sights (A–G)?*

***b)*** *Which five sights are on their final list? Listen again if you need to.*

***c)*** *Are these sentences right or wrong? Listen and check your answers.*

1 Ruth's cousin is coming to New York.
2 You go to Ellis Island and the Statue of Liberty by boat.
3 Ruth thinks Central Park is boring.
4 Both girls love shopping.
5 Caitlin loves the Brooklyn Bridge.
6 They want to take Ryan to a deli.

► *P 1 (p. 20) • WB 1–2 (p. 6) • SF Listening (p. 141)*

C Tourists love the Brooklyn Bridge.

D The Statue of Liberty stands on Liberty Island in New York Harbor.

E Skating in Central Park in the heart of Manhattan.

F Fifth Avenue is famous for shopping!

G Times Square at night

The five boroughs of New York

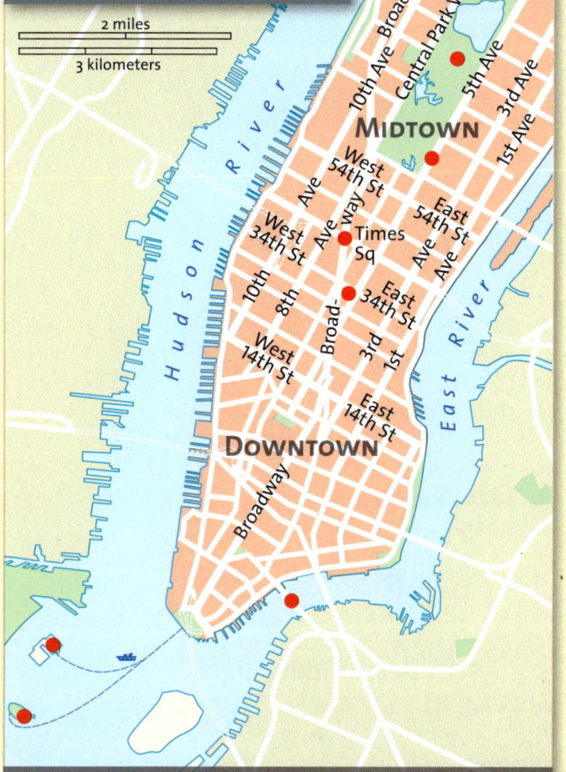


The streets go from west to east. They usually have numbers. The avenues go from north to south. Some have names, others have numbers too.

# All about ... getting around an American city

## 1 Understanding directions

*Follow the woman's directions on the map. Choose the correct German translations for the phrases **1–4**.*

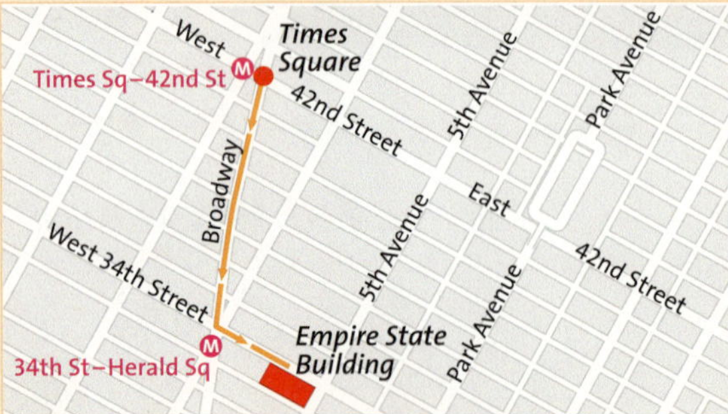

1 *downtown* Ⓐ unter der Stadt Ⓑ im Zentrum

2 *eight blocks* Ⓐ das achte Haus Ⓑ acht Straßen weiter

3 *34th and Broadway* Ⓐ Broadway, Ecke 34. Straße Ⓑ 34. Straße oder Broadway

4 *the subway* Ⓐ die U-Bahn Ⓑ die Unterführung

## 2 Understanding signs

***a)*** *What do you think the signs mean? Discuss with your partner.*

***b)*** *Guess where you can find each of these signs.*

on the street • on the pavement • outside a shop • in a hospital • ...

1

2

4

3

5

6

## 3 American and British English

*Copy and complete the chart below.*

| American English (AE) | German | British English (BE) |
| --- | --- | --- |
| subway | U-Bahn | ... |
| downtown | | |
| sidewalk | | |
| line | | |
| cellphone | | |

U-Bahn • Warteschlange • Handy • Bürgersteig • Stadtzentrum

city centre • pavement • queue • underground • mobile phone

► P 2–3 (p. 20–21) • WB 3–4 (p. 7)

## 4 Travelling is great

'How was the trip?' Caitlin asked Ryan, her cousin from Ireland.

'Great,' said Ryan. 'Travelling is always great. Flying into New York was really special. But getting up at 4 o'clock this morning was hard!'

'And then there's the time difference between Ireland and New York,' said Caitlin.

'That's right,' said Ryan. 'In Ireland we're five hours later. It's time to go to bed in Ireland now!'

'Well, don't go to bed now. You'll wake up in the middle of the night and think it's morning. – I know. Let's walk over to the fire station and say hi to Dad.'

'Good idea!' said Ryan. He wanted to know all about his uncle's job as a New York firefighter.

> *When it's 5 o'clock pm in New York, what time is it in Ireland?*

## 5 I love being a firefighter

My dad and grandpa were both firefighters. And I can't imagine doing anything else. I love being a firefighter. Yes, it's hard work. And nobody likes getting up in the middle of the night. But it feels good when you put out a fire and maybe save somebody's life.

We work 15-hour shifts, but we spend a lot of that time at the station. I enjoy spending time at the fire station with the men and women on my shift. We don't just work together – we live together. Some of the guys are great cooks. There was this one guy, Ricardo. He made the best chili con carne. Good old Ricardo. He's not with us any more – he died on 9/11.

> *What are the hard things about being a firefighter? What are the good things?*

**Looking at language**

***a)*** Suche alle Sätze mit *-ing*-Formen in 4 und 5 und schreibe sie auf.
*Travelling is ...*

***b)*** Nach welchen Verben in 5 steht eine *-ing*-Form?

▸ GF 1a–b: Gerund (p. 154) • P 4–7 (pp. 21–22) • WB 5–7 (pp. 8–9)

**Extra Americana ★ ★ ★**

### 9/11 and Ground Zero

On September 11th (9/11), 2001, nineteen hijackers took over four US planes. They flew two of them into the Twin Towers of the World Trade Center in downtown Manhattan. Both towers burned and collapsed. Almost 3000 people died, 343 of them were firefighters.

The place where the Towers stood is now called Ground Zero. Every year, on 9/11 the 'Tribute in Light' takes place and people remember the men and women who died there.

## 6 At the deli

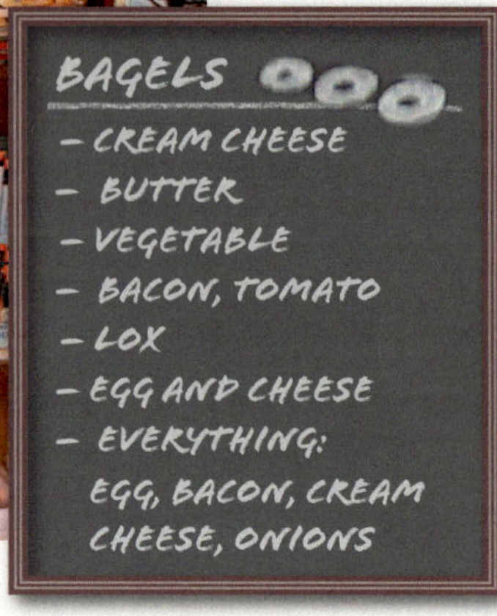


The next day Caitlin and Ryan met Ruth for a late breakfast at her local deli.

'Quick,' said Ruth. 'If you grab that table over there, I'll order. What would you like?'

'A bagel and lox for me, please,' said Caitlin. 'And a water. What about you, Ryan?'

'A small coffee for me, please. And I'll have a bagel too. What's lox?' Ryan asked.

'Salmon – in Yiddish,' explained Ruth.

'Oh,' said Ryan, 'I don't really like fish. The bagel with everything looks good. Can I have it without the onions?'

'No problem,' said Ruth. She went to order.

'Hi, Aaron. Two regular waters, a small coffee and three bagels, please.'

'Hi, Ruthy. What would you like on your bagels?'

'Two with lox, and one with everything, but without onions.'

'Sure, Ruthy. No onions on the bagel with everything. Is this for here or to go?'

'For here,' said Ruth.

'Great. I'll bring the bagels.'

Five minutes later they had their food.

'Wow,' said Ryan. 'You can't get bagels like this in Ireland. This is a great start to our day out in New York. What's next on your list?'

> *What was the deli like? (big/small, busy/empty, unfriendly/friendly, good/bad food, ...)*

**Extra Americana ★ ★ ★**

**Delis and bagels**

New Yorkers often eat bagels for breakfast. They run into a deli (the name comes from the German *Delikatessen*) on their way to work and grab a bagel and coffee to go.

Jewish immigrants brought the bagel with them from Europe in the 19th century. It's like a bread roll with a hole in it.

▸ *P 8 (p. 22) • P 9–10 (p. 23) • WB 8 (p. 9)*

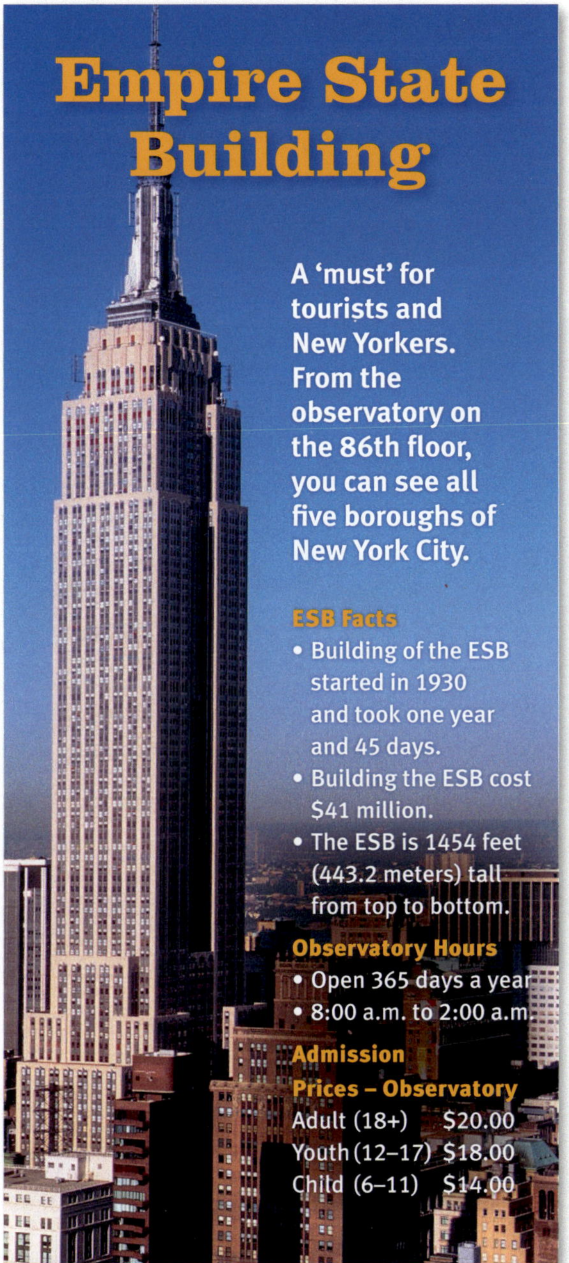

► *P 13–14 (pp. 24–25)* • *WB 11–13 (pp. 11–12)* •
**Text File 3** *(pp. 120–121)*

## 7 On top of the world

'Well, it's a perfect day for the Empire State Building,' Caitlin said. 'Come on, the elevators are over there.'

'Can we take the stairs?' asked Ryan. 'I'm not very good at going in lifts.'

'You want to walk up 86 floors?' Ruth said. 'Come on, Ryan. You'll be OK.'

Ryan was OK in the end. He didn't enjoy going up in the lift. But he closed his eyes and in only a minute they were on the 86th floor.

The views from the top were fantastic. They could see 45 miles.

'I'm so glad that I came up,' said Ryan. 'This is brilliant.'

'Are you scared of going down again?' asked Ruth.

'Yes!' said Ryan. 'Of course. But what can I do?'

*1 Find the different words that Ruth and Ryan use for 'Aufzug'.*
*2 What have these numbers got to do with the ESB? 365 – 1454 – 86 – 41*

► *GF 1c: Gerund after prepositions (p. 155)* • *P 11–12 (p. 24)* • *WB 9–10 (p. 10)*

## 8 Extra SONG A heart in New York

New York
To that tall skyline I come
flying in from London
To your door

New York
Lookin' down on Central Park
Where they say you should not wander
After dark

New York
Like a scene from all those movies
But you're real enough to me
But there's a heart
A heart that lives in New York

*by Benny Gallagher and Graham Lyle*

*Does the singer love or hate New York? Which of the photos in the unit go with the song?*

## Extra Background File A COUNTRY OF IMMIGRANTS

★ ★ ★

The US is a country of immigrants. In a population of 300 million, only four million are Native Americans – all the rest have their roots in other countries around the world.

### A BETTER LIFE

★ Many immigrants came to America because in their own countries they were not free to practise their religion or take part in politics. Other immigrants came because they were poor. They hoped for a better life in America.

### ARRIVING AT ELLIS ISLAND

★ For many immigrants Ellis Island was their first stop. Ellis Island Immigration Station opened in 1892.

The immigrants were all tired when they arrived on Ellis Island after weeks on the open sea. Many of them were children.

The immigrants were nervous. 'Will I be allowed into America? Will all my family be allowed in? What will happen to us after this?'

### ELLIS ISLAND TODAY

★ More than 12 million people went through Ellis Island. Most of them came between 1892 and 1924. The Ellis Island Immigration Station closed in 1954 and is now a museum.

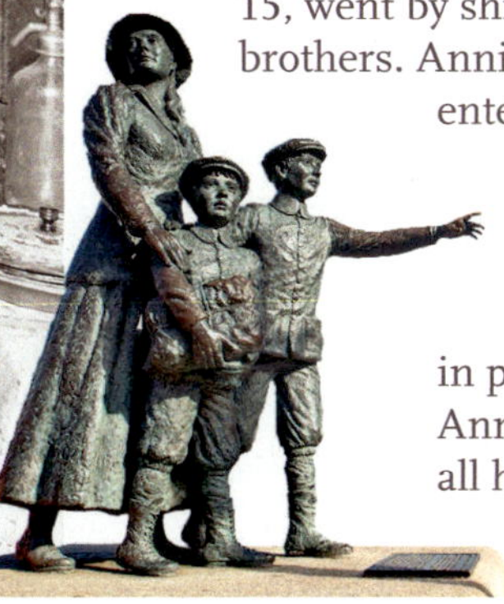

## Annie Moore

★ Annie Moore's parents moved to America in 1891, but they left Annie in Ireland with her two younger brothers. A year later Annie's parents sent money for tickets and Annie, who was only 15, went by ship to New York with her brothers. Annie was the first person who entered Ellis Island when it opened on January 1st 1892. Life was hard for immigrants in those days. They often started their life in America in poor flats in New York City. Annie Moore lived in New York all her life. She didn't make a lot of money. She was only 47 when she died.

*Look at all the photos on pp. 18–19. How do you think Annie felt:*
- *when her parents left her in Ireland?*
- *on the ship with her brothers?*
- *when she arrived at Ellis Island?*
- *when she saw her parents again in New York?*

### Immigration then and now

In 1900 13.6 % of the US population was born outside the US. The three biggest groups were from:

Germany 2.66 million
Ireland 1.62 million
Canada 1.18 million

In 2000 10.8 % of the US population was born outside the US. The three biggest groups were from:

Mexico 9.18 million
China 1.52 million
The Philippines 1.37 million

*Which of the five continents did the immigrants come from in 1900? And in 2000?*

Europe • Asia • America • Africa • Australia

### 1 Visit Ellis Island

*Go to www.ellisisland.org. Put your surname into the search engine there. Find out if someone with your name went through Ellis Island.*

### 2 Immigration and you

*Has anybody you know ever gone to live in another country? Check with your parents or grandparents. Try and find out:*
- What country did they leave?
- What country did they go to?
- When did they go?
- What was their journey like?

▸ WB 14 (p. 13) • **Text File 4** (p. 122)

## 1 The five boroughs of New York

*There are five New York boroughs. Manhattan is one of them. The other four are A–D on the map.*

***a)*** *Partner B: Go to p. 103.*
*Partner A: Read out boxes **1** and **2** to your partner. Does your partner know the answers?*

**1** Queens is the biggest New York borough. John F. Kennedy Airport is in Queens. Is Queens A, B, C or D?

**2** Brooklyn is south of Manhattan. To get from Manhattan to Brooklyn you can go over the Brooklyn Bridge to cross the East River. Is Brooklyn A, B, C or D?

***b)*** *Now listen to your partner. Answer the questions.*

*The answers: Queens is B, Brooklyn is C.*

## 2 LISTENING Different words

***a)*** *Write down the names of the things **1–11**. Use the British English (BE) words in the green box.*

1 rucksack
2 …

biscuit • chips • crisps • mobile phone • pavement • rubber • rubbish • rucksack • timetable • trousers • underground

***b)*** *Listen to the two dialogues. The people use the American English (AE) words for **1–11**. They are all in the yellow box. Match the AE words to the BE words.*

⁺backpack • cellphone • ⁺cookie • ⁺eraser • ⁺French fries • ⁺garbage • ⁺pants • ⁺potato chips • ⁺schedule • sidewalk • subway

## 3 WORDS Verbs and nouns that go together

*a)* ◯ *Choose one verb from the box that goes with with all the words in one group.*

catch • take • visit • wait

1 ... a bus, the underground, a photo = *take*
2 ... a train, a cold, a thief
3 ... at the bus stop, in a queue, for a friend
4 ... a museum, a city, an aunt

*b) Find at least one more word that goes with each of these verbs.*

1 arrive at *a station, ...*
2 eat at *a deli, ...*
3 ride *a bike, ...*
4 walk *a mile, ...*

*c)* 👥 *Compare with a partner.*

## 4 //◯ WORDS Jobs in the city

▸ D p. 106

*What are the jobs?*

1 a person who puts fires out
2 a person who catches thieves
3 a person who helps you in a shop
4 a person who puts on the music at the disco
5 a person in an ambulance who helps people who are hurt
6 a person at a national park who gives people information
7 a person who cuts your hair
8 a person who helps people who are ill

DJ • doctor • firefighter • +hairdresser • paramedic • park ranger • policeman • shop assistant

## 5 //◯ Being a paramedic is great (Gerund)

▸ D p. 106

*a) Complete the interview with the New York paramedic. Use the -ing-forms in the boxes.*

being • doing • meeting • saving

**What are the best things about your job?**
*Saving* people's lives. That's the best thing.
... part of a great team is important too.
... new people every day. I really enjoy that.
... different things every day. It's really interesting.

driving • getting • waiting • working

**What are the worst things about your job?**
... up in the middle of the night. I hate that.
... long shifts is hard.
... for a call. That can be very boring.
... very fast through the city can be dangerous.

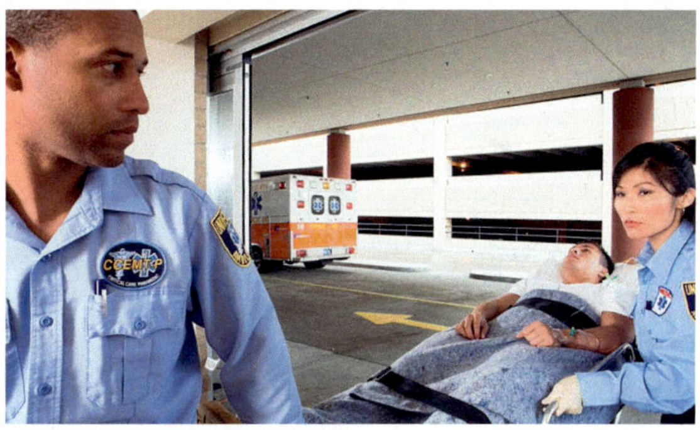

*b)* **Extra** ● 👥 *Choose a job. What's the best thing and the worst thing about it? Can your partner guess the job?*

Meeting people is the best thing about it. Washing other people's hair is the worst thing.

Oh, that's a ...

## 6 //O What does Caitlin like doing? (Gerund) ▸ D p. 106

*Finish these sentences. Use the -ing-forms in the box.*

cooking • driving • going • hearing • meeting • sleeping • visiting

1 Caitlin likes *going* on vacation with her family every summer.
2 She loves ... in a tent and ... meals outside.
3 But she doesn't like ... for days in the car to get there.
4 She really enjoyed ... the Grand Canyon this summer.
5 She also enjoyed ... her Irish cousin Ryan for the first time.
6 Ryan loved ... about his uncle's job as a firefighter.

## 7 I like watching ... (Gerund)

**a)** O *Finish these sentences. Use the -ing-forms of the verbs in the box.*

1 (+) I like ...
2 (++) I love ...
3 (–) I don't like ...
4 (– –) I hate ...

argue with my parents • camp • cut grass • clean my room • cook • eat spicy food • hike • do tests • have sleepovers • go on holiday • hang out with friends • sleep in a tent • spend time at home • play football • get up late • ...

**b)** *Tell your partner what you like/don't like. Listen to his or her ideas. Take notes.*

A: I love/like ... – What about you?
B: Oh no, I hate it. / Yes, I like it too. / It's OK.

| | Markus | me |
|---|---|---|
| camping | + | – |
| swimming | ++ | + |
| eating spicy food | – | + |

**c)** *Tell the class about your partner.*

Markus likes camping.
He loves ...
He doesn't like eating spicy food.
He hates ...

**d)** **Extra** *Write about your partner.*

## 8 WORDS Ordering food

**a)** *Who says it – the customer or the waiter at the deli?*

No cheese, thanks.
Next, please?
Large, please.
Thanks. I'll sit over there.
For here or to go?
OK. I'll bring it to your table.
OK. Would you like something to drink?
I'll have the bagel with egg.
Can I have a bagel, please?
What would you like on your bagel?
I'll have a coffee, please.
Would you like cheese with that?
It's for here.
Regular or large?

**b)** *Write a dialogue with the phrases. Practise it with your partner.*

## 9 MEDIATION At the deli

*a) Imagine you are in a New York deli. You hear another German. He wants to order. Try and help him.*

*German man* ___ Die Frau spricht so schnell. Kannst du sie bitten, ihre Frage zu wiederholen?
*You* ___ Excuse me, can you ...
*Woman at deli* ___ Sure. Is this for here or to go?
*You* ___ Sie will wissen, ...
*German man* ___ Ach so, ich möchte hier essen. Ich hätte gern einen Bagel mit Käse, aber kein Ei, wenn's geht.
*You* ___ It's for ...

*b) Listen to the rest of the dialogue. Listen again and help the man.*

▸ SF Mediation (p. 152)

## 10 SPEAKING Making plans together

*Partner B: Look at p. 103.*
*Partner A: You and your partner are on holiday in New York. You want to spend a day together.*

*a) Choose one of the activities. Tell your partner about it.*

– I'd like to go to ...
– It's in the Bronx/near ... Park.
– It costs ... for adults/for children. / It's free.
– You can go every day/from ... to ...
– I think it looks good/interesting/fun/...
– I love going to the zoo/going on boats.

### THE BRONX ZOO

The Bronx Zoo is the largest city zoo in the United States, home to over 4000 animals.
The zoo is open 365 days a year!
10:00 a.m. – 5:00 p.m.
Admission: Adult $ 14.00
Child (Ages 3–12) $ 10.00

### STATEN ISLAND FERRY

If you just want to have the views and a fun time on the water, take the Staten Island Ferry. Ferries leave from Battery Park every day and they are free!

*b) Listen to your partner and take notes like this.*

| What? | Where? | How much? | When? |
|---|---|---|---|
| | | | |

▸ SF Taking notes (p. 144)

*c) Plan your day. Do one activity in the morning and one in the afternoon.*

*A:* What time can we go there?
*B:* We can go to ... in the morning/in the afternoon.
*A:* What about going to ... in the morning and to ... in the afternoon?

## 11 Lisa is good at ... (Gerund with prepositions)

***a)*** *Complete these sentences with the -ing-form of the verb in brackets.*

1 Lisa is good at ... (speak) English.
*Lisa is good at speaking English.*
2 She's tired of ... (live) in Germany.
3 So she dreams of ... (work) in New York.
4 She's thinking of ... (become) a rapper!
5 But how will she get to NYC? She's scared of ... (fly).

***b)*** *Write sentences about yourself. You can use the -ing-forms of the verbs in the box.*

| | |
|---|---|
| I'm good/bad at ... | I dream of ... |
| I'm interested in ... | I'm scared of ... |

sing • play the piano • ski • write stories • tell jokes • play in a band • sleep on the beach • ...

## 12 REVISION A letter from New York (Simple past)

**Tipp**

*Wenn du über etwas schreibst, das in der Vergangenheit liegt, verwende das* ***simple past****.*
- *regelmäßige Verben: mit* ***-d/-ed***
  I enjoyed the trip. / Did you enjoy the trip?
- *unregelmäßige Verben* ▸ *S. 238–239*
  I didn't go to New York. I went to Las Vegas.

*Complete Ryan's letter to his sister with the simple past of the verbs in brackets.*

Dear Sarah
Yesterday Caitlin and her friend Ruth ... (take) me on a sightseeing trip. They ... (plan) it together! We ... (start) the day in a deli. We ... (have) breakfast there. I ... (eat) my first New York bagel. Yummy! Next we ... (go) to the Empire State Building. I ... (not enjoy) going up in the lift. But the views from the top ... (be) brilliant. ... (you go) up there last year?
See you soon, Ryan

## 13 WRITING Taking a break in Central Park

**Tipp**

*Wenn du einen Text schreibst,*
- *sammle und ordne deine Ideen (Mindmap, Liste, die 5 Ws)*
- *benutze* ***Adjektive****,* ***Adverbien*** *und* ***Bindewörter*** *(****first****,* ***later****,* ***and****, ...):*
  First it was a sunny day and very hot. Later ...
- *überlege dir einen guten Anfang und ein interessantes Ende.*

*Look at the photo. Imagine you are one of the people on the grass. Write a text of about 60–80 words about your day in the park. Use questions like these to get ideas for your writing:*
**Who** was in the park with you? **What** was the weather like? **Where** did you sit? **How** did you like it there? **When** did you leave?

more help ▸ *D (p. 107)*

▸ *SF: The steps of writing (pp. 146–147)*

## 14 READING Fire safety (Working out the meaning of words) ▸ SF p. 142

***a)*** *Read these fire safety instructions. Try to understand them with the help of the tips. Then explain (in German) what you have to do if there's a fire.*

**Tipp**

*Folgende Tipps helfen dir, unbekannte Wörter zu verstehen.*

1. *Schau dir die* ***Bilder*** *an:*
   *Was ist wohl ein* **high-rise building***?*
2. *Manche Wörter sind ähnlich wie* ***deutsche*** *Wörter:*
   *Was könnte* **second** *bedeuten?*
3. *Der* ***Kontext*** *(Wörter, die in der Nähe des unbekannten Wortes stehen) hilft ganz oft:*
   *Was könnte* **alert** *bedeuten?*
4. *Manchmal kennst du* ***Teile des Wortes*** *oder der Wortgruppe:*
   *Du kennst* **stairs** *und* **way**. *Was könnte* **stairway** *bedeuten?*
   *Du kennst* **direction**. *Was könnte* **directed** *bedeuten?*

***b)*** **Extra** *Try to explain these words from the instructions (page 1):* exit, report a fire, dial

***c)*** *Use the tips to explain the highlighted words in the safety instructions on the right.*

- *Du kennst* **hall** *und* **way**. *Was könnte* **hallway** *bedeuten?*
- *Schau dir das Bild an. Was könnte* **wet cloth** *bedeuten?*
- *Du kennst einen Teil des Wortes* (**bath**). *Was könnte* **bathtub** *bedeuten?*
- *Welchen Teil deines Bettes kannst du als Signal für die Feuerwehr aus dem Fenster hängen?*

**1**

### Fire safety in high-rise buildings

FIRE DEPARTMENT CITY OF NEW YORK

**If the fire is IN your room**

- If there is a fire, stay calm and think about what to do. Act quickly because every second counts.
- Get everybody out. Stay low, where air is fresher – smoke rises.
- Use your safest and nearest exit.
- CLOSE ALL DOORS as you leave.
- Knock on other guests' doors on your way out and alert them to the danger.
- DO NOT USE THE ELEVATOR.
- Go down the nearest STAIRWAY.
- To report a fire, dial 911. Firefighters will be directed to your location.

**2**

### Fire safety in high-rise buildings

FIRE DEPARTMENT CITY OF NEW YORK

**If the fire is NOT in your room**

- If the hallways are full of smoke, stay in your room.
- Place a wet cloth over your mouth and nose.
- Fill your bathtub with water. If your door gets hot, wet it down.
- If you are in great danger, hang a bedsheet out the window so that firefighters can spot you.

## You can tell me From *Kelly 'n' Me* by Myron Levoy (adapted)

*Anthony (15) meets a girl in the park. She says that her name is Kelly Callahan and that her family is poor, like Anthony's. She shows Anthony a beautiful apartment near Central Park and says that her mother works for the rich Lawrence family that lives there.*
*Anthony likes spending time with Kelly. They both love music. They often sing and play for people and earn money that way.*

▸ SF Working out the meaning of words (p. 142)

"Hey, Kelly," I said. "Let's go and play at the zoo."

"How about the subway, Anthony?"

"OK, if you really want to," I said.

"I do! It's fun. You can sing really loud down there. Come on!"

I hate the subway. I hate being underground. But there were crowds of people down there. We did some of our loudest songs and the money was good.

Some people stopped. One of them seemed drunk or on drugs. He was looking at our money. I wanted to move, but Kelly said no.

"Don't worry, Anthony," she said. "If he takes any money, it means he needs it more than we do."

We sang for another hour and a half. Then I couldn't take it any more. The noise, the smells, the crowds. I shouted to Kelly.

"I quit! Please, Kelly! Let's get out of here!"

"You look white."

"I feel sick. I mean it. I'm going to throw up."

"Okay! Gig ended."

I felt better up on the street. It was after five. And I was hungry.

"Say, Kelly," I said. "Let's eat."

"You want to have a picnic in the park? I know a good private spot."

Our picnic was a lot of fun. We got eight pieces of chicken and some chocolate milk. We went to a wild section of the park called the Ramble. I wouldn't go there after dark, but it was safe in the evening, I thought.

As Kelly threw her head back to drink the chocolate milk, I put my arm around her.

"Give me a chocolate mustache," I said.

Kelly leaned over and gave me a very good kiss. And I moved closer.

"Anthony, we really should talk," she said.

"You always want to talk."

"There are things I want to do, Anthony. I want to take off and be the new me. But I'm scared."

"You don't look scared to me."

"Well, I am. I'm scared of everything. Of my parents. And of being on my own. And of going to the West Coast. And now I'm scared of losing you."

"Kelly? Why are you crying? Tell me. What is it? Please!"

"I want to tell you. I really do!"

"Kelly, you can tell me anything. Anything."

"I can and I can't. Why did I have to meet you now?" She seemed angry.

"Hey, come on. It's not my fault."

"I know. It's – I guess I need some time to think about what I'm doing, and about you and me. I – I'm really falling for you, Tony, Anthony. I am. I am."

"And me for you," I said.

"Oh God, I know. I ..."

She was looking past me. "Uh-oh ..."

I followed her eyes. There were two guys out on the path, one with a red beard and one blond. They were watching us.

"Yo, blondie!" said Redbeard to Kelly. "You got a nice bod. You ever use it?"

"L-leave us alone," I said. It was dumb to be in this part of the park this late!

"I like your guitar, blondie," said Redbeard. "It's nice, just like your ass." He walked slowly towards her.

When I get really angry, I don't think, I just explode! I jumped up and hit Redbeard with everything I had. He was surprised and he fell. Kelly screamed. And she can scream! She tried to hit Blondbeard with her guitar, but he grabbed the guitar. Redbeard was getting up. I kicked him. He fell back down. I didn't care if it was fair or not. I prayed that they didn't have knives. Or guns.

I turned towards Blondbeard, but it was too late. He hit Kelly. She fell against a tree.

Then I heard some people shouting. The people got closer, and Blondbeard and Redbeard took off, with Kelly's guitar.

I sank down next to Kelly. Three or four people were around us now.

"Call the police!" said a woman.

"Are you OK?" I asked.

"I'm – I'm f-fine," said Kelly.

She was shivering.

"Don't call the – the police," said Kelly. "They'll n-never catch them. And I'm f-fine."

We started walking slowly.

"Take me to Fifth Avenue and I'll get a cab," Kelly said.

"No, I'm going all the way home with you!"

"Please. Please, Anthony."

"No! Enough's enough, Kelly. I'm going with you."

As we walked slowly towards the park exit I asked Kelly again and again if she was all right.

"It's nothing, Anthony."

"You were as brave as hell."

"Thanks. So were you."

"I'm sorry about your guitar," I said.

"I've got another guitar," she said. "No problem."

We got to Fifth Avenue.

"OK ... Anthony, can we sit here a minute?"

We sat. Kelly turned towards me.

"This is what – what I was going to tell you," she said. "We won't have to walk far. Because I live there." She pointed to a building across the street, one of three huge apartment houses.

"What? But that's where your mother works. The Lawrences live there."

"I'm sorry, Anthony. I live there. And my name isn't really Kelly Callahan. My name's Kelsey. Kelsey Lawrence. I'm sorry ..."

## Working with the text

### 1 What happened?

*Put the pictures in the correct order.*

### 2 True or false?

*Read the story carefully. Which statements are true? Correct the false ones.*

1 Anthony and Kelly played music for money.
2 They didn't get much money in the subway.
3 Anthony was hungry so they left the subway.
4 Anthony thought the park was safe in the evening.
5 The two men took Kelly's guitar.
6 Kelly wanted to call the police.
7 Anthony wanted to go home with Kelly.
8 Anthony wasn't surprised when Kelly told him where she lived.

### 3 Guess the meanings

*Guess the meanings of these words and phrases.*

*p. 26, l. 17* – drunk
*p. 26, l. 27–28* – throw up
*p. 26, l. 52* – leaned over
*p. 27, l. 73* – I'm really falling for you.
*p. 27, l. 83* – dumb
*p. 27, l. 107* – She was shivering.

more help ► *D (p. 107)*

### 4 How did he feel?

***a)*** *Find one point in the story when Anthony felt:*
*1* nervous *2* scared *3* ill *4* happy
– I think Anthony felt ... when ...

***b)*** *What should you do if somebody tries to rob you? Do you think Anthony's reaction was good?*
– I think Anthony's reaction was good/stupid/dangerous/ ...
– I think you should/shouldn't ...

shout for help • do nothing • fight • run • talk to the person • ...

### 5 Extra What will happen next?

*What do you think Anthony said to Kelly/Kelsey? What do you think she said to him?*

Why did you tell me your name was Kelly?
I wanted to tell you.
I feel stupid.
It's OK.
I don't want to talk to you.
I was scared of telling you.
I don't like being Kelsey Lawrence.

► *WB 15 (p. 14)* • **Checkpoint 1** *WB (p. 15)*

## How am I doing?

▸ SF Check yourself (p. 137)

**STUDY SKILLS** Check yourself

***Remember: Stop – Check – Go!***
*Überprüfe dich nach jeder Unit selbst. Finde heraus, wo du Probleme hast und plane, wie du dein Englisch verbessern kannst.* ***How am I doing?*** *hilft dir dabei.*

***a)*** *Choose or find the correct answers.*

### New York

1 The city of New York has five ...
A towns. B villages.
C boroughs. D cities.

2 Many of the famous sights in New York (like the Empire State Building) are in ...
A Staten Island. B Queens.
C Brooklyn. D the Bronx.
E Manhattan.

3 Downtown Manhattan is in the ... of the island.
A north B south C east D west

4 When Americans speak of 9/11, they mean the date when planes flew into ...
A the Empire State Building.
B the World Trade Center.
C Ground Zero. D Times Square.

5 What can't you get in a deli?
A a bagel with cream cheese
B a bagel with lox
C a sandwich D a book

6 The place where immigrants came into the USA is called ...
A the Statue of Liberty. B Ellis Island.
C Liberty Island.
D the Brooklyn Bridge.

### American English

7 For an American what are chips?

A  or B  ?

8 What words do the British use for these American words?
a) elevator b) vacation c) subway

### Words

9 Which word does not mean 'very good'?
A awesome B awful C great
D fantastic

10 The job of a firefighter is to ... fires.
A put on B put off C put out
D put up

11 Where can you not sleep?
A motel B tent C hotel D deli

### Grammar

12 ... in the Grand Canyon is very exciting.
A Hike B Hiked C Hiking
D Hikes

13 I'm good ... swimming.
A in B on C at D to

### Everyday English

14 Du möchtest den Bagel nicht im Deli essen, sondern mitnehmen, deshalb sagst du: A bagel ..., please.
A for here B to stay C to go
D to take

15 What would you like on your bagel?
A Yes, please.
B Egg and tomato, please. C No, thanks.
D I'm sitting over there

***b)*** *Check your answers on p. 235 and add up your points – one point for each correct answer.*

***c)*** *If you had 14 or more points, well done!*
*Where did you make mistakes? The chart below will tell you what you can do to improve your English.*

| No. | Areas | Find out more | Exercises |
|---|---|---|---|
| 1– 6 | New York | Unit 1 (pp. 12–17) | P 1 (p. 20), WB 1–2 (p. 6), 13 (p. 12) |
| 7– 8 | American English | Unit 1 (p. 14) | P 2 (p. 20), WB 3 (p. 7) |
| 9–12 | Words | Unit vocabulary (pp. 166–168) | WB 3–5 (pp. 7–8), 12 (p. 11) |
| 13–14 | The gerund | GF 1 (pp. 154–155) | P 5–7 (pp. 21–22), WB 6–7 (pp. 8–9), 9–10 (p. 10), |
| 15 | Everyday English | P 9 (p. 23) | P 8 (p. 22), WB 8 (p. 9) |

## 1 WORDS In a city

*Look at this picture of an American city. Write down words for as many things or people as you can.*

## 2 WORDS Describing towns and cities

***a)*** *Complete the sentences with words that mean the opposite.*

1 A town can be large or *small*.
2 It can be in the east or the ... of a country.
3 It can be exciting or ...
4 It can be noisy or ...
5 The buildings can be old or ...
6 The streets can be clean or ...

***b)*** *Write a text about the picture in 1.*

– The city is old/clean/...
– In the foreground/middle of the picture/...
– On the left/right there's a ... /there are some ...
– Some people are waiting/skating/...
– A young man/girl is singing/... near the ...
– It looks like a nice/friendly/boring/... city.
– I'd like/I wouldn't like to live there.

▸ *SF Describing pictures (p. 140)*

## 3 You aren't allowed to park here! (Modal verbs)

*Complete the sentences.*

1 Look at that NO PARKING sign! You (are allowed to / aren't allowed to) park here!
2 They drive on the right in the US, but in England you (have to / are allowed to) drive on the left.
3 You can play football in the park. And you (are allowed to / have to) skate there too.
4 Central Park is only two blocks away. So you (have to / don't have to) take the subway. You can walk.
5 The sports museum is free on Saturday. You (have to / don't have to) buy a ticket.
6 Sorry, no cameras, please. You (aren't allowed to / don't have to) take photos here.

## 4 What did you do last weekend? (Simple past)

*Rachel is telling her friend what she did last Saturday morning. Finish the sentences with the correct forms of the verbs. Use the **simple past** forms of the verbs in brackets.*

1 On Saturday morning I ... (get up) at 7 o'clock.
*On Saturday morning I got up at 7 o'clock.*
2 After breakfast I ... (take) the bus into town.
3 First, I ... (go) to Jeans World because I ... (want) to buy some jeans.
4 I ... (see) some nice jeans, but I ... (~~buy~~) them because they ... (~~have~~) my size.
5 Outside in the street, I ... (meet) Karen and Amy from our class.
6 We ... (go) to a café and ... (had) a drink and ... (chat).
7 Then I ... (look) at my watch. It ... (be) already 1.30 pm.
8 When I ... (get) home, my parents ... (~~be~~) happy because I ... (be) late for lunch!!

## 5 STUDY SKILLS Writing better sentences (Linking words)

*In a test, you might have to write an e-mail or a letter. Remember that **linking words** can make them more interesting. Link the pairs of sentences with the correct **linking word**.*

1 I like my town (because/but) it's big and exciting.
*I like my town because it's big and exciting.*
2 I often look at expensive clothes (because/but) I never buy them!
3 I don't eat chips too often (because/but) I know they're bad for me.
4 We can go to the cinema (and/or) we can watch a DVD at home.
5 My mum often gives me money (or/so that) I can go out with my friends.
6 My favourite place in town is the park (so/because) it's quiet and really pretty.
7 The film was long (and/but) it was boring too.

▸ *SF Writing course (p. 146)*

## 6 What do you like doing? (Gerunds)

***a)*** *Work with a partner. Brainstorm ideas about things you like doing. Make a network.*

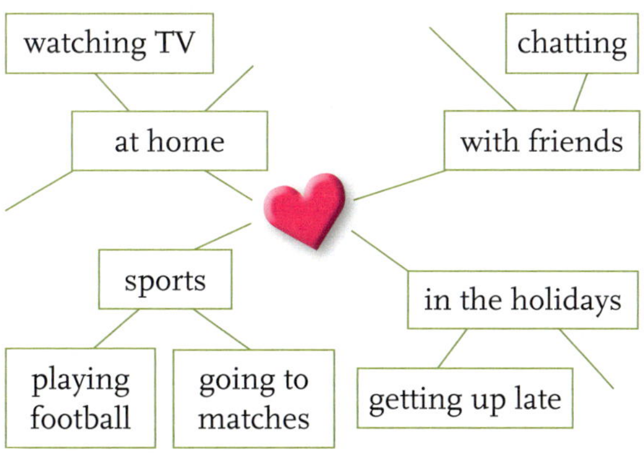


***b)*** *Make sentences that are true for you with words and phrases from your network.*

– I like ... when I'm at home/with friends.
– I (really) like/love/enjoy ...
– I'm (very) interested in ...
– My hobby/My favourite activity is...

**STUDY SKILLS** **How to do well in a test**

*Wenn ein Test ansteht, solltest du*
*– wissen, wie du dich darauf vorbereiten kannst*
*– darauf achten, dass du die Aufgaben richtig verstanden hast*
*– wissen, worauf du bei Multiple-Choice-Aufgaben achten solltest.*
*Im **Skills File** findest du Hilfe für all dies und mehr.*

▸ *WB 1–5 (pp. 16–17) • SF How to do well in a test (pp. 150–151)*

## 1 Reading

*Greg Zimmermann is a teenager from New York. Read his blog this week and do the tasks below.*

**New York's yellow taxis are going green!**

Hi! What do you think of when you hear the words New York? Skyscrapers? Delis? Central Park? The Statue of Liberty? I love all those things too, but for me, there's another thing that is so typical of the city. Taxis. The famous yellow New York taxicabs.

Taxicabs are everywhere in New York. In fact, there are 13,000 of them. Over half of all the cars you see in Manhattan are taxis. That's great if you need a cab. But there's a problem. They use a lot of gas[1]. And all that gas makes the air in New York dirty. Very dirty!

But now something interesting is happening. The cabs are going green. No, I don't mean that people are painting them a different color. The cabs will still be yellow like always. But they'll be 'environmentally friendly'[2]. The old cabs will slowly go, and there'll be new ones.

The new cabs (there are almost 400 of them in the city already) will be 'hybrid cabs'. What does that mean? Well, a normal cab uses gas all the time. A hybrid cab uses gas and electricity. It has a normal gas motor, and then it also has an electric motor. It uses the electric motor when it's going slowly – and when it stops at a traffic light. And it uses the gas motor when it travels more quickly. Result: cleaner air! Cool.

Everybody is excited about the new cabs. The mayor[3] was on TV yesterday. He thinks that New York's image is really important. When tourists come here, they don't want to visit a dirty city. They want to find a place that's modern and that cares about[4] the environment.

And what do the cab drivers think? Our neighbor, Mr. Janjma, drives one of the new cabs, so I asked him. "Cab drivers have to buy their cabs," he said, "and the new ones cost more than the old ones. But they don't use so much gas. I save about 30 dollars a day now. I'm really happy!"

Until next week! Stay safe! Greg

***a)*** *Choose the right answers:*

*1* New York taxicabs ...
- A aren't typical of the city.
- B don't use much gas.
- C make the city's air dirty.
- D aren't a problem.

*2* In future, New York's taxicabs will ...
- A be green in colour.
- B be environmentally friendly.
- C travel slowly.
- D only drive in Manhattan.

*3* A hybrid taxi ...
- A has two motors.
- B has got one motor.
- C uses only gas.
- D uses only electricity.

*4* The mayor of New York says that the city should be ... for tourists.
- A dirty B famous C cool D clean

*5* Mr Janjma ...
- A pays $ 30 a day for his green taxi.
- B likes his green taxi.
- C never drives his green taxi.
- D hasn't got a green taxi.

***b)*** *Finish the sentences with information from the text.*

*1* There are ... taxis in New York.
*2* There are already amost ... hybrid cabs.
*3* A hybrid cab only uses gas when it ...

[1] gas [gæs] *Benzin* [2] environmentally friendly [ɪnˌvaɪrənmentəli 'frendli] *umweltfreundlich* [3] mayor [meə] *Bürgermeister/in*
[4] (to) care about ['keər_əbaʊt] *achten auf*

## 2 Reading

*Here are some signs that you can see in town. Write down what they mean.*
*Sign 1: You aren't allowed to ...*

- You are/aren't allowed to ...
- You (don't) have to ...

Signs

... stop when you see this sign.
... park where you see this sign.
... put your rubbish here.
... drive on the left here.
... use your mobile in this area.
... get off your bike when you see this sign.

1

2

3

4

5

6

## 3 Writing

*Choose one of the tasks below. Write an e-mail of 80–100 words. Count the words at the end.*

***a)*** *Chloe is your new American penfriend[1] and she wants to know something about the place where you live. Write about the following things*

I live in/near a village/town/city/in the country.

It's in the north/south/... of Germany.

It's old/famous/...

There are lots of shops/buildings/...

You can do lots of things here, for example you can ...

I like/don't like it because ...

***b)*** *Your British penfriend Robert wants to know what you did last weekend. Tell him:*
- what you did on Saturday or Sunday
- who you did it with
- if it was fun/boring/...

Hello from Germany!

Dear ...

My name is ...
I want to tell you about ...
...

Write soon.
Best wishes

## 4 Speaking

*You're starting an internet project with a school in Boston in the US. In your class you are making sound files about yourselves.*
*Talk about 'What I like doing' for about one minute.*

Hello, my name is ...
I'm in class ... I want to talk to you about ...
Well, at the weekend/at home/
when I'm with my friends ...
I also love/enjoy ...
Goodbye and thanks for listening!

[1] penfriend ['penfrend] *Brieffreund/in*

# California, the 'Golden State'?

**1 Did you know?**

***a)*** *Look at the photos and read the information about California.*

***b)*** *What did you know already? What didn't you know before?*

I knew/I didn't know that ...
- Hollywood is part of Los Angeles.
- California is near Mexico.
- the Golden Gate Bridge is in San Francisco.
- there are mountains/beaches there.
- they have earthquakes/tsunamis.
- they grow fruit/vegetables there.
- the weather can be sunny/foggy.

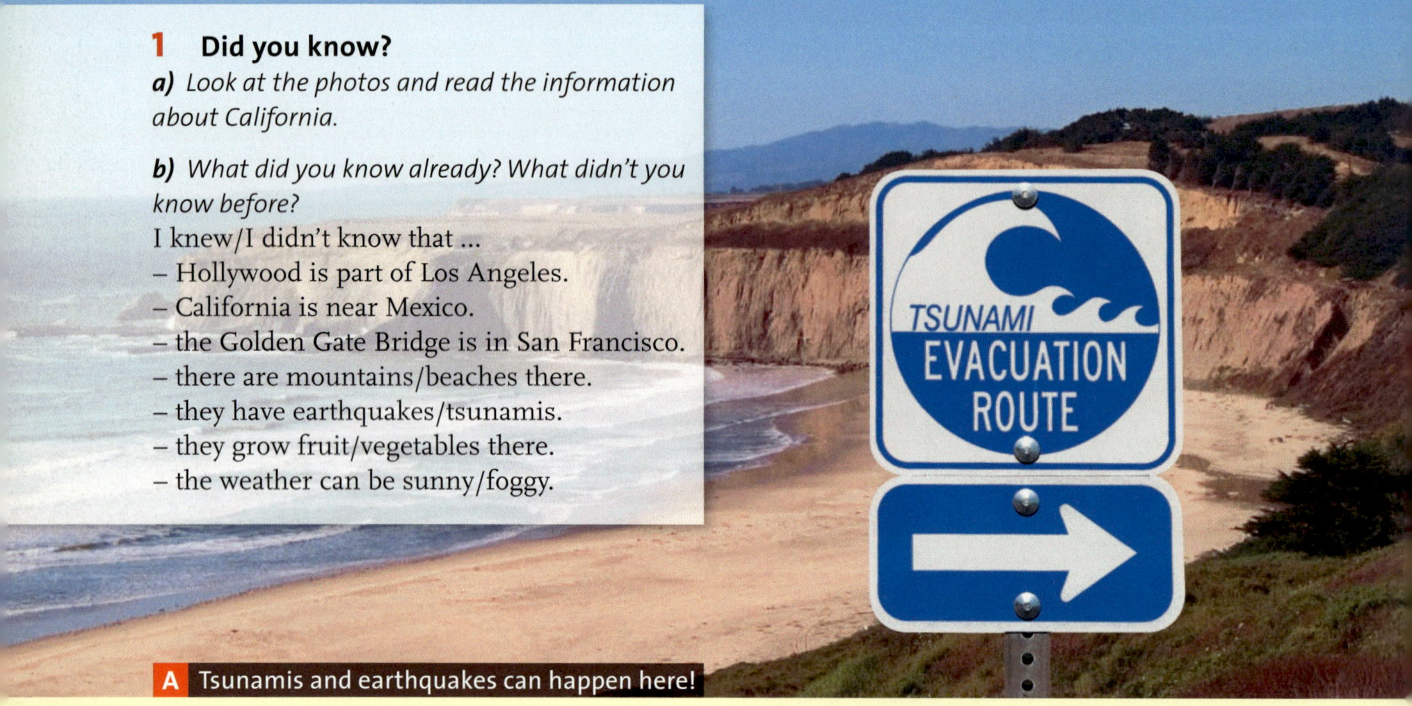


**A** Tsunamis and earthquakes can happen here!

**B** Everyone goes to the beach. You see lots of homeless people there too.

**C** You can drive 1200 miles along the coast of California on Highway 101.

**D** San Francisco is famous for the Golden Gate Bridge – and for fog!

E This is Yosemite National Park. It's just one of eight national parks in California.

F Hollywood is part of L.A. – tourists come here to see the stars.

G They grow all kinds of fruit and vegetables in California. Lots of Mexicans cross the border to work on the farms.

## 2 California sounds

*Listen. Which sound file (1–7) goes with which photo (A–G)?*

▸ *SF Listening (p. 141)*

## 3 Extra SONG California

*Listen to the theme song from the popular TV series 'The OC'.*

***a)*** *Which photo goes best with the song?*

***b)*** *How do you feel when you listen to the song? What comes to your mind?*

I feel happy/excited/relaxed ...
I think of ...

▸ *P 1–2 (p. 42)* • *WB 1 (p. 18)* • **Text File 5** *(p. 123)*

## 1 Business in California

Geography Today • 29

### General facts

Farmers grow all kinds of fruit and vegetables in California because the weather is very warm and sunny. Central Valley is California's most important farming area. Strawberries, lettuce and oranges are grown on huge farms. Over 85 % of America's strawberries are produced in California.

A lot of wine is produced there too. Have a look in your local supermarket. Maybe they sell wine from California. Californian wine is sold all over the world.

'Silicon Valley' is a big industrial area near San Francisco. Lots of famous computer and hi-tech companies are found there.

Tourists are very important for California. Theme parks like Disneyland and Six Flags Magic Mountain are very popular. Of course the visitors have to eat. Four million burgers are eaten in Disneyland every year.

*Strawberry fields in Central Valley*

*Growing grapes in Napa Valley*

*Hi-tech companies in Silicon Valley*

*Six Flags Magic Mountain, near Los Angeles*

**a)** *Skim the text and answer this question. Where do you think this text is from?*

- A a story book
- B a school book
- C a brochure

**b)** *Scan the text and find the answers to these questions:*

1. What is grown on Californian farms?
2. Where can you buy Californian wine?
3. What kind of companies are there in Silicon Valley?
4. How many burgers are eaten in Disneyland in one year?

► SF Scanning/SF Skimming (p. 142)

**Looking at language**

**a)** *Vergleiche diese Sätze aus Text **1**:*

1 Farmers **grow** all kinds of fruit and vegetables in California.

2 Strawberries **are grown** there.

*Die Verbform **grow** in Satz 1 drückt aus, was die Landwirte **tun**. **(Aktiv)***

*Die Verbform **are grown** in Satz 2 drückt aus, was mit den Erdbeeren **geschieht**. **(Passiv)***

**b)** *Finde mehr Sätze im Passiv in Text **1** und schreibe sie auf.*

► GF 2a–c: Passive (p. 156) • P 3–5 (pp. 42–43) • WB 2–8 (pp. 18–21)

**All about ...** growing up in two cultures

## 2 Letters to the editor

*Before you start, read only the headings of the two letters. Are the writers happy or unhappy in California? Now read the letters. Were you right?*

*Last week we asked our readers about their attitudes to minorities and immigration. This is what two young Californians wrote.*

### "Lucky to live in America"

I was born here in California, so I'm a US citizen, but I'm proud to be a Latino too. Growing up in two cultures is interesting. Speaking two languages is an advantage. It will be useful when I look for a job.

Where I live, relations between Latinos and other people are very good. I feel very lucky to live in America, where everyone can be successful if they have the right attitude.

*Luis M. (14), San Clemente, CA*

### "I feel different"

I was born in Korea. My parents brought my sisters and me to the US when I was 7 years old. When I started school, some of the students laughed at me because I only spoke Korean. Learning a new language was hard.

I was an illegal immigrant for 9 years, but in the end I got my papers. Now I'm a US citizen, but I still feel different. I hate being a member of a minority. In my opinion, there is a lot of prejudice against Koreans and other minorities.

*Kim L. (16), Eureka, CA*

**Extra** **Americana ★ ★ ★**

**Californians**

About 37 million people live in California. One in three Californians is Latino. 'Latino' means that they, or their families, are from Spanish-speaking countries like Mexico or Puerto Rico. (Another word for Latino is Hispanic.)

## 3 Words and phrases

***a)*** *Find at least two phrases in each letter that show the writer's opinion.*

***b)*** *Find words which mean:*

- a good thing – an ...
- it will help me – it will be ...
- everyone can do well – everyone can be ...
- immigrants who don't have papers – ... immigrants
- people think bad about people who are different – there is a lot of ...
- a small group of people – a ...

## 4 Extra Role play

***a)*** *Prepare a role play. One of you is a reporter, one is Kim or Luis. Make questions for the interview.*

- Where – you born?
- Where – you live now?
- What languages – you speak?
- Do you – like – speak – two languages?
- Do you think – prejudice – against minorities?
- Do you like – live – in California?

more help ▸ D p. 109

***b)*** *Together prepare answers for Kim or Luis. Then practise your role play. Swap roles.*

▸ P 6–8 (p. 44) • WB 9–11 (pp. 22–23)

## 5 How was your day?

Every morning at seven o'clock Mrs Morales takes the bus to the rich area of the town. She works as a maid in two different houses. She cleans and cooks all day, then at six o'clock she goes home. Three days a week she has a third job in the evening – as a waitress.

'Hi!' Mrs Morales called out as she opened the front door.

Luis Morales was watching a film, but he turned off the TV when he heard his mum.

'Hey, Mom! How was your day?'

'Ah, hijo mio! It was OK. Did you have time to go to the supermarket for me?'

'Of course,' said Luis. 'Are you working tonight?'

'Yes,' said his mother. 'I have to leave in half an hour.'

'Oh Mama, Mama, will you tell us a story?' begged Maria.

'First dinner, then a story, if there's time,'

Mrs Morales said. 'Which story do you want, bebita mia?'

'The story about you and Papa when you came across the border to California.'

'Again?' smiled Mrs Morales.

> *What jobs does Mrs Morales do?*

## 6 A family story

*Listen to Mrs Morales's story.*
*Which one is true – A or B?*

1 Mr and Mrs Morales got married ...
   A before they left Mexico.
   B after they left Mexico.
2 She and her husband crossed the border ...
   A as legal immigrants.
   B as illegal immigrants.
3 When the border guards stopped ...
   A they saw Mr and Mrs Morales.
   B they didn't see them.
4 Mr and Mrs Morales found work ...
   A quickly.
   B after a long time.
5 Their first job was ...
   A in a factory.
   B on a farm.
6 The amnesty meant that ...
   A they got their papers.
   B they had to leave the US.

► *P 9–11 (pp. 45–46)* • *WB 12 (p. 23)* • *SF Listening (p. 141)* • **Text File 6** *(pp. 124–125)*

**Extra Americana ★ ★ ★**

**The border**

The border between the US and Mexico is over 3000 kilometres long. Thousands of Mexican immigrants cross the border illegally every year. They dream of a new life in the US. But the US Border Patrol catches a lot of them. The US government has built a high fence along parts of the border to stop the immigrants.

## 7 The California dream

# VISIT COLOMA,

## WHERE THE CALIFORNIA GOLD RUSH BEGAN

**The Marshall Gold Discovery State Historic Park, Coloma, California**

GOLD! A piece of gold was discovered in Coloma in 1848 by James Marshall. This changed the history of California. 300,000 people rushed to California to look for gold between 1849 and 1855. They were called the 'forty-niners' because a lot of them arrived in that year.

Like many other Californian towns, Coloma was built during the Gold Rush. When there was no more gold, most of the people left the town. Today Coloma is one of California's popular state parks. Visit us to see how people lived in the 1850s.

Some forty-niners found gold, most didn't. Why not try it? You can buy a pan in the park and look for gold in the river. You might be lucky!

Discover the history of California's gold towns and have fun at the same time

*a) Would you like to visit this state park? Skim the brochure, then say why/why not.*

I'd like to ...
I'm (not) interested in ...
It looks fun/boring/...

▸ *SF Skimming (p. 142)*

*b) True or false? Correct the false statements.*

1 Gold was found in Coloma in 1948.
2 The first gold was found by James Marshall.
3 Coloma was built after the Gold Rush.
4 You can't look for gold in Coloma now.

## 8 Now you

*a) Find out at least two interesting facts about your town or your area.*

| | | | |
|---|---|---|---|
| Potatoes<br>Cars<br>Wine<br>... | is<br>are | grown<br>produced<br>found<br>... | in this area. |

| | | | |
|---|---|---|---|
| Our school<br>The old castle<br>The old buildings<br>... | was<br>were | built | in ... |

*b)* **Extra** *Put your facts together. Find some pictures and make a brochure.*

▸ *GF 2d: Passive (p. 157) • P 12–14 (pp. 46–47) • WB 13–16 (pp. 24–25)*

**Extra** Background File **WELCOME TO CALIFORNIA!**

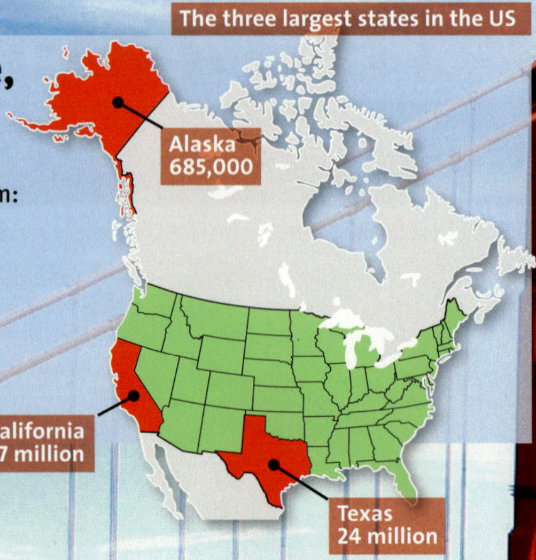


## California, the Golden State,

is the third largest of the fifty states of the US, and it has more people than any other state.

Today California is very rich. Its money comes from:

- farming: fruit, vegetables and wine
- the computer industry in Silicon Valley
- the entertainment industry – films and TV
- tourism – the national parks, San Francisco, Hollywood and much more

### *Let's go to San Francisco ...*

... where you can see the Golden Gate Bridge, gateway to the Pacific Ocean. It's known for its beautiful views.

When you're in San Francisco don't forget to take a ride on a cable car – it's the best way to see the city.

San Francisco is one of the richest areas in California. But not everyone is rich. In the streets you will see lots of homeless people.

### *... where the earth moves ...*

One problem for the people who live in San Francisco – and in large parts of California – is earthquakes. In 1906 about 3000 people were killed by the great earthquake and the fire that followed it. More than half of San Francisco's population lost their homes. In the 1989 earthquake 57 people died and again there was a lot of damage.
Remember the rule:
'Drop, cover and hold on!'

- drop down under a heavy table
- cover your eyes
- hold on to a table leg

► **Text File 7** *(pp. 126–127)*

### ... or to the world-famous Sequoia National Park ...

where the giant sequoias grow. They are the tallest (up to 110 metres) and oldest trees in the world – some are over 2000 years old!

### ... and maybe end up in Los Angeles.

It's the largest city in California and it has a very famous suburb: Hollywood.

The first Hollywood movie was made here in 1910. The sunshine and the wonderful locations (sea, mountains, deserts) brought movie makers and stars to L.A. – Hollywood has always been the most important place in the world for films and TV.

## 1 A poster about California

*a) In groups of four fill in a placemat with interesting topics about California. Look through the unit to get ideas. Agree on one or two topics.*

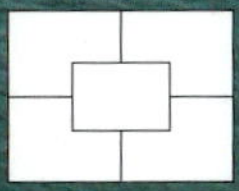

*b) Find pictures and information for your poster.*

*c) Prepare your poster. Write captions for the pictures. Check what you have written.*

## 2 Gallery walk

*a) Hang your posters on the classroom wall. In your group go and look at each poster.*

*b) Write a short comment for each poster on a piece of paper (Say what you like or ask a question.) Stick your comment next to the poster.*

*c) Go back to your poster. Read the comments. Try and answer the questions.*

► WB 17 (p. 25)

## 1 WORDS California words

***a)*** *Group the words from the box in a chart or a mind map. You can use the group words on the right. Collect more words as you work through the unit.*

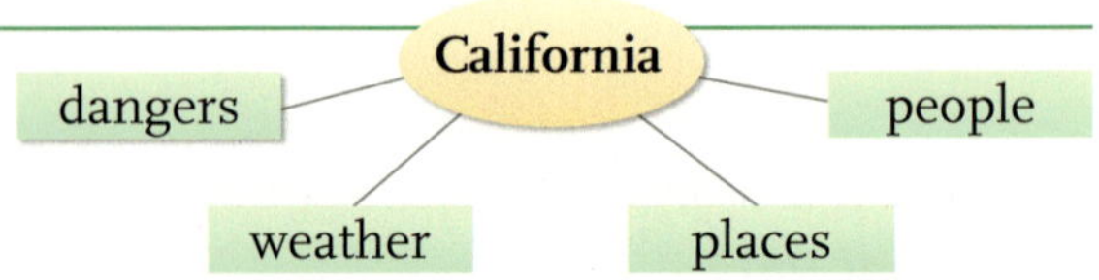


beach • drive along the coast • actors • the border • earthquakes • film stars • fog • go surfing • hot • Golden Gate Bridge • Hollywood • Mexicans • homeless people • look after national parks • Sacramento • relax in the sun • park rangers • rain • sunny • surfers • tourists • be careful • tsunamis • act in films • state capital • warm • Yosemite National Park • work on farms • forest fires • grow fruit and vegetables

***b)*** *Complete the sentences about California with words from your chart or mind map.*

1 California is very popular. Tourists can visit famous places like ...
2 Many people come to work in California: For example, they ...
3 Both Californians and tourists spend lots of time outside. They ...
4 There are some dangers in California. For example, there are ...

## 2 //O WORDS Word building (-less) ▸ D p. 108

**Tipp**

*Bei manchen Wörtern entsteht durch das Anhängen der Nachsilbe **-less** ein neues Wort, z.B.* Water is colourless. *(= farblos, ohne Farbe)*

*Was heißt z.B.* **hairless** *im folgenden Satz?*
Baby cats are blind and hairless.

*Match the sentences.*

1 I didn't get much sleep.
2 It's a warm and sunny day.
3 That man hasn't got a home.
4 Nobody scored a goal yesterday.
5 I want a new mobile.

He's homeless.
I had a sleepless night.
It was a scoreless match.
My old one is useless.
The sky is cloudless.

## 3 //O A quiz (Passive – simple present) ▸ D p. 108

***a)*** *Choose the correct answer.*

1 Spanish is spoken in Portugal **(I)**/Mexico **(H)**/Italy **(J)**.
2 Oscars are given to film stars **(O)**/good sportsmen or sportswomen **(P)**/famous painters **(Q)**.
3 Computer software is made in Napa Valley **(K)**/Silicon Valley **(L)**/Central Valley **(M)**.
4 Four million sausages **(C)**/burgers **(L)**/cookies **(G)** are eaten in Disneyland every year.
5 Most US strawberries are grown in Alaska **(X)**/California **(Y)**/New York **(Z)**.
6 Californian wine is sold in the US **(U)**/in the US and Canada **(V)**/all over the world **(W)**.
7 California is called the Yellow State **(S)**/Orange State **(T)**/Golden State **(O)**.
8 Park rangers are found at all American beaches **(N)**/national parks **(O)**/stations **(P)**.
9 Most of the big films are made in Los Angeles **(D)**/San Francisco **(E)**/New York **(F)**.

***b)*** *Look at the letters behind your correct answers. What word do they make?*

## 4 READING Endless summer surf camp (Skimming and scanning) ▸ SF p. 142

***a)*** *Skim the text. Where is it from?*

A a guidebook for a town by the sea
B a newspaper article about surfing
C a brochure for a summer camp

**Tipp Skimming**

*Du überfliegst einen Text, um herauszufinden, worum es geht.*
*→ Lies schnell, nicht Wort für Wort. → Sieh dir Überschriften und Bilder an, achte auch auf Wörter in **Fettdruck** oder GROSSBUCHSTABEN.*

***b)*** *Skim again. Your friend is interested, but only …*
– if you can sleep at the camp.
– if they give you meals.
– if it is fun for young people.
*Has the camp got what your friend is looking for?*

***c)*** *Your friend has some more detailed questions. Scan the brochure. Look for the **key words**.*

1 How many **days** is this surf camp?
2 How many **meals** do you get every day?
3 Do they have **vegetarian** food?
4 How big are the **groups**?
5 What about **prices**?

**Tipp Scanning**

*Du suchst nur nach bestimmten Informationen:*
*→ Denke an Schlüsselwörter **(key words)** und suche nach ihnen. → Geh dabei mit deinen Augen sehr schnell durch den Text:*
*• diagonal, jeweils über einen Absatz*
*• s-förmig, über die ganze Seite*
*Such dir die für dich beste Methode aus.*

**At our 5-day surf camps we offer**
- quality surfing lessons
- great surfing equipment
- expert surf coaches
- comfortable tents
- delicious meals

***Surf training***
You've never surfed before? You can already surf and want to learn some new tricks? We can help you.
Our coaches work with you in small groups (3 students per coach), so all students get individual help.

***Relaxing and sleeping***
You sleep in comfortable tents (guys and girls separate). At the campsite you can play table tennis and volleyball. There's a TV lounge with sofas where you can relax.

***Meals***
You get three meals a day, plus snacks and drinks:
- *big breakfast every morning*
- *lunch of sandwiches, summer fruits and other snacks at the beach*
- *great dinner every evening.*

There's a vegetarian alternative at every meal.
*Prices on our website or by phone*

## 5 More facts about California (Passive – simple present) ▸ D p. 108

*Match the sentence halves.*

1 Millions of dollars …
2 Software from California …
3 A lot of rubbish …
4 Most of California's fruit and vegetables …
5 English and Spanish …
6 Mexican food …

is used all over the world.
is eaten in many Californian restaurants.
are grown in Central Valley.
are spoken in many Californian families.
is picked up from the Californian coast.
are spent every year to fight forest fires.

## 6 WORDS Countries and people

***a)*** ◻ *Copy and complete the chart. If you need help, look at the list on p. 231.*

***b)*** ◻ *Add at least six countries to the chart, e.g. Germany, France, Poland, Turkey, ...*

| Country | Person/People | Language |
|---|---|---|
| Spain | Spanish | Spanish |
| Mexico | ... | ... |
| the US | ... | ... |
| Great Britain | ... | ... |

***c)*** *Complete the text below.*

Luis's parents were born in Mexico, so they're ...
Luis was born in California, so he's ...
He and his parents speak two languages: ... and ...
His grandparents still live in Mexico. They don't speak English. They only speak ...

***d)*** **Extra** *Write a short text about your family. (The text on the right can help you.) You can add a picture and put your text in your DOSSIER.*

My parents were born in ..., so they're ...
They speak ...
I was born in ..., so I'm ...
I speak ... At school we learn ...
My uncle/sister/... was born in ... He's/She's ...
My grandpa/aunt lives in ... He/She speaks ...

## 7 Extra WRITING More about 'Growing up in two cultures' (Writing letters)

**STUDY SKILLS Writing letters**

*Beim Briefeschreiben musst du unterschiedliche Regeln beachten, je nachdem ob du einen persönlichen, informellen Brief **(informal letter)** an Freunde oder Verwandte schreibst oder einen förmlichen Brief **(formal letter)** an unbekannte Personen, Behörden usw. Besonders bei formalen Briefen sind **Anfang** und **Ende** sehr wichtig.*

*What do you think about growing up in two cultures? Write a (formal) letter to the editor. Look at the letters on p. 37 (and the two letters on the right) to get some ideas. You can add your letter to your DOSSIER.*

more help ▸ D p. 109

20 April ...
Dear Sir or Madam

I am not a member of a minority, but a lot of my friends are.
In my opinion, speaking two languages can be a great advantage because ...

Yours faithfully
...

...

Dear Ms Winter

I don't live in the US, but I am a member of a minority.
I think that there is a lot of prejudice against minorities.
I often feel different from the other kids because ...

Yours sincerely
...

▸ **Extra** *SF Writing letters (p. 148)*

## 8 REVISION Learning English is ... (Gerund)

*Complete the sentences. Use the -ing-form of the verb in brackets and add an adjective from the box.*

1 ... (learn) English is ... – *Learning English is easy.*
2 ... (eat) lots of burgers and chips is ...
3 ... (write) letters is ...
4 ... (send) text messages is ...
5 ... (go) to school by bike is ...
6 ... (surf) is ...

boring • brilliant • cool • dangerous • difficult • easy • expensive • hard • healthy • nice • old-fashioned • safe • silly • slow • trendy • uncool • unhealthy • useful

## 9 MEDIATION Sale!

***a)*** *There are some interesting special offers in the supermarket this week. Listen to the announcements (1–4) and match them to the posters (A–D).*

A

B

C

D

***b)*** *Now listen to Mr Walther's questions and try to answer them.*

## 10 SPEAKING A picture story

***a)*** *Partner B: Go to p. 104.*
*Partner A: Look at pictures 1–3. Tell the story to your partner. The green boxes will help you.*

1

- Tom and Debbie – to a new café – went
- a nice table – in front of the pictures – found – They

2

- drank – They – their colas
- laughed – talked and – They
- lots of fun – had – And they

3

- a bright light – there was – Suddenly
- 'Stop him!' – shouted – Someone
- shocked – Tom and Debbie – were

***b)*** *Look at pictures 4–6. Listen to your partner's story. Is it the same as the story in the orange boxes?*

4

At that moment Tom and Debbie saw a gun. It was on the floor near their table.

5

Then a man ran towards them. Tom picked up the gun. Debbie screamed loudly.

6

Someone shouted angrily, 'Cut!' It was a film director! Tom and Debbie felt really silly.

***c)*** **Extra** *Try and tell the whole story.*

## 11 WORDS Who uses these things? (Jobs)

***a)*** ◯ healthy *Match the jobs and the pictures.*

*1 a waiter/waitress*

*2 ...*

actor • photographer • farmer • maid • robber • singer • teacher • waiter/waitress

1

2

3

4

5

6

7

8

***b)*** **Extra** ◉ *Write one or two sentences about where these people work and what they do.*

## 12 LISTENING Welcome to San Clemente cinemas

**Tipp**

*Bei **automatischen Telefonansagen** sind die gewünschten Informationen auf Band aufgezeichnet. Meist wirst du aufgefordert, bestimmte Tasten auf deinem Telefon zu drücken. **Keine Panik**, wenn du etwas nicht verstanden hast. Du kannst es so oft abspielen lassen wie du willst.*

*Imagine you want to take your ten-year-old cousin to the cinema on Saturday afternoon.*

***a)*** ◯ *Listen to **part 1** and fill in a copy of the chart.*

| *What number do I have to press?* | |
|---|---|
| *– Which movies can I see?*<br>*– I want to hear the information again.*<br>*– How can I get tickets?*<br>*– When do the movies start?* | ... |

***b)*** *Look at the poster on the right. What kind of films can your cousin go to?*

***c)*** ◉ *Listen to **part 2**. Find out which of the three movies you can see with your cousin.*

***d)*** *Listen to **part 3**. What time do you have to be at the cinema for that film?*

▸ SF Listening (p. 141)

## 13 //○ California was discovered by ... (Passive – simple past) ▸ D p. 110

*Look at the pictures. Write down what happened when. Use **was** or **were**.*

1 California ... discovered by Spanish explorers in 1769.

2 The Golden Gate Bridge ... built by Joseph Strauss.

3 The first film ... made in Hollywood in 1910.

4 The first gold ... found in Coloma in 1848.

5 The first jeans ... made by Levi Strauss during the Gold Rush.

6 Fourteen people ... killed by the forest fires last summer.

*1 California was discovered by Spanish explorers in ...*

## 14 Extra ● An accident – young man crashed into ... (Active and passive)

*Complete the report. Choose the correct verb form – active or passive.*

**Remember**

***Aktiv:*** *Es drückt aus, was jemand tut.*
A young woman saw the accident.
***Passiv:*** *Es drückt aus, was mit wem oder womit etwas geschieht.*
The accident was seen by a young woman.

*An accident happened on Park Road yesterday morning.*
*1 A young man on a bike crashed into ...*
*2 The woman ...*

1. A young man on a bike (crashed/was crashed) into an old woman.
2. The old woman fell. She (hurt/was hurt) her head.
3. The man (left/was left) quickly.
4. He (didn't help/wasn't helped) the old woman.
5. The accident (saw/was seen) by a young woman.
6. She (called/was called) an ambulance.
7. The old woman (took/was taken) to hospital.
8. The young woman (interviewed/was interviewed) by the police.
9. Descriptions of the man (send/were sent) to all police stations.
10. The same man (saw/was seen) at the station minutes after accident.
11. He (left/was left) his bike there.
12. The police (didn't find/weren't found) the man.

## Santa Monica – Episode 1 of a TV series

*Teen TV* is a new TV station for teenagers in Los Angeles. It wants to make a new teen soap. People are sending in lots of scripts. This is one of them.

*Is this script good enough to be the new teen soap? Read it and give your opinion. Some of the new words aren't in the Dictionary of this book. Try and guess what they mean.*

▸ *SF Working out the meaning of words (p. 142)*

### Scene 1 At the beach

*Three cool, beautiful rich kids – Josh, Cindy, and Lara – are walking along the beach in Santa Monica, laughing.*

*Cindy* ... so I'm going to Alaska with my parents in the summer.

*Lara* You poor thing – I hate the cold.

*Cindy* It's not cold in Alaska in the summer ... is it?

*Lara and Josh look at each other.*

*Josh* Hey, there's Luke!

*Luke is waving to them from the road.*

*Josh* He wants us to go surfing with him.

*Lara* Well, aaaall right! Let's go.

*We see the group walk off the beach.*

### Scene 2 At Luke's car

*Luke, cool like the others, stands by an expensive car. On top of it are surfboards.*

*Luke* Hey, guys. The surf's good over at Malibu. Make yourselves comfortable and let's go.

*Josh* Is this the new car?

*Luke* Sure is.

*Cindy* Wow! It's real nice, Lukey. *It's clear Cindy likes Luke a lot. He's relaxed.*

*Luke* Thanks, Cindy.

### Scene 3 On the road

*We're inside the car as it drives along by the sea. Lots of laughter. Josh is in the front with Luke. Lara and Cindy are in the back.*

*Josh* Look, that girl needs help. *He points to a car at the side of the road. A girl is looking at the engine.* Stop a minute.

*Luke* Fine, whatever, but be quick!

*Josh gets out and goes over to the girl.*

*Lara* Josh is a real nice guy.

*Luke* Too nice! Look at the car – it's all old and dirty!

*Luke and Cindy laugh, Lara doesn't.*

### Scene 4 By the road

*Jenna is looking at the engine. She's very pretty. She wears the uniform of a coffee shop waitress – a short skirt and blouse. Josh walks over.*

*Josh* Hi, can I help you?

*She looks up.*

*Jenna* If I don't get to Santa Monica in five minutes, I'll lose my job.

*Josh quickly begins to check the engine.*

*Luke* *Calls from SUV.* Hey, Josh, hurry up!

*Josh looks up.*

*Josh* Go on, I'll meet you there.

*He turns back to the car.*

*Josh* By the way, my name's Josh.

*Jenna* I'm Jenna.

*Josh* Nice to meet you Jenna.

*Jenna looks nervously at her watch.*

*Josh* There you go!

### Scene 5 A street in Santa Monica

*A café with tables on the street. The old car arrives. Jenna and Josh get out.*

*Josh* Go! Go! I'll wait.

*Boss* Well, you won't have to wait long! Jenna, this is the third time you've been late. I warned you: you're fired!

*Jenna* Larry, please ...

*The boss goes back into the café.*

## Scene 6 In Jenna's car

*Josh* I'm sorry. But it was only a café job.

*Jenna* *Angrily.* But I needed the money! You and your friends don't have to work – you just ask your parents for your money.

*Josh* *Feeling guilty.* I'm sorry.

*Jenna* *Still angry.* Yeah. You know... *bitterly* ... I live with my mom in Inglewood – but I guess you never go to *that* part of town. My mom doesn't have a job. My dad's in jail. He stole a car and then got into a fight. I have to pay for everything ...

*Josh* I'm sorry ...

*Jenna* It's not your fault.

*Jenna turns off the road. We see Luke's SUV and Josh's friends with their surfboards on the beach.*

*Jenna* Your friends are waiting for you.

*Josh opens his door.*

*Josh* Do you have a boyfriend, Jenna?

*Jenna* Why?

*Josh* *Smiling.* What are you doing tonight?

*Jenna looks at him. She's clearly nervous.*

*Jenna* I'm babysitting for our neighbor.

*Josh* Can I come too?

*Jenna* Are you serious?

*Josh* I'm serious.

*Jenna* Mrs Alvarez won't like it.

*Josh* Please, Jenna. What's the address?

*Jenna* *Pause.* 41 Hayden Street.

*Josh* 41 Hayden Street. *He jumps out.* Thanks for the ride.

*He closes the door and Jenna drives off.*

## Scene 7 The kitchen at Jenna's house

*Jenna is cleaning the small, cheap kitchen. We hear the front door open.*

*Mom* *Calling.* Hi baby! I'm home.

*Jenna* Hi, Mom.

*She goes through to the living room.*

## Scene 8 The living room at Jenna's house

*Jenna's mom sits down on the sofa and drops her keys on the table.*

*Jenna* Oh, Mom. You're drunk again. You promised ...

*Mom* Oh, Jenna baby, don't get angry. *She tries to get up.* Where are my cigarettes? *She sees them on the table next to her, takes one and lights it.*

*Jenna* I lost my job today.

*Mom* *Opens eyes.* My poor baby. Hey, let's go out for a drink tonight, just you and me ...

*Jenna* *Sadly.* I'm babysitting for Mrs Alvarez tonight, Mom. *Gets ready to go.*

*Mom* Aw, don't go, baby. Stay with me.

*Jenna kisses her mom.*

*Jenna* I'm sorry, Mom. I promised Mrs Alvarez. She has to work and her niece doesn't have time tonight. And it's ten dollars. See you.

## Scene 9 Malibu Beach

*Luke* So, what are we doing tonight, guys?

*Cindy* There's a party over at Melissa's house. We could ...

*Josh* *Angry.* Hey Cindy, all you ever think about is parties and surfing ... don't you believe in anything more important?

*Cindy* — Shopping?

*Cindy and Luke laugh. Josh gets up angrily.*

*Lara* — I believe in lots of things, Josh.

*He looks down at her.*

*Josh* — I know.

*Lara* — So, what do you want to do tonight?

*Josh* — I'm busy. I'll call you tomorrow, OK?

*He walks off.*

*Cindy* — Don't worry, Lara. He'll be back.

*Lara* — I'm not so sure ...

### Scene 10 The Alvarez house – the living room

*Somebody knocks at the door. Jenna goes over, checks who it is and opens the door. Josh stands there with boxes of Chinese food.*

*Josh* — Hi.

*Jenna* — Hi. You shouldn't be here.

*Josh* — Hungry?

*Jenna* — *Smells the food.* OK, just this one time.

*She lets him come in. They sit down.*

### Scene 11 Party at a rich house

*One of the guests is standing alone. It's Lara. A waiter offers her some food.*

*Lara* — No, thanks.

*Waiter* — *Whispers.* You OK?

*Lara* — Yeah. *She smiles weakly.* Thanks.

### Scene 12 The Alvarez house – the living room

*The meal is finished. Jenna and Josh are on the white sofa. She's drinking a coffee. Josh suddenly turns to her, the coffee goes on the sofa.*

*Jenna* — *Jumps up.* Oh, no!

*Josh* — It's only coffee!

*Jenna* — Only coffee! Look at the sofa. It's new.

*Josh* — *Gets up.* I'll clean it up.

*Jenna* — *Angry and worried.* I'll do it! You shouldn't even be here.

*Josh* — Hey, let's not get into an argument over a little coffee.

*Jenna* — This was a bad idea. Just go, Josh!

*Josh goes to the door, his feelings hurt.*

*Josh* — Bye Jenna.

*Jenna* — Bye.

## Working with the text

### 1 The scenes

*Say what each scene is about (1–2 sentences).*

1: Josh, Cindy and Lara meet at the beach.

2: Luke invites them to go to Malibu in his car. They want to go surfing.

3: They see a girl at the side of ...

more help ► D p. 110

### 2 The characters

**a)** *How do these people feel about each other?*

1 Josh and Lara 2 Luke and Cindy 3 Josh and Jenna

– He likes her more than she likes him.
– She likes him more than he likes her.

**b)** *Why do you think that? Find examples in the script.*

### 3 Extra Act it out

*Learn and act your favourite scene for the class.*

### 4 Soap operas

**a)** *Think of soaps you know. What is typical for them?*

love stories • music • everyday life • money problems • fights • arguments • social problems • jealousy • ...

**b)** *Finish this statement. You can use the ideas in the box or your own ideas.*

*I like/don't like watching soaps because ...*

they are just like real life • they aren't like real life at all • the stories are interesting/boring • the actors in them are nice/stupid/... • they are on every day

► WB 18 (p. 26) • **Checkpoint 3** WB (p. 27) • Selbsteinschätzung 1–2 WB (pp. 28–29)

## How am I doing? ▸ SF Check yourself (p. 137)

***a)*** *Find or choose the correct answers.*

### California

1 California is sometimes called ...
A the Golden State. B the Orange State. C the Sunny State. D the Surfing State.

2 There are lots of computer companies in ...
A San Clemente. B Yosemite. C Silicon Valley. D San Diego.

3 Many people in California come from Mexico. They speak ...
A Italian. B English. C French. D Spanish.

4 Some people cross the ... from Mexico to the US to look for work.
A road B highway C sea D border

5 The most famous bridge on the west coast of the US is ...
A the Brooklyn Bridge. B Tower Bridge. C the Golden Gate Bridge.

### Study Skills

6 Beim **Skimming** solltest du *nicht* ...
A die Überschriften lesen. B die Bilder anschauen. C Wort für Wort lesen.

7 Beim **Scanning** suchst du nach ...
A schönen Bildern. B bestimmten Informationen. C einer Übersetzung.

### Words

8 People who come from another country are called ...
A homeless people. B immigrants. C Mexicans. D Latinos.

9 I think there's a lot of ... against people who are different.
A prejudice B advantages C minority

10 Silicon Valley is a big ... area in California.
A farming B industrial C theme D filming

11 Which word fits in this sentence?
Most US strawberries are ... in California.
A made B eaten C done D grown

12 Which word doesn't fit?
A mountain B tsunami C earthquake D forest fire

### Grammar

13 Most American films ... in Hollywood.
A make B made C are made

14 Gold ... in California in 1848.
A was found B found C is found

15 That film was made ... Steven Spielberg.
A from B by C through

16 Which means the same as 'My camera was stolen'?
A I stole a camera.
B A camera stole me.
C Someone stole my camera.

***b)*** *Check your answers on p. 235 and add up your points – one point for each correct answer.*

***c)*** *If you had 13 or more points, well done!*
*Where did you make mistakes? The chart below will tell you what you can do to improve your English.*

| No. | Areas | Find out more | Exercises |
|---|---|---|---|
| 1– 5 | California | Unit 2 (pp. 34–38) | P1, P3 (p. 42), WB 1–2 (p. 18), 17 (p. 25) |
| 6– 7 | Study Skills | SF Skimming/scanning (p. 142) | P4 (p. 43), WB 8 (p. 21) |
| 8–12 | Words | Vocabulary (pp. 170–172) | P6 (p. 44), WB 2 (p. 18), 7 (p. 20), 9 (p. 22), 13 (p. 24) |
| 13–16 | The passive | Unit 2 (p. 36), GF 2 (pp. 156–157) | P3, P5, P13, P14 (pp. 42, 43, 47), WB 4–6 (pp. 19–20), 16 (p. 25) |

# Hermann says 'Willkommen'

**A** Market Street is the main street of Hermann, Missouri.

**C** The town on the Missouri River was founded in 1837 by German immigrants.

Hermann's **D** Festhalle – keeping German traditions alive

Wineries are one of **B** Hermann's most important industries.

**E** Hermann High School is a modern school with about 400 students.

F German festivals like Maifest and Oktoberfest are very popular with visitors.

G These beautiful old houses were built in the 19th century.

Arriving at the Krugers' farmhouse, outside Hermann H

## 1 What's Hermann like?

***a)*** *Look at the photos of Hermann, Missouri.*

| | |
|---|---|
| *What's the town like?*<br>The town looks ...<br>The countryside is ... | busy • quiet • hilly • nice • old-fashioned • pretty • boring • ... |
| In photo ... you can see ...<br>There is/There are ... | a school • tourists • a bridge • old buildings • ... |

***b)*** *Talk to a partner.*
*Say as many things as you can about Hermann.*

*A:* I think Hermann is quite small.
*B:* Yes, and there are ...

## 2 Arriving in Hermann

***a)*** *Listen and answer the questions.*

1 Are the Schmidts going to Hermann on holiday or to live there?
2 Do people in Hermann speak German?

***b)*** *Listen again and answer these questions:*

1 What's the temperature in St. Louis when they arrive?
2 How long does it take from St. Louis airport to Hermann?
3 What river is Hermann on?
4 Name one event that takes place in the Festhalle.
5 How many people live in Hermann?
6 Who's going to start at the high school?

***c)*** **Extra** *Would you like to start a new life In Hermann?*

I don't want to leave Germany.
I think it's too quiet.
I'd like to live there. I think it looks nice. What about you?
...

► P 1–2 (p. 60) • WB 1 (p. 30) • SF Listening (p. 141)

## All about ... American schools

### 1 A brochure about Hermann High School

> *If you were in the US, which school and grade would you be in?*
*Who has more school holidays – American or German students?*

Home of the Bearcats

## Hermann High School

Hermann MO

## Information for international exchange students

**The school system**

| | | |
|---|---|---|
| High School | Grades 9-12 | Ages 14-18 |
| Middle School | Grades 6-8 | Ages 11-14 |
| Elementary School | Grades 1-5 | Ages 6-11 |
| Kindergarten | | Ages 5-6 |

**The school year**

The school year starts at the beginning of September and goes to the end of May. It has two semesters. The summer vacation is three months: June, July and August. There is also a week off for Christmas and a week for Easter.

**The school day**

The school day starts at 8:20 a.m. and finishes at 3:00 p.m. Most students come by school bus or drive to school. You can get hot lunches in the school cafeteria, or you can bring your own lunch from home. Check the bulletin board in the cafeteria for the lunch menu.

**Grades**

At Hermann High we use the same grades that are used in all American schools:

**A** 'excellent' – **B** 'good' – **C** 'average' – **D** 'below average' – **F** 'failure'

If you want to take part in extracurricular activities, you can't have any grade below a C.

### 2 Jake's schedule

**Hermann High School** **Jake Kruger** **Grade: 9**

**Monday – Friday**

| Period | Time | Subject | Rm. |
|---|---|---|---|
| 1 | 08:20–09:10 | English 1 | 31 |
| 2 | 09:15–10:05 | Science | 36 |
| 3 | 10:10–11:00 | Algebra | 16 |
| 4 | 11:05–11:55 | Health | 28 |
| 5 | Lunch/study hall | | |
| 6 | 01:15–02:05 | American History | 21 |
| 7 | 02:10–03:00 | Boys' PE | Gym |

> 1 *Are your subjects like Jake's?*
2 *Are your lessons longer or shorter?*
3 *Would you like to have the same timetable every day? Why (not)?*

### 3 School words

***a)*** *Copy the chart. Find the American English words on this page and complete the AE section.*

| German | AE | BE |
|---|---|---|
| Jahrgangsstufe | grade | ... |
| Stundenplan | ... | ... |
| Unterrichtsstunde | ... | ... |
| (Schul-)Note | ... | ... |
| Schwarzes Brett | ... | ... |

***b)*** *Complete the BE section with the British English words from the box.*

year • timetable • lesson • grade • notice board

► P 3–6 (pp. 60–62) • WB 2–5 (pp. 30–32)

## 4 Extracurriculars

It was Timo Schmidt's first week at Hermann High School. He had lots of questions for his classmate Jake Kruger.

'What extracurriculars do you do?' Timo asked.

'Cindy and I go to the FFA. There's a meeting this afternoon. Do you want to join us?'

'FFA? What's that?' Timo asked.

'Future Farmers of America,' Jake told him.

'But I'm not a farmer!'

'No problem,' said Cindy.

There were a lot of students at the meeting. They were talking about their hogs.

'Sorry,' Timo said to Jake, 'what's a hog?'

'It's a word for a pig.'

Timo was surprised. 'You mean, students have their own hogs?'

'Sure,' said Jake.

'How many hogs have you got?' asked Timo.

'Just one.'

'And you look after it? How much time does that take every day?' asked Timo.

'I feed her twice a day,' Jake told him. 'Before and after school.'

'Wow,' said Timo. 'This is all new for me!'

*What is the FFA? Do you think people at your school would like it?*

**Extra | Americana ★ ★ ★**

**Extracurricular activities**
Sport and other extracurricular activities are just as important as lessons at American high schools. Students should be good at their school subjects, good at sport and interested in other things. The FFA is only one of these activities – there are usually foreign language clubs, debate teams, dance groups, a school band, a drama group, cheerleaders and teams for every kind of sport.

A

B

C

D

*Name these activities.*
*Which extracurriculars would you like to do?*

## 5 Extra Now you

***a)*** *Make notes about your school in Germany and Hermann High School. Think about: the school day, the timetable, how students get to school, lunch break, activities in school, ...*

more help ▸ D p. 111

***b)*** *Work with another group. Compare notes.*

▸ GF 3: Countable/uncountable nouns (p. 158) • P 7–8 (p. 62) • WB 6–8 (pp. 32–33)

## 6 In Jake's Health class

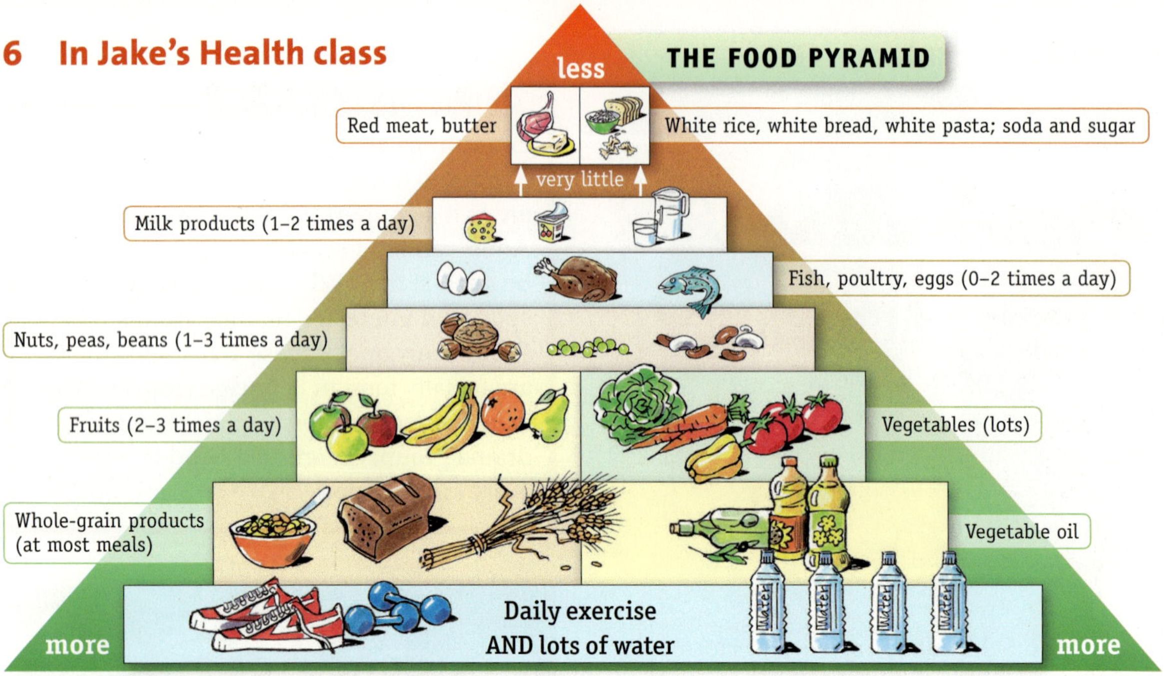


*What can you eat and drink a lot of? What shouldn't you eat and drink a lot of?*

► P 9 (p. 63) • WB 9 (p. 33)

## 7 Now you

***a)*** *Write down everything that you ate and drank yesterday. Think of the different meals and the snacks between meals.*

– *breakfast: muesli, a glass of milk, a banana, ...*

***b)*** *How healthy was your food yesterday?*

– I think it was (quite) healthy/unhealthy.
– I ate lots of/too much ...
– I didn't eat/drink enough ...
– I should eat more/less ...

## 8 Talking about health

'OK, we've talked a lot about food and health in general,' said Ms. Meerbusch, the Health class teacher. 'Now let's talk about the food that we eat. Is it healthy? – Yes, Cindy?'

'Well, the food that I eat at home is very healthy. Every morning my mom gives me a piece of fruit. And for dinner we always have vegetables or a salad. But school lunches are a problem. Most of the food that students choose is unhealthy.'

'Thank you, Cindy. – Yes, Jake?'

'I think fitness is important,' said Jake. 'If you play sports and eat good food, you feel great. But if you sit and watch TV and eat fast food, you feel bad.'

Timo smiled, 'What about that hamburger and fries you had for lunch today, Jake?'

Jake just laughed.

*Why is Cindy's food healthy? What else is important for your health?*

► **Extra** *GF 4: Definite article (p. 159) • P 10 (p. 63)*

► *P 11–12 (pp. 63–64) • WB 10–12 (pp. 34–35)*

## 9 From the local paper

Scrapbook — Hermann Advertiser-Courier — Wedne

### Hermann says a big 'Willkommen!' to new German family

**When Andreas Schmidt first visited Hermann 20 years ago, he had never heard of Missouri wine. But now he has a job at the Hermannthal Winery, and he's living here with his family.**

Andreas Schmidt first visited Hermann with a school group from Bad Arolsen, Germany, 20 years ago. And he's happy to be back! "Leaving your home and your country is a big step," Schmidt says. "But it's very exciting too."

Karla, Andreas's wife, says that moving to the US was an adventure. "At first I was worried, but now I'm happy. Everyone in Hermann is very friendly."

Son Timo (14) likes his new school. "A lot of things seemed strange at first, but I really like it here now." Timo loves soccer. "We've started a soccer team at the high school," he says. "We weren't very good at first. You see, the boys

hadn't played soccer before. But they're quite good now!"

His younger sister Anna (12) was homesick at first, but now has lots of friends. She already speaks English with a Missouri accent!

**To Andreas, Karla, Timo and Anna: Hermann says 'Willkommen!'**

*How do the Schmidts feel in their new home?*

► GF 5: Past perfect (p. 160) • P 13 (p. 64) • WB 13–14 (pp. 35–36)

## 10 Did you see the article?

*Jake calls Timo. He wants to tell him about the article. What can he say?*

Hi Timo, there's an article in the paper about ...

A your family. B Bad Arolsen.
C Hermann.

The first part is about ...

A Bad Arolsen. B your dad. C the winery.

It says that ... and it says that ...

... Bad Arolsen is in Germany.

... your dad visited Hermann 20 years ago.

... he has a job in a winery here.

... your dad's name is Andreas.

The rest of the article is about ...

A Hermann. B soccer.
C you, your mom and your sister.

It says that ...

A you're all happy in Hermann.
B you like hockey.
C your sister hasn't found friends.

**STUDY SKILLS** Summarizing texts

*Wenn du einen Text (mündlich oder schriftlich) zusammenfasst, gibst du die **wichtigsten Informationen** in kürzerer Form wieder. Schreibe keine Sätze aus dem Originaltext ab, sondern verwende deine eigenen Worte.*

► SF Summarizing texts (p. 149) • P 14–15 (p. 65) • WB 15 (p. 36)

## Extra | Background File | Going west

### 1 READING Group puzzle (part 1)

*Divide the class into four groups (A, B, C, D). Each person in the group has a number (1, 2, 3, ...). Group A reads the text about Hermann, Group B reads the text about Missouri, etc. Then go to **2** on p. 59.*

### A HERMANN

In the 18th and early 19th centuries, many German immigrants were unhappy because their children grew up with English traditions and the English language. They wanted them to grow up with the German traditions and the German language. So a group of Germans bought land in Missouri in 1837 and the town of Hermann was founded.

Hermann stayed very German until World War I (1914–1918). The US was fighting against the Germans in Europe, so Germans weren't popular. The school in Hermann was not allowed to teach in German. The people of Hermann stopped speaking German and gave up their traditions for many years.

*The first settlers in Hermann thought it looked like the Rhine Valley.*

### B THE ROLE OF MISSOURI

The first states of the United States of America were on the east coast. Then, in 1848, thousands of people wanted to go west because gold was discovered in California. Not everybody went west to look for gold. Lots of people were looking for free or cheap land so they could start a farm. Missouri was a good place to start a journey to the West, so it became the 'Gateway to the West'.

In St. Louis people bought everything that they needed for the journey. Then they went up the Missouri River to Independence, where they joined a wagon train. These 'trains' were the safest way to travel. There was no railway across the country until 1869.

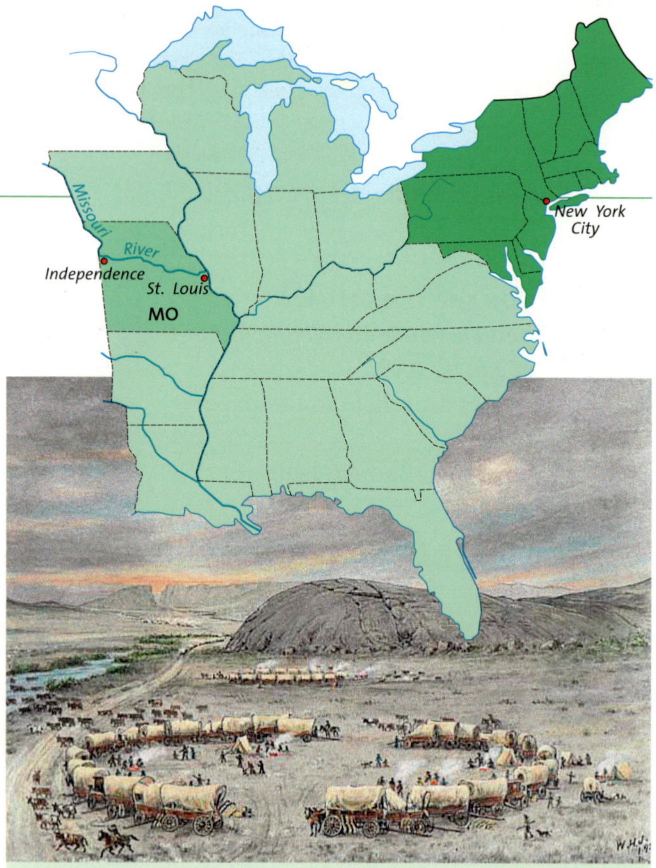


*Settlers got off the Missouri river boats and formed wagon trains for the journey to the West.*

► **Text File 8** *(pp. 128–129)*

## C THE TRAILS TO THE WEST

The wagon trains followed one of many trails to the West. The most famous one is the Oregon Trail. It was 2000 miles long, and the journey took five months. Many of the pioneers walked all the way – their wagons were full of the things that they needed for their new lives in the West.

More than half a million people went west with the wagon trains. But it was a dangerous trip. 50,000 of them didn't make it. Many died of accidents or illnesses. Some were killed by animals or died in fights with Native Americans.

## D THE NATIVE AMERICANS

When the first Europeans came to North America, there were already millions of people there – the 'Native Americans' (or 'American Indians').The arrival of the Europeans brought trouble for the Native Americans. First, millions of them died of illnesses that the Europeans brought with them. Later, as more and more Europeans arrived, the Native Americans were forced out of their traditional land by the white settlers. There were a lot of fights between white settlers and Indians.

Today there are about four million Native Americans in the US, about 1.5 % of the population. Some live in or near reservations. Some have moved to big cities. ■

### 2 Group puzzle (part 2)

***a)*** *In your group, answer the two questions on the right about your text. Make sure that all of you have understood the main points.*

***b)*** *Make new groups of four (A1, B1, C1, D1; A2, B2, ...). Tell each other the important information from your text. Take notes on the other texts.*

***c)*** *Go back to your first group (A, B, C or D) and compare your information. Did you all understand the same things? If not, read the texts again and check your information.*

▸ **Text File 9** *(pp. 130–131)* • *WB 16 (p. 37)*

**Group A**
- When did German immigrants found Hermann?
- Why did people in Hermann stop speaking German?

**Group B**
- Why was Missouri called the 'Gateway to the West'?
- When could people cross the country by railway?

**Group C**
- What was the most famous trail? How long was it?
- How many people went west on the trails?

**Group D**
- Why did the arrival of the Europeans bring trouble for the Indians?
- How many Native Americans are there today?

## 1 //O REVISION More about Hermann (Passive) ▸ D p. 111

*Complete the sentences about Hermann.*

1. The area around Hermann **(is/are)** called 'the US Rhineland'. A lot of wine **(is/are)** grown there.
2. The first houses in Hermann **(was/were)** built by German immigrants. This house **(was/were)** built in 1880.

3. German traditions **(is/are)** kept alive in Hermann. The Oktoberfest **(is/are)** visited by lots of tourists every year.
4. In the 1800s German **(is/was)** spoken by the people of Hermann. Today only English **(is/was)** spoken there.

## 2 WORDS Hermann in numbers: average temperature, population, ...

*Partner B: Look at p. 104.*

***a)*** *Partner A: Look at the list. What can you tell your partner about Hermann?*

- Hermann was founded in ...
- The average temperature in winter is minus ... degrees Celsius.
- ... per cent of the people have German names.

***b)*** *Listen to your partner. Fill in a copy of the chart.*

HERMANN

| | |
|---|---|
| Founded in: | 1837 |
| Population today: | ? |
| Average temperature: | – 7 °C (winter)<br>? °C (summer) |
| People with German names: | 54.4 % |
| Wine made in Missouri: | ? million litres a year |

## 3 //O WORDS School in the US and Britain ▸ D p. 112

*Complete the sentences with words from the boxes.*

schedule • bulletin board • grades • periods • vacation

holidays • grades • lessons • notice board • timetable

1. American students say *schedule* when they tell you what they do every day at school and when. British students use the word ___.
2. At Hermann High School there are seven of these in a school day and each one is 50 minutes long. They are called ___. In Britain they are called ___.
3. In America they talk about the summer ___. In Britain they usually talk about the summer ___.
4. In every school you can find this on the wall. Teachers and students put information on it so that everyone can read it. In America it's called a ___. In Britain, it's called a ___.
5. In Britain and America teachers give you ___ to tell you how good or bad a piece of work is.

## 4 SPEAKING If you're not sure, ask!

*a) Timo is new in Jake's class. Jake tells him about school but Timo doesn't always understand. Make Timo's questions. Then listen and check.*

Well, the school year starts every year in September. We have school till the end of May.

Sorry – when – school year – finish?

At the end of May. The summer vacation is from June to August.

Sorry – how long – summer vacation?

Three months from June to the end of August. And at Christmas and Easter we get a week off.

Sorry – how long – you get off – at Christmas and Easter?

*b) Jake tells Timo about his school day. What questions might Timo ask? Make the questions and write them down.*

| | | | | |
|---|---|---|---|---|
| Sorry, | when<br>what<br>how much | do you get to school?<br>does the bus leave? | homework do you do?<br>do you have after lunch?<br>can you get for lunch? | is lunch?<br>do you get home? |

*c) Listen again. You are Timo and you don't always understand what Jake says. Ask questions. Use your questions from b).*

## 5 WRITING A letter to Hermann High (Letter for information)

*Write a letter to Jake Kruger to find out more about Hermann High.*

***In your letter you should say:***

– who you are and why you're writing

***You can say something about yourself:***

– where you go to school
– what grade/year you're in / how old you are
– why you are writing
– ...

***In your letter you should ask questions.***
***You could ask about:***

– the school day
– how students get to school
– school subjects
– vacations/holidays
– extracurricular activities
– ...

*You can put your letter in your DOSSIER.*

more help ► *D p. 112*

► **Extra** *SF Writing letters (p. 148)*
► *SF Correcting your text (p. 147)*

Willy-Brandt-Str. 14
34454 Bad Arolsen
Germany
May 27 ...

Dear Jake

My name is Julia Gieseler and I'm writing to you because I'd like to know more about Hermann High School.
...

Best wishes
Julia

**Tipp**

– *Beginne deinen Brief mit der richtigen Anrede und beende ihn mit einer Grußformel.*
– *Lies den fertigen Brief noch einmal genau durch. Überprüfe dabei Schreibung, Grammatik usw.*
– *Unterschreibe deinen Brief.*

## 6 Extra LISTENING School announcements and 'Thought for the day'

*Read the statements below. Then listen. Are the statements true (T) or false (F)?*

1 Hermann played well, but lost the game against Washington.
2 The Hermann High School team is called the Bearcats.
3 The school band will meet in the music room this Saturday.
4 The band is going to play at Maifest.
5 The school play is called 'TV Hour'.
6 The play will be on Friday, Saturday and Sunday evenings.
7 Today's 'Thought for the day' comes from the writer Robert Collier.
8 Collier thinks that we shouldn't try too hard.

## 7 How much time? How many hours? (Countable/uncountable nouns)

**a)** *Copy the chart below and put the nouns from the box in two groups.*

apples • cheese • e-mails • homework • milk • hours • DVDs • time • water • subjects • pocket money • sandwiches • text messages

| *Countable (how many? = wie viele)* | *Uncountable (how much? = wie viel)* |
|---|---|
| *apples* | *cheese* |
| ... | ... |

**b)** *Write questions with* **How much?** *and* **How many?**

*How many* apples do you eat in a week?
... milk or water do you drink in a day?
... subjects do you learn at school?
... homework do you do every day?
... text messages do you get in a day?
... pocket money do you spend on CDs and DVDs in a month?
... DVDs do you watch in a week?
... time do you spend in front of the computer in a week?

**c)** Extra *Ask a partner your questions. Answer your partner's questions.*

## 8 Do you need some money? (Countable/uncountable nouns)

*Complete the sentences with* **a/an** *or* **some**.
*Then read the dialogue.*

*Mom* Do you need ... money for a hot lunch today, Cindy?
*Cindy* No thanks, Mom. We've got ... bread. I'll make ... sandwich.
*Mom* You should take ... fruit. It's good for you.
*Cindy* OK, I'll take ... apple and ... banana.
*Mom* Do you want ... bottle of orange juice?
*Cindy* It's OK. I can get ... water at school.

**Tipp**
*Bei zählbaren Nomen* **(countable nouns)** *kannst du* **a/an** *verwenden:* **a cake, an apple**
*Unzählbare Nomen* **(uncountable nouns)** *darfst du nur mit* **some** *oder* **lots of** *verwenden:* **some sugar, lots of sugar**

## 9 WORDS Food

***a)*** *Put the food and drink words in a chart like the one below. Then add your favourite food.*

beans • beef • biscuits • bread • butter • carrots • +cereals • cheese • chicken • coffee • crisps • curry • eggs • fish • fruit • juice • lamb • marmalade • meat • milk • muesli • nuts • pasta • peas • pork • potatoes • poultry • rice • rolls • salad • salami • sausages • soup • spaghetti • steak • sweets • tea • toast • turkey • vegetables • water

| breakfast | lunch | dinner | snacks between meals |
|---|---|---|---|
| cereals<br>... | ... | ... | ... |

***b)*** *Talk to your partner like this.*

What do you usually eat for breakfast/lunch/... ?

I usually eat ...

What's your favourite food/drink/dish?

I like/love ...

How often do you eat fruit/vegetables/sweets/...?

Every day/once a week/twice a week/ ...

***c)*** **Extra** *Write a short text about the food that you eat.* more help ▸ D p. 113

## 10 Extra Money is a problem (Definite article)

*Add* **the** *where you need it.*

1 ? money really is a problem for my family because we aren't rich.
2 I've spent all ? money that you gave me yesterday.
3 I love ? pizza. It's my favourite food.
4 ? pizza that we had for lunch was delicious.
5 ? life of a farmer must be very hard.
6 Is ? life easier if you're rich?

## 11 WORDS Word building (Noun suffixes)

**Tipp**

*Wenn ein Nomen die Nachsilbe **-ness** hat, kannst du es meist verstehen, wenn du den ersten Teil des Wortes kennst,*

*z. B. happ**iness** = happ**y** + **ness***
*Du weißt, dass **happy** 'glücklich' heißt.*
*Also heißt **happiness** 'Glück'.*

***a)*** *Copy and complete. Work without the dictionary first. Then check in the dictionary.*

| | | |
|---|---|---|
| madness → | mad: verrückt → | Verrücktheit |
| fitness → | fit: ... → | ... |
| illness | ... | |
| nervousness | | |
| weakness | | |

***b)*** *Complete the sentences with words from the green box in a).*

1 I want to be in the school baseball team, but I'm not sure about my ...
2 ... before a test is a problem for some students.
3 I usually eat healthy food, but I have a ... for hamburger and chips.

## 12 READING Soft drinks, hard facts (Finding the main ideas of a text) ► SF p. 143

**Finding the main ideas of a text**
*In vielen Texten findest du in jedem Abschnitt einen Satz, der den Hauptgedanken (***main idea***) dieses Abschnittes enthält.*

# Where's the soda machine?

(1) **Experts agree that American teenagers drink too many sugary drinks. A study in California found that six out of ten teenagers drink at least some soda every day, and some of them drink two or more soft drinks a day.**

(2) The same study found out that if it's easy to buy soda, teenagers drink more. If it's difficult to buy it, they drink less. In other words, if you don't sell soda in school, students will drink less of it.

(3) That's why some schools have stopped selling soft drinks. These schools don't have soda machines any more. Under the new rules, students can still bring soft drinks with them from home, but they can't buy them in school.

(4) The idea is that the new rules will help all children, not just those who are already fat. Maybe the fat kids will lose a few pounds. And everybody will learn more about healthy and unhealthy food.

(5) Experts agree that soda is bad for your health. So yes, if you want to be healthier, it's a good idea to drink less soda. But you can do more. If you want to be really healthy, you must also eat less unhealthy food. That means no biscuits, cakes, white bread, burgers and chips – all the things that teenagers love!

***a)*** *Which of the main ideas below* (A–D) *goes with which paragraph* (1–4)*?*

(A) The experts hope that the new rules will be good for everybody.
(B) Experts think that students will drink less soda if they can't buy it in school.
(C) In some schools students can't buy soda any more.
(D) Teenagers in America drink too much soda.

***b)*** *Find the sentence in each paragraph that gives you the main idea of that paragraph.*

***c)*** *Which of the two marked sentences gives you the main idea in the last paragraph* (5)*?*

## 13 What a nice little party! (Past perfect)

*Complete the sentences. Use the* ***past perfect****.*

1. I went to Lea's birthday party with Tom. He was excited because *he had never met* (never/meet) her before.
2. When we arrived at the party Tom couldn't find his present. He ... (leave) it on the bus.
3. Sandra was late. She ... (forget) Lea's address.
4. At the party I ate chicken curry. I ... (never/try) Indian food before. It was delicious.
5. Lisa couldn't eat the chicken curry. She ... (eat) too many biscuits.
6. Peter played Lea's guitar. It was awful. He ... (never/play) before.

## 14 STUDY SKILLS Summarizing texts

***a)*** *Read the story.*

### The rafting trip

Carrie was nervous.

'Why are you going on the rafting trip if you're scared of water?' her friend Cindy asked. 'The Castor River is pretty wild.'

'Everybody says it's fun,' said Carrie.

She didn't tell Cindy the real reason: Jim Nielson. Jim was at Hermann High too, but he was two grades above Carrie. Carrie thought he was really nice. And Jim was one of the guides on the rafting trip ...

On the bus to the river Carrie sat next to Sue. She talked and talked about Maifest. Carrie didn't talk. She was thinking about the river.

At first the water was slow, so they talked and laughed in the raft. But after an hour it got faster. Suddenly Jim shouted, 'Go left, left!' – but it was too late. The raft hit a rock and Carrie fell in the water. 'This is the end,' she thought. But then she felt a hand. It was Jim. He pulled her back onto the raft.

'Sorry about that. Were you scared?' he said.

'No, I'm fine,' said Carrie. 'Thanks for saving me.'

'No problem,' said Jim. 'That was the easy bit. The next bit is really fast.'

'Oh no,' Carrie thought. 'Never again!'

***b)*** *Put the sentences in the right order and retell the story.*

- **A** On the bus Carrie is worried about the trip.
- **B** The story is about a girl called Carrie.
- **C** At first everything is OK because the water is slow.
- **D** The problem is that Carrie is scared of water.
- **E** She goes on a rafting trip because she wants to meet Jim, a boy from school.
- **F** But Carrie doesn't want to go rafting ever again.
- **G** Then the raft hits a rock and Carrie falls into the water.
- **H** Jim saves her.

► *SF Summarizing texts (p. 149)*

## 15 MEDIATION American tourists in Germany

***a)*** *You're at the train station in Bad Arolsen. On the platform two American tourists ask you for help. Look at the first announcement and help the man.*

**Announcement 1:**

Bitte beachten Sie: Der Regionalexpress von Bad Arolsen nach Kassel-Wilhelmshöhe fährt heute ausnahmsweise nicht von Gleis 1 ab, sondern von Gleis 4.

*Man* Excuse me, can you help me, please? We're going to Kassel. I think we need platform 1. Is that right?

*You* No, that isn't right. The train to ...

***b)*** *Now listen to the announcements on the CD. How can you help the tourists?*

- The train to ... is ... minutes late.
- You can get a cup of coffee in ...
- We have to get out on the ... side.
- We'll ... in Frankfurt in a few minutes.

► *SF Mediation (p. 152)*

## Angus Bethune's moment by Chris Crutcher (adapted)

> *Angus Bethune is a boy at an American high school. Before you read the text, look at the pictures on pp. 66–67. What do you think the boy is like? Choose from the ideas in the box.*

boring • brave • clever • clumsy • cool • friendly • funny • happy • nervous • nice • popular • rich • rude • shy • sporty

I'm a big kid and my name is Angus. Which is a cow's name. So I have my problems. But it isn't all bad. I have great reflexes and I'm a good football player. And I get good grades at school. But I'd be happy to swap reflexes and good grades for a little beauty.

That brings me to tonight. Tonight is a big night. See, I was elected Winter Ball King. That means for about one minute I will be on the dance floor at Lake Michigan High School with Melissa Lefevre, the girl of my dreams. She was elected Winter Ball Queen.

I don't know how I was elected. It's a joke, I know that. But tonight I will get my moment with Melissa Lefevre.

But there's a problem. I can't dance.

I fell in love with Melissa in kindergarten. She was a blond girl with long legs and brown eyes. I've never even talked to her. Until tonight. Tonight I'll *have* to talk to her. It's my moment with Melissa.

What is Melissa thinking? She's probably thinking that it's like a trip to the dentist. It will hurt, but soon it will be over and she'll still be alive.

Of course, Melissa hasn't seen me dance.

I walk into the gym. I'm scared but I try to look cool. I see Melissa on the dance floor with her boyfriend, Rick Sanford – a real jerk. I hear the announcement: the King and Queen have to be on the stage in five minutes.

I'm sweating. I want my moment.

Melissa and Rick are walking toward me. I want to run. What am I doing here?

They stand in front of me. "Angus," Rick says. "I'm giving you this pretty thing for a few minutes. So she can compare."

Melissa smiles. She says, "Hi. Don't listen to him. He's drunk. And rude."

I smile. I can't speak.

Melissa says, "Why don't we go?"

"Yeah," Rick says, "you go with my girl, snowball king."

Melissa whispers, "Shut up, Rick."

"Have fun," Rick says to me. "Your election cost me a lot of money. And don't put your big fat hands on my girl."

Melissa takes my arm and says, "Let's go."

We're waiting to go onto the stage. I say, "By the way, there's something you should know. I can't dance."

Melissa smiles. "We'll survive," she says.

"What did he mean, my election cost him a lot of money?" I whisper.

"Never mind. He's rich, and he's rude," she says. "I'm embarrassed I'm with him." She pauses and puts her arm in mine. "I'm not with him."

The curtains open and the trumpets play. We get our crowns. I feel stupid. King Angus the Fat.

Melissa says, "I chose a slow song. We don't have to move much. Dance close to me. Don't listen to the music. Just follow me."

We go to the dance floor. She smiles, then pulls me close. She says, "Follow me."

I'm in heaven. In my wildest dreams I never imagined that Melissa Lefevre would be nice to me. She whispers, "Relax," into my ear, and I follow her.

"Angus?"

"Yeah?"

"Do you ever get tired of who you are?"

I say, "Yeah."

She says, "I want to tell you something. I'm bulimic. Do you know what that is?"

"Yes, I know what that is. It means when you eat too much, you throw up so you don't look like me."

"Don't worry, I'm in therapy for it," she says.

"Actually," I say, "I even tried it once, but when I put my finger down my throat, I was still hungry and I nearly ate my arm."

Melissa laughs and holds me closer. "You're the only person who I've ever told. Would you do something for me?"

"OK."

"Would you leave with me?"

"You mean leave this dance? Leave this dance with you?"

She nods.

The music ends. "I want to dance one more," Melissa says. "A fast one."

"I'll wait."

"No. I want to dance it with you."

"You don't understand," I say. "When I dance rock and roll, people across the country feel earthquakes."

She takes my hand. "Listen. Do what you do on the football field. Follow me like you follow the guy from the other team."

The band starts to play "Bad Moon Rising", and the dance floor is full. Melissa starts to dance, and I watch her the way I would watch a player on the football field. I do everything that she does. Soon lots of kids are watching us. I'm in a circle of kids, and they're cheering. I'm Angus Bethune, Fat Man Extraordinaire, in the spotlight with Melissa Lefevre.

When the band finishes, everyone is clapping, even Melissa. I tell God he can take me now.

"You bitch!" Rick shouts. "You practiced with him. You planned this." He turns to me. "I'm gonna kill you, fat boy," he says.

I say, "Don't even think it. After dancing, fighting is what I do best."

## Working with the text

### 1 Your first reaction to the story

***a)*** *Go back to the question at the beginning of the story. Were you right about Angus?*

I thought Angus was ... – I was right/wrong about that. Now I think he's ...

***b)*** ◯ *What do you think of the ending?*

brilliant • funny • good • realistic • sad • silly • surprising • unrealistic • ...

### 2 In the story or not?

*Look at the pictures. Some of these things didn't happen in the story. Which ones?*

### 3 //◯ Tell the story ▸ D p. 113

*Match the sentence parts.*

| | |
|---|---|
| 1 This story is about a boy called ... | ... Melissa Lefevre. |
| 2 He says that he has problems because ... | ... Rick. |
| 3 But he's good at football and ... | ... Winter Ball King. |
| 4 Angus is elected ... | ... Angus. |
| 5 The Winter Ball Queen is ... | ... he's big. |
| 6 Melissa's boyfriend is called ... | ... he gets good grades at school. |
| 7 Angus is elected because Rick gave people ... | ... Melissa helps him. |
| 8 Angus is OK on the dance floor because ... | ... is clapping. |
| 9 Melissa tells Angus that ... | ... very angry. |
| 10 After the fast dance everyone ... | ... very happy. |
| 11 At the end Rick is ... | ... money. |
| 12 And Angus is ... | ... she's bulimic. |

### 4 ● Extra The next day

*Write a dialogue between two of the characters the next day.*

– Angus and Melissa
– Angus and Rick
– Melissa and Rick

Hi, how are you today?

I can't believe it happened.

That was a brilliant/terrible/fantastic evening.

I felt really nervous/surprised/shocked/embarrassed/... when ...

You were awesome/great/rude/...

Everybody is talking about last night.

▸ WB 17 (p. 38) • **Checkpoint 3** WB (p. 39)

## How am I doing?

***a)*** *Find or choose the correct answers.*

### Hermann and Missouri

1 Missouri is a state in the ... of the US.
A middle B south C east D west

2 The people who founded Hermann where from ...

3 'Missouri' is the name of a state, but also the name of a big ...
A national park. B forest. C river. D city.

### American schools

4 The school before middle school is called ...

5 High school starts with the 9th ...

6 In the US sports and school clubs are called ...

7 There are five grades in US schools, the best grade in a test is ...

### Words

8 Write down four school words from the unit.

9 Which word in the box goes with 'poultry'?
poultry – ...

pig • cow • chicken

10 What's your daily ...? – I ride my bike every day.

11 How do you say this? %

12 How do you say this? 1.8

### Summarizing texts

13 Welche Aussage trifft *nicht* zu? Wenn du einen Text zusammenfasst, solltest du ...
A die wichtigsten Informationen des Originaltexts wiedergeben.
B deine eigenen Worte verwenden.
C alle Einzelheiten des Originaltexts wiedergeben.

### Grammar

14 Add ***a/an*** or ***some***:
a) Can I have ... glass of milk, please?
– Of course, there's ... milk in the fridge.
b) Would you like ... fruit with your sandwich?
– Yes, ... apple would be nice.
c) Dad, can I have ... money for school lunch?

15 Timo couldn't open the door. He ... his key.
A loses B had lost C lost D will lost

### Everyday English

16 You didn't understand. What can you say?

I get to school at eight o' clock.

Sorry, ... do you get to school?
A where B what C when D how

***b)*** *Check your answers on p. 235 and add up your points – one point for each correct answer.*

***c)*** *If you had 16 or more points, well done!*
*Where did you make mistakes? The chart below will tell you what you can do to improve your English.*

| No. | Areas | Find out more | Exercises |
|---|---|---|---|
| 1– 3 | Hermann and Missouri | Unit 3 (pp. 52–53) | WB 1 (p. 30) |
| 4– 7 | American schools | Unit 3 (pp. 54–55) | P 3 (p. 60), WB 2–4 (pp. 30–31), 12 (p. 35) |
| 8–10 | Words: school, food | All about (p. 54), A6 (p. 56) | P 3 (p. 60), P 9 (p. 63), WB 2–3 (pp. 30–31), 9 (p. 33) |
| 11–12 | Words: numbers | P 2 (p. 60) | |
| 13 | Summarizing texts | Unit 3 (p. 57), SF (p. 149) | P 14 (p. 65), WB 15 (p. 36) |
| 14 | Countable/uncountable nouns | GF 3 (p. 158) | P 7–8 (p. 62), WB 6–8 (pp. 32–33) |
| 15 | Past perfect | GF 5 (p. 160) | P 13 (p. 64), WB 13–14 (pp. 35–36) |
| 16 | Everyday English | P 4 (p. 61) | WB 4–5 (pp. 31–32) |

## 1 WORDS Holidays

***a)*** *Collect ideas about holidays in four lists.*

| Getting there | Where to stay | Things to do | Describing things |
|---|---|---|---|
| fly / go by plane<br>go by ... | stay with friends<br>stay at a ... | see the sights<br>relax on the beach<br>visit a ... | It's fun / cool / ... here.<br>The beach is beautiful / ...<br>The weather is ... |

***b)*** *Write a short text for a brochure for an exciting holiday place. Use ideas from your lists.*

Come to ...!
It's easy to get here. You can ...
Stay at ... or ...
There's lots to do. You can ...
This is a great place. There's ...

## 2 WORDS Numbers

*Dates, times and prices are important on holidays.*

***a)*** *Practise these numbers.*

What's the time?

It's ...

| | | |
|---|---|---|
| 8:04 | 12:04 | 20:00 |
| 9:36 | 15:30 | 22:45 |
| 11:15 | 18:27 | 22:49 |

18th April • 12 May • 1 July • 2nd October •
23/8 • 3/1 • 25/12 • 30/11 • 29/2 • 21/9

| | | | | | |
|---|---|---|---|---|---|
| $1.50 | $8.30 | $15 | $17.56 | $44.99 | $71.65 |

***b)*** *Write down ...*

– *the times of two things you're doing next week*
– *the birthdays of two people*
– *the price of one thing that you bought last week.*

*Read everything to your partner.*

– I'm going to ... on Sunday/... at ...
– ...'s birthday is on ...
– I bought a ... It cost ...

**Tip**

| | You see | You say |
|---|---|---|
| Times | 6:00 | six o'clock/six am |
| | 9:30 | nine thirty/half past nine |
| | 10:47 | ten forty-seven |
| | 17:00 | five o'clock/five pm |
| | 19:08 | nineteen oh eight |
| | 22:15 | quarter past ten/ten fifteen |
| Dates | 17 March | the seventeenth of March |
| | 14th June | the fourteenth of June |
| Prices | $1 | a/one dollar |
| | $1.20 | a/one dollar twenty |
| | $5 | five dollars |
| | $8.59 | eight dollars fifty-nine |

## 3 My school holidays start ... (Prepositions in time phrases)

*Complete the sentences with* at *(2x),* in *(5x ), or* on *(4x).*

*1* My school holidays start ... Thursday.
*2* I want to relax ... the first day of the holidays.
*3* Visit Las Vegas ... May – it's too hot ... July.
*4* We often go to the beach ... the summer.
*5* Hurry! The train leaves ... 8:04.
*6* We arrived in London ... Monday morning.
*7* We arrived in London ... the morning.
*8* When's the concert? – It's ... 10 June.
*9* We spent two weeks in the US ... 2006.
*10* What do you want to do ... the weekend?

## 4 SPEAKING Let's go to the park

***a)*** *Matt and Jon are talking about what they want to do today. Read their conversation.*

*Matt* Let's go to the park. We can skate there.
*Jon* No, I don't really want to do that again. We went to the park yesterday. What about going to the cinema today?
*Matt* Sorry, I can't. I haven't got any money. We could go back to my house. I've got a new computer game.
*Jon* That's a good idea. Let's do that.
*Matt* Cool. Come on then. Let's go.

**Tip**

**Say what you want to do:**
– Let's go/watch/...
– We could/go/watch/...
– What about going/watching/...?

**Maybe you don't like the idea:**
– I don't really want to do that.
– Sorry, I can't.

If you don't like the idea, try and give a reason:
– We went there yesterday.
– I haven't got so much money.

**Maybe you like the idea:**
– That's a good/great/... idea.
– Yes, let's do that.

***b)*** *Make a conversation like the one on the left. Here are some ideas for things to do.*

go shopping/swimming/... • go on a trip to ... • make a pizza • watch a film • play football/... • go to a basketball/... match • ...

## 5 STUDY SKILLS Writing (Linking sentences)

*A good text needs linking words and time phrases.*

***a)*** *Use these time phrases to complete the text.*

At about one o'clock • before they went to bed • Last year • later in the afternoon • 90 minutes later • One morning in July

1 there was a competition in UK schools. It was organized by the German Tourist Information and the first prize was four days in Germany. 2 the 15 winners left London and just 3 they arrived at Cologne Bonn Airport. They went into Cologne and left their bags at their hotel.

4 they had lunch in town and 5 they visited the cathedral and a sports museum. They had dinner at a restaurant with German food and 6 they went for a short walk through the old town.

***b)*** *Complete the text with these linking words.*

and • because • but • but • so • when • where

The next day they all went shopping. (They had to use their German 1 not all the shop assistants spoke English!) Later they went up the Rhine on a boat 2 visited a chocolate museum. Everyone ate lots of chocolate.

On the third day they travelled to Bonn. There they saw the house 3 Beethoven was born, 4 there wasn't enough time to go to the city's other museums. In the evening they had tickets for a rock festival. It wasn't over until 1 am, 5 they all went to bed really late.

Everyone was very tired 6 they arrived back in London the next day, 7 they had all had a fantastic time in Germany.

▸ *WB 1–4 (pp. 40–41)*

## 1 Listening

*You will hear five travel announcements and mini-dialogues.*
*For each one choose the correct picture: A, B, or C. At the end you will hear the recordings again.*

*1* Which gate at the airport must passengers for Denver go to?

A 8 B 18 C 8A

*2* Where is the ticket office at this railway station?

A Platform 6 B Platform 9 C Ticket Office next to café →

*3* How much does the man pay for his tickets?

A $ $ $ $8 B $ $ $ $10 C $ $ $ $25

*4* Which platform must the woman go to?

A S3 Stadtmitte/City Centre 11:07 Gleis 16

B S3 Stadtmitte/City Centre 11:17 Gleis 6

C S3 Stadtmitte/City Centre 11:20 Gleis 2

*5* When does the man want a hotel?

A 8 May 12 May B 18 May 20 May C 18 March 20 March

## 2 Listening

*You will hear a radio programme from the US. Read the questions below. Then listen and choose the correct answer: A, B or C. You will hear the programme twice.*

*1* You can hear the programme once a …
A day. B week. C month.

*2* Later in the show Annie will talk about …
A school grades. B sport. C fashion.

*3* Katie went on an interesting vacation last …
A summer. B winter. C autumn.

*4* She was a … for a week.
A pop singer B circus clown C cowgirl

*5* She went with her …
A uncle and aunt. B parents. C sisters.

*6* On the vacation, Katie … every day.
A cooked B ran 20 miles C rode horses

*7* One day she helped Ben and Ted with a …
A baby cow. B baby horse. C baby lion.

*8* Once they had a … in the mountains.
A camp fire B concert C picnic

*9* During the vacation Katie slept in a …
A hostel. B tent. C cabin.

*10* Katie says the vacation is great if you can …
A swim. B ride horses. C ride a bike.

► *SF How to do well in a test (pp. 150–151)*

## 3 Speaking

*You're on holiday with your partner. You want to discuss things to do tomorrow.*
*– Look at the pictures below. Choose three things that you'd like to do.*
*– Tell your partner about your ideas. How many things can you find that you both want to do?*

*Give reasons why you want (or don't want) to do something.*
*Partner A begins:* *A:* Let's … *B:* …

1

2

3

4

5

6

7

8

9

## 4 Writing

Buddy *is a magazine for teenagers. They want to publish letters from their readers about 'The best holiday I've ever had'.*
*Write a short letter to the magazine. Say …*
*– when the holiday was*
*– where you went*
*– who you went with*
*– some things you did*
*– why you liked the holiday so much.*

… (date)

Dear Buddy

You wanted to know about the best holiday I've ever had. It was …

…

# My life in Atlanta, GA

WATCH THIS VIDEO

## 1 Madison's life

***a)*** *Madison Young lives in Atlanta, GA. Find Atlanta on the map at the front of the book. What US state is it in?*

***b)*** *These photos are from a video that Madison made about her life. What do they show? Choose captions for the photos from the box.*

at church • doing volunteer work • a busy street downtown • hanging out in the shopping mall • a place that tourists visit • my favourite music • where my mom works

A

C

B

D

## 4 Have you been home long?

'Hi Madison. Am I late? Have you been home long?'
'Don't worry, Marcia. I've only just arrived.'
'I wanted to call you. I tried your cellphone but there was no answer.'
'Oh ... that's the problem. I've lost it. I haven't told my parents yet. Anyway, we're both here now. Come in and we can start working on our project.'
'That TV is unbelievable, Madison,' said Marcia. 'I haven't seen it before. Is it new?'
'We've had it for two weeks. Mom says it's embarrassing. But Dad and I like seeing her on the big screen.'
'Your mom is a reporter with CNN, right? How long has she worked there?'
'For three months,' Madison said.
'Wow, that's so exciting.'

'Maybe she'll be on now. She's at the airport. She's been there for hours. There was an explosion or something. I hope she's OK.'
'Look, there she is now!' Marcia said.

### Looking at language

***a)*** *Beantworte die folgenden Fragen:*
- How long has Madison's family had the big TV?
  *for two weeks*
- How long has Madison's mother been at the airport?
  ...

***b)*** *Finde den passenden englischen Satz in Text 4. Was ist im Englischen und Deutschen unterschiedlich?*
- Wir haben den Fernseher seit zwei Wochen.
- We ... it for two weeks.

***c)*** *Say it in German.*
- Mom has been at the airport for hours.
- Mama ... ... Stunden am Flughafen.

► *P 9 (p. 85) • WB 9 (p. 46)*

*True or false?*
1 *Madison and Marcia meet at Marcia's house.*
2 *Madison's mother wants to catch a plane.*

► *P 6–8 (pp. 84–85) • WB 7–8 (pp. 45–46)*

## 5 Take Your Child to Work Day

Madison and her friend Marcia were talking about Take Your Child to Work Day.
'Well, Madison. I bet you want to go to CNN with your mom on TYCTWD?'
'Yeah. But she might be too busy. Then I'll have to go with Dad. His job is so boring.'
'Where does he work?' Marcia asked.
'At the King Center. It's just books and old papers.'
'But that's perfect!'
'Why?' Madison asked, puzzled.
'Have you forgotten that our project is about Martin Luther King? Perfect timing, girl! You can get lots of great information about Dr King and our project will be the best.'

1 *Madison really wants to go to work with ...*
A her mother. B her father.

2 *Marcia thinks she should go with ...*
A her mother. B her father.

**Extra Americana ★ ★ ★**

**Take Your Child to Work Day**

TYCTWD is a day when parents can take their children to their workplace. Every year more than 25 million children go to work with their mother or father on this special day. It takes place on the fourth Thursday in April.

*Think of a workplace you'd like to visit.*
– I'd like to visit a hospital/TV studio/farm/...
– I'd like to go to work with my brother/a hairdresser/a paramedic/...

## 6 At the King Center

'I hope you're not disappointed, Madison. I know you really wanted to go to work with Mom,' said Madison's dad.

'It's OK, Dad. Anyway, we're doing a class project on Martin Luther King. So it's a good time to come.'

'Well, come and look at some of Dr King's letters if you like,' said her dad. 'They've been on display for a few weeks – since the anniversary of his death.'

'Since April 4th,' Madison said.

'That's right.' Her dad was impressed. 'How do you know the date?'

'I've known it since Monday. That's when my class started the project!'

'Really?'

'No,' said Madison laughing. 'I've known that for a long time, Dad.'

*How long has Madison known the date that Martin Luther King died?*
A since Monday B for a long time

**Looking at language**

**a)** *Schreib die Tabelle ab. Ergänze alle Ausdrücke mit* **since** *und* **for** *aus Text* **6**:

| for | since |
|---|---|
| for a few weeks | since the anniversary ... |
| for ... | since ... |

**b)** **since** *und* **for** *bedeuten beide 'seit'. Was benutzt du für einen* ***Zeitpunkt*** *und was für einen* ***Zeitraum?***

► GF 6: German 'seit' (p. 161) • P 10–12 (p. 86) • WB 10–11 (pp. 46–47)

## 7 Important African Americans

*a)* *Do some internet research to complete the text. Use the key words in the boxes.*

I have a dream that my … little children will one day live in a nation where they will not be judged by the color of their skin but by the content of their character.

**Martin Luther King, Jr.**

Martin Luther King was a black leader who wanted the same rights for all people – black, white, rich and poor. On August 28, 19 … , 250,000 people listened to Martin Luther King's speech in Washington. This was when he said the famous words 'I have a dream'. Martin Luther King was shot on April 4, 1968. The name of the man who killed him was …

Key Words:
"Martin Luther King" dream "little children"

Key Words:
"Martin Luther King" "August 28" Washington

Key Words:
"Martin Luther King" "who shot" name

*b)* *Compare your answers.*

*c)* *Do some internet research and find the answers to these questions. Before you start, note down the key words you want to use.*

- How old was Martin Luther King when he died?
- Martin Luther King Day is a holiday in the US. When is it? Why was this day chosen?

**STUDY SKILLS** **Internet research**

1 *Bevor du beginnst, mach dir eine Liste mit Schlüsselwörtern (**key words**), die du für deine Suche verwenden willst.*
2 *Beachte: Nicht alles, was im Internet steht, ist richtig! Daher solltest du mehr als eine Website anschauen, um sicherzugehen, dass die Informationen stimmen.*
3 *Du musst nicht jedes Wort auf einer Website lesen. Scanne den Text gezielt nach den Informationen (**key words**), die du brauchst.*

► *SF Internet research (p. 139) 2–5 (pp. 82–83) • WB 12 (p. 47)*

*d)* **Extra** *Barack Obama became the first African-American president of the United States of America in 2009.*

Barack Obama

*Do some research and answer the questions.*

- Where was Barack Obama born?
- In which country was Barack Obama's father born?
- How old was Barack Obama when he became president?

## Extra Background File An Atlanta timeline

### 1 Welcome to Atlanta

**a)** *Copy the Atlanta timeline. Try to complete the notes under the timeline. Use the pictures and what you already know about Atlanta.*

**b)** *Listen to the CD. Check your timeline.*

► *SF Listening (p. 141)*

**Atlanta timeline**

1847 – before 1861 – 1861 – 1864 – 1865 – 1886

1847: The city of Atlanta ...

before 1861: Black slaves ...

1861: The American Civil War ...

1864: The city of Atlanta ...

1865: The American Civil War ... Black slaves ...

1886: Coca Cola ...

... worked on cotton plantations.

... were free.

... ended.

... started.

... was first made.

... was founded.

... was burned down.

## 2 Now you

*Make a timeline for your town or area.*

| 1929 | 1968 | 1980 | 1996 | 2002 |
|---|---|---|---|---|
| *Martin Luther King …* | *Dr Martin Luther King …* | *CNN …* | *The Olympic Games …* | *Shirley Franklin …* |

… took place in Atlanta.

… was born.

… became the first black woman mayor of Atlanta.

… was founded in Atlanta.

… was shot.

▸ *WB 13 (p. 48)* • **Text File 11** *(pp. 134–135)*

## 1 WORDS My life

**a)** ☐ *Complete the mind map with these words.*

my activities • my family • famous for ... • my city • my favourite music • places that I go

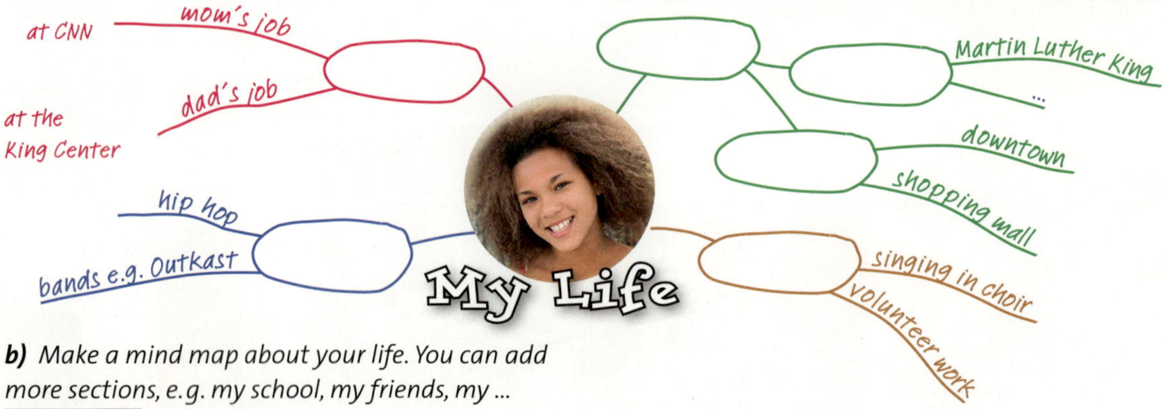


**b)** *Make a mind map about your life. You can add more sections, e.g. my school, my friends, my ...*

more help ▸ D p. 114

## 2 WORDS Good programmes – bad programmes

**a)** ☐ *You can use these words to talk about good and bad programmes. Make two lists.*

awesome • awful • brilliant • cool • fantastic • funny • great • silly • stupid • terrible

**b)** ☐ *Find the opposites.*

*best – worst; interesting – ...*

best • interesting • modern • recorded

boring • live • old-fashioned • worst

**c)** *Write three sentences about different TV programmes.*

| | | |
|---|---|---|
| Game shows<br>Reality shows<br>Soaps<br>Documentaries<br>Live concerts<br>... | are<br>(sometimes/<br>often/<br>always) | awesome<br>boring<br>brilliant<br>terrible<br>... |

**d)** *Read your sentences to your partner. Tell him/her what you think about his/her sentences.*

I agree. I like game shows/... too.

I don't agree. I don't like reality shows/...

## 3 WORDS More TV words

**a)** *Check the meaning of the words in the box.*

+(to) change channels • +flat screen • +(to) receive • +remote control • +satellite • +(to) turn up/down • +volume

**b)** *Write sentences about yourself.*

1. We have cable TV/satellite TV/...
   *We have cable TV.*
2. We can receive 20/30/... channels.
   *We can ...*
3. We have a flat screen/an old-fashioned TV.
4. I use the button on the TV/the remote control to turn the volume up or down.
5. I check/don't check the TV listings before I change channels.

## 4 SPEAKING Talking about films or TV shows

**a)** //O ▸ D p. 115

*Complete the dialogue between Emma and her friend Sally. Use phrases from the box below.*

*Emma* 1 the Simpsons last night?
*Sally* No, I didn't. What 2 ?
*Emma* Oh, Marge opened her own women-only fitness centre.
*Sally* And, 3 ?
*Emma* It wasn't bad. The 4 was really funny.
*Sally* Well, I was watching a documentary on tigers. I'm really 5 that kind of programme.
*Emma* I'm going to watch that Brad Pitt movie 6 tonight. Maybe we can watch together?
*Sally* I don't know. I 7 those big Hollywood movies.
*Emma* What 8 then?
*Sally* Well, I 9 documentaries on TV. And 10 music programmes.

Did you watch • don't really like • I love • do you like • ending • interested in • how was it? • on TV • was it about? • watch

**b)** *Listen to the dialogue. Check your notes.*

**c)** *Prepare a dialogue like the one between Emma and Sally. Then act it out in class.*

more help ▸ D p. 113

## 5 MEDIATION TV in America

**a)** *Todd, an American boy, is staying with the Kleins, a German family that you know. But Todd doesn't speak German and the family doesn't speak English. Help them in this conversation.*

*Fr. Klein* Kannst du Todd bitte fragen, wie er deutsches Fernsehen findet?
*You* She wants to know what you think of ...
*Todd* Well, my problem is that I don't understand very much. But I think it's funny when I hear American actors speaking German. I watched the Simpsons and Bart Simpson was speaking German. That was so funny.
*You* ...
*H. Klein* Ich habe irgendwo gelesen, dass Amerikaner vier Stunden pro Tag fernsehen. Ist das wahr?
*You* He has read that Americans watch ...
*Todd* Four hours, wow! Some people watch a lot of TV, but four hours every day? The people I know don't watch so much TV.
*You* ...

**b)** *Listen to the rest of the conversation and help Todd and the Klein family.*

**Tipp**
*Übersetze nicht jedes Wort, sondern gib nur das Wesentliche wieder.*

▸ SF Mediation (p. 152)

## 6 READING The price of work for high school students (Drawing conclusions) ► SF p. 143

**1** *Fragen zu einem Text sind manchmal so, dass du die Antworten sofort und direkt im Text findest.*

***a) What do students spend their money on? Find three things.*** *– Look at paragraph 1.*

**2** *Für andere Fragen findest du die nötigen Informationen an verschiedenen Textstellen.*

***b) Why do students work?*** *– Look at paragraphs 1 and 6.*

*– Because they want to …*

*– Because they have to help …*

***c) What are the advantages of having a job?*** *Complete the answer below. Which paragraphs do you have to look at?*

*Students are more … and they learn how to … They also get … that will help them in their future jobs.*

**3** *Manchmal steht die Antwort auf eine Frage nicht direkt im Text. Aber du findest bestimmte Fakten, die etwas mit der Frage zu tun haben, und daraus kannst du deine Schlussfolgerungen ziehen.*

***d) Why can a job be bad for students' school work?*** *Look at the facts. Choose a conclusion.*

**Facts**

– 'an 11-hour work day'

– 'I'm often too tired to do my schoolwork'

**Conclusion:** When students work …

A they're often late for classes.

B they don't have enough time for schoolwork.

C they get average grades in their schoolwork.

***e) ● Does the writer think that it is a good thing or a bad thing for students to have a job?***

**Facts**

– 'they could have problems finding a good job in the future'

– 'many teens pay a high price: their education'

**Conclusion:** The writer thinks …

A schoolwork is more important than a job.

B students need money to pay for their education.

C if students want a job in the future, they need work experience.

# The price of work for high school students

(1) A lot of students work after school because they want to buy things like cars, clothes or iPods without having to ask their parents for money.

(2) We talked to one hundred students from Watsonville High School in California and found that 30% work. That's a lot of students with jobs. But is it bad for their schoolwork when they work?

(3) "A student who wants to be allowed to work has to have certain grades," Ms. Viotti, a counsellor at Watsonville High, said. But you don't have to be a good student. Average grades are OK.

(4) "Having a job can have advantages. Students who work are more disciplined and learn how to organize their time," a chemistry teacher at Watsonville High said.

(5) But having a job has disadvantages too. Students go to school for seven hours, and some of them work for four hours a day after school. That's an 11-hour work day.

(6) Many students have no choice. "Some students have to work to help their families," Ms. Viotti told us. "A lot of parents in Watsonville are poor or don't have jobs, so their kids have to help out."

(7) Many students who work don't know the price they are paying. Some get bad grades. Others don't finish high school. And that means that they could have problems finding a good job in the future. "When I get home from my job at 10 p.m., I'm often too tired to do my schoolwork," Kim, who works at a local supermarket, told us.

(8) Millions of teens like Kim work after school in the US. Some of them get useful work experience that will help them in their future jobs. But many teens pay a high price: their education.

## 7 ○ WORDS believable/unbelievable (Word building)

**Tipp**

*-able am Ende eines Wortes heißt meistens 'you can do this'. 'A believable story' ist also eine Geschichte, die man glauben kann.*

*un- am Anfang heißt das Gegenteil. 'An unbelievable story' ist also eine Geschichte, die man nicht glauben kann.*

*Say what these sentences mean.*

1 That plate is unbreakable. – You can/can't break that plate.
2 Ben is a likeable guy. – People like/don't like Ben.
3 The name on the book is unreadable. – You can/can't read the name.
4 There are downloadable ringtones at this website. – You can/can't download the ringtones.

## 8 REVISION Madison's dreams (Present perfect)

**a)** *Look at Madison's list. What has she already done? What hasn't she done done yet? Write sentences.*

My dreams
1 stay in a hotel in Las Vegas ✓
2 see the Grand Canyon from a helicopter ✗
3 walk on the Grand Canyon skywalk ✓
4 visit the CNN studios ✗
5 make a video diary ✓
6 spend a holiday at Disney World in Florida ✗
7 travel to Europe ✗

*Madison has already stayed in a hotel in Las Vegas.*
*She hasn't … yet.*

**b)** *What interesting thing have you already done? What haven't you done yet? Write two sentences.*
*I've seen / been to / visited / made / …*
*I haven't seen / been to / … – but I want to one day.*

**c)** ● *Talk to three different partners. Ask what they have done and haven't done yet. Take notes.*

**d)** ● *Tell the class. Who has done the most interesting things? Who has the most interesting dreams?*

Simon has been to Paris. That's cool.

Muriel hasn't visited Disneyland yet, but she wants to one day.

## 9 //○ How long …? (Present perfect with 'for') ▸ D p. 115

*Complete the dialogues. Use the present perfect.*

1 I'm sorry I'm late! Have you been here long?
– No, I … (only/be) here for five minutes.
*No, I've only been here for five minutes.*
2 How long have you and Madison been friends?
– We … (be) friends for years.
3 Have you seen Madison this week?
– No, I … (see) her for days.
4 How long has Rob been in hospital?
– He … (be) in hospital for months.
5 I like your cap. How long have you had it?
– I … (have) it for a week.

6 And your skateboard? Is that new too?
– No, I … (have) it for two years.
7 How long have you lived in Atlanta?
– I … (live) here for five years.

## 10 How long have you had it? (since/for)

**a)** *Write five sentences about your things:*

*I've had my pencil case for nearly a year. I've had my trainers since the summer holidays. ...*

| | |
|---|---|
| **since** | yesterday • last week • last month • Monday • April • 2008 • the summer holidays • ... |

| | | |
|---|---|---|
| **for** | about nearly over | three days • two weeks • three months • a year • two years • ... |

**b)** *Make a chart like the one on the right and fill it in for yourself.*

**c)** *Make appointments with two classmates. Ask and answer questions and fill in your chart.*
How long have you been at this school? ...

**d)** **Extra** *Write sentences about you and your partners.*
*I've been at this school for four years. Anne has been here since last year. Timo has ...*

| How long ...? | Me | Partner 1 |
|---|---|---|
| have you been at this school | 4 years | last year |
| have you been at school today | | |
| have you known your best friend | | |
| have you lived in this town | | |
| have you had your mobile | | |

## 11 Mr Young at the King Center (since/for)

*Mr Young is telling Madison about his job. Add* since *or* for *to complete the sentences.*

1 I've been in my job ... 1999.
2 I've known my boss ... about five years.
3 I need a new computer. I've had this one ... almost seven years.
4 Martin Luther King's wife started the Center, but she's been dead ... 2006.
5 The King Center has been part of the National Park system ... more than twenty years.
6 Martin Luther King's birthday has been a holiday in the US ... 1986.

## 12 Washington has been the capital ... (since)

The White House in Washington, D.C.

**a)** *Partner B: Look at* *p. 105.*
*Partner A: Ask questions. Note down your partner's answers.*
1 A: How long has the US had 50 states?
B: ...
2 How long has Washington been the capital of the US?
3 How long has the US had the dollar for its money?

**b)** *Answer your partner's questions. Use* since *and the date.*
4 1788: Georgia became a US state
5 1868: Atlanta became capital of Georgia
6 1980: CNN opened its studios in Atlanta

**Remember**

*So werden Jahreszahlen im Englischen ausgesprochen:*
*1900 → nineteen hundred*
*1803 → eighteen oh three*
*1759 → seventeen fifty-nine*

# Melba's story

## Background

It's hard to believe now, but before the 1960s America was a very different place. In many states, especially in the South, public places were segregated. This meant that black – or 'colored' – people and white people couldn't go to the same places. There were cinemas, shops, buses, hotels, restaurants and even park benches for whites only.

Black and white children went to different schools too. Black schools were often older and smaller than white schools. Black students had to use old school books that the white schools didn't use any more.

Little Rock is a town in the state of Arkansas. In the 1950s it had a big modern high school, but there were no black students at this school. That's because Arkansas was a segregated state with segregated schools. But in 1954 the law changed. The new law said that segregated schools were wrong. Black and white children should go to the same schools everywhere in the US.

Three years later, on 3rd September, 1957, the first black students were ready for their first day at the high school in Little Rock. But many white people didn't want black kids in their school. And that's where Melba's story begins.

Classroom in a black school

Classroom in a white school

◄ Central High School, Little Rock, Arkansas

*What was segregation? Collect as many examples as you can.*

Black people couldn't ...

## The story (adapted from an interview with Melba Pattillo Beals)

*Look at the photos. What do you think Melba's story is about?*

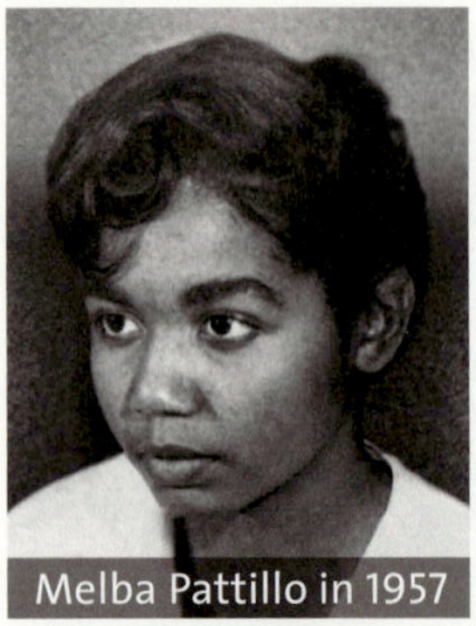
Melba Pattillo in 1957

This is the story of Melba Pattillo Beals. When she was a girl she lived in Little Rock, Arkansas. In 1957, nine black students were chosen to go to Central High School in Little Rock. Melba Pattillo, who was then 15 years old, was one of those students. They were called the Little Rock Nine.

The Little Rock Nine in 1957

In September 1957 Melba and the other black students tried to enter the high school. A big crowd of white people tried to stop them. They shouted and threw things at the teenagers.

In the end the US President had to send soldiers to help the black students. The soldiers drove them to school and protected them during the day.

The US president sent soldiers to help the black students.

Melba remembers how she felt on that first day:

"I felt nervous. My face was hot. I was so frightened about what might happen to me. I still remember that. I was right to feel like that. On the first day I had to run away from men who said they would kill me."

A crowd of white people tried to stop the Little Rock Nine

At first Melba thought that everything was going to be OK.
"When the soldiers came to protect us I felt proud to be an American. I thought that integration could work. I thought: The white students need to get to know me. When they see that I am smart, that I wear nice clothes, then they will understand that I'm really not so different. I just have brown skin. That's all."

But it wasn't like that. At first a few white students were nice to the black teenagers.
"They smiled and they wanted to talk to us, to be friends with us. But then it became too dangerous for them too. They had to turn away from us."

Melba often wanted to give up.
"When someone called me names, or kicked me, I thought I can't do this any more."

But Melba's grandmother wouldn't let her give up.
"She said: Don't quit. Don't let them win."

Melba and the other students never gave up.
"We wanted to make it to the end of the year and we did that."

But it was too dangerous for Melba to stay in Little Rock. A group of white people had a price on her head – $ 10,000 dead and $ 5000 alive.

When Melba was 16 years old she left Little Rock and went to an integrated school in California. She had to leave her family and live with a different family in California.
"I am very lucky – I have two moms and two dads."

Her new family was white.
"That is why I don't want people to think that I hate white people. Lots of white people have helped me and looked after me."

## Forty years later

Forty years later Melba returned to the high school in Little Rock. She walked up the stairs of the school and she remembered how she had felt in 1957 – she had felt scared.

But when she got to the top of the stairs she saw a young black boy. He said, 'Welcome to Central High. I'm the president of the student body.'
Melba felt very proud.
"There were tears in my eyes. This was my dream. This was why I did it. So that this boy could stand there and say that. It was amazing."

The Little Rock Nine in 2007

## Working with the text

### 1 Headlines

*Which headline fits Melba's story best?*

Little Rock Nine welcomed at Central High School

☆ LITTLE ROCK NINE ENTER HIGH SCHOOL WITH HELP OF US SOLDIERS

President says black students can't go to Little Rock high school

### 2 Tell the story

*Put the sentences in the right order.*

1 The black students finish a year at Central High School.
2 Fifty years later, the Little Rock Nine return to Central High School.
3 Melba goes to school in California.
4 Angry white people stop the nine teenagers.
5 Melba wants to give up, but she doesn't.
6 The US President sends soldiers to help the black students.
7 Nine black students are chosen to go to the white high school in Little Rock.
8 Melba has to leave Little Rock.

### 3 Talking to Melba

*This student has got a lot of things wrong. Look at the text and complete Melba's sentences.*

*Student* Nothing has changed in America since the 1960s.
*Melba* You're wrong! Before the 1960s America was *a very different place*.
*Student* The black schools were as good as the white schools.
*Melba* You're wrong! Black schools were ... and ... than white schools.
*Student* Everyone was happy when the law said segregated schools were wrong.
*Melba* You're wrong! A lot of white people were ...
*Student* The soldiers were there to stop the black students going to school.
*Melba* You're wrong! They were there to ...

*Student* The Little Rock Nine were at Central High for a week or two.
*Melba* You're wrong! We were at Central High ...
*Student* Dreams don't come true!
*Melba* You're wrong! My dream...

### 4 ● Extra Melba's feelings

*Say how you think Melba felt. You can use the words in the box.*

amazed • angry • disappointed • excited • fed up • frightened • glad • happy • nervous • proud • sad • scared • shy • unhappy • upset

She felt ...
1 ... when she saw the angry white people at the school.
2 ... when the President sent the soldiers.
3 ... when she heard that there was a price on her head.
4 ... when she had to leave Little Rock.
5 ... when she went back to the school years later.

▸ WB 14–16 (pp. 48–50) • **Checkpoint 4** WB (p. 51) • Selbsteinschätzung 3–4 WB (pp. 52–53)

## How am I doing?

***a)*** *Find or choose the correct answers.*

**Atlanta and its history**

1 Atlanta is a city in ...
A California. B Missouri. C Georgia.

2 Martin Luther King's dream was ...
A to build hospitals.
B to get the same rights for all people.
C to be President of the US.

3 Which of these is not at home in Atlanta?
A the White House B CNN
C the King Center

**TV words**

4 Choose words that match the definitions:

documentary • comedy show • drama • presenter • series • viewer

a) a TV show that's on once a week
b) a show with lots of jokes and funny scenes
c) a film or TV show that tells you about things that really happened
d) a person who watches TV

5 Which is not a good way to find out about something that happened yesterday?
A newspaper B radio C TV D books

6 A good place to find out what's on TV is ...
A a TV show. B a book.
C the TV listings. D CNN.

7 Which is not a job in television?
A reporter B presenter C actor
D waiter

8 You need it to change channels:
A flat screen B satellite
C remote control D volume

**Internet research**

9 Wenn du eine Recherche im Internet machst, ist es besser, wenn du ...
A nur bei Wikipedia suchst.
B nur eine Webseite nutzt.
C mehr als eine Webseite nutzt.
D nur Webseiten auf Deutsch nutzt.

10 Es ist nicht unbedingt nötig, dass du ...
A Schlüsselwörter benutzt.
B Notizen machst.
C alle Informationen auf einer Webseite liest.
D die Informationen überprüfst.

11 Informationen im Internet sind ...
A niemals richtig.
B niemals falsch.
C nicht immer richtig.
D immer richtig.

**Reading**

12 Da deine Frage nicht direkt im Text beantwortet wird, musst du Schlussfolgerungen ziehen. Was hilft dir dabei?
A Bilder B einzelne Beispiele
C Fakten, die mit der Frage zu tun haben
D Überschrift des Textes

**Grammar**

13 Put in the correct form of the verb:
We ... in the same flat for six years.
A live B have lived C living D lives

14 Put in the correct form of the verb:
My parents ... married for 15 years.
A are B is C have been D has been

15 Decide: ***since*** or ***for***? I have been here ...
a) yesterday. b) an hour. c) two days.
d) Monday.

***b)*** *Check your answers on p. 236 and add up your points – one point for each correct answer.*

***c)*** *If you had 17 or more points, well done!*
*Where did you make mistakes? The chart below will tell you what you can do to improve your English.*

| No. | Areas | Find out more | Exercises |
|---|---|---|---|
| 1– 3 | Atlanta and its history | Unit 4 (pp. 74–75, 77–79) | P 1 (p. 82), WB Info Box (p. 43), 13 (p. 48) |
| 4– 8 | TV words | Unit 4 (p. 76) | P 2–3 (p. 82), WB 2–3 (pp. 42–43) |
| 9–11 | Internet research | Unit 4 (p. 79), SF (p. 139) | WB 12 (p. 47) |
| 12 | Reading | P 6 (p. 84) | WB 7 (p. 45) |
| 13–15 | Grammar: since/for | GF 6 (p.161) | P 9–12 (pp. 85–86), WB 9–11 (p. 46–47) |

## Extra Who did it? A mystery game[1]

### 1 The mystery

Mo, the reporter

Hi! I'm Mo. I write for the student newspaper at Westwood High. There's a big story this week. There is a cheat[2] in Mr Bell's class! On Thursday the class took a test. But afterwards a student found a copy of the test in a book in the library. It seems that someone had the test paper[3] *before* the test. But who? OK, let's meet the suspects[4] ...

1 Sam

2 Jacko

3 Flash

4 Nat

5 CJ

6 Scott

7 Cindy

8 Mr Bell

[1] mystery game ['mɪstri geɪm] *Detektivspiel* [2] (to) cheat/cheat [tʃi:t] *schummeln, betrügen / Schummler/in, Betrüger/in*
[3] test paper ['test peɪpə] *Klassenarbeit* [4] suspect ['sʌspekt] *Verdächtige(r)*

## 2 Who's who?

***a)*** *Match the photos (1–8) and the speech bubbles (A–H).*

***b)*** *What do you learn about the suspects?*

good/bad at school • popular • interested in ... • works hard for school • stressed • clever • nervous • ...

***c)*** *Choose one of the suspects. Read their part out loud to the class. Who is the best actor?*

**A** Mr Bell says I talk too much in class. But his class is so easy for me. If any student gets a better grade than me, I'll give them my MP3 player!

**B** I usually get A's. But now my family has money problems and I have to work at Mack's Burger Bar in my free time to earn money. I'm always tired and I don't have much time to study. Cindy is my girlfriend.

**C** I usually get D's or F's in tests. I'm interested in photography [1]. I'm really excited about the school trip to Atlanta and the King Center.

**D** I'm new to Westwood High. I don't have any friends here. I really don't like Jacko. He's really a big mouth and he thinks he's so smart.

**E** I'm popular. Everyone likes me. I would do anything for Scott. He's my boyfriend. I usually get C's in class.

**F** I don't study for tests! I'm only interested in basketball. My family is rich, so I don't have to work hard. I like Cindy, but she's only interested in Scott.

**G** This is a very difficult job. The students give me a hard time. They always talk and laugh and they don't listen to me.

**H** I study REALLY hard, but I never get A's. I usually get C's. I never get an F, but my parents always say I must do better.

### Americana ★ ★ ★

In the US lots of schools have an honor code [2] to stop cheating. The students sign a promise. The teacher might not be in the room when a class takes a test. The students in the class must tell the teacher if another student breaks [3] the honor code.

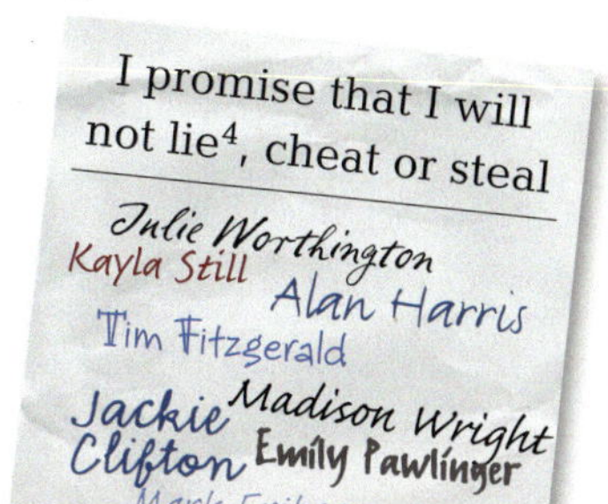


---

[1] photography [fəˈtɒgrəfi] *Fotografie* [2] honor code [ˈɒnə kəʊd] *Ehrenkodex* [3] (to) break [breɪk] *brechen* [4] (to) lie [laɪ] *lügen*

## 3 The scene of the crime

*Before the game starts, study Mo's notes.*

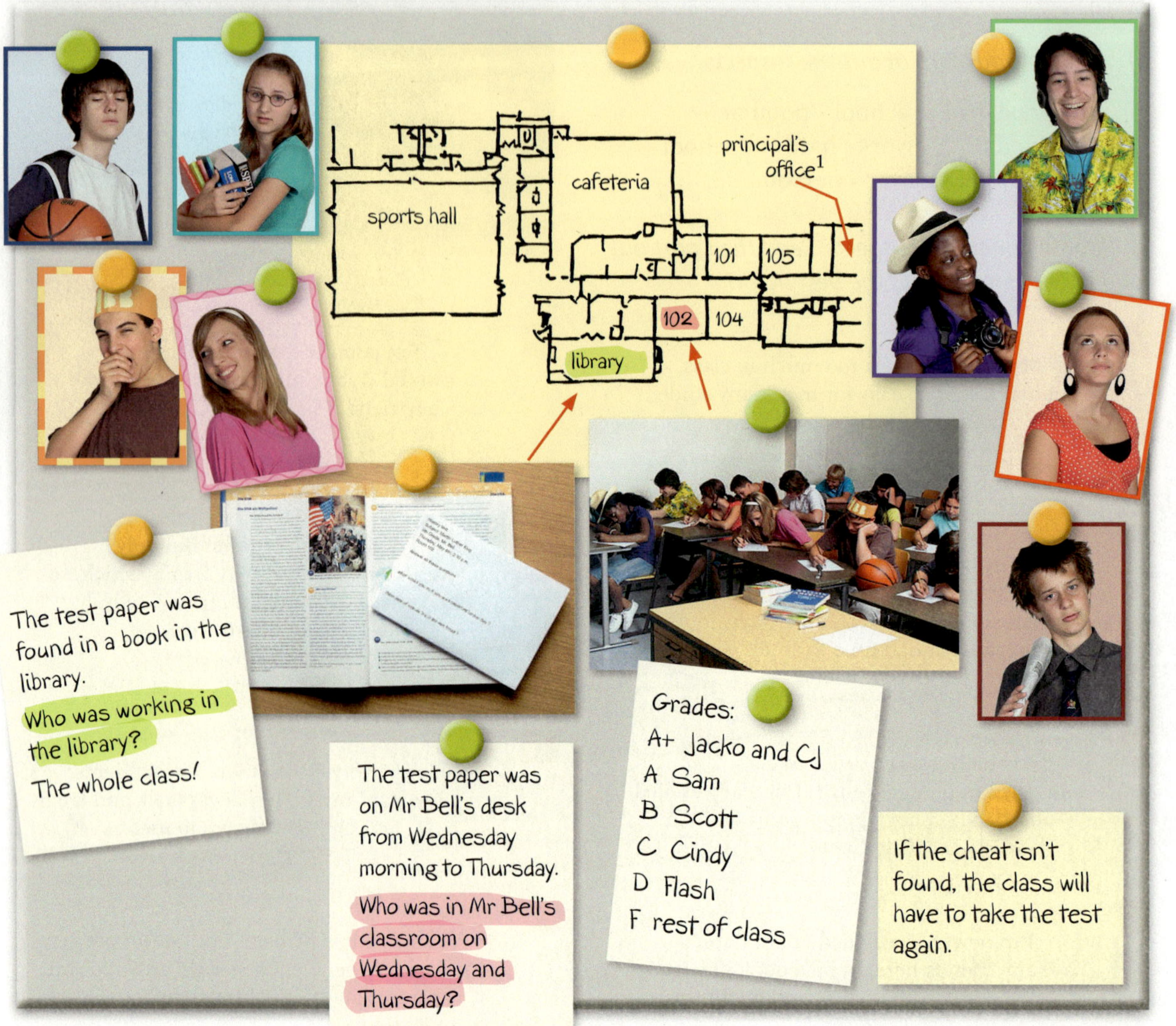


## 4 What do we know so far[2]?

***a)*** *Fill in the first two columns*[3] *on a copy of this chart. Use the information from this page.*

| Suspects | Got a good grade | Other comments |
|---|---|---|
| Sam | yes | |
| Jacko | ... | |

***b)*** *Add the information below to the chart.*

Scott's girlfriend

Got an F. Usually gets C's.

New to Westwood High.

Usually gets D's.

His job is very difficult. Students give him a hard time.

Not interested in tests. Likes Cindy.

Mr Bell's class is easy for him.

Cindy's boyfriend. Works, very tired. Not much time to study.

[1] principal's office [ˌprɪnsəpl ˈɒfɪs] *Büro des/der Schulleiters/in* [2] so far [ˈsəʊ ˈfɑː] *bis jetzt, bisher* [3] column [ˈkɒləm] *Spalte*

## 5 How the mystery game works[1]

**Tipp**

*Nur die Person, die es getan hat, wird lügen. Also musst du entscheiden, wer lügt.*

[1] how the game works *wie das Spiel funktioniert/geht*

## Scene 1

*It's Friday, the day after the test. All the suspects are in Mr Bell's classroom.*

*Mr Bell* Nat, please tell everyone where you found the test paper.

*Nat* Well, after the test I went to the library. I found the test paper inside a book about Martin Luther King.

*Scott* So someone had the questions before the test and was looking for the answers.

*Mr Bell* Yes, Scott, and the person who did this is in a lot of trouble! Remember the honor code! And if we don't find the cheat, the whole class will take the test again.

*Sam* *(worried)* Oh no, I don't want to take the test again! I got an A! My grandmother will be really proud of me. Maybe I won't get an A on a second test.

*Mr Bell* Yes, Sam. Your A grade was a big surprise. Especially after that letter from Ms Hammer. Can I read it out?

*Sam* No problem.

*Mr Bell reads the letter out loud.* →

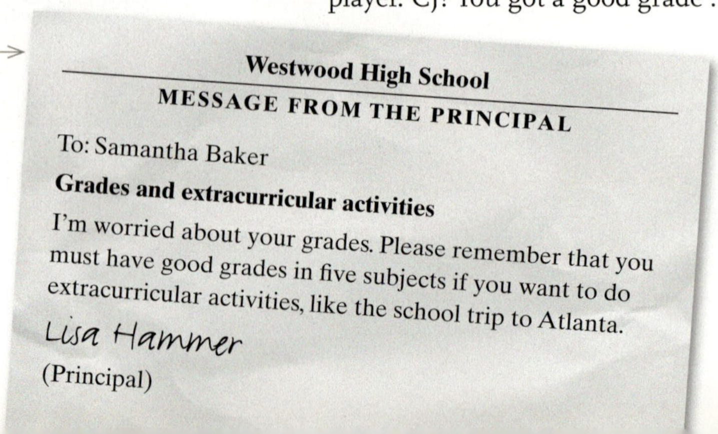

**Westwood High School**

**MESSAGE FROM THE PRINCIPAL**

To: Samantha Baker

**Grades and extracurricular activities**

I'm worried about your grades. Please remember that you must have good grades in five subjects if you want to do extracurricular activities, like the school trip to Atlanta.

*Lisa Hammer*

(Principal)

*Jacko* I'm not sure if this is important, but err ... Sam was in this room on Wednesday morning ... alone ... Sorry Sam, but what were you doing here?

*Sam* *(not smiling)* I had a photo and I wanted to show it to Mr Bell. But you were in the room alone when I arrived, Jacko. And you got an A$^{+}$ in the test. Why were you here?

*Jacko* I had one of Mr Bell's books. I left it on his desk. I had to study extra hard because of that stupid bet that I made!

*Mr Bell* Bet? What bet?

*Cindy* Oh, don't you know, Mr Bell? Jacko said he'd give his MP3 player away if anyone got a better grade than him.

*Mr Bell* So that's why the test was so important to you, Jacko!

*Nat* *(sadly)* You're lucky, Jacko. You always get good grades. You don't have to work hard. Not like me.

*Jacko* Hey, I've just had an idea. Maybe the person wanted to get a good grade because they wanted to win my MP3 player. CJ! You got a good grade ...

*CJ* *(angrily)* So what? I always got good grades at my old school.

*Flash* What about Scott? He got a good grade too.

*Cindy* It wasn't Scott! Maybe you did it, Flash. Maybe the letter that you gave me in class on Wednesday is a clue[1]?

*Cindy reads the letter out loud.*

> Cindy
>
> I think you're amazing. Forget Scott!
> He isn't as perfect as you think. I'm better than him. I can give you everything that you need.
>
> Flash

*Flash* What has my letter got to do with it? I didn't get a good grade. I got a D. Anyway, I don't care about tests. Basketball is important for me – not tests!

*Scott* You're so stupid, Flash!

*Flash* Listen! I was in school on Wednesday evening for basketball training. I saw Scott. Maybe he took the test paper then.

*Jacko* Why were you in school on Wednesday evening, Scott?

*Scott* I came back because I forgot a book for homework, that's all.

*Nat* I was in the library on Wednesday evening. When I went home I saw Flash and Scott. Flash wanted to fight with Scott. He pushed him.

*CJ* What did Scott do?

*Nat* Nothing. He walked away.

*Scott* That's true. I didn't want to fight Flash ... not in school anyway. That would be stupid! I could get into trouble for that.

*CJ* Hmm. You've just given me an idea. Maybe the person who stole the test didn't do it to get a good grade.

*Nat* Err ... What do you mean?

*CJ* Well, Flash hates Scott. So he steals the paper, and we all think it was Scott.

*Nat* *(excited)* Oh, yes!

*Cindy* I don't understand.

*CJ* Oh Cindy, think about it! *(slowly)* If you think Scott is a cheat, you might not like him so much. And Ms Hammer might throw him out of school. You know, because of the honor code.

*Flash* Look, it's all lies[2]! I didn't take the test paper! You're all mad!

---

[1] clue [kluː] *Hinweis* [2] lie [laɪː] *Lüge*

## 6 What do we know so far?

***a)*** *Look at the statements below. Which suspects are they true for? Why?*

1 He/She needed a good grade in the test.
2 He/She got a grade that was higher/lower than usual.
3 He/She was in Mr Bell's room.
4 He/She was in school after class on Wednesday.
5 He/She has enemies in the class.
6 He/She might want to win Jacko's MP3 player.

***b)*** *Add to the chart that you started in* **4** *(on p. 94) like this:*

| Suspects | Got a good grade | Other comments |
|---|---|---|
| Sam | yes | Usually gets D's. Needed a good grade on the test. Wants to go on school trip. Was in Mr Bell's room. Wanted to show a photo to Mr Bell. |
| Jacko | ... | |

## 7 Questions and answers

***a) Suspects:*** *Go to the* ***role cards*** *on p. 233. You have to answer some questions. You'll find your answers on your role card.*

***Detectives:*** *Ask one or more of the suspects these questions:*

Why do you think Sam got a good grade on the test?

Did you want to win Jacko's MP3 player?

***b)*** *Report back to the others. Is there any important new information? Add it to your chart.*

## 8 What do we know so far?

*Listen to Mo and check your notes. Have you got everything?*

*Mo* OK. So what do we know so far? We know that Sam has to get good grades because she wants to go to Atlanta on the school trip. So she's lucky that her grandmother met Martin Luther King and told Sam about him.
And then there's Jacko. He made a silly bet and was scared of losing his MP3 player. But who was interested? Everyone in the class has an MP3 player. But CJ likes the same music as Jacko. She'd like to have his playlist.
What about Flash? He really likes Cindy. *(Other people laugh and whistle.)* But Cindy has already got a boyfriend – Scott. Maybe Flash wants to get Scott into trouble? What do *you* think?

### Scene 2

*Flash has got something to tell everyone.*

*Flash* Hey, listen everyone! This is interesting. *(He reads.)*

**$ 2000**
**Dunn Prize**
**for Best Student at Westwood High School**
This prize is given at the end of the school year to the student with the best grades.

*Jacko* Why's that interesting Flash? You don't need the money!

*Sam* Do you think the person who stole the paper wants to win the prize?

*Jacko* Exactly! And who could win the prize?

*Sam* *(laughs)* Not me!

*Nat* *(sadly)* Not me.

*Scott* Say it, Flash. You think I did it for the prize money.

*Flash* That's right! We all know you need the money. Sorry Cindy, but your Mr Perfect is a cheat!

*Cindy* But Scott will win the prize anyway. He doesn't have to cheat. He's so smart, he's the best.

*Flash* Hah! But he works at Mack's Burger Bar now and he's too tired to study. Maybe he needed a little extra help.

*Scott* Oh, Flash! Shut up! Yes, I want to win the prize. Yes, I need the money. But I'm not a cheat!

*Nat* What about Cindy? She would do anything to help Scott. Before the test she talked about stealing the paper for him.

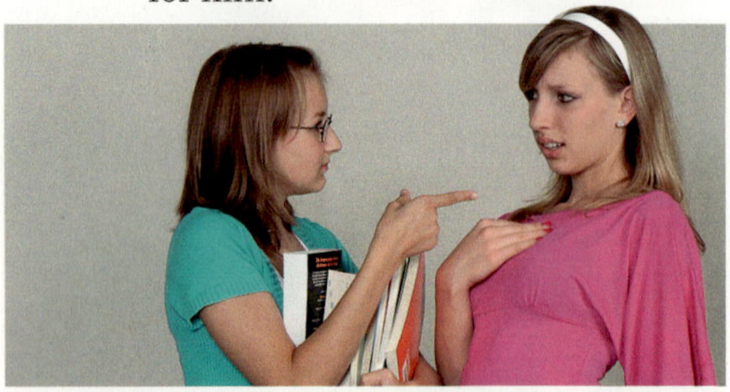

*Cindy* It's true. I said that. But I was only joking. I didn't take the test paper.

*Nat* I thought you were joking, but maybe you were serious?

*Cindy* Thanks, Nat, I thought you were a friend. I was so sorry for you when you started to cry in the test.

*Jacko* You were worried about the test too, Nat. Maybe you took the paper.

*Nat* But I got an F, remember? Sam got the A ... and the letter from the principal.

*Sam* Hey! I've just remembered something! When I was waiting to see Mr Bell, I saw that he had a letter from Ms Hammer too. I think it was about our grades.

*CJ* That's interesting!

*Mr Bell* It's true, I got a letter from Ms Hammer. You can read it if you want.

*CJ reads the letter out loud.*

**Westwood High School**

**MESSAGE FROM THE PRINCIPAL**

To: Mr Bell

Please come to see me at 3:15 p.m. on Friday. I would like to talk to you about your classes. Please bring your grade book.

Lisa Hammer

(Principal)

*Mr Bell* But surely you don't think I stole my own test paper?

*CJ* Maybe not.

*Jacko* No, I don't think so.

*Scott* Aha! But maybe the test paper wasn't stolen at all.

*Nat* What do you mean?

*Scott* Well, twenty students in the class got an F. That was bad for the students, but it was bad for Mr Bell too.

*CJ* Yeah! I never thought of that.

*Jacko* That's true! What will the principal say?

*Scott* And if we do the test again, the grades will probably be better!

## 9 What do we know so far?

*a) Who is it?*

1 She's stressed about her school work.

2 She'll do anything for Scott.

3 He's worried because his class got really bad grades.

4 He's a bit crazy. He made a stupid bet.

5 He wants to win the Dunn Prize.

6 He doesn't like Scott, but he likes Cindy a lot.

7 She needs good grades so that she can do extracurriculars.

8 She likes Jacko's music.

*b) Talk about the mystery with your partner.*

Maybe ... What do you think?

I agree. Or maybe ...

I don't agree. I think ...

| | |
|---|---|
| Cindy | ... wanted Jacko's MP3 player because he has good music. |
| CJ | ... is crazy enough to cheat. After all he made that silly bet. |
| Flash | ... really wanted to win the Dunn Prize. |
| Jacko | ... took the paper for Scott. |
| Nat | ... took the paper because she was so stressed by her bad grades. |
| Sam | ... wants the class to do the test again. |
| Scott | ... wants to get Scott into trouble. |
| Mr Bell | ... cheated because she needed good grades to go to Atlanta. |

## 10 Questions and answers

***a) Suspects**: Go to the **role cards** on p. 234. You have to answer some questions. You'll find your answers on your role card.*

***Detectives**: Ask one or more of the suspects these questions:*

Do you want to take the test again?

Who do you think did it?

***b)** Report back to the others. Is there any important new information?*

***c)** Go back to your chart in 6b). Can you fill in any more gaps?*

## 11 Who do you think did it?

***a)*** *Listen to Mo and the suspects.*

***b)*** *Say who you think did it and why. Your notes might help you.*

– I think it was … because …
– I don't think it was … because …
– I think … is lying when he/she says …
– I believe … when he/she says …
– I think/don't think … is a cheat.

It's nearly time to decide who did it. Who is lying? I think I know.

Mo, the reporter

I didn't cheat. The test was easy, and I worked extra hard to get the best grade. I didn't want to lose my MP3 player.

1 Sam

2 Jacko

I was amazed when I got the A. I didn't cheat. My grandmother told me all about Martin Luther King.

I didn't steal the test paper. I hope Scott did it. Then the principal will throw him out.

3 Flash

4 Nat

5 CJ

I didn't cheat. I always get good grades. Do you think Jacko will give me his MP3 player? I got the same grade as him!

Of course I didn't do it. I got an F in the test, remember?

6 Scott

7 Cindy

8 Mr Bell

I didn't steal the test paper. I want to win the Dunn Prize, but I'm not a cheat.

I didn't steal the test paper for Scott. It was a joke.

I really don't know what's going on [1]. I need some help with this class.

## 12 Who was it?

*Now listen to Mo and find out if you were right.*

[1] What's going on? *Was ist hier los?*

# Unit 1

## 1 The five boroughs of New York

▸ Unit 1 (p. 20)

*There are five New York boroughs. Manhattan is one of them. The other four are A–D on the map.*

***a)*** *Partner B: Your partner has information about two New York boroughs. Listen and answer your partner's questions.*

***b)*** *Now read out boxes **3** and **4** to your partner. Does your partner know the answers?*

**3** Staten Island is south-west of Manhattan. A famous ferry goes between Staten Island and Manhattan. It goes past the Statue of Liberty. Is Staten Island A, B, C or D?

**4** The Bronx is north of Manhattan. There's a river between the Bronx and Manhattan. Is the Bronx A, B, C or D?

*The answers: Staten Island is D, the Bronx is A.*

## 10 SPEAKING Making plans together

▸ Unit 1 (p. 23)

*You and your partner are on holiday in New York. You want to spend a day together.*

***a)*** *Listen to your partner and take notes like this:*

| What? | Where? | How much? | When? |
|---|---|---|---|
| | | | |

▸ SF Taking notes (p. 144)

***b)*** *Choose one of the activities. Tell your partner about it.*

- I'd like to go to ...
- It's in/at ...
- It costs ... for adults/for students. / It's free.
- It's open every day/from ... to ...
- I think it looks good/interesting/fun/...
- I love shopping/scycrapers/going to museums.

***c)*** *Plan your day. Do one activity in the morning and one in the afternoon.*

*A:* What time can we go there?

*B:* We can go to ... in the morning/in the afternoon.

*A:* What about going to ... in the morning and to ... in the afternoon?

EVERYDAY ENGLISH

**SKYSCRAPER MUSEUM**

The Skyscraper Museum – the only museum of its kind – explores the history of tall buildings.
It's at 39 Battery Place in Manhattan.
Museum hours are 12–6 p.m., Wednesday–Sunday.
Admission is $5, $2.50 for students.

**The World's Largest Department Store**

Macy's – New York's most famous department store! With 10 floors and half a million things for sale – you'll need lots of time!
Open 9 to 9!
Herald Square (6th Avenue and 34th Street)

## Unit 2

EVERYDAY ENGLISH

### 10 SPEAKING A picture story ▸ Unit 2 (p. 45)

***a)*** *Partner B:*
*Look at pictures 1–3. Listen to your partner's story. Is it the same as the story in the green boxes?*

1 Tom and Debbie went to a new café. They found a nice table in front of the pictures.

2 They drank their colas. They talked and laughed. And they had lots of fun.

3 Suddenly there was a bright light. Someone shouted, 'Stop him!' Tom and Debbie were shocked.

***b)*** *Look at pictures 4–6. Tell the story to your partner. The orange boxes will help you.*

4
- saw – At that moment – a gun – Tom and Debbie
- near – It was – their table – on the floor

5
- a man – towards them – Then – ran
- picked up – Tom – the gun
- screamed – Debbie – loudly

6
- shouted – 'Cut!' – Someone – angrily
- a film director! – was – It
- really – Tom and Debbie – silly – felt

## Unit 3

### 2 WORDS Hermann in numbers: average temperature, population, ... ▸ Unit 3 (p. 60)

***a)*** *Partner B: Listen to your partner and fill in a copy of the chart.*

***b)*** *Look at the chart. What can you tell your partner about Hermann?*
- ... people live in Hermann today.
- The average temperature in summer is ... degrees Celsius.
- ... litres of wine are made in Missouri every year.

| HERMANN | |
|---|---|
| Founded in: | ? |
| Population today: | 2684 |
| Average temperature: | ? °C (winter)<br>30.5 °C (summer) |
| People with German names: | ? % |
| Wine made in Missouri: | 1.9 million litres a year |

## Unit 4

### 12 Washington has been the capital ... (since) ▸ *Unit 4 (p. 86)*

***a)*** *Answer your partner's questions. Use* **since** *and the date.*

*1* 1959: Hawaii became the 50th state
A: How long has the US had 50 states?
B: Since 1959.
*2* 1800: Washington became the US capital
*3* 1785: US chose the dollar for its money

***b)*** *Ask questions. Note down your partner's answers.*

*4* How long has Georgia been a US state?
*5* How long has Atlanta been the capital of Georgia?
*6* How long has CNN had studios in Atlanta?

**Remember**

*So werden Jahreszahlen im Englischen ausgesprochen:*

*1900 ⟶ nineteen hundred*
*1803 ⟶ eighteen oh three*
*1759 ⟶ seventeen fifty-nine*

Georgia State Capitol, Atlanta

## TF 1

### US facts ▸ *Text File 1 (p. 117)*

### 2 US quiz – Correct answers

*1* 13 stripes
*2* United States of America
*3* Washington, D.C.
*4* two nickels in a dime
*5* 50 states
*6* Kentucky, Kansas
*7* 27 times
*8* Katrina
*9* 4th July
*10* White House (Washington, D.C.)

## Unit 1

### 4 //● WORDS Jobs in the city ▸ Unit 1 (p. 21)

*What are the jobs?*

1 a person who puts fires out
2 a person who catches thieves
3 a person who helps you in a shop
4 a person who puts on the music at the disco
5 a person in an ambulance who helps people who are hurt
6 a person at a national park or monument who gives people information
7 a person who cuts your hair
8 a person who helps people in the hospital who are ill

### 5 //● Being a paramedic is great (Gerund) ▸ Unit 1 (p. 21)

***a)*** *Complete the interview with the New York paramedic. Use the -ing-form of the verbs in the boxes.*

be • do • meet • save

**What are the best things about your job?**
*Saving* people's lives. That's the best thing.
... part of a great team is important too.
... new people every day. I really enjoy that.
... different things every day. It's really interesting.

drive • get • wait • work

**What are the worst things about your job?**
... up in the middle of the night. I hate that.
... long shifts is hard.
... for a call. That can be very boring.
... very fast through the city can be dangerous.

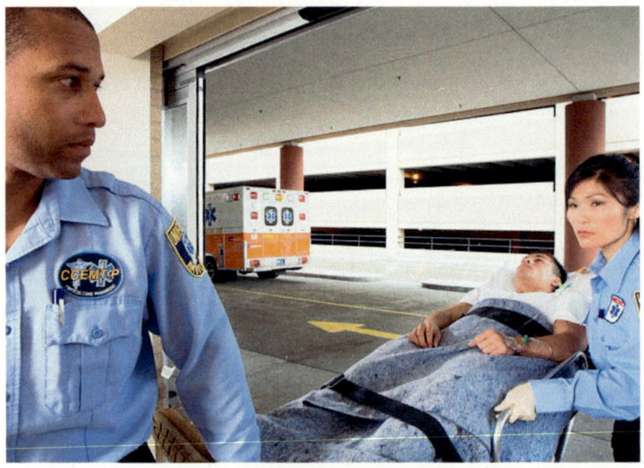

### 6 //● What does Caitlin like doing? (Gerund) ▸ Unit 1 (p. 22)

*Finish these sentences. Use the -ing-form of the verbs in the box.*

1 Caitlin likes *going* on vacation with her family every summer.
2 She loves ... in a tent and ... meals outside.
3 But she doesn't like ... for days in the car to get there.
4 She really enjoyed ... the Grand Canyon this summer.
5 She also enjoyed ... her Irish cousin Ryan for the first time.
6 Ryan loved ... about his uncle's job as a firefighter.
7 He enjoyed ... time at the firestation too.
8 Caitlin's dad loves ... a firefighter.

be • cook • drive • go • hear • meet • sleep • spend • visit

## Unit 1

### 13 more help WRITING Taking a break in Central Park ► Unit 1 (p. 24)

***a)*** *Before you write, get some ideas. Look at the picture. Try to answer these questions.*
- **Who** was in the park with you? Who did you meet there?
- **What** was the weather like? What did you do there? What did you eat?
- **Where** did you sit?
- **When** did you go to the park? When did you leave?
- **Why** were you there?
- **How** did you like it? How long did you stay? How did you feel when you got home?

***b)*** *Use your ideas from a) and complete this text.*

*I was in the park because I wanted to meet …*
*I got there at about …*
*The weather was …*
*We really enjoyed sitting in the sun and …*
(What did you do? Hang out, play football, listen to music, …?)
*We stayed there for about … hours.*
*Later we were hungry so we …*
*I had a … time.* (brilliant, awesome, terrible, … )
*I went home at about …*
*When I got home I was …* (Say how you felt.)

## Working with the text

### You can tell me From *Kelly 'n' Me* by Myron Levoy (adapted) ► Unit 1 (p. 28)

### 3 more help Guess the meanings

*One partner has the book open at this page. The other partner finds the words in the story. Read the tips for each word or phrase here. Then read the word in the text again. Together try and guess the meaning.*

*p. 26, l. 17*
**drunk:** Das englische Wort ist dem deutschen Wort ähnlich. Lest den Text erneut. Anthony hatte Angst, dass der Mann das Geld stehlen würde. Was war mit dem Mann wohl los?

*p. 26, l. 27–28*
**throw up:** Anthony ging es schlecht. Er war weiß im Gesicht. *Throw* heißt werfen. Wollte er etwas werfen? Nein, das ergibt keinen Sinn …

*p. 26, l. 52*
**leaned over:** Das englische Wort ist dem deutschen Wort ähnlich. Anthony und Kelly sitzen nebeneinander. Anthony möchte einen Kuß von Kelly haben. Was muss sie machen?

*p. 27, l. 73*
**I'm really falling for you:** Das hat doch nichts mit „fallen" zu tun, oder? Es ist nicht leicht, den Begriff zu raten. Probiert es trotzdem, dann schlagt im Wörterbuch nach.

*p. 27, l. 83*
**dumb:** Klingt fast genau wie das deutsche Wort. War es klug, sich so spät in diesem Teil des Parks aufzuhalten?

*p. 27, l. 107*
**She was shivering:** Kelly steht unter Schock. Das merkt man daran, dass sie stottert (*I'm – I'm f-fine*). Woran merkt man das noch? Was tun Menschen häufig, wenn sie unter Schock stehen?

## Unit 2

### 2 //● WORDS Word building (-less) ▸ Unit 2 (p. 42)

**Tipp**

*Bei manchen Wörtern entsteht durch das Anhängen der Nachsilbe* ***-less*** *ein neues Wort, z. B.* Water is colourless. *(= farblos, ohne Farbe)*

*Was heißt z. B.* ***hairless*** *im folgenden Satz?*
Baby cats are blind and hairless.

*Complete the sentences with the words from the box.*

cloudless • homeless • scoreless • sleepless • useless

1 I didn't get much sleep. – I had a ... night.
2 It's a warm and sunny day. The sky is ...
3 That man hasn't got a home. He's ...
4 Nobody scored a goal yesterday. It was a ... match.
5 I want a new mobile. My old one is ...

### 3 //● A quiz (Passive – simple present) ▸ Unit 2 (p. 42)

**a)** *Complete the sentences with* ***is*** *or* ***are****.*
1 Spanish is/are spoken in Portugal **(I)**/Mexico **(H)**/Italy **(J)**.
*Spanish is spoken in ...*
2 Oscars is/are given to film stars **(O)**/good sportsmen or sportswomen **(P)**/famous painters **(Q)**.
3 Computer software is/are made in Napa Valley **(K)**/Silicon Valley **(L)**/Central Valley **(M)**.
4 Four million sausages **(C)**/burgers **(L)**/cookies **(G)** is/are eaten in Disneyland every year.
5 Most US strawberries is/are grown in Alaska **(X)**/California **(Y)**/New York **(Z)**.
6 Californian wine is/are sold in the US **(U)**/in the US and Canada **(V)**/all over the world **(W)**.
7 California is/are called the Yellow State **(S)**/Orange State **(T)**/Golden State **(O)**.
8 Park rangers is/are found at all American beaches **(N)**/national parks **(O)**/stations **(P)**.
9 Most of the big films is/are made in Los Angeles **(D)**/San Francisco **(E)**/New York **(F)**.

**b)** *Look at the letters behind your correct answers. What word do they make?*

### 5 //● More facts about California (Passive – simple present) ▸ Unit 2 (p. 43)

*Complete the sentences with the correct form the the verb.*
1 Millions of dollars ... (spend) every year to fight forest fires.
2 Software from California ... (use) all over the world.
3 A lot of rubbish ... (pick up) from the Californian coast.
4 Most of California's fruit and vegetables are ... (grow) in Central Valley.
5 English and Spanish ... (speak) in many Californian families.
6 Mexican food is ... (eat) in many Californian restaurants.

## Unit 2

# All about … growing up in two cultures

### 4 Extra Role play ▸ Unit 2 (p. 37)

**a)** more help *Match the sentence halves. Write the questions for an interview with Kim or Luis.*

1 Where were … — living in California?
2 Where do you … — you born?
3 What languages … — against minorities?
4 Do you like speaking … — do you speak?
5 Do you think there is prejudice … — live now?
6 Do you like … — two languages?

**b)** *Together write answers to the questions for Kim or Luis. Choose from these ideas. Then practise your role play. Swap roles.*

### 7 Extra WRITING More about 'Growing up in two cultures' (Writing letters) ▸ Unit 2 (p. 44)

more help *What do you think about growing up in two cultures? Write a (formal) letter to the editor. The flow chart below will help you. For steps **1–3**, choose sentences from the boxes each time. You can add your letter to your DOSSIER.*

Dear Sir or Madam ▼ 20 April …

**Step 1**
- I am not a member of a minority, but a lot of my friends are.
- I don't live in the US, but I am a member of a minority.

▼

**Step 2**
- I think that speaking two languages is very useful.
- Learning two languages can be very hard.
- For example, I make a lot of mistakes in both languages. At school I have to learn English, so that is my third language.
- I also think that …
- In my opinion, there is a lot of prejudice against minorities.
- In my opinion, there is not a lot of prejudice against minorities.
- For example, it can be an advantage when you are looking for a job.

▼

**Step 3**
- So I think that living in two cultures is a good / difficult thing.
- So I like / do not like living in two cultures.

Yours faithfully ◀

## Unit 2

### 13 //● California was discovered by ... (Passive – simple past) ▸ Unit 2 (p. 47)

*Look at the pictures. Write down what happened when. Use the passive of the verbs in brackets.*

1 California ... (discover) by Spanish explorers in 1769.

2 The Golden Gate Bridge ... (build) by Joseph Strauss.

3 The first film ... (make) in Hollywood in 1910.

4 The first gold ... (find) in Coloma in 1848.

5 The first jeans ... (make) by Levi Strauss during the Gold Rush.

6 Fourteen people ... (kill) by the forest fires last summer.

## Working with the text

## Santa Monica – Episode 1 of a TV series ▸ Unit 2 (p. 50)

### 1 more help The scenes

*Match the sentence halves and say what each scene is about.*

| | | | |
|---|---|---|---|
| **Scene** | 1: | Josh, Cindy and Lara meet ... | with her old car. |
| **Scene** | 2: | Luke invites them to go to Malibu in ... | her job. |
| **Scene** | 3: | They see a girl at the side of the road. She has problems ... | his new car. |
| **Scene** | 4: | Josh helps the girl. He finds out her name is ... | at home. |
| **Scene** | 5: | Josh and the girl drive to the café, but they're too late. She loses ... | to go out. |
| **Scene** | 6: | Jenna tells Josh about her family. She takes him back ... | some food. |
| **Scene** | 7: | We see Jenna ... | leaves. |
| **Scene** | 8: | Jenna's mom doesn't want her ... | angry. |
| **Scene** | 9: | The rich kids talk about their plans for the evening. Josh gets ... | to his friends. |
| **Scene** | 10: | Josh brings Jenna... | Jenna. |
| **Scene** | 11: | Lara is at a party. She's ... | lonely. |
| **Scene** | 12: | Josh puts coffee on the sofa. Jenna is angry. Josh ... | at the beach. |

## Unit 3

### 1 //● REVISION More about Hermann (Passive) ▸ Unit 3 (p. 60)

*Complete the sentences about Hermann.*
*Use* **is/are** *or* **was/were**.

1 The area around Hermann ... called 'the US Rhineland'. A lot of wine ... grown there.

2 The first houses in Hermann ... built by German immigrants. This house ... built in 1880.

3 German traditions ... kept alive in Hermann. The Oktoberfest ... visited by lots of tourists every year.

4 In the 1800s German ... spoken by the people of Hermann. Today only English ... spoken there.

### 5 Extra Now you

**a)** more help ▸ Unit 3 (p. 55)
*Complete the notes. Divide up the work among the members of your group.*
*Add more information from the unit if you can.*

**IN HERMANN HIGH SCHOOL, MISSOURI**

*The school day*
- starts at ... am
- finishes at ... pm
- students get to school by ... or ...
- lessons are ... minutes long
- ... lessons in the morning
- ... lessons in the afternoon

*Timetable*
- subjects at Hermann High, for example: ...

*Lunch*
- lunch break at ...
- students eat in the school cafeteria

*Activities in school*
- different activities / extracurriculars, for example: ...

**IN OUR SCHOOL IN GERMANY**

*The school day*
- starts at ... am
- finishes at ... pm
- students get to school by ... or ...
- lessons are ... minutes long
- ... lessons in the morning
- ... lessons in the afternoon

*Timetable*
- subjects at our school, for example: ...

*Lunch*
- lunch break at ...
- students eat in ... / at home / ...
- they can eat for example: ...

*Activities in school*
- different activities / extracurriculars, for example: ...

## Unit 3

### 3 //● WORDS School in the US and Britain ▸ Unit 3 (p. 60)

*Complete the sentences with school words.*

1. American students say *schedule* when they tell you what they do every day at school and when. British students use the word ___.
2. At Hermann High School there are seven of these in a school day and each one is 50 minutes long. They are called ___. In Britain they are called ___.
3. In America they talk about the summer ___. In Britain they usually talk about the summer ___.
4. In every school you can find this on the wall. Teachers and students put information on it so that everyone can read it. In America it's called a ___. In Britain, it's called a ___.
5. In Britain and America teachers give you ___ to tell you how good or bad a piece of work is.

EVERYDAY ENGLISH

### 5 WRITING A letter to Herman High (Letter for information) more help ▸ Unit 3 (p. 61)

*Write a letter to Jake Kruger to find out more about Hermann High. You can use the ideas below. (Think of a good order for the sentences in the green boxes.)*

... (your address)
... (today's date)

Dear Jake

I hope you can write back soon.
How do students get to school?
My name is ... and I'm ... years old.
What subjects are there at Hermann High?
I'm writing to you because I'd like to know more about Hermann High School.
What extracurriculars are there? I'm very interested in computers / music / ...
I'm in ... class, that's ... grade in a US High School.
Can you answer some questions about your school? Here are my questions: ...
How long is a school day?
I'm a student at ... School in the town of ... in Germany.

Best wishes
... (your name)

## Unit 3

### 9 WORDS Food

*c)* **Extra** more help ▸ *Unit 3 (p. 63)*

*Write a short text about the food that you eat. You can use these ideas.*

*I don't like …*

*I drink / eat lots of (some / too much / too many) …*

*I think the food that I eat is (quite / very) healthy / unhealthy.*

*I usually / sometimes eat … for breakfast (lunch / dinner).*

*I should eat / drink more …*

*My favourite food is …*

*I don't eat / drink any (enough) …*

### Working with the text

### Angus Bethune's moment by Chris Crutcher (adapted) ▸ *Unit 3 (p. 68)*

**3** //● **Tell the story**

*Finish these sentences.*

1. This story is about a boy called …
2. He says that he has problems because …
3. But he's good at football and …
4. Angus is elected …
5. The Winter Ball Queen is …
6. Melissa's boyfriend is called …
7. Angus is elected because Rick gave people …
8. Angus is OK on the dance floor because …
9. Melissa tells Angus that …
10. After the fast dance everyone …
11. At the end Rick is …
12. And Angus is …

## Unit 4

### 4 SPEAKING Talking about films or TV shows

EVERYDAY ENGLISH

*c)* more help ▸ *Unit 4 (p. 83)*

*Complete the dialogue with a partner. Then practise it and act it out in class.*

*A:* Did you watch … last night?
*B:* No, I didn't. What was it about?
*A:* Oh, …
*B:* And, how was it?
*A:* It wasn't bad. The ending was really … What about you? What did you watch?
*B:* Well, I watched …
*A:* How was it?
*B:* It was …
*A:* I'm going to watch … on TV tonight. Maybe we can watch together?
*B:* Great idea. I love that kind of programme.

## Unit 4

### 2 Extra My video diary

***b)*** more help ▸ *Unit 4 (p. 75)*

*Here are some phrases you could use in your script:*

Hi, this is …
I'm from …
I want to tell you about …

This is my …
There's a … over there.
My … are over here/on the wall.
I'm interested in …

This is where …
This is the best place for …
I come here every Saturday/Sunday/… with …

When people think of my town, they think of …
Did you know that … comes from here?
My area is famous for …

### 1 WORDS My life

***b)*** more help ▸ *Unit 4 (p. 82)*

*Here are some words you could add to your mind map. Only choose words that are important to you. Add as many words and phrases as you can.*

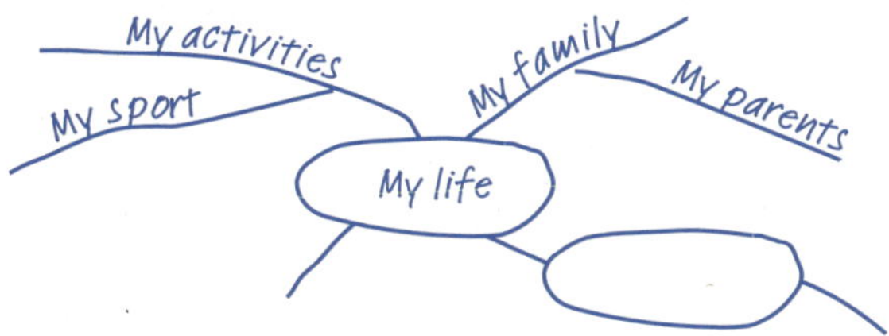


**my sport:**

stadium • team • coach • go to training • score a goal • play in a match • …

**my school:**

best friends • favourite subjects • how I get to school • at break • clubs • …

**my family:**

parents • brother/sister • share a room • fight • argue • parents' jobs • our flat • …

**my friends:**

we usually/often meet at • hang out • go to the shopping mall • go to the cinema • chat online • …

**my favourite music:**

bands • buy CDs • download songs from the internet • singer • kind of music • pop • put posters on the wall • …

## Unit 4

EVERYDAY ENGLISH

### 4 SPEAKING Talking about films or TV shows

▸ Unit 4 (p. 83)

**a)** *Complete the dialogue between Emma and her friend Sally.*

*Emma* ... the Simpsons last night?
*Sally* No, I didn't. What ...?
*Emma* Oh, Marge opened her own women-only fitness centre.
*Sally* And, ...?
*Emma* It wasn't bad. The ... was really funny.
*Sally* Well, I was watching a documentary on tigers. I'm really ... that kind of programme.
*Emma* I'm going to watch that Brad Pitt movie ... tonight. Maybe we can watch together?
*Sally* I don't know. I ... those big Hollywood movies
*Emma* What ... then?
*Sally* Well, I ... documentaries on TV. And ... music programmes.

### 9 How long ...? (Present perfect with 'for')

▸ Unit 4 (p. 85)

*Complete the dialogues. Use the* **present perfect**.

1 I'm sorry I'm late! Have you been here long?
– *Sag, nein, du bist erst seit fünf Minuten hier.*
No, I've only been here for ...

2 How long have you and Madison been friends?
– *Sag, dass ihr seit Jahren Freunde seid.*
We've been ...

3 Have you seen Madison this week?
– *Sag nein, du hast sie seit Tagen nicht gesehen.*
No, I haven't ...

4 How long has Rob been in hospital?
– *Sag, dass er seit Monaten im Krankenhaus ist.*
He's ...

5 I like your cap. How long have you had it?
– *Sag, dass du sie seit einer Woche hast.*
I've ...

6 And your skateboard? Is that new too?
– *Sag nein, du hast es seit zwei Jahren.*
No, I've ...

7 How long have you lived in Atlanta?
– *Sag, dass du seit fünf Jahren hier wohnst.*
I've ...

## TF 1 US facts

### 1 Before you read

***a)*** *Name as many US states as you can. Then look at the US map on the front inside cover of this book. How many did you get right?*

***b)*** *Name other US places and people that you know.*

### Fast facts

**Country name:** United States of America
**Other names:** USA, US, US of A, America, The States
**Population**[1]**:** 305.8 million
**Capital:** Washington, D. C.
**Largest city:** New York City
**Area**[2]**:** 9.8 million square kilometres[3]
**Money:** 1 dollar ($ or USD) = 100 cents (¢)

### ★ The US flag

The US flag has 50 stars – one for each of the 50 states today. It also has 13 stripes – that's one for each of the states in 1776.

### ★ Did you know?

- ★ Another name for the US flag is the Stars and Stripes.
- ★ The US is 27 times bigger than Germany.
- ★ 1 cent is also called a penny, 5 ¢ is a nickel, 10 ¢ is a dime[4] and 25 ¢ is a quarter.

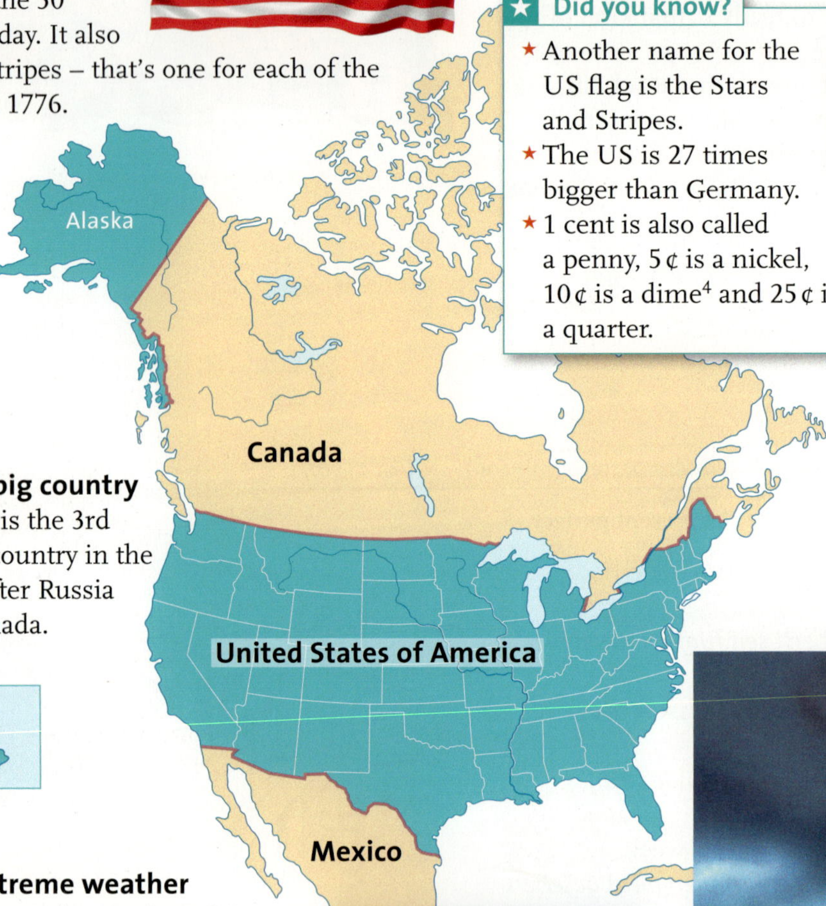


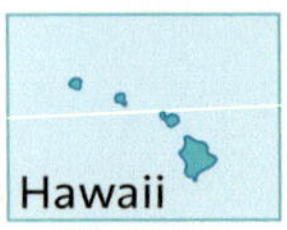


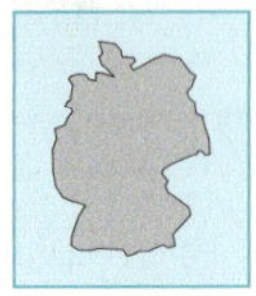

Germany

### ★ A big country

The US is the 3rd largest country in the world after Russia and Canada.

### ★ Extreme weather

The hottest place in the US is Death Valley in California. In 2001 the highest temperature there was 57.2 °C.

Three out of four of all the tornadoes in the world hit[5] the US.

In 2005 Hurricane Katrina was the worst hurricane in US history.

[1] population [ˌpɒpjuˈleɪʃn] *Bevölkerung, Einwohner(zahl)* [2] area [ˈeəriə] *Fläche* [3] square kilometres [skweə] *Quadratkilometer* [4] dime [daɪm] [5] (to) hit [hɪt] *hier: treffen*

## Some important dates

### ▼ About 30,000 BC or earlier
The ancestors[1] of modern Native Americans came to Alaska from Russia by a land bridge.

### ▼ 1492
Christopher Columbus arrived in America.

### ▼ 1607
The British founded[2] Jamestown in Virginia.

**★ Did you know?**

Columbus thought that he was in India. That's why he called the people who lived there 'Indians'.

### ▼ 1619
The first slaves arrived from Africa.

### ▼ 1776
On 4th July, in the Declaration of Independence[3], thirteen states said that they wanted to be free from Britain. This was Independence Day – the birthday of the US!

### ▼ 1776–1783
The Americans fought a war[4] against Britain. America won in the end.

### ▼ 1838
Thousands of Native Americans died on the Trail of Tears.

### ▼ 1848
The Californian Gold Rush began.

### ▼ 1861–1865
The Northern states and the Southern states fought against each other in the Civil War[5].

Mount Rushmore, South Dakota

### ★ US Presidents
You can see the heads of four US Presidents at Mount Rushmore. They are George Washington, Thomas Jefferson, Theodore Roosevelt and Abraham Lincoln.

**★ Did you know?**

The US President lives in the White House in Washington, D.C.

## 2 US quiz
*Use the facts on these pages to answer the quiz questions. Check your answers on page 105.*

1. How many stripes are there on the US flag?
2. What do the letters 'USA' stand for?
3. What is the capital of the US?
4. How many nickels are in a dime?
5. How many states are there in the US?
6. Name a state that begins with the letter 'K'?
7. How much bigger than Germany is the US?
8. What is the name of the hurricane that hit the US in 2005?
9. When is the birthday of the US?
10. Where does the US President live?

[1] ancestor ['ænsestə] *Vorfahre* [2] (to) found [faʊnd] *gründen* [3] Declaration of Independence [ˌdekləˈreɪʃn‿əv ˌɪndɪˈpendəns] *Unabhängigkeitserklärung* [4] war [wɔː] *Krieg* [5] civil war [ˌsɪvl ˈwɔː] *Bürgerkrieg*

## TF 2 The President and Mr Muir

*Read this page about President Roosevelt and John Muir. Find out what both men found interesting.*

Theodore Roosevelt at age 25

**Theodore Roosevelt (1858–1919, US President 1901–1909)**

When he was young, Theodore Roosevelt was often ill. He wasn't as strong as other boys. So his father sent him to boxing lessons, which made him strong and fit. He also enjoyed other sports like walking and mountain climbing.

Theodore loved nature[1]. When he was seven, he started his own natural history[2] museum, and at age nine he wrote about insects. Later he wrote books about birds. Roosevelt's other great love was books. He read one book every day for most of his life. One day he discovered[3] the books of John Muir, who wrote about nature.

In 1901 Theodore Roosevelt became the President of the United States. Two years later he met John Muir for the first time.

John Muir at age 23

**John Muir (1838–1914)**

John Muir was born in Scotland. When he was eleven years old his family moved to the US. As a boy John worked on his family's farm in Wisconsin. He loved being outdoors.

In 1863 John Muir decided[4] to walk from Indiana to Florida. He wanted to spend time in the wilderness[5].

When John Muir visited California in 1868, he walked to Yosemite Valley. Muir thought Yosemite was a very special place and he wanted to protect[6] it. He wrote books, articles and letters and told people that they must protect not only Yosemite, but nature everywhere.

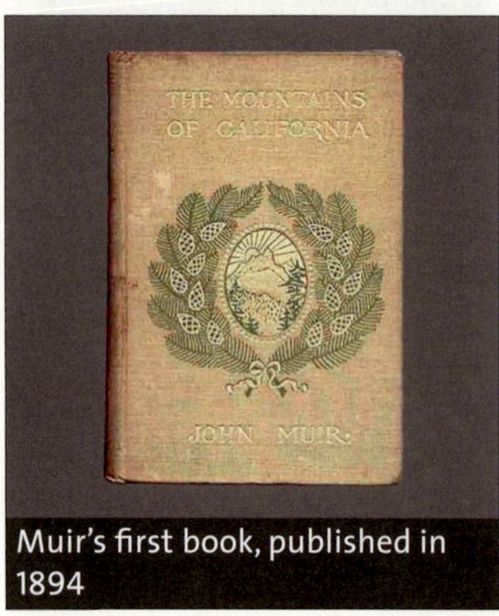


Muir's first book, published in 1894

Roosevelt and Muir at Glacier Point, Yosemite, in 1903

[1] nature ['neɪtʃə] [2] natural history ['nætʃrəl 'hɪstri] *Naturkunde* [3] (to) discover [dɪ'skʌvə] *entdecken* [4] (to) decide [dɪ'saɪd] *beschließen*
[5] wilderness ['wɪldənəs] *Wildnis* [6] (to) protect [prə'tekt] *(be)schützen*

### A famous camping trip

In 1903 President Roosevelt and Mr Muir spent four days and three nights in Yosemite. They slept under the stars, without a tent.

Muir talked to the President about nature and how important it was to protect it. And the President listened.

When he got back to Washington, D.C., Roosevelt started the work that saved Yosemite, and other important natural places in the US. There were national parks in the US before the famous camping trip, but Muir and Roosevelt did more to protect nature in the US than anyone before or after them. Thanks to these two men, land was protected and many new national parks and forests were created[1].

Today millions of people enjoy visiting America's national parks. The Grand Canyon and Yosemite are two of the most popular national parks, but visitors today can choose from almost 400 national parks, forests and nature reserves[2]. About 3.5 million people visit Yosemite National Park every year.

## 1 Right or wrong?

*Are these sentences right or wrong?*

1. Theodore Roosevelt's father wanted Theodore to be fit and strong.
2. Yosemite is in the state of Florida.
3. Roosevelt started the first national park in the US after the camping trip.

## 2 Protecting nature

***a)*** *Which organisations or people try to protect nature today? Do you support them?*

***b)*** *Find out about a US national park. Where is it? What can you see and do there?*

Glacier Bay National Park

Everglades National Park

Yosemite National Park

[1] created [kriːˈeɪtɪd] *geschaffen* [2] nature reserve [ˈneɪtʃə rɪˈzɜːv] *Naturschutzgebiet*

## TF 3 New York – three poems, an essay and a song

### Skyscraper

Skyscraper, skyscraper
Scrape[1] me some sky:
Tickle[2] the sun
While the stars go by[3].
Tickle the stars
While the sun's climbing high,
Then skyscraper, skyscraper
Scrape me some sky.

*Poem by Dennis Lee*

> *What do you think of skyscrapers?*
I think skyscrapers are beautiful/big/exciting/modern/terrible/...

### The city

If flowers[4] want to grow
right out of the concrete[5] sidewalk cracks[6]
I'm going to bend down[7] to smell them.

*Poem by David Ignatow*

> *If you saw a flower that is growing out of a crack in the sidewalk, what would you do?*
(A) walk on it (B) smell it (C) take it home

### Subway rush hour[8]

Mingled[9]
breath[10] and smell
so close
mingled
black and white
so near
no room for fear[11]

*Poem by Langston Hughes*

> *What does the poem say?*
(A) The subway rush hour is terrible because there are too many people.
(B) The subway rush hour brings people together.
(C) There are bad smells in the subway during rush hour.

### 1 The poems

***a)*** *Learn your favourite poem.*

***b)*** *Say your poem for your partner.*

---

[1] (to) scrape [skreɪp] *(ab)kratzen* [2] (to) tickle [tɪkl] *kitzeln* [3] (to) go by *vorüberziehen, -gehen* [4] flower [flaʊə] *Blume*
[5] concrete [ˈkɒŋkriːt] *Beton* [6] crack [kræk] *Riss* [7] (to) bend down [bend] *sich hinunterbeugen* [8] rush hour [ˈrʌʃ‿aʊə] *Hauptverkehrszeit*
[9] mingled [ˈmɪŋɡld] *vermischt* [10] breath [breθ] *Atem* [11] fear [fɪə] *Angst*

### To the visitor

Visitors force[1] you to think. When you ask what they'd like to do or see they say, 'Oh, what's good?'

What's good? In New York?

You tell them that this is New York where everything is good. Everything, baby.

A hot dog at Nathan's in Coney Island is good.

A walk on the Brooklyn Bridge when the sun is setting is good.

A ride on the Staten Island Ferry at sunset past the Statue of Liberty and Ellis Island is very good.

Walk down Broadway. Just look at the people. Look. You're looking at the country's history. And listen to them in their various tongues[2].

And all that is good.

*From an essay by Frank McCourt*

> *Would you like to do the things Frank McCourt describes? Why? If not, what would you like to do in New York?*

### New York, New York

Start spreading[3] the news, I'm leaving today
I want to be a part of it –
New York, New York

These vagabond shoes, are longing to stray[4]
Right through the very heart[5] of it –
New York, New York

I want to wake up in a city that doesn't sleep
And find I'm king of the hill –
top of the heap[6]

These little town blues[7], are melting away[8]
I'll make a brand new start of it –
in old New York
If I can make it[9] there, I'll make it anywhere
It's up to you – New York, New York

*Song by Fred Ebb*

> 1 *Where do you think the singer comes from?*
> (A) a big city (B) a small town
> (C) another country
> 2 *Why do you think the singer wants to go to New York?*
> Maybe the singer wants to find work/ see the sights/visit a friend/ go shopping/...

## 2 A word picture of New York

**a)** *What picture of New York did the texts give you? Write down words and phrases that come to your head.*

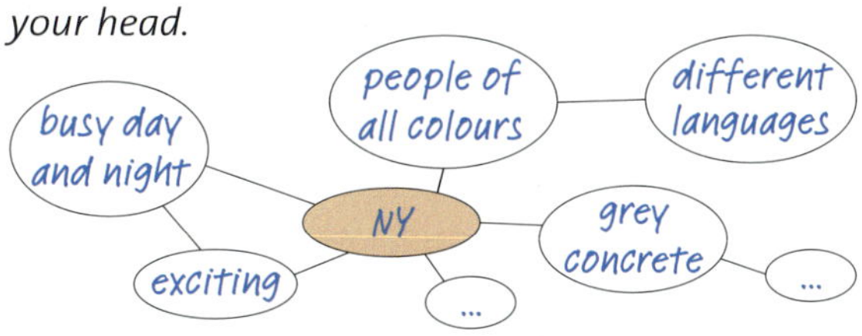


**b)** *Use the words and phrases that you have collected to describe your picture of New York.*
It's a place that is ... There are lots of ...
You can see/hear/smell/...

[1] (to) force [fɔːs] *zwingen* [2] tongue [tʌŋ] *hier: Sprache* [3] (to) spread [spred] *hier: verbreiten* [4] ... are longing to stray [lɒŋɪŋ], [streɪ] *etwa: ... wollen in die Welt hinaus* [5] right through the very heart *mitten durchs Herz* [6] top of the heap [hiːp] *ganz oben* [7] blues [bluːz] *pl etwa: Eintönigkeit* [8] (to) melt (away) [melt] *(weg)schmelzen* [9] (to) make it *es schaffen*

## TF 4 'How about them Yankees?' by Louie D'Agostino (adapted)

*When you meet somebody for the first time, what do you usually talk about? (music, football, the weather, school, politics, TV, ...)*

"'How about them Yankees?' That's all you need." said my old English teacher, Signor Bertanelli. I was visiting him before leaving our little town in Sicily to go to the US – I was emigrating.

"You never were very good at English, Luigi." he said. "Just remember this: 'How about them Yankees?'" He said it again slowly. "Then you will be fine when you get to New York."

I had no idea what the old man was talking about. But I remembered the question: "How about them Yankees?" And very soon I understood why it was a good sentence to know. Even before I learned that the Yankees are a baseball team from the Bronx in New York City.

On the plane I was sitting between two American men from Brooklyn. They asked me lots of easy questions, but after a few minutes, my English was no longer enough. I almost panicked, but then I thought of Signor Bertanelli's question.

"How about them Yankees?" I asked. And just as my old teacher said, everything was fine. The two men talked the rest of the way to New York – I didn't have to say anything. Yes, this one sentence was going to help me a lot.

When I got to New York, I used Signor Bertanelli's question with the Immigration man at JFK airport. I used it to get a room and when I went to get my first job in America. For three months I washed dishes[1] in a restaurant. (Now I have my own restaurant.)

I'll never forget the night when I went to my first bar in America. I was talking to a group of guys. When I couldn't think of anything to say, I asked them, "So, how about them Yankees?"

I became everybody's best friend! They bought me drinks. And they gave me my American name: Louie. As in "Hey, Joe. Meet Louie. Louie here's a big baseball fan."

After a few months in the US, I was a big Yankees fan and and I often went to their home games at Yankee Stadium in the Bronx.

I still am. And now I have lots to say when somebody uses that great conversation opener[2], "How about them Yankees?" Thank you, Signor Bertanelli.

Yankee Stadium is the home of the New York Yankees – the most famous baseball team in the US.

### 1 Understanding the text

*Right or wrong? Correct the wrong statements.*

1 Louie has always spoken English well.
2 Louie is a baseball fan today.
3 Louie has been successful in the US.

### 2 Conversation openers

***a)*** *How many conversation openers can you think of? Write them down. The ideas below may help you.*

- *Ask a question.* (Where are you from?)
- *Talk about the weather.* (It's hot/... today, isn't it?)
- *Talk about the other person's clothes.* (That's a nice ... Where did you get it?)
- *Talk about sport/TV.* (Did you watch ...?)

***b)*** *Read out your best conversation opener. Decide in your group which is the best and the worst conversation opener.*

[1] dishes ['dɪʃɪz] *pl Geschirr* [2] conversation opener [ˌkɒnvəˈseɪʃn ˌəʊpənə] *Satz, mit dem man ein Gespräch beginnen kann*

## TF 5 Life of Ryan

**When you walk around San Clemente, California, you sometimes see famous TV stars. That's not unusual[1] in southern California.**

**But** this star is different: he's only 17, and he's not an actor. In the MTV reality show "Life of Ryan", Ryan Sheckler plays himself, skateboarding star Ryan Sheckler. The cameras follow him everywhere.

**Ryan** first got on a skateboard when he was 18 months old. When he was four, he could already do tricks on the board. He became a professional skateboarder at age 13. Ryan has skated all over the world, in Europe, China, and Australia.

**Ryan** has won lots of competitions, but he also earns money from his sponsors. Lots of companies are happy to pay him so he'll wear their clothes.

**What** about school? Like lots of young celebrities[2], Ryan goes to Futures High School in California. Futures is a private high school where he meets alone with a teacher twice a week for an hour and a half at a time. He goes away "with a pile of[3] homework" after every meeting. But does he do it? You bet![4] Ryan is "really good" at Math, his favorite subject is Science, and he takes English very seriously. He wants to have his own business, and good English is important for that.

### 1 Ryan Sheckler's life

*What's the most surprising thing about Ryan's life?*

– I think the most surprising thing is that ...
– I think it's more surprising that ...

### 2 Reality TV

**a)** *Which reality TV shows do you watch? What do/don't you like about them?*

– I sometimes/never/always watch ...
– I like/don't like reality shows because they're interesting/boring/funny/stupid/...

**b)** *Think of an idea for a reality TV show that you'd like to see. Make notes (who? what? where? when? how?) and tell your group about your idea.*

My idea is a show called 'Back to school'. I think it would be fun to see my parents back at school and doing homework. I'd like to see ...

[1] unusual [ʌnˈjuːʒʊəl] *ungewöhnlich* [2] celebrity [sɪˈlebrɪti] *Berühmtheit* [3] pile [paɪl] *Stapel, Stoß* [4] you bet! [ˌjʊ ˈbet] *und ob!*

# TF 6 Child labour[1]

## 1 Child labour on the US-Mexican border

Many Californian farmers have large fruit and vegetable farms in northern Mexico. One of the main reasons is that labour is cheaper in Mexico. Farm workers are paid about US $ 9 an hour in California, but only US$ 11 a day in Mexico. Most of the fruit and vegetables that are grown on these farms in Mexico are exported back to the US.

### A case study[2]: Adriana Salgado, Mexico

Adriana Salgado, 10, spends her days in a field in north-western Mexico, picking vegetables for US salad bowls.

Adriana goes to school for one hour a day (from 6 pm to 7 pm) and she doesn't know how to read. Her 15-year-old sister, who works with her, also can't read. Adriana had an 8-year-old brother too, but he was killed by a tractor while he was working in a tomato field last year.

Cruz Salgado, Adriana's father, says his family needs the extra $ 7 a day that Adriana earns. The $ 20 a day that he and his wife earn wouldn't be enough to live.

'I wish they didn't have to work,' said Adriana's father. 'But we need the money'.

Does Adriana enjoy working? 'Not much,' she said, 'I like school'.

*Source[3]: Chris Hawley, The Arizona Republic, May 8, 2008*

***a)*** *Compare the labour law information on the right to the information in the case study. What do you notice?*

Child labour is not legal in Mexico. Children must be over 14 to work. Children between 14 and 16 can only work 6 hours a day and they must have finished secondary school.

***b)*** *Look at the circle diagram[4] and use the words in the box to complete the sentences.*

school • job • read • work • money

***c)*** *Describe the circle diagram.*

***Activate your English***

- The circle diagram shows ...
- Because parents ... their children have to ...
- And because of this the children can't ...
- The diagram is a circle because ...

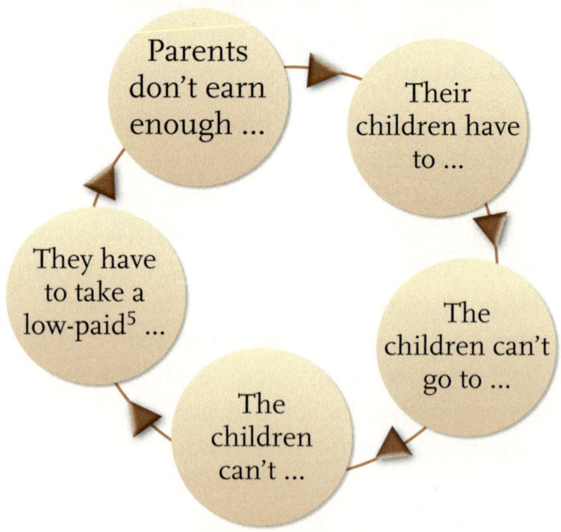


[1] labour ['leɪbə] *Arbeit* [2] case study ['keɪs stʌdi] *Fallstudie* [3] source [sɔːs] *Quelle* [4] circle diagram ['sɜːkl ˌdaɪəgræm] *Kreisdiagramm*
[5] low-paid [ˌləʊ 'peɪd] *schlecht bezahlt*

## 2 Child labour around the world

*Describe what the map below shows. In which regions do children most often have to work?*

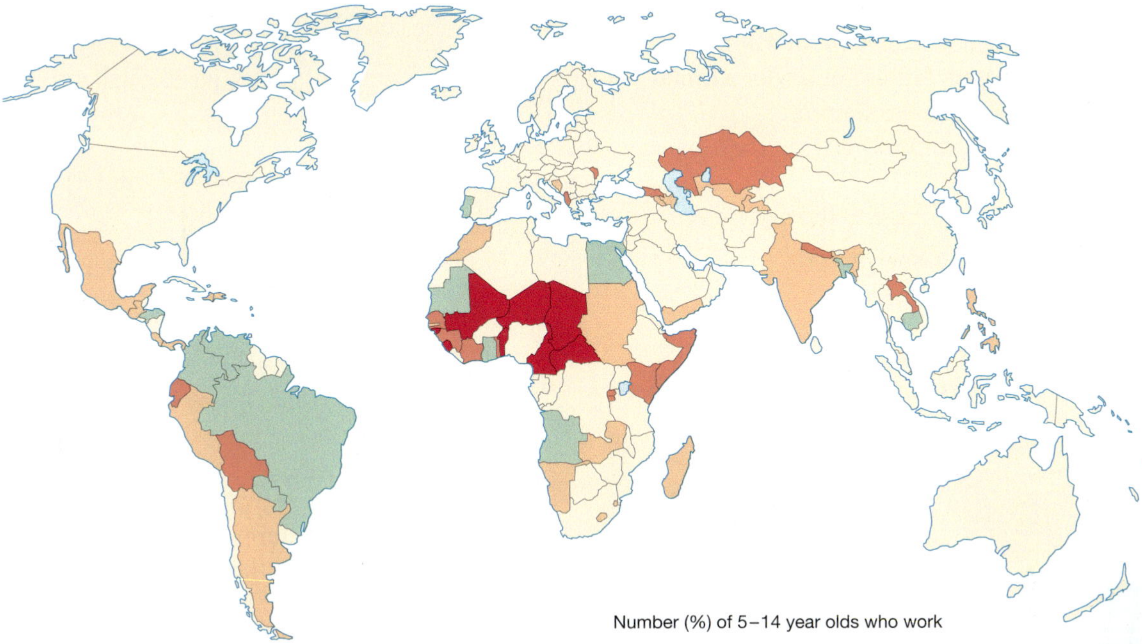


**GEOGRAPHY SKILLS Karten beschreiben**

*Wenn du eine Karte beschreibst, solltest du Folgendes beachten:*

- *Schau dir die Überschrift und die Legende an. Verstehst du, was die Karte darstellt?*
- *Mache zuerst eine allgemeine Aussage über den Inhalt der Karte. Gehe dann auf Einzelheiten ein.*

***Activate your English***

– The map shows/gives information about ...
– This is a map of ...
– It shows how many children ...
– You can see that the situation is ...

## 3 Now you

***a)*** *This is a UNICEF poster against child labour. Describe what it shows. What could be its message[1]?*

– The poster shows a jeans label[2]. On the label you can see ...
– I think the poster wants to tell us ...

***b)*** *What can you do to stop child labour? Think about the poster's message.*

[1] message ['mesɪdʒ] *hier: Botschaft, Aussage* [2] label ['leɪbl] *Etikett, Schild*

## TF 7 Earthquakes in California

### 1 An eyewitness account[1]

*Read what a teenager said after the Northridge earthquake in 1994. True or false?*

1 The boy and his father got under a table when the earthquake started.
2 The electricity went off during the earthquake.
3 There was no damage to the apartment building.

"I was asleep when the earthquake came. I was so scared and I didn't know what to do. The house was shaking[2] so bad that I couldn't even walk. My dad came into my room and got me and we got under the table. We could see the refrigerator[3] sliding back and forth across the kitchen with its door opening and shutting and all of the stuff falling out onto the floor. Our TV went flying across the room and smashed into[4] the wall. All over we could hear things breaking. Then the lights went out. After it stopped we went outside. We could see all of the other people outside too. They were crying and looking around. Part of our apartment building fell down and now those people have to find another place to live. We might have to too."

### 2 After an earthquake

*Describe these photos of earthquakes in California.*

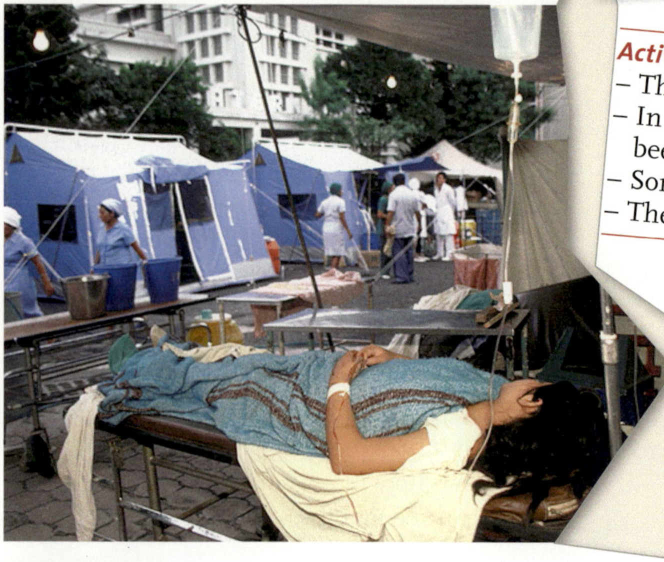

**Activate your English**

- The photos show different results of an ...
- In the first/second/... photo a road/ ... has been destroyed[5] and ...
- Some people are injured[6] ...
- There is a lot of rubble[7] everywhere ...

[1] eyewitness account [ˈaɪwɪtnəs‿əˈkaʊnt] *Augenzeugenbericht* [2] (to) shake [ʃeɪk] *wackeln, beben* [3] refrigerator [rɪˈfrɪdʒəreɪtə] *Kühlschrank* [4] (to) smash into sth. [smæʃ] *gegen etwas krachen* [5] (to) destroy [dɪˈstrɔɪ] zerstören [6] injured [ˈɪndʒəd] *verletzt* [7] rubble [rʌbl] *Schutt, Trümmer*

## 3 Southern California earthquakes

***a)*** *Read the text and look at the map and diagram and answer these questions:*
- When do earthquakes happen?
- Which plate is San Francisco on? And which plate is Los Angeles on?
- What does the diagram show?

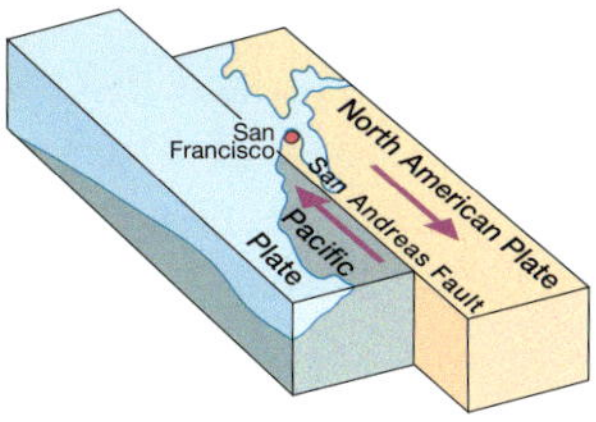


Southern California has thousands of earthquakes every year. People don't feel most of them, but every year there are two or three earthquakes that are large enough to damage[1] buildings.

Part of California is on the Pacific Plate, and part is on the North American Plate. The San Andreas Fault is the border between these two plates. The fault is more than 1000 km long. Earthquakes happen when the two plates scrape[2] against each other.

All the land to the west of the San Andreas Fault is moving slowly north-west past all the land to the east of the fault. The land is moving about 50 mm per year. That is about as fast as your fingernails grow. Today, Los Angeles City Hall is 2.7 metres closer to San Francisco than when it was built in 1924.

The San Andreas Fault

***Activate your English***
- The diagram shows ...
- The land on the ... side of the San Andreas Fault is moving past the land on the ... side of the fault.

## 4 What to do before, during and after an earthquake

***a)*** *Find more examples of things that you should ...*
- *fix[3] to the walls or the floor*
- *put in a disaster kit[4]*
- *do after an earthquake.*

***b)*** *Discuss your results in class.*

***c)*** *Design a poster to help people prepare for an earthquake. Add little drawings like this one.*

### Before an earthquake
**1** Look around your home. Is there any heavy furniture and equipment that could fall and hurt you? Make sure they are fixed to the walls or the floor. Think about things like cupboards, TVs, ...
**2** Make disaster kits with food, water, ...

### During an earthquake
Drop, cover and hold on! Drop to the floor, take cover under a desk or table and hold on to it.

### After an earthquake
**1** Check whether anyone is injured.

[1] (to) damage ['dæmidʒ] *beschädigen* [2] (to) scrape [skreɪp] *scheuern, reiben* [3] (to) fix [fɪks] *hier: befestigen, sichern*
[4] disaster kit [dɪ'zɑːstə kɪt] *Katastrophenausrüstung*

## TF 8 Building the Gateway Arch[1]

The Gateway Arch is the symbol[2] of St. Louis, Missouri. The Arch is the tallest monument[3] in the US. It was built in 1965 as a monument to the first settlers who came to the western US.

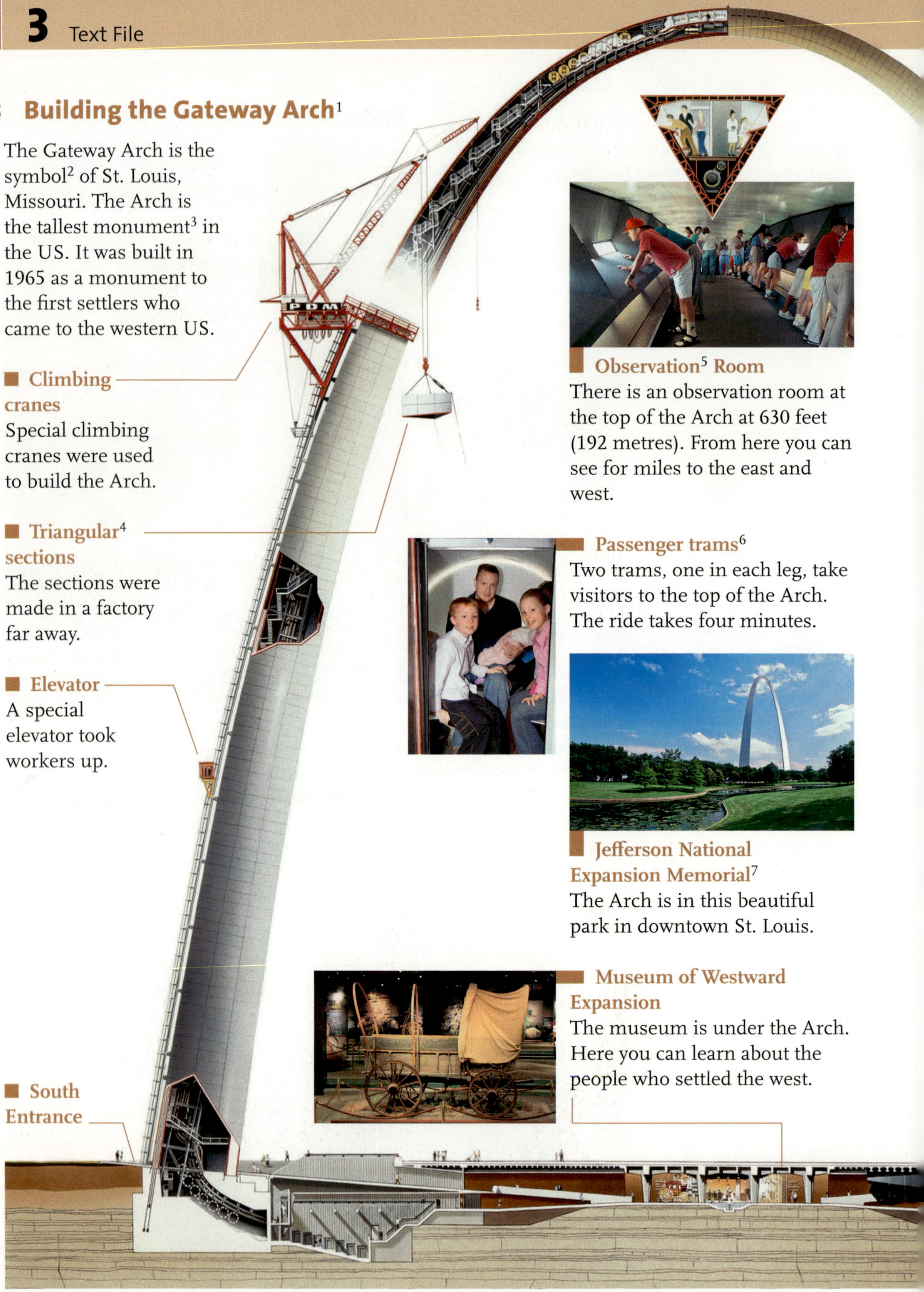


**Observation[5] Room**
There is an observation room at the top of the Arch at 630 feet (192 metres). From here you can see for miles to the east and west.

**Climbing cranes**
Special climbing cranes were used to build the Arch.

**Triangular[4] sections**
The sections were made in a factory far away.

**Passenger trams[6]**
Two trams, one in each leg, take visitors to the top of the Arch. The ride takes four minutes.

**Elevator**
A special elevator took workers up.

**Jefferson National Expansion Memorial[7]**
The Arch is in this beautiful park in downtown St. Louis.

**Museum of Westward Expansion**
The museum is under the Arch. Here you can learn about the people who settled the west.

**South Entrance**

[1] gateway arch ['geɪtweɪ ˌɑːtʃ] *Torbogen* [2] symbol ['sɪmbl] *hier: Wahrzeichen* [3] monument ['mɒnjʊmənt] *Denkmal*
[4] triangular [traɪ'æŋgjələ] *dreieckig* [5] observation [ˌɒbzə'veɪʃn] *Aussichts-* [6] passenger tram ['pæsɪndʒə ˌtræm] *Schienenbahn für Passagiere*
[7] memorial [me'mɔːriəl] *Denkmal, Mahnmal*

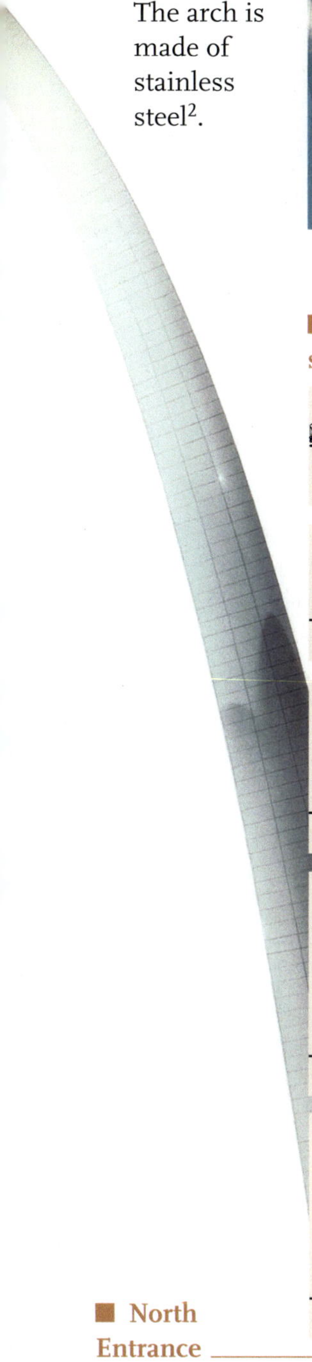

■ **The skin**[1]
The arch is made of stainless steel[2].

■ **Construction steps**[3]

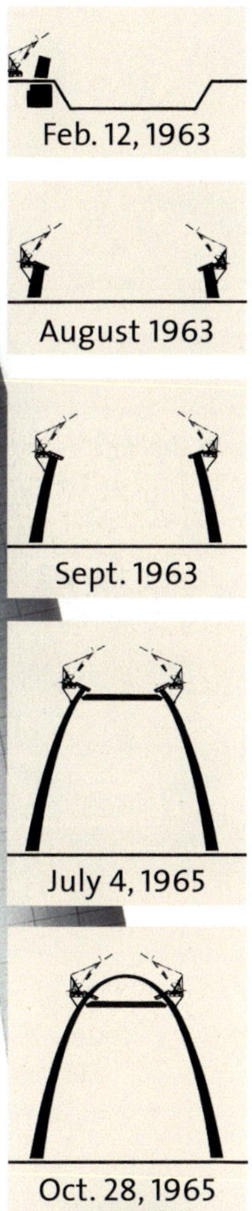


■ **North Entrance**

1 First the two legs were built.

2 In the last few months the two halves were brought together at the top.

3 A triangular section

4 The last piece of the Arch

## 1 Understanding the pictures and texts

*Look carefully at the drawings, photos and texts and answer the following questions:*

1 How tall is the Arch in feet? In metres?
2 How long did it take to build the Arch?
3 What can visitors to the Arch see and do?

## 2 Surprise!

*Do you think the Arch is taller than it is wide, or wider than it is tall? Use your ruler to check.*

---

[1] skin [skɪn] *hier: (Außen-)Hülle* [2] stainless steel [ˌsteɪnləs ˈstiːl] *rostfreier Stahl, Edelstahl* [3] construction steps [kənˈstrʌkʃn] *Baufortschritte*

## TF 9 The Trail of Tears[1] – Georgia to Oklahoma

The darkest time in the history of the Cherokee people was the 'Trail of Tears'. In 1838 16,000 of them were moved[2] from the south-eastern US. In their language this journey of nearly 2000 kilometres is called 'the trail where they cried'.

[1] trail of tears [ˌtreɪl‿əv 'tɪəz] *Pfad der Tränen* [2] (to) move *hier: umsiedeln, vertreiben* [3] law [lɔː] *Gesetz* [4] territory ['terɪtərɪ] *Gebiet*
[5] Supreme Court [sʊ'priːm ˌkɔːt] *Oberster Gerichtshof (US)* [6] (to) leave sb. alone *jn in Ruhe lassen*

5 New Echota, Georgia, November 1838

6 Somewhere in Kentucky, January 1839

7 Somewhere in Missouri, February 1839

8 New Echota Historic Site[3], today

## 1 What happened?

*Match these headings to the pictures.*

*A* The Cherokee were cold and hungry.
*B* The President sent the army to move the Cherokee.
*C* A law said that the Cherokee had to move away.
*D* People come to New Echota today to remember what happened.
*E* Many Cherokee died on the journey.
*F* Gold was found in Georgia.
*G* The US Supreme Court said that the new law was wrong.
*H* The Cherokee were good farmers.

---

[1] make sure (that) *dafür sorgen, dass* [2] cholera ['kɒlərə] *Cholera (Krankheit, die von starkem Durchfall und Erbrechen begleitet wird)*
[3] historic site [hɪ'stɒrɪk ˌsaɪt] *historische Gedenkstätte*

## TF 10 Black music

For 400 years, since the first black slaves arrived in America in 1619, black music has changed the look[1] and sound of music in the US. From spirituals to contemporary[2] R&B, here are ten important black music styles.

**1 SPIRITUALS** The earliest black songs in the US were the work songs and spirituals that the slaves sang in the fields. Spirituals were religious songs that gave hope of a better future to the slaves. One very famous spiritual is 'Swing low, sweet chariot'[3]. Gospel music, which started in the African American churches in the early 1900s, comes from the spirituals sung by southern slaves.

Slaves in the fields

**2 BLUES** Slavery was abolished[4] in 1865. As blacks moved north to the towns, a new type of black music was born – the blues. Robert Johnson was one of the most famous blues musicians[5], and there were many more great blues singers, like Ma Rainey and Bessie Smith.

Bessie Smith

Robert Johnson

Louis Armstrong

**3 JAZZ** In the 1920s jazz music was very popular in the US. Buddy Bolden, Jelly Roll Morton and Louis Armstrong were some of the first stars of this amazing new music style.

Bo Diddley

**4 R&B** Rhythm and blues was a music style that started in the 1930s and 1940s. It was a mix of jazz, gospel and blues music. Ruth Brown, Bo Diddley and Fats Domino were popular R&B artists at that time.

**5 ROCK 'N' ROLL** In the 1950s, the first rock 'n' roll songs were played by black artists. 'Tutti Frutti' by Little Richard and 'Johnny B. Goode' by Chuck Berry were two of the first rock 'n' roll songs.

Chuck Berry

[1] look [lʊk] *Aussehen* [2] contemporary [kən'temprəri] *zeitgenössisch, modern* [3] Swing low, sweet chariot [ləʊ], ['tʃæriət] *etwa: Schwing dich herab, du himmlischer Wagen* [4] (to) abolish [ə'bɒlɪʃ] *abschaffen* [5] musician [mju:'zɪʃn] *Musiker(in)*

Aretha Franklin

**6 SOUL** Soul came from R&B and gospel. It was started in the late 1950s by black artists like Sam Cooke, Ray Charles and James Brown. In the 1960s one of the most popular soul stars was Aretha Franklin. People call her 'The Queen of Soul'.

Kool and the Gang

**7 DISCO** In the 1970s, black disco stars, like B.T. Express, Kool and the Gang, Sister Sledge and Donna Summer, were popular.

**8 RAP AND HIP HOP** In 1979, The Sugar Hill Gang produced the first rap hit, 'Rapper's Delight'. This was the start of a new sound in the music world.

Alicia Keys

**9 NEO SOUL** In the late 1990s there was a new mix of sounds which people called neo soul. It was made up of hip hop, reggae, jazz, soul and Latin music. Lauryn Hill, Erykah Badu and Alicia Keys are famous neo soul artists of the 1990s and 2000s.

Usher

LeToya

**10 CONTEMPORARY R&B** Contemporary R&B is a style of music that comes from soul, funk and disco. Today, black R&B singers like Beyoncé, LeToya, Usher and Ne-Yo are continuing[1] the black music tradition in the US.

## 1 Black music quiz

*Answer the quiz questions.*

1 What were the religious slave songs called?
A the blues B spirituals C gospels
2 What came first? The blues, soul or jazz?
A the blues B soul C jazz
3 What music came from jazz, gospel and the blues and was popular in the 1930s and 1940s?
A R&B B rock 'n' roll C soul
4 Who first sang the rock 'n' roll song 'Johnny B. Goode'?
A Chuck Berry B Little Richard C Bo Diddley
5 She was born on March 25, 1942 and they call her 'The Queen of Soul'. What's her name?
A Beyoncé B Alicia Keys C Aretha Franklin
6 Which trio[2] had the first rap hit?
A Kool and the Gang B Sister Sledge C Sugar Hill Gang

## 2 Radio quiz show

*Listen to the quiz show. Check your answers and correct any wrong answers.*

[1] (to) continue [kən'tɪnjuː] *fortführen* [2] trio [triː'əʊ] *Trio (Gruppe, die aus drei Mitgliedern besteht)*

# TF 11 The American Civil War[1] (1861–1865)

## 1 Causes[2] of the Civil War

*Read the text and find the answers to these questions: Where were slaves used – in the North or the South? How many states left the Union[3]? Who won the war?*

The Civil War (1861–1865) was a conflict between the North and the South in the US. At that time, the Northern states and the Southern states were very different. In the South, there were big plantations[4] that used black slaves to do the work. In the North, industry was more important than farming and most of the Northern states did not use slaves. A lot of people in the North thought that slavery was wrong.

The South thought that the US government wanted to end slavery. Between 1860 and 1861, 11 Southern states left the Union to make the 'Confederate States[5] of America'.

The President, Abraham Lincoln, sent soldiers[6] to the South to try to bring the Confederate states back into the Union. The fighting started in April 1861 and went on for four years.

In April 1865, the Union won the war and North and South were united again. 620,000 American soldiers died in the Civil War – more than in any war in the history of the US. In the South, many farms and cities were destroyed[7]. In December 1865, slavery was abolished[8] in the US.

## 2 Causes and effects[8]

*Copy the diagram and fill in the missing words.*

| main causes | | Civil War (1861–1865) | | main effects |
|---|---|---|---|---|
| | The plantations in the ... used slaves. Many people in the ... thought that slavery was wrong. | → | ... was abolished | |
| | 11 Southern ... left the Union. The President sent ... to the South. | → | North and South were ... again. | |

## 3 The United States – divided[9] by war

***a)*** *Describe the map.*

***b)*** *Find the following states on the map: California, Missouri, New York, Georgia. Which side were they on in the Civil War? Were they for or against slavery?*

The United States of America 1861–1865

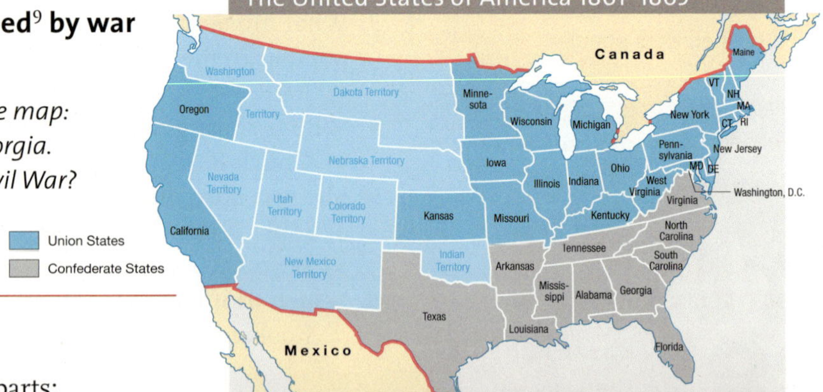


Before 1861, the US was made up of 19 free states, 15 slave states and some territories. Then 11 slave states left the Union to form the Confederate States of America.

*Activate your English*
- The map shows...
- The US was divided into two parts: the Union states and territories and ...
- The blue states were in the ...
- The grey states were in the ...

[1] civil war [ˌsɪvl 'wɔː] *Bürgerkrieg* [2] cause [kɔːz] *Ursache* [3] the Union ['juːnjən] *die Unionsstaaten* [4] plantation [plæn'teɪʃn] *Plantage* [5] Confederate States [kən'fedərɪt steɪts] *Konföderierte (d.h. verbündete) Staaten* [6] soldier ['səʊldʒə] *Soldat* [7] (to) destroy [dɪ'strɔɪ] *zerstören* [8] (to) abolish [ə'bɒlɪʃ] *abschaffen* [9] effect [ɪ'fekt] *Wirkung* [10] (to) divide [dɪ'vaɪd] *teilen*

## 4 A photo from 1865

*Before you read the text, try to answer these questions: Who are the men in the photo? How do they feel?*

*a) Now read the text on the right and try to find the answers to these questions.*

1 The men in the photo are ...
- A soldiers.
- B officers.
- C slaves.

2 They fought for ...
- A the North.
- B the South.

3 They felt...
- A afraid to fight against slavery.
- B proud to fight against slavery.

*b) In your group talk about the photo and the information in the text.*

The photo shows soldiers of Company E, 4th Colored Infantry Regiment[1] at Fort[2] Lincoln. It was taken in 1865, after the end of the Civil War.

About 200,000 (10%) of the soldiers in the Union army were black. Nearly 40,000 black soldiers died in the war.

Black people were afraid that if the South won the war, slavery would continue[3]. They thought that if the North won the war, the US government would stop slavery. Although they didn't have the same rights as white soldiers, they felt proud to fight for the Union.

### Activate your English
- The photo was taken in ... at ...
- I think the photo was taken by ...
- The photo shows ...
- They fought in the ... army.

### HISTORY SKILLS Historische Fotos

*Historische Fotos können uns viel über vergangene Zeiten erzählen. Aber Vorsicht: um wirklich zu verstehen, was diese Fotos zeigen, musst du die Hintergründe kennen:*
- *Wer ist auf dem Foto zu sehen?*
- *Wann wurde das Foto aufgenommen?*
- *Was geschah zu dieser Zeit?*
- *Wo (und von wem) wurde das Foto aufgenommen?*

[1] infantry regiment ['ɪnfəntrɪ ˌredʒɪmənt] *Infanterieregiment (Fußtruppe)* [2] fort [fɔːt] *Fort (kleine Befestigungsanlage)*
[3] (to) continue [kən'tɪnjuː] *fortdauern*

## Skills File – Inhalt



Im **Skills File** findest du Hinweise zu Arbeits- und Lerntechniken. Was du in den Skills-Kästen der Units gelernt hast, wird hier näher erläutert.

Was du bereits aus Band 3 von English G 21 kennst, ist mit **REVISION** gekennzeichnet,
z. B.
– **REVISION Describing pictures**, Seite 140
– **REVISION Giving a presentation**, Seite 140.

Viele neue Hinweise helfen dir bei der Arbeit mit Hör- und Lesetexten, beim Sprechen, beim Schreiben von eigenen Texten, bei der Sprachmittlung und beim Lernen von Methoden.

Manchmal gibt es auch Aufgaben dazu.

# STUDY AND LANGUAGE SKILLS

## SF REVISION Learning words

### Worauf solltest du beim Lernen und Wiederholen von Vokabeln achten?

- Lerne immer 7–10 Vokabeln auf einmal.
- Lerne neue und wiederhole alte Vokabeln regelmäßig – am besten jeden Tag 5–10 Minuten.
- Lerne mit jemandem zusammen. Fragt euch gegenseitig ab.
- Schreib die neuen Wörter immer auch auf und überprüfe die Schreibweise mithilfe des *Dictionary* oder *Vocabulary*.

### Wie kannst du Wörter besser behalten?

Wörter kannst du besser behalten, wenn du sie in Wortgruppen sammelst und ordnest:

- **Gegensatzpaare** sammeln, z. B. alive ◂▸ dead, majority ◂▸ minority, forget ◂▸ remember
- Wörter mit **gleicher Bedeutung** sammeln, z. B. (to) train – (to) practise
- Wörter in **Wortfamilien** sammeln, z. B. (to) dance, dance, dancer, dancing lessons; friend, boyfriend, girlfriend, friendly, unfriendly, ...
- Wörter in **Wortnetzen** *(networks)* sammeln und ordnen.

## SF Check yourself ▸ *Unit 1, p. 29*

### How am I doing?

Damit du weißt, in welchen Bereichen des Englischen du noch Schwächen hast und welche du schon beherrschst, solltest du dich immer wieder selbst überprüfen. Das kannst du auf unterschiedlichen Wegen tun. Eine Reihe von Tipps kennst du schon vom **Stop-Check-Go** aus Band 1–2.
Du kannst dich auch nach jeder Unit mithilfe der *How am I doing*-Seiten selbst überprüfen, die du schon aus Band 3 kennst. Dabei gehst du wie folgt vor:

1. Du machst die einzelnen Aufgaben und überprüfst deine Ergebnisse.
2. Dann schaust du dir die Bereiche, in denen du Fehler gemacht hast, nochmal an. Halte dich dabei an die Hinweise in der Spalte *Find out more*.
3. Nun übst du gezielt diese Bereiche. Dazu schaust du in der Spalte *Exercises* nach, wo du im Englischbuch und *Workbook* Übungen dazu findest.
4. Nach einiger Zeit machst du die Aufgaben in *How am I doing?* noch einmal und vergleichst die Lösungen mit deinen Ergebnissen vom ersten Mal.

### Die Arbeit mit einer persönlichen Fehlerliste

Führe eine Liste der Fehler, die du oft machst, und nutze sie beim Schreiben von Texten als persönliche Checkliste. Hefte diese Listen in deinem Englischordner ab oder lege dir dafür ein extra Heft an (z.B. in DIN-A5).
Das Heft kannst du z.B. nach folgenden Schwerpunkten unterteilen:

1. Drittel: *Words* 2. Drittel: *Grammar* 3. Drittel: *Spelling*

Dann untersuchst du deine Klassenarbeiten und andere schriftliche Arbeiten auf deine Fehlerquellen hin. Dein/e Englischlehrer/in zeigt durch Abkürzungen am Rand, was für eine Art Fehler du gemacht hast.

WORDS

| Wrong | Correct | REMEMBER |
|---|---|---|
| He goes to school ~~with the~~ bus. | He goes to school by bus. | mit dem Bus fahren – go by bus |
| We've got a ~~strong~~ teacher. | We've got a strict teacher. | Nicht verwechseln! streng – strict / strong – stark |
| I climbed ~~on~~ a tree. | I climbed a tree. | auf einen Baum klettern – climb a tree |

**Tipp**

- Ergänze das Heft jedes Mal, wenn du eine Klassenarbeit oder einen Text von deinem Lehrer/deiner Lehrerin zurückbekommen oder wenn du eine *How am I doing*-Seite bearbeitet hast.
- Überprüfe, ob du bestimmte Fehler immer wieder machst. Wenn ja, such dafür Übungen in deinem Englischbuch, deinem *Workbook*, deinem *e-Workbook* oder frag deinen Lehrer/deine Lehrerin nach Übungen.
- Schau dir vor jeder Klassenarbeit die Fehler an, die du oft machst.
- Mach dir mithilfe des Grammatikteils die Regeln, die dir besonders schwerfallen, noch einmal bewusst.

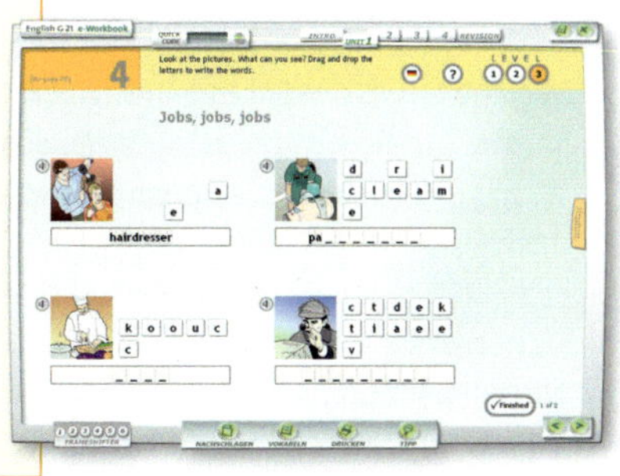

# SF REVISION Using a bilingual dictionary

## Wann brauche ich ein zweisprachiges Wörterbuch?

Du verstehst einen Text nicht, weil er zu viele Wörter enthält, die dir unbekannt sind, und die Worterschließungstechniken (▸ *SF Working out the meaning of words, p. 142*) helfen dir nicht weiter?
Du sollst einen Text auf Englisch schreiben, und dir fehlt das eine oder andere Wort, um deine Ideen auszudrücken? Du willst z.B. über die Ankunft eines Einwanderers in einem neuen Land schreiben (vgl. S. 18–19) und kennst das englische Wort für „Grenze" nicht?
In jedem Fall hilft dir ein zweisprachiges Wörterbuch.

## Wie benutze ich ein zweisprachiges Wörterbuch?

- Die **Leitwörter** oben auf der Seite helfen dir, schneller zu finden, was du suchst. Auf der linken Seite steht das erste Stichwort, auf der rechten Seite das letzte Stichwort der Doppelseite.
- **Grenze** ist das **Stichwort**. Alle Stichwörter sind alphabetisch geordnet: **g** vor **h**, **ga** vor **ge** und **gre** vor **gri** usw.
- Die **kursiv gedruckten** Hinweise helfen dir, die für deinen Text passende Bedeutung zu finden.
- Die **Ziffern** 1, 2 usw. zeigen, dass ein Stichwort mehrere ganz verschiedene Bedeutungen hat.
- **Beispielsätze** und **Redewendungen** sind dem Stichwort zugeordnet. In den Beispielsätzen und Redewendungen ersetzt eine **Tilde** (~) das Stichwort.
- Im englisch-deutschen Teil der meisten Wörterbücher findest du außerdem Hinweise auf **unregelmäßige Verbformen**, auf die **Steigerungsformen der Adjektive** und Ähnliches.
- Die **Lautschrift** gibt Auskunft darüber, wie das Wort ausgesprochen und betont wird. (→ *English sounds, p. 206*)

**gottlos**

divinely
**gottlos** godless, wicked
**gottverlassen** *umg.* godforsaken
**Götze, Götzenbild** idol ['aɪdl]
**Gouverneur** governor

**Grazie** grace
**graziös** **1** *Adj* graceful (⚠ *nicht* gracious) **2** *Adv* gracefully; **~ tanzen** dance gracefully
**greifen** **1** *Verb mit Obj* seize, take* hold of **2** *Verb ohne Obj; übertragen: von Maßnahmen* take* effect; **~ nach** reach for; *fest* grab at; ***sie griff in ihre Handtasche*** she reached into her handbag
**Greis** old man
**greisenhaft** senile (*auch* MED)
**Greisin** old woman
**grell** *Licht* glaring, harsh; *Farbe* garish; *Ton* shrill
**Grenze** border; *Linie* boundary; *übertragen* limit; ***es hält sich in Grenzen*** it's not too bad
**grenzen:** **~ an** border on (*auch übertragen*)
**grenzenlos** **1** *Adj* boundless **2** *Adv*; seh-

Bei kniffligen Wörtern gibt es in vielen Wörterbüchern **Info-Boxes**, in denen dir mehr Hilfen und Hinweise gegeben werden, hier z.B. für das deutsche Wort „schwer".

**schwer krank**

**schwer**

Das deutsche **schwer** hat drei Hauptbedeutungen:
1) *schwer von Gewicht*: **heavy**;
2) *schwerwiegend, ernst*: **serious**, **bad**;
3) *schwierig*: **difficult**, **hard**, **tough**.

Welche englische Entsprechung von **Grenze** brauchst du in diesen Sätzen?
1. The ... between the US and Mexico is over 3000 km long.
2. In yesterday's run he pushed himself to his ...

**Tipp**

Nimm nicht einfach die erste Übersetzung, die dir angeboten wird! Lies den Wörterbucheintrag, bis du die richtige Übersetzung gefunden hast.

## Internet research ▸ *Unit 4 (p. 79)*

### Wie kann ich das Internet zur Recherche nutzen?

*Find some information about African Americans in the 1960s* – so oder so ähnlich lauten Aufgaben, die dir oft als Hausaufgabe gestellt werden. Wenn du nun nach Informationen suchst, dann ist das Internet ist eine wichtige Quelle. Aber manchmal findest du dort so viele Informationen, dass du schnell den Überblick verlierst. Diese Tipps sollen dir helfen, damit du nicht im *world wide web* verloren gehst.

- Bevor du ins Internet gehst, mach dir eine Liste mit Schlüsselwörtern (**key words**) zu deinem Thema: *African Americans, history, USA, discrimination, ...*
- Überlege, welches Schlüsselwort oder welche Kombination von Schlüsselwörtern am besten sein könnte:
  **„African Americans" history** oder **African+Americans+history**
- Wenn du dir zunächst einen Überblick verschaffen willst, kannst du auch ein Nachschlagewerk im Internet anklicken:
  www.infoplease.com www.en.wikipedia.org
  Manchmal gibt es dort auch Links, die dir weiterhelfen können.
- Suchmaschinen (wie z.B. *Google, Altavista* oder *Yahoo*) helfen dir, Websites zu deinem Thema zu finden. Verwende eine Suchmaschine und gib deine Schlüsselwörter in das Suchfenster ein.
- Wenn die angezeigten Websites dir nicht helfen oder zu umfangreich sind, versuch es noch einmal, indem du deine Schlüsselwörter präzisierst.

**Tip**

- Beachte: Nicht alles, was im Internet steht, ist richtig! Daher solltest du immer mehr als eine Website anschauen, um sicherzugehen, dass die Informationen stimmen.
- Suche Antworten auf die **5 Ws** (**who**, **what**, **where**, **when**, **why**).
- Bei englischen Quellen musst du nicht jedes Wort auf einer Website verstehen. Konzentrier dich auf das Wesentliche. Scanne den Text gezielt nach Informationen (**key words**), die du brauchst (▸ *Reading Course S. 142*).
- Schreib die Quellen nicht wortwörtlich ab, sondern mach dir Notizen.

### Wo kann ich noch Informationen finden?

Neben dem Internet gibt es natürlich weitere Quellen, wo du Informationen zu deinem Thema findest, z.B. in einem Lexikon, Atlas, Wörterbuch, Schulbuch oder auch in Zeitschriften oder Zeitungen. Auch CDs und DVDs sind mögliche Quellen. Benutze auch möglichst englische Quellen, das kann dir beim Ausformulieren deines englischen Textes helfen.

- Internet/Lexikon: alle Wissensgebiete, wichtige Personen und Ereignisse
- Atlas: geografische und politische Übersichten, Städte, Flüsse
- Wörterbücher: Rechtschreibung und Bedeutung von Wörtern
- Schulbücher: verschiedene Wissensgebiete
- Zeitungen/Zeitschriften: aktuelle Informationen zu allen Themenbereichen

## SF REVISION Describing pictures

### Wie kann ich Bilder beschreiben?

- Um zu sagen, wo genau etwas abgebildet ist, benutze:
  **at the top/bottom • in the foreground/background • in the middle • on the left/right**
- Diese Präpositionen sind auch hilfreich:
  **behind • between • in front of • next to • under**
- Um zu beschreiben, was die Personen auf dem Bild tun, benutze das **present progressive**.
  **The girl is looking down into the Grand Canyon.**

### Wie kann ich beschreiben, was die Personen fühlen?

Oft sollst du dich in eine Person auf einem Foto hineinversetzen und beschreiben, was sie fühlt oder denkt. Schau dir das Foto genau an und nimm dir Zeit, dir die Situation vorzustellen. Beim Formulieren helfen dir *phrases* wie:
**Maybe the woman/man in the photo feels ... /is thinking about ... •**
**I think he/she feels/wants to/...**

## SF REVISION Giving a presentation

### Wie mache ich eine gute Präsentation?

**Vorbereitung**
- Schreib die wichtigsten Gedanken als Notizen auf, z. B. auf nummerierte Karteikarten oder als Mindmaps.
- Übe deine Präsentation zu Hause vor einem Spiegel. Sprich laut, deutlich und langsam.

**Folien oder Poster**
- Overhead-Folien oder Poster sind gut, um
  - zu zeigen, wie dein Vortrag aufgebaut ist
  - Tabellen, Diagramme usw. für alle lesbar zu präsentieren
  - die wichtigsten Punkte zusammenzufassen.
- Schreib groß und für alle gut lesbar.

**Durchführung**
- Bevor du beginnst, leg deine Folie auf den ausgeschalteten Projektor bzw. häng das Poster auf und sortiere deine Vortragskarten.
- Warte, bis es ruhig ist. Schau die Zuhörer an.
- Erkläre zu Anfang, worüber du sprechen wirst. Lies nicht von deinen Karten ab, sondern sprich frei, nutze deine Karten nur als Gedankenstütze.

My presentation is about ... First, I'd like to talk about ... Second, ...

This picture/photo/ ... shows ...

**Schluss**
- Sag, dass du fertig bist.
- Frag die Zuhörenden, ob sie Fragen haben. Bedanke dich fürs Zuhören.

That's the end of my presentation. Have you got any questions?

# LISTENING AND READING SKILLS

## SF REVISION Listening

### Was muss ich allgemein beim *Listening* beachten?

**Vor dem Hören:**
- Überlege, worum es in dem Hörtext gehen wird. Frag dich, was du schon über das Thema weißt.
- Lies die Aufgabe gut durch, damit du weißt, worauf du achten sollst:
  - auf die Hauptgedanken oder
  - auf bestimmte Informationen, wie z.B. Namen, Uhrzeiten, Jahreszahlen.
- Bereite dich darauf vor, Notizen zu machen. Leg z.B. eine Tabelle oder Liste an.

**Beim Hören:**
- Keine Panik! Du musst nicht alles verstehen. Konzentriere dich auf das Wesentliche. Oft werden wichtige Informationen auch wiederholt.
- Achte auf Geräusche und unterschiedliche Stimmen. Was ein Sprecher/eine Sprecherin besonders betont, das ist wichtig!
- Wenn du gezielt nach Informationen suchst, denk an die Aufgabe und lass dich von anderen Einzelheiten nicht ablenken.
  Aufgepasst! Die Informationen, die du suchst, kommen vielleicht in einer anderen Reihenfolge vor, als du sie erwartest.

- Manche Signalwörter machen es dir leichter, den Hörtext zu verstehen:
  - Aufzählung: **and**, **another**, **too**
  - Gegensatz: **but**
  - Grund, Folge: **because, so**
  - Vergleich: **larger/older/... than**, **more**, **most**
  - Reihenfolge: **before**, **after**, **then**, **next**, **later**, **when**, **at last**
- Mach nur kurze Notizen, z.B. Anfangsbuchstaben, Symbole oder Stichworte, schreib keine ganzen Sätze.

**Nach dem Hören:**
- Vervollständige deine Notizen sofort.
- Konzentriere dich beim zweiten Hören auf das, was du zuerst nicht gut verstanden hast.

### Worauf sollte ich bei automatischen Telefonansagen achten?

Wenn du eine telefonische Auskunft einholen willst, hörst du manchmal eine automatische Telefonansage.
- Keine Panik! Du kannst eine automatische Telefonansage mehrmals hören.
- Achte besonders auf Zahlen! Meist wirst du aufgefordert, bestimmte Tasten auf deinem Telefon zu drücken, um die gewünschte Information zu erhalten. Oft werden diese Zahlen wiederholt.
- Überlege dir vorher, welche Informationen du suchst und auf welche Schlüsselwörter du dafür achten solltest. Schreib sie auf.
- Höre dann besonders genau zu, wenn deine Schlüsselwörter genannt werden und mach dir Notizen zu ihnen. ▸ *Unit 2, p. 46*

# READING COURSE – Zusammenfassung

## REVISION Working out the meaning of words ▸ Unit 1, p. 25

Das Nachschlagen unbekannter Wörter im Wörterbuch kostet Zeit und nimmt auf Dauer den Spaß am Lesen. Oft geht es auch ohne Wörterbuch!

### Was hilft dir, unbekannte Wörter zu verstehen?

1. **Bilder** zeigen oft die Dinge, die du im Text nicht verstehst. Wenn es Bilder zum Text gibt, dann schau sie dir vor dem Lesen genau an.
2. Oft hilft dir der **Textzusammenhang**, z.B. *When we* ***reached*** *the station, Judy went to the ticket machine to buy our tickets.*
3. Manche englischen Wörter werden **ähnlich wie im Deutschen** geschrieben oder ausgesprochen, z.B. **excellent**, **millionaire**, **nation**, **reality**.
4. Manchmal stecken in unbekannten Wörtern **bekannte Teile**, z.B. **friendliness**, **helpless**, **understandable**, **gardener**, **tea bag**, **waiting room**.

## REVISION Skimming and Scanning ▸ Unit 2, p. 43

### *Skimming:* Lesen, um sich einen Überblick zu verschaffen

Beim **Skimming** überfliegst du einen Text schnell, um dir einen ersten **Überblick** zu verschaffen, worum es geht. Du willst herausfinden, ob ein Text, den du im Internet oder in einem Buch gefunden hast, überhaupt nützliche Informationen zu deinem Thema (z.B. für ein Referat) enthält. Achte beim Skimming auf:
- die **Überschrift**
- die **Zwischenüberschriften** und **hervorgehobene** Wörter oder Sätze
- die **Bilder** und **Bildunterschriften**
- den **ersten** und **letzten Satz** jedes Absatzes
- **Grafiken**, **Statistiken** und die **Quelle** des Textes.

### *Scanning:* Lesen, um nach bestimmten Informationen zu suchen

Beim **Scanning** suchst du in einem Text nach **bestimmten Informationen**, die z.B. für ein Referat wichtig sind. Dazu brauchst du nicht den gesamten Text zu lesen, sondern du suchst nach Schlüsselwörtern (**key words**) und liest nur dort genauer, wo du sie findest. Geh dabei so vor:

**Schritt 1:** Denk an das Schlüsselwort, nach dem du suchst, oder schreib es auf.

**Schritt 2:** Geh mit den Augen und dem Finger schnell durch den Text, in breiten Schlingen wie bei einem „S" oder „Z" oder von oben nach unten wie bei einem „U". Dabei hast du das Schriftbild oder das Bild des Wortes, nach dem du suchst, vor Augen. Das gesuchte Wort wird dir sofort „ins Auge springen". Lies nur dort weiter, um Näheres zu erfahren.

**Schritt 3:** Wenn das Schlüsselwort, nach dem du suchst, im Text nicht vorkommt, überleg dir, welche anderen Wörter mit den benötigten Informationen zu tun haben, und such nach diesen.

## Finding the main ideas of a text ▸ *Unit 3, p. 64*

Wenn du Texte wie Zeitungsartikel, Berichte oder Kommentare richtig verstehen willst, ist es gut, wenn du ihre Hauptaussagen erkennst und nachvollziehst, wie sie zusammenhängen. Dabei hilft dir ein Blick auf die Struktur dieser Texte.

### Wie finde ich die Hauptaussagen eines Textes?

1. Jeder Text dreht sich um ein Thema oder hat eine Hauptaussage, z. B.
   *Experts agree that American teenagers drink too many sugary drinks.*
   Diese Hauptaussage findest du oft im **ersten Absatz**. Lies ihn deshalb besonders gründlich durch.

2. Die Hauptaussage wird in der Regel durch weitere Aussagen bzw. Gedanken unterstützt, z. B.
   *If you don't sell soda in school, students drink less of it.*
   Du findest sie oft im ersten oder letzten Satz der nachfolgenden Absätze.

3. Diese weiteren Aussagen bzw. Gedanken werden meist durch Beispiele und Begründungen ergänzt, z. B.
   *Under the new rules, students can still bring soft drinks with them from home, but they can't buy them in school.*

**Tipp**

Die folgenden Wörter oder Wendungen werden oft im Zusammenhang mit Begründungen oder Beispielen verwendet:
**... % of ... are ...** • **and so** • **because** • **e.g. / for example** • **etc.** • **for lots of reasons** • **this shows that** • **that's why**

## Drawing conclusions ▸ *Unit 4, p. 84*

Wenn du bei einer Arbeit Fragen zu einem Text beantworten sollst oder bei einer Recherche Informationen zu einer bestimmten Frage in einem Text suchst, kann es gut sein, dass du an mehreren Stellen schauen musst oder dass die Antwort nicht 1:1 im Text steht.

### Wie funktioniert schlussfolgerndes Lesen?

1. Die einfachste Form des schlussfolgernden Lesens besteht darin, die Informationen aus verschiedenen Textstellen zusammenzuführen. Im Text auf S. 84 z. B. musst du mehrere Textstellen anschauen, wenn du alle Gründe finden willst, warum Schüler/innen in den USA arbeiten gehen.

2. Manchmal steht die Antwort auf eine Frage nicht direkt im Text. Dann musst du sie dir erschließen. Im Text auf S. 84 geht es um die Frage, welche Auswirkungen das Arbeiten auf die schulischen Leistungen hat. Dafür musst du Fakten im Text finden, die etwas mit dieser Frage zu tun haben:

*FACTS: students have an 11-hour work day; they're often too tired to do their school work*
*CONCLUSION: jobs can be bad for students' school work*

## SF REVISION Taking notes

### Worum geht es beim Notizenmachen?

Wenn du beim Lesen oder Zuhören Notizen machst, kannst du dich später besser an das Gehörte oder Gelesene erinnern, wenn du etwas vortragen, nacherzählen oder einen Bericht schreiben sollst.

### Wie mache ich Notizen?

In Texten oder Gesprächen gibt es immer wichtige und unwichtige Wörter. Die wichtigen Wörter werden Schlüsselwörter (**key words**) genannt und nur die solltest du notieren. Meist sind das Substantive und Verben, manchmal auch Adjektive oder Zahlen.

**Tipp**

- Verwende Ziffern (z. B. „7" statt „seven").
- Verwende Symbole und Abkürzungen, z. B. ✔ (für „ja") und + (für „und") oder US für United States, C. für Caitlin.
  Du kannst auch eigene Symbole erfinden.
- Verwende **not** oder ✗ statt „doesn't" oder „don't".

## SF REVISION Marking up a text

### Wann sollte ich einen Text markieren?

Du hast einen Text mit vielen Fakten vor dir liegen und sollst später über bestimmte Dinge berichten. Dann wird es dir helfen, die für die Aufgabenstellung wichtigen Informationen im Text zu markieren.

### Wie gehe ich am besten vor?

Lies den Text und markiere nur die für dein Thema wichtigen Informationen. Nicht jeder Satz enthält für deine Aufgabe wichtige Wörter, und oft reicht es aus, nur ein oder zwei Wörter in einem Satz zu markieren.

- Du kannst wichtige Wörter einkreisen.
- Du kannst sie unterstreichen.
- Du kannst sie mit einem Textmarker hervorheben.

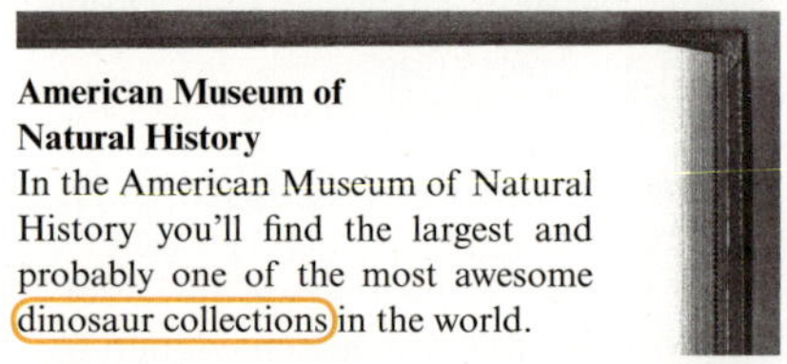
**American Museum of Natural History**
In the American Museum of Natural History you'll find the largest and probably one of the most awesome dinosaur collections in the world.

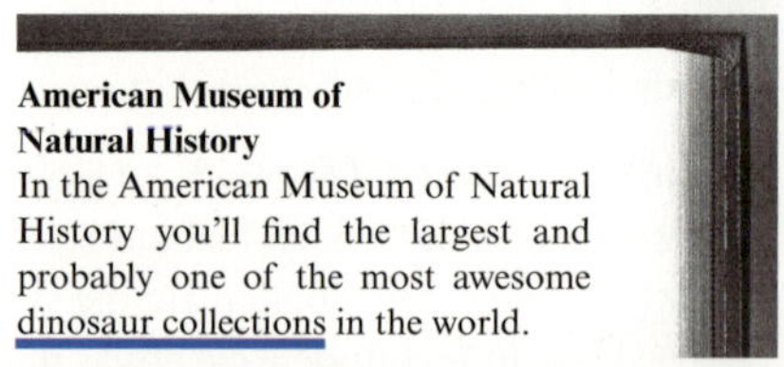
**American Museum of Natural History**
In the American Museum of Natural History you'll find the largest and probably one of the most awesome dinosaur collections in the world.

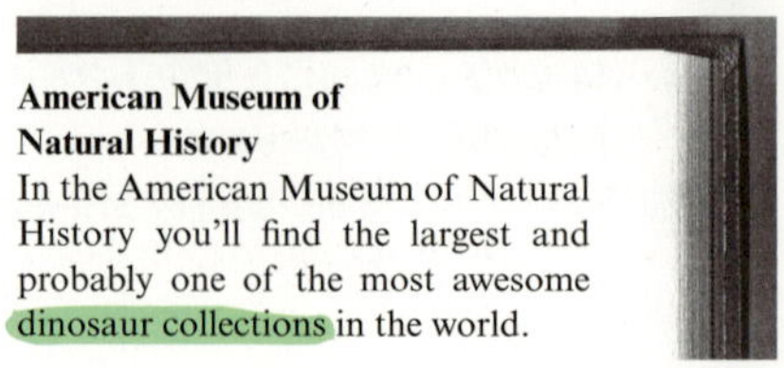
**American Museum of Natural History**
In the American Museum of Natural History you'll find the largest and probably one of the most awesome dinosaur collections in the world.

**ABER:**
Markiere nur auf Fotokopien von Texten oder in Büchern, die dir gehören, oder verwende eine Folie und einen wasserlöslichen Folienstift.

# SPEAKING AND WRITING SKILLS

## SF REVISION Paraphrasing

### Worum geht es beim Paraphrasing?

Paraphrasing bedeutet, etwas mit anderen Worten zu erklären. Das ist hilfreich, wenn dir ein bestimmtes Wort nicht einfällt oder wenn dein Gegenüber dich nicht verstanden hat (siehe auch ▸ *SF Mediation, p. 152*).

### Wie gehe ich beim Paraphrasing vor?

- Man kann mit einem Wort umschreiben, das dieselbe Bedeutung hat:
  **to train is the same as to practise**
  Oder man sagt das Gegenteil: **alive is the opposite of dead**
- Manchmal braucht man mehrere Wörter, z. B. wenn man etwas beschreibt oder erklärt. Dabei benutzt man ein allgemeines Wort (**general word**) und nennt weitere Eigenschaften.
  **A skyscraper is a very tall building.**
- Oder du umschreibst das Wort mit **... is/are like ...**
  **A cabin is like a small house, it's in the country.**
- Du kannst zum Umschreiben auch ein allgemeines Wort nehmen (z.B. **person**, **something**) und dieses mit einem durch **who**, **that** oder **where** eingeleiteten Satz näher erklären: **A ranger is a person who works in national parks and protects the parks and helps visitors.**
  **A ticket office is a shop where you can buy tickets for shows and concerts.**

## SF REVISION Brainstorming

### Wofür ist Brainstorming gut?

Bei vielen Aufgaben ist es nützlich, wenn du im ersten Schritt möglichst viele Ideen zum Thema sammelst. Dabei hilft dir das Brainstorming.

### Wie gehe ich beim Brainstorming vor?

**Schritt 1:**
Schreib alle Ideen so auf, wie sie dir einfallen. Es ist zunächst völlig egal, ob sie gut sind oder nicht. Du kannst die Ideen durcheinander auf einen Zettel schreiben oder schon etwas geordnet, z.B. für jede eine neue Zeile.

**Schritt 2:**
Lies alle deine Ideen durch und wähle die besten aus. Dann sortiere sie und fasse sie sinnvoll zusammen. Dabei kannst du folgende **Techniken** anwenden:

1. Leg eine **Mindmap** an. Schreib das Thema in die Mitte eines Blattes Papier. Überlege, welche Oberbegriffe zu deiner Sammlung von Ideen passen. Verwende unterschiedliche Farben. Ergänze jede Idee, die zu einem Oberbegriff passt, auf einem Nebenast. Nimm dafür nur wichtige Schlüsselwörter. Du kannst statt Wörtern auch Symbole verwenden und Bilder ergänzen.
2. **The 5 Ws**: Schreib die **5** W-Fragen **Who? What? When? Where? Why?** in eine Tabelle. Die Ideen, die dir zu jeder Frage kommen, kannst du darunter schreiben.

# REVISION WRITING COURSE – Zusammenfassung

**The steps of writing**

1. Brainstorming – Ideen sammeln, dann sortieren (► *SF Brainstorming, p. 145*).
2. Schreiben. Dabei achte darauf,
   - deine Sätze zu verbinden und auszubauen (*Writing better sentences*)
   - deinen Text gut zu strukturieren (*Using paragraphs*)
   - bei einem Bericht die 5 Ws abzudecken (*Writing a report*)
3. Deinen Text inhaltlich und sprachlich überprüfen (*Correcting your text*)

## Writing better sentences

### Linking words

Eine Geschichte klingt interessanter, wenn du die Sätze mit **linking words** miteinander verbindest. Dabei gibt es mehrere Möglichkeiten:
- **Time phrases** wie **at 7 o'clock**, **every morning**, **a few minutes later**, **then**, **next** ...
- **Konjunktionen** wie **although**, **because**, **but**, **so ... that**, **that**, **when**, **while**
- **Relativpronomen** wie **that** und **who**

### Adjektive und Adverbien

- Mit Adjektiven kannst du Personen, Orte oder Erlebnisse genauer und interessanter beschreiben. Vergleiche: **The man looked into the room.**
  ► **The young man looked into the empty room.**
- Mit Adverbien kannst du beschreiben, **wie** jemand etwas macht:
  **The young man looked nervously into the empty room.**

## Using paragraphs

### Structuring a text

Ein längerer Text ist besser zu verstehen, wenn er in mehrere Absätze unterteilt ist:
- eine Einleitung (**beginning**) – hier schreibst du, worum es geht
- einen Hauptteil (**middle**) – hier schreibst du mehr über dein Thema
- einen Schluss (**end**) – hier bringst du den Text zu einem interessanten Ende.

### Topic sentences

Am Anfang eines Absatzes sind kurze, einleitende Sätze (**topic sentences**) gut, weil sie den Lesern sofort sagen, worum es geht, z. B.
1. Orte: **My trip to ... was fantastic. / ... is famous for ... / ... is a great place.**
2. Personen: **... is great/funny/interesting/clever ...**
3. Aktivitäten: **... is great fun. / Lots of people ... every day.**

### Wie kann ich meine Absätze interessant gestalten?

- Beginne mit einem interessanten Einstiegssatz:
  **You'll never guess what happened to me today! / Did I tell you that ...?**
- Fang für jeden neuen Aspekt einen neuen Absatz an.
- Beende deinen Text mit einer Zusammenfassung oder etwas Persönlichem.

## Writing a report – collecting and organizing ideas

### Worauf kommt es bei einem Bericht an?

- Gib dem Leser **eine schnelle Orientierung**, was passiert ist.
- Beginne mit **wichtigen Informationen** und gib erst dann Detailinformationen.
- Ein Bericht gibt immer Antworten auf die **5 Ws**:
  **Who? What? When? Where? Why?** und manchmal auch auf **How?**
- Verwende das **simple past**.

## Correcting your text

Ein Text ist noch nicht „fertig", wenn du ihn zu Ende geschrieben hast. Du solltest ihn immer mehr als einmal durchlesen:
- einmal, um zu sehen, ob er vollständig und gut verständlich ist
- noch einmal, um ihn auf Fehler zu überprüfen, z. B. **Rechtschreibfehler *(spelling mistakes)*** oder **Grammatikfehler *(grammar mistakes)***.

**tomato** [tə'mɑːtəʊ], *pl* **tomatoes** Tomate II

**wife** [waɪf], *pl* **wives** [waɪvz] Ehefrau II

**drop (-pp-)** [drɒp] fallen lassen I

**forget (-tt-)** [fə'get] vergessen I

### Spelling mistakes

Lies deinen Text langsam, Wort für Wort, Buchstabe für Buchstabe. Wenn du unsicher bist, hilft dir ein Wörterbuch. Beachte folgende Regeln:

**Tipp**

- Manche Wörter haben Buchstaben, die man nicht spricht, aber schreibt, z. B. **knife**, **climb**.
- Manchmal ändert sich die Schreibweise, wenn ein Wort eine Endung erhält, z. B. **take** → **taking**, **terrible** → **terribly**, **lucky** → **luckily**, **try** → **tries** (**aber stay** → **stays**), **run** → **running**, **drop** → **dropped**.
- Beim Plural tritt manchmal noch ein **-e** zum **-s**, z. B. **church** → **churches**.

### Grammar mistakes

Diese Tipps helfen dir, typische Fehler zu vermeiden:

**Tipp**

- Im **simple present** wird in der 3. Person Singular **-s** angehängt: **she knows**
- **Unregelmäßige Verben:** Manche Verben bilden die Formen des *simple past* und des Partizip Perfekt *(past participle)* unregelmäßig. Die unregelmäßigen Formen musst du lernen. Die Liste steht auf S. 238–239.
  **go – went – gone; buy – bought – bought**
- **Verneinung bei Vollverben:** Im *simple present* mit ***don't/doesn't***, im *simple past* mit **didn't**, z. B. **He doesn't speak French**, **he didn't learn it at school**.
- **Satzstellung**: Im Englischen gilt immer (auch im Nebensatz):
  a) subject – verb – object (SVO) **... when I saw my brother.**
  **... als ich meinen Bruder sah.**
  b) Orts- vor Zeitangabe **I bought a nice book in the city yesterday.**

## SF Extra Writing formal and informal letters ▸ Unit 2, p. 44

Beim Briefeschreiben musst du unterschiedliche Regeln beachten, je nachdem ob du einen förmlichen Brief (*formal letter*) an unbekannte Personen, Behörden, Zeitschriften usw. schreibst oder einen persönlichen, informellen Brief (*informal letter*) an Freunde oder Verwandte.

### Worauf kommt es bei förmlichen Briefen an? (Formal letters)

(1) Schreibe deine Adresse (ohne Namen) und das Datum in die rechte obere Ecke. Verwende keine typisch deutschen Buchstaben wie z.B. ß, ä, ö, oder ü.
(2) Die Anschrift steht links.
(3) Die Anrede lautet *Dear Sir or Madam*. Wenn du den Namen des Adressaten kennst, beginne deinen Brief mit *Dear Mr/Mrs/Ms ...*
(4) Nenne zu Beginn den Grund deines Briefes.
(5) Bedanke dich bei Bitten und Anfragen im Voraus (*I look forward to hearing from you. Thank you.*).
(6) Beende den Brief mit *Yours faithfully*, wenn du den Adressaten nicht kennst. Hast du den Adressaten am Anfang des Briefes mit Namen angeredet, dann schreibe *Yours sincerely*.
(7) Unterschreibe den Brief und tippe zusätzlich deinen Namen.

(1) Waldstr. 5
50933 Koeln
Germany

(2) 1532 Beachview Place
Los Angeles, CA
94832 - 1384
USA

20 May 2009

(3) Dear Sir or Madam

I am writing to you because I am really interested in an article I read in your newspaper (May 2009). The title of the article is "New World, New Hopes, and New Problems" and it is about three immigrant families living in America. I have some questions and I hope that you can answer them. (4)

I know that a lot of Americans are proud of their country. What about people who live in America but were not born there? Are they proud of America? Have you asked the families from the article how they feel about America? I would really like to know what they think.

Thank you very much. (5)

(6) Yours faithfully

(7) *Tom Winter*
Tom Winter

**Tipp**

Beachte, was du zum Schreiben von Texten gelernt hast:
- Vor dem Schreiben: Ideen sammeln, dann sortieren.
- Während des Schreibens: Sätze verbinden und ausbauen; strukturieren.
- Nach dem Schreiben: Überprüfe deinen Brief inhaltlich und sprachlich. ▸ *SF Writing course, pp. 146–147*

### Was ist bei persönlichen Briefen anders? (Informal letters)

Hier sind die Regeln nicht ganz so streng. Aber beachte Folgendes:
- Schreibe deine Adresse (ohne Namen) und das Datum in die rechte obere Ecke.
- Verwende keine typisch deutschen Buchstaben wie z.B. ß, ä, ö, oder ü.
- Du benötigst keine Anschrift.
- Du kannst deinen Brief mit *Dear/Hello/Hi ...* beginnen.
- Nenne zu Beginn den Grund deines Briefes, stelle auch Fragen.
- Beende den Brief mit einem freundlichen Gruß/Ausblick/Erwartungen/...
- Schließe deinen Brief mit *Yours/Best wishes/Love/...* ab.

Alles klar? Wohin gehören die Wendungen im blauen Kasten?

| | Formal letter | Informal letter |
|---|---|---|
| Briefanfang | Dear Mr Smith, ... | Dear Pete, ... |
| Briefende | ... | ... |

Best wishes • Dear Pete •
Yours faithfully • Dear Mr Smith •
Yours sincerely • Lots of love • Love •
Dear Sir or Madam • See you soon! •
Hello Sarah • Thank you very much. •
Happy birthday! I've just heard ...

## SF Summarizing texts ▸ *Unit 3, p. 57*

Wenn du einen Text (mündlich oder schriftlich) zusammenfasst, gibst du die wichtigen Informationen oder Ereignisse in kürzerer Form wieder.

### Wie gehe ich beim summarizing vor?

**1.** Lies den Text mindestens einmal genau durch, damit du verstehst, worum es geht. Mach dir noch keine Notizen.

**2.** Lies den Text erneut, Satz für Satz, durch und mach dir Notizen zu den 5 Ws:

| | |
|---|---|
| **Who?** | Who is the text about? |
| **What?** | What happens?/What does he/she do? |
| **Where?** | Where does it happen? |
| **When?** | When does it happen? |
| **Why?** | Why does it happen? / Why does he/she do this? |

Was auf diese Fragen Antwort gibt, ist wichtig. Auslassen solltest du dagegen Beispiele, Vergleiche, Zitate, direkte Rede, ausschmückende Adjektive und andere Textteile, die der Beschreibung dienen.

**3.** Leg den Text nun beiseite und schreib mithilfe deiner Notizen eine Zusammenfassung des Texts in deinen eigenen Worten.

– Erklär in den ersten ein oder zwei Sätzen, worum es in dem Text geht.

• Vergleiche diese drei Anfänge einer Zusammenfassung von *You can tell me* (S. 26–27). Welcher gibt am besten das Thema der Geschichte wieder?

*YOU CAN TELL ME is a story about New York.*

*YOU CAN TELL ME is a story about Anthony and Kelly, two teenagers from New York.*

*Anthony and Kelly play music together. They have a nice picnic in the park.*

Du kannst für deine einleitenden Sätze die folgenden phrases verwenden:
**The story is about ... • The text describes ... • The article shows ... • In the story we get to know ...**

– Im Hauptteil solltest du die wichtigen Ereignisse (z.B. einer Geschichte) oder die Hauptpunkte eines Textes (z.B. eines Zeitungsartikels) wiedergeben. Bring die Informationen in eine logische Reihenfolge.
  - Verwende dafür deine Notizen zu den **5 Ws**.
  - Schreib den Text nicht ab, sondern benutze deine eigenen Worte.

She didn't tell Cindy the real reason: Jim Nielson. Jim was at Hermann High too, but he was two grades above Carrie. Carrie thought he was really nice. → *Carrie thinks Jim is nice.*

– Schreib im **simple present**, auch wenn die Geschichte oder der Artikel in der Vergangenheit spielt. Nicht vergessen: im **simple present** wird in der 3. Person Singular **-s** angehängt: **Carrie thinks.**

# EXAM SKILLS

## SF How to do well in a test

▸ *Getting ready for a test (p. 31)*

### Countdown zum Testerfolg

Ein Test ist angekündigt? Kein Grund zur Panik. Wichtig ist, dass du weißt, worauf du dich vorbereiten musst. Im Zweifelsfall frag deine Lehrerin oder deinen Lehrer. Der Countdown kann beginnen!

**Eine Woche vor dem Test**

1. Lies noch einmal die **Texte** der zuletzt durchgenommenen Unit (vor allem *Lead-in*, *A-Section* und *Text*, eventuell auch das *Background File*). Fasse mündlich oder schriftlich zusammen, worum es ging.

2. Wiederhole den **Wortschatz** der Unit mithilfe des *Vocabulary*, des *Wordmaster* oder des *English Coach*. Schreibe dir die Wörter und Wortverbindungen, die du immer wieder vergisst, auf ein Blatt Papier. Eine Mindmap oder ein Wortfeld helfen beim Behalten.

3. Geh noch einmal die neue **Grammatik** durch. Aufgaben zur Selbstüberprüfung und zum Üben findest du im *Practice*-Teil, auf der *How am I doing?*-Seite, im *Grammar File*, in deinem *Workbook* und im e-*Workbook*.

**Zwei oder drei Tage vor dem Test**

1. Wiederhole den **Wortschatz**. Manche Wörter sitzen noch nicht? Schreibe einen kurzen Text, in dem du sie verwendest.

2. Lies die **Schülerbuch-Texte** ein weiteres Mal.

3. Erkläre einem Freund oder einer Freundin die neue **Grammatik**. Klappt nicht richtig? Dann lies nochmal im *Grammar File* nach.

**Am Abend vor dem Test**

1. Entspanne dich. Du kannst lesen, dich in die Badewanne legen, Musik hören, fernsehen, ...

2. Geh zur gewohnten Zeit ins Bett.

**Am Morgen des Tests**

1. Steh rechtzeitig auf, damit du nicht hetzen musst.

2. Lies etwas „zum Aufwärmen", aber schau nicht mehr in dein Schülerbuch.

**Während des Tests**

1. Denk daran: Du hast dich gut vorbereitet. Es gibt keinen Grund, nervös zu sein.

2. Konzentriere dich auf den Test, lass dich nicht ablenken.

3. Lies dir die Aufgaben genau durch. Dann löse zuerst die Aufgaben, die dir einfach scheinen. Wende dich erst danach den schwereren Aufgaben zu.

4. Aufgaben, die du bearbeitet hast, hakst du ab. So siehst du, wie du vorankommst, und behältst den Überblick.

5. Schau ab und zu auf die Uhr. Du solltest dir für den Schluss noch Zeit einplanen, um deine Antworten noch einmal durchzulesen und zu korrigieren.

Good luck!

## Aufgabenstellungen verstehen

Bevor du damit anfängst, die Aufgaben zu bearbeiten, stell sicher, dass du genau weißt, was du machen sollst. Lies die Aufgabenstellung Wort für Wort langsam und gründlich und von Anfang bis Ende durch. Du kannst besonders wichtige Dinge der Aufgabenstellung unterstreichen und die Aufgabe, wenn nötig, für dich in einzelne Schritte unterteilen.

## Worauf sollte ich bei Multiple-Choice-Aufgaben achten?

- Lies die Frage oder den Satz sehr genau durch.
- Bevor du dir die Lösungsangebote anschaust, deck sie mit Papier ab. Überleg dir, was die richtige Antwort sein könnte. Wenn das dann auch als eine Lösungsmöglichkeit angeboten wird, ist es meistens richtig.
- Lies immer alle vorgegebenen Lösungen, bevor du dich entscheidest.
- Achte darauf, dass du nur **eine** der Antworten ankreuzt – es sei denn, dass in der Aufgabenstellung ausdrücklich gesagt wird, dass mehrere Antworten richtig sein können.
- Mach erst alle Aufgaben so gut du kannst. Lass keine Aufgabe aus, aber geh zum Schluss zu den Fragen zurück, bei denen du unsicher bist.
- Wenn das alles nicht hilft, such nicht mehr nach der richtigen Antwort, sondern nach den falschen Antworten. Weil drei Antwortmöglichkeiten falsch sein müssen, kannst du erschließen, dass die vierte Antwort richtig ist. Hier ist ein Beispiel. Stell dir vor, du hörst folgenden Dialog.

  Boy *Wow, that was great, Dad. Thanks. Can we do it again next weekend?*

  Dad *Sure, Greg – if the weather's nice. But let's find an easier tour then – I'm a bit tired.*

Dazu wird dir die Multiple-Choice-Frage hier unten gestellt.
Greg und sein Vater müssen etwas im Freien gemacht haben, denn Gregs Dad spricht über das Wetter. Also sind die Antworten **B** und **C** falsch. Man schwimmt keine Touren, also ist **A** auch falsch. Daher muss **D** die richtige Antwort sein.

**1.** Greg and his dad have just
- A been swimming.
- B been to a fitness club.
- C seen a movie.
- D been on a bike ride.

# MEDIATION SKILLS

## SF REVISION Mediation

### Wann muss ich zwischen zwei Sprachen vermitteln?

Manchmal musst du zwischen zwei Sprachen vermitteln. Das nennt man mediation.

1. Du gibst englische Informationen auf Deutsch weiter:
   Du fährst z. B. mit deiner Familie in die USA und deine Eltern oder Geschwister wollen wissen, was jemand in einem Café gesagt hat oder was an einer Informationstafel steht.
2. Du gibst deutsche Informationen auf Englisch weiter:
   Vielleicht ist bei dir zu Hause eine Austauschschülerin aus den USA oder Dänemark zu Gast, die kein Deutsch spricht und Hilfe braucht.
3. In schriftlichen Prüfungen musst du manchmal in einem englischen Text gezielt nach Informationen suchen und diese auf Deutsch wiedergeben. Oder du sollst Informationen aus einem deutschen Text auf Englisch wiedergeben.

### Worauf muss ich bei *mediation* achten?

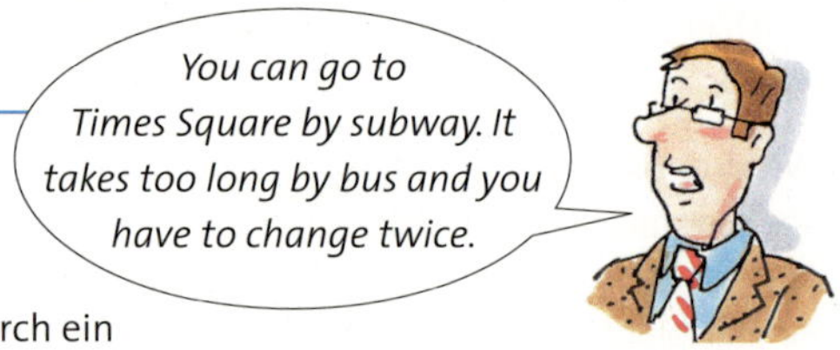


- Übersetze nicht alles wörtlich.
- Gib nur das Wesentliche weiter, lass Unwichtiges weg.
- Verwende kurze und einfache Sätze.
- Wenn du ein Wort nicht kennst, umschreibe es oder ersetze es durch ein anderes Wort.

### Was kann ich tun, wenn ich ein wichtiges Wort nicht kenne?

Vielleicht findest du es manchmal schwer, mündliche Aussagen oder schriftliche Textvorlagen in die andere Sprache zu übertragen, z. B. weil:
- dein Wortschatz nicht ausreicht
- dir bekannte Wörter „im Stress" nicht einfallen
- spezielle Fachbegriffe auftauchen.

Manche Wörter kannst du umschreiben, z. B. mithilfe von Relativsätzen wie:
**It's somebody/a person who ...**
**It's something that you use to ...**
**It's an animal that ...**
**It's a place where ...**

▸ *SF Paraphrasing, p. 145*

# Grammar File – Inhalt



---

Im **Grammar File** (S. 154–163) wird zusammengefasst, was du in diesem Band **über die englische Sprache** lernst.

In der **linken Spalte** stehen Beispielsätze und Übersichten.

In der **rechten Spalte** stehen Erklärungen und nützliche Hinweise.

Would you like a glass of **milk**?
Möchtest du **ein Glas Milch**?

| Countable nouns | Uncountable nouns |
|---|---|
| **how many girls?** | **how much bread?** |
| wie viele Mädchen? | wie viel Brot? |

► *Unit 3 (p. 55)* • *P 7–8 (p. 62)*

! *many* heißt „**viele**“ und steht nur mit **Nomen im Plural**. *much* heißt „**viel**“ und steht nur mit **nicht zählbaren Nomen**.

Dieser **Grammar-File**-Abschnitt gehört zu Unit 3, S. 55, und den Übungen 7 und 8 auf S. 62.

Das **rote Ausrufezeichen** macht dich auf besondere Fehlerquellen aufmerksam.

*Vervollständige die Sätze in deinem Heft*

1 … alone to New York was ve‑
2 He didn't enjoy … in the c

Am Ende der Abschnitte stehen kleine Aufgaben zur Selbstkontrolle. Schreib die Lösungen in dein Heft. Überprüfe sie dann auf Seite 162.

## Unit 1

# GF 1 The gerund Das Gerundium

### *a)* Use and form

Flying is exciting.
**Fliegen** ist aufregend.

Travelling makes me tired.
**Reisen** macht mich müde.

Taking **a taxi** is quite expensive.
**Mit dem Taxi zu fahren / Taxifahren** ist ziemlich teuer.

Cycling **in New York** can be dangerous.
**In New York Rad zu fahren / Radfahren in New York** kann gefährlich sein.

### Gebrauch und Form

Als **Gerundium** *(gerund)* bezeichnet man die *-ing*-Form, wenn sie als **Nomen** verwendet wird.

Auf das Gerundium kann – wie bei einem Verb – ein Objekt *(a taxi)* oder eine Orts- oder Zeitangabe *(in New York)* folgen.

Im Deutschen wird das Gerundium oft durch einen Infinitiv mit „zu“ oder durch ein Nomen wiedergegeben.

### *b)* The gerund as subject and object

### Das Gerundium als Subjekt und als Objekt

Das Gerundium (und seine Erweiterung) kann im Satz **Subjekt** (Frage „Wer oder was?“) oder **Objekt** (Frage „Wen oder was?“) sein:

| Subjekt | |
|---|---|
| ***Flying*** | *is exciting.* |
| ***Cycling in a big city*** | *isn't very healthy.* |

| | Objekt |
|---|---|
| *My sister likes* | ***skating.*** |
| *I like* | ***riding my bike in Central Park.*** |

Ich wohne gern in einer Großstadt. / Ich genieße es, in einer Großstadt zu wohnen.
Ich kann mir nicht vorstellen, auf dem Land zu leben.

**!** Beachte:

◄ **1** Nach einigen Verben – z.B. ***enjoy, finish, imagine, miss, practise*** – steht ein weiteres Verb als Gerundium:

*I **enjoy** living ..., I can't **imagine** living ...*

Anders als im Deutschen darf nach diesen Verben **kein Infinitiv** stehen!
Also nicht: *I ~~enjoy to live~~ ..., I can't ~~imagine to live~~ ...*

When I got to Times Square, it **started** raining. / to rain.

I **like/love** riding / to ride my bike in the rain.

◄ **2** Nach ***begin/start, hate, like, love*** kann – bei gleicher Bedeutung – ein Gerundium oder ein *to*-Infinitiv stehen.

**I'd like/love** to ride in a New York taxi too.
I **would hate** to live in the country.

◄ **3** Nach ***would** like*, ***would** love*, ***would** hate* kann nur der *to*-Infinitiv stehen.

► *Unit 1 (p. 15)* • *P 5–7 (pp. 21–22)*

### c) The gerund after prepositions

After so much walking, we were tired.
Nach all der Herumlauferei ... /
Nachdem wir so viel herumgelaufen waren, ...

Never cross a street without looking.
Überquere nie eine Straße, ohne zu schauen.

Ryan is **scared** of going in lifts.
Ryan hat Angst davor, mit dem Lift zu fahren.

Ryan was **excited** about going to the fire station.
Ryan freute sich darauf, die Feuerwache zu besuchen.

Das Gerundium nach Präpositionen

Nach einer Präposition *(after, without, for, of, ...)* steht ein Verb immer in der *-ing*-Form.

Beachte die verschiedenen deutschen Entsprechungen:

| englisch | | deutsch |
|---|---|---|
| – ***after walking*** | → | „nach der Herumlauferei" *oder* „nachdem wir herumgelaufen waren" |
| – ***without looking*** | → | „ohne zu schauen" |
| – *scared* ***of going ...*** | → | „Angst, ... zu fahren" |

Nützliche Wendungen mit Präposition + Gerundium sind:

Ryan is **interested** in learning about New York firefighters.
Ryan ist daran interessiert, etwas über ... zu erfahren.
He's **excited** about meeting some of them.
Er freut sich sehr darauf, einige von ihnen zu treffen.

| | | |
|---|---|---|
| – *(to) be* | ***interested in*** <br> ***excited about*** <br> ***afraid of*** <br> ***good/bad at*** <br> ***tired of*** | ***doing*** *sth.* |

Ryan's **reason** for going to New York was to visit family. Sein Grund, dort hinzufahren, war ...
Caitlin had the **idea** of visiting the fire station.
Caitlin hatte die Idee, die Feuerwache zu besuchen.

| | | |
|---|---|---|
| – *the* | ***reason for*** <br> ***idea of*** | ***doing*** *sth.* |

Caitlin **was** against going to Brooklyn Bridge.
Caitlin war dagegen, zur Brooklyn Bridge zu gehen.
Ryan and Caitlin **talked** about meeting Ruth.
Ryan und Caitlin sprachen darüber, Ruth zu treffen.

| | | |
|---|---|---|
| – *(to)* | ***be against*** <br> ***talk about*** <br> ***dream of*** <br> ***think of*** | ***doing*** *sth.* |

► *Unit 1 (p. 17) • P 11 (p. 24)*

*Vervollständige die Sätze in deinem Heft. Wähle ein Verb aus dem Kästchen. Achte auf die richtige Form.*

1 ... alone to New York was very exciting for Ryan.
2 He didn't enjoy ... in the queues at the airport.
3 At first he was a bit afraid of ... up the ESB in a fast lift.
4 He was very interested in ... all the sights.

(to) fly • (to) go • (to) see • (to) wait

# Unit 2

## GF 2 The passive Das Passiv

### *a)* Active and passive

**Active:** **Farmers in California** grow strawberries on huge farms.
Landwirte in Kalifornien bauen Erdbeeren auf großen Farmen an.

**Passive:** **Strawberries** are grown on huge farms.
Erdbeeren werden auf großen Farmen angebaut.

#### Aktiv und Passiv

◄ Mit einem **Aktivsatz** drückst du aus, **wer oder was etwas tut**:

| **Subjekt** | **Verb** | **Objekt** |
|---|---|---|
| *Farmers in California* | *grow* | *strawberries …* |

◄ Mit einem **Passivsatz** drückst du aus, **mit wem oder womit etwas geschieht**:

| **Subjekt** | **Verb** | |
|---|---|---|
| *Strawberries* | *are grown* | *on huge farms.* |

### *b)* Form

… wird produziert …
… wird verkauft …
… wurden angebaut …

#### Form

Das Passiv bildest du mit einer **Form von *be*** und der 3. Form des Verbs*.

**Simple present:** *am/are/is* + **3. Form des Verbs**
*A lot of wine is **produced** …*

**Simple past:** *was/were* + **3. Form des Verbs**
*700,000 tons were **grown** …*

* Die 3. Form des Verbs heißt **Partizip Perfekt** *(past participle)*. Sie wird bei regelmäßigen Verben mit ***-ed*** gebildet: *(to) produce, produced, produced.* Unregelmäßige Verben haben eigene Formen: *(to) grow, grew, grown.*

► *Unregelmäßige Verben (pp. 238–239)*

### *c)* Use

At 8.45 yesterday morning a 12-year-old boy was hurt in a car accident on Duke Street. The police were called and the boy was taken to hospital.

► *Unit 2 (p. 36)* • *P 3, 5 (pp. 42–43)*

#### Gebrauch

In einem Passivsatz steht nicht, wer die Handlung ausführt. Oft ist das unwichtig oder gar nicht bekannt. Du findest daher das Passiv oft in Nachrichten und in Zeitungsberichten (z. B. über Unfälle, Verbrechen) oder auf Schildern.

Ein englischer Passivsatz wird im Deutschen oft durch einen Aktivsatz mit „man“ wiedergegeben:

*The boy **was taken** to hospital.*
***Man brachte** den Jungen ins Krankenhaus.*

### *d)* Passive sentences with *by* ...

Passivsätze mit *by* ...

The cable cars in San Francisco **are used** by lots of tourists.
Die Kabelbahnen in San Francisco werden von vielen Touristen benutzt.

The Golden Gate Bridge **was built** by Joseph Strauss.
Die Golden Gate Bridge wurde von Joseph Strauss erbaut.

My parents' house **was destroyed** by fire.
Das Haus meiner Eltern wurde durch ein Feuer zerstört.

Wenn du in einem Passivsatz den „Täter" oder „Verursacher" nennen willst, verwendest du ***by*** („von", „durch").

▸ *Unit 2 (p. 39)* • *P 13–14 (p. 47)*

*Sieh dir die Bilder und den Kasten mit den Verben und den Namen an. Schreib die richtigen Passivsätze in dein Heft.*

1 

2 

3 

1 The telephone was ... by ...
2 'We will rock you!' was ...
3 Clifton Suspension Bridge ...

**build** • **invent** • **sing**
**Alexander Bell** • **Brunel** • **Queen**

## Unit 3

## GF 3 Countable and uncountable nouns — Zählbare und nicht zählbare Nomen

### *a)* Countable nouns — Zählbare Nomen

a friend – two friends
a CD – lots of CDs
one hour – many hours

◄ Die meisten Nomen sind **zählbar**, d.h., sie kommen im Singular und im Plural vor.

### *b)* Uncountable nouns — Nicht zählbare Nomen

| | | | |
|---|---|---|---|
| **bread** | Brot | **money** | Geld |
| **butter** | Butter | **music** | Musik |
| **cheese** | Käse | **news** | Nachricht(en) |
| **homework** | Hausaufgabe(n) | **sugar** | Zucker |
| **information** | Information(en) | **traffic** | Verkehr |
| **love** | Liebe | **water** | Wasser |
| **milk** | Milch | **work** | Arbeit |

◄ **Nicht zählbare** Nomen stehen **nie** im Plural.
Zu den nicht zählbaren Nomen gehören viele Bezeichnungen für Lebensmittel und viele abstrakte Begriffe, z.B. *love*.

! Auch die Nomen ***homework, information*** und ***news*** sind nicht zählbar – anders als ihre deutschen Entsprechungen.

***not:*** ~~a bread; breads~~
~~an information; many informations~~
~~a homework; two homeworks~~

That's too much **homework**. I can't do it.
Das sind zu viele **Hausaufgaben**. Ich kann sie nicht machen.

Where did you get this **information**?
Wo hast du diese **Information(en)** her?

◄ Die zugehörigen **Begleiter, Verben und Pronomen** stehen auch immer **im Singular**.

Would you like a glass of **milk**?
Möchtest du **ein Glas Milch**?

That's a useful piece of **information**.
Das ist **eine** nützliche **Information**.

◄ Wenn du **bestimmte Mengen** oder eine **bestimmte Anzahl** nennen willst, musst du passende Wendungen wie ***a glass of …, a kilo of …, a piece of …*** verwenden.

### *c)* Quantifiers: *some, lots of, many, much* — Mengenangaben: *some, lots of, many, much*

| Countable nouns | Uncountable nouns |
|---|---|
| some **girls**<br>einige/ein paar Mädchen | some **bread**<br>etwas Brot |
| lots of **girls**<br>viele Mädchen | lots of **bread**<br>viel Brot |
| **how** many **girls?**<br>wie viele Mädchen? | **how** much **bread?**<br>wie viel Brot? |

Die Mengenangaben *some* und *lots of* (oder *a lot of*) verwendest du mit **zählbaren Nomen** und **nicht zählbaren Nomen**.

! *many* heißt „**viele**" und steht nur mit **Nomen im Plural**.
*much* heißt „**viel**" und steht nur mit **nicht zählbaren Nomen**.

► *Unit 3 (p.55) • P 7–8 (p.62)*

*Sieh dir die Bilder an und vervollständige die Sätze mit* a *(1x)*, an *(1x)*, some *(2x)*, many *(1x)*, much *(3x)*.

1 There's ... milk but there isn't ... bread.

2 Here's ... information about the Grand Canyon. I'm doing ... project on it.

3 We haven't got ... eggs, and we haven't got ... butter.

4 I haven't got ... homework, just ... exercise for French.

## GF 4 Extra The definite article *the* Der bestimmte Artikel *the*

**1** For Timo and his family, life is exciting at the moment.
... ist das Leben im Moment aufregend.

**2** Clean water is important to health.
Sauberes Wasser ist wichtig für die Gesundheit.

**3** American students do lots of extracurricular activities.

◄ Wenn ein Nomen **ganz allgemein** gebraucht wird, steht es **ohne den bestimmten Artikel** *the*.
Das gilt insbesondere für

**1** **abstrakte Begriffe** wie *life, history, health, traffic*

**2** **Stoffbezeichnungen** wie *oil, water, coffee, bread*

**3** **Nomen im Plural** (hier: *students*).

**1a** At the FFA meeting Timo learned a lot about the life **of Missouri farmers.**
... über das Leben der Farmer in Missouri.

**2a** Don't worry, the water **in Hermann** is clean.
... das Wasser in Hermann ...

**3a** The students **who went to the FFA meeting** were very interested in hogs.

◄ Wenn diese Nomen aber **näher bestimmt** sind, stehen sie **mit bestimmtem Artikel**.
Die nähere Bestimmung erfolgt z.B. in Satz 1a durch eine *of*-Fügung *(of Missouri farmers)* und in Satz 3a durch einen Relativsatz *(who went to the FFA meeting)*.

Vergleiche die Sätze 1a–3a mit den Sätzen 1–3.

► *Unit 3 (p.56)* • *P 10 (p.63)*

*Mit oder ohne* the? *Schreib die Sätze in dein Heft.*

1 We can learn a lot from ... history.
2 What do you know about ... history of England?
3 ... tourists like to visit Hermann's Festhalle.
4 ... tourists who asked us the way were from Germany.

## GF 5 The past perfect Das *past perfect*

### *a)* Use — Gebrauch

Andreas Schmidt first **visited** Hermann 20 years ago.
... besuchte ...
He **stayed** with the Kruger family.
... wohnte ...

◄ Du benutzt das *simple past* für **Handlungen, Ereignisse und Zustände in der Vergangenheit**.

He had never heard of Missouri wine when he first **visited** Hermann 20 years ago.
... hatte noch nie von Wein aus Missouri gehört, ...

They had already sold their house in Germany when Karla Schmidt **got** a bit worried.
Sie hatten ihr Haus in Deutschland bereits verkauft, ...

◄ Mit dem *past perfect* drückst du aus, dass etwas noch **vor etwas anderem in der Vergangenheit** stattgefunden hatte.
Die Handlung/das Ereignis im *past perfect* geschah zuerst:

| 1 | 2 |
|---|---|
| *They had already sold ...* | *when she **got worried**.* |
| (geschah zuerst) | (geschah danach) |

| Simple past | Past perfect |
|---|---|
| 1 **The concert began when he arrived.** *Das Konzert begann, als er ankam.* | 2 **The concert had begun when he arrived.** *Das Konzert hatte begonnen, als er ankam.* |

– In **Satz 1** begann die Band erst zu spielen, als er ankam.
– In **Satz 2** hatte die Band bereits angefangen zu spielen, als er ankam.

### *b)* Form — Form

**Regular verb:** (to) **play** – I/you/he/... **had played**
**Irregular verb:** (to) **sell** – I/you/he/... **had sold**

Das *past perfect* bildest du mit ***had*** und der 3. Form des Verbs (Partizip Perfekt, *past participle*).
(Zur Bildung der 3. Form des Verbs siehe S. 156, GF 2b.)
► *Unregelmäßige Verben (pp. 238–239)*

Had they already moved to Hermann in 1998?
Waren sie 1998 schon nach Hermann gezogen?

**!** Beim *past perfect* must du immer ***had*** verwenden, egal ob im Deutschen „hatte" oder „war" steht.

► *Unit 3 (p. 57)* • *P 13 (p. 64)*

*Schreib die vollständigen Sätze in dein Heft.*

**A horrible evening for Tim and his band ...**
1 Tim couldn't play the guitar because he (leave) it on the bus.
2 Julie couldn't play the drums because she (break) her arm.
3 Max couldn't play the piano because he (hurt) his finger.
4 Fiona couldn't play the trumpet because she (have) an accident.

## Unit 4

## GF 6 The present perfect with *since* and *for* (German 'seit')

### Das *present perfect* mit *since* und *for* (Deutsch „seit")

Dad ist **seit** 1999 beim King Center.
Er kennt seinen Chef **seit** fünf Jahren.

Du kannst das *present perfect* verwenden, um über einen **Zustand** zu sprechen, der in der Vergangenheit begonnen hat und jetzt noch andauert.

**!** Wenn du sagen willst, **seit wann** oder **wie lange** der Zustand bereits andauert, musst du aufpassen – es gibt zwei englische Wörter für das deutsche „seit":

◄ **1** Mit *since* gibst du einen **Zeit**punkt an *(since 1999; since May; since 12 o'clock).*
***since* + Zeitpunkt** drückt also aus, **seit wann** ein Zustand andauert.

◄ **2** Mit *for* gibst du einen **Zeit**raum an *(for five years; for a month; for a long time).*
***for* + Zeitraum** drückt also aus, **wie lange** ein Zustand bereits andauert.

***since* + Zeitpunkt** | ***for* + Zeitraum**

Madison and her mom are in the car on the way to the CNN studios. **It's 8.20.**

They'**ve been** in the car since 8 o'clock.
... seit 8 Uhr.

They'**ve been** in the car for 20 minutes.
... seit 20 Minuten.

We've lived in this house since 2004.
Wir wohnen seit 2004 in diesem Haus.

I've had my computer for three years.
Ich habe meinen Computer schon seit drei Jahren.

**!** Achtung:
Im **Deutschen** benutzt man meist das **Präsens**:
*Wir **wohnen** seit ... / Ich **habe** ... seit ...*

Im **Englischen** muss das ***present perfect*** stehen:
*We'**ve lived** ... since ... / I'**ve had** ... for ...*

How long **have** you **lived** in Atlanta?
– Since 2005. / For a few years.
Wie lange **wohnt** ihr in Atlanta?
– Seit 2005. / Seit ein paar Jahren.

Mit ***How long ...?*** + *present perfect* fragst du, seit wann oder wie lange ein Zustand schon andauert.

► *Unit 4 (pp. 77–78)* • *P 9–12 (pp. 85–86)*

*Since oder for? Schreib die vollständigen Sätze in dein Heft.*

1 We've lived here ... four years.
2 Madison has been at her school ... 2005.
3 I've known my best friend ... five years.
4 The weather has been bad ... over a week.

## Lösungen der Grammar-File-Aufgaben

p.155
1 **Flying** alone to New York was very exciting for Ryan.
2 He didn't enjoy **waiting** in the queues at the airport.
3 At first he was a bit afraid of **going** up the ESB in a fast lift.
4 He was very interested in **seeing** all the sights.

p.157
1 The telephone **was invented by Alexander Bell.**
2 'We will rock you!' **was sung by Queen.**
3 Clifton Suspension Bridge **was built by Brunel.**

p.159/1
1 There's **some** milk but there isn't **much** bread.
2 Here's **some** information about the Grand Canyon. I'm doing **a** project on it.
3 We haven't got **many** eggs, and we haven't got **much** butter.
4 I haven't got **much** homework, just **an** exercise for French.

p.159/2
1 We can learn a lot from history.
2 What do you know about **the** history of England?
3 Tourists like to visit Hermann's Festhalle.
4 **The** tourists who asked us the way were from Germany.

p.160
1 Tim couldn't play the guitar because he **had left** it on the bus.
2 Julie couldn't play the drums because she **had broken** her arm.
3 Max couldn't play the piano because he **had hurt** his finger.
4 Fiona couldn't play the trumpet because she **had had** an accident.

p.162
1 We've lived here **for** four years.
2 Madison has been at her school **since** 2005.
3 I've known my best friend **for** five years.
4 The weather has been bad **for** over a week.

## Grammatical terms (Grammatische Fachbegriffe)

| | | |
|---|---|---|
| **active** ['æktɪv] | Aktiv | *Shakira **sang** that song.* |
| **adjective** ['ædʒɪktɪv] | Adjektiv | *good, red, new, boring, ...* |
| **adverb** ['ædvɜːb] | Adverb | *always, badly, here, really, today* |
| **adverb of frequency** ['friːkwənsi] | Häufigkeitsadverb | *always, often, never, ...* |
| **adverb of indefinite time** [ɪnˌdefɪnət 'taɪm] | Adverb der unbestimmten Zeit | *already, ever, just, never, ...* |
| **adverb of manner** ['mænə] | Adverb der Art und Weise | *badly, happily, quietly, well, ...* |
| **article** ['ɑːtɪkl] | Artikel | *the, a/an* |
| **comparison** [kəm'pærɪsn] | Steigerung | *old – older – oldest* |
| **conditional sentence** [kənˌdɪʃənl 'sentəns] | Bedingungssatz | *I'd call him if I knew his number.* |
| **conjunction** [kən'dʒʌŋkʃn] | Konjunktion | *and, or, but; because, before, ...* |
| **countable noun** ['kaʊntəbl] | zählbares Nomen | *girl – girls, pound – pounds, ...* |
| **definite article** ['defɪnət] | bestimmter Artikel | *the* |
| **gerund** ['dʒerənd] | Gerundium | *I like **dancing**. **Dancing** is fun.* |
| ***going to*-future** | Futur mit *going to* | ***I'm going to watch** TV tonight.* |
| **imperative** [ɪm'perətɪv] | Imperativ (Befehlsform) | *Open your books. Don't talk.* |
| **infinitive** [ɪn'fɪnətɪv] | Infinitiv (Grundform des Verbs) | *(to) open, (to) see, (to) read, ...* |
| **irregular verb** [ɪˌregjələ 'vɜːb] | unregelmäßiges Verb | *(to) go – went – gone* |
| **main clause** | Hauptsatz | ***I like Scruffy** because I like dogs.* |
| **modal** ['məʊdl] | modales Hilfsverb, Modalverb | *can, could, may, must, ...* |
| **noun** [naʊn] | Nomen, Substantiv | *Sophie, girl, brother, time, ...* |
| **object** ['ɒbdʒɪkt] | Objekt | *My sister is writing **a letter**.* |
| **passive** ['pæsɪv] | Passiv | *That song **was sung** by Shakira.* |
| **past participle** [ˌpɑːst 'pɑːtɪsɪpl] | Partizip Perfekt | *cleaned, planned, gone, seen, ...* |
| **past perfect** [ˌpɑːst 'pɜːfɪkt] | Plusquamperfekt, Vorvergangenheit | *I couldn't sing because I **had lost** my voice.* |
| **past progressive** [ˌpɑːst prə'gresɪv] | Verlaufsform der Vergangenheit | *At 7.30 I **was having** dinner.* |
| **personal pronoun** [ˌpɜːsənl 'prəʊnaʊn] | Personalpronomen (persönliches Fürwort) | *I, you, he, she, it, we, they; me, you, him, her, it, us, them* |
| **plural** ['plʊərəl] | Plural, Mehrzahl | |
| **possessive determiner** [pəˌzesɪv dɪ'tɜːmɪnə] | Possessivbegleiter (besitzanzeigender Begleiter) | *my, your, his, her, its, our, their* |
| **possessive form** [pəˌzesɪv fɔːm] | *s*-Genitiv | *Jo's brother; my sister's room* |
| **possessive pronoun** [pəˌzesɪv 'prəʊnaʊn] | Possessivpronomen | *mine, yours, his, hers, ours, theirs* |
| **preposition** [ˌprepə'zɪʃn] | Präposition | *after, at, in, next to, under, ...* |
| **present perfect** [ˌpreznt 'pɜːfɪkt] | *present perfect* | *We**'ve made** a cake for you.* |
| **present progressive** [ˌpreznt prə'gresɪv] | Verlaufsform der Gegenwart | *The Hansons **are having** lunch.* |
| **pronoun** ['prəʊnaʊn] | Pronomen, Fürwort | |
| **quantifier** ['kwɒntɪfaɪə] | Mengenangaben | *some, a lot of, many, much, ...* |
| **regular verb** [ˌregjələ 'vɜːb] | regelmäßiges Verb | *(to) help – helped – helped* |
| **reflexive pronoun** [rɪˌfleksɪv 'prəʊnaʊn] | Reflexivpronomen | *myself, yourself, themselves, ...* |
| **relative clause** [ˌrelətɪv 'klɔːz] | Relativsatz | *There's the girl **who helped me**.* |
| **relative pronoun** [ˌrelətɪv 'prəʊnaʊn] | Relativpronomen | *who, that, which* |
| **short answer** [ˌʃɔːt_'ɑːnsə] | Kurzantwort | *Yes, I am. / No, I don't. / ...* |
| **simple past** [ˌsɪmpl 'pɑːst] | einfache Form der Vergangenheit | *Jo **wrote** two letters yesterday.* |
| **simple present** [ˌsɪmpl 'preznt] | einfache Form der Gegenwart | *I always **go** to school by bike.* |
| **singular** ['sɪŋgjələ] | Singular, Einzahl | |
| **statement** ['steɪtmənt] | Aussage(satz) | *I like tea. I don't like coffee.* |
| **subject** ['sʌbdʒɪkt] | Subjekt | ***My sister** is writing a letter.* |
| **uncountable noun** [ʌn'kaʊntəbl] | nicht zählbares Nomen | *bread, milk, money, news, work, ...* |
| ***will*-future** | Futur mit *will* | *I think it **will be** cold tonight.* |

**Diese Wörterverzeichnisse findest du in deinem Englischbuch:**

- Das **Vocabulary** (Vokabelverzeichnis – S.164–179) enthält alle Wörter und Wendungen, die du lernen musst. Sie stehen in der Reihenfolge, in der sie in den Units vorkommen.
- Das **Dictionary** besteht aus zwei alphabetischen Wörterlisten zum Nachschlagen:
  Englisch – Deutsch: S.180–206
  Deutsch – Englisch: S.207–230.

**So ist das Vocabulary aufgebaut:**

- Hier siehst du, wo die Wörter vorkommen:
  p.17/A 7 = Seite 17, Abschnitt 7
  p.21/P 4 = Seite 21, Übung 4
- Die Lautschrift zeigt dir, wie ein Wort ausgesprochen und betont wird.
  (→ Englische Laute: S.206)
- Eingerückte Wörter lernst du am besten zusammen mit dem vorausgehenden Wort, weil die beiden zusammengehören.
- Die blauen Kästen solltest du dir besonders gut ansehen.

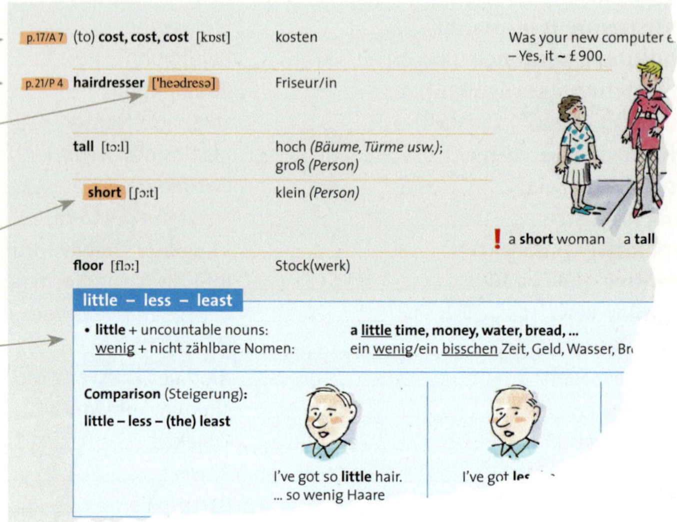


Tipps zum Wörterlernen findest du im Skills File auf Seite 136.

**Abkürzungen:**

| | | | |
|---|---|---|---|
| *n* = *noun* | | *v* = *verb* | |
| *adj* = *adjective* | | *adv* = *adverb* | |
| *prep* = *preposition* | | *conj* = *conjunction* | |
| *pl* = *plural* | | *no pl* = *no plural* | |
| p. = page | | pp. = pages | |
| sb. = somebody | | sth. = something | |
| jn. = jemanden | | jm. = jemandem | |
| *AE* = *American English* | | *BE* = *British English* | |

*infml* = *informal* (umgangssprachlich, informell)

**Symbole:**

**!** Hier stehen Hinweise auf Besonderheiten, bei denen man leicht Fehler machen kann.

◄► ist das „Gegenteil"-Zeichen:
(to) **begin** ◄► (to) **stop**
(**begin** ist das Gegenteil von **stop**)

~ Die **Tilde** in den Beispielsätzen steht für das neue Wort. Beispiel:
**downtown** – Dad works at a bank **~**.

## Introduction – Welcome to the United States of America

| | | | |
|---|---|---|---|
| p.6 | **canyon** ['kænjən] | Schlucht | |
| p.8 | **close (to)** [kləʊs] | nahe (bei, an) | It's not far. The shop is very **~ to** our home. |
| | **awesome** ['ɔːsəm] *(AE, infml)* | klasse, großartig | very good, great |
| | **hometown** ['həʊmtaʊn] | Heimatstadt | |
| | **three and a half days** | dreieinhalb Tage | **!** With **and**: **three and a half days** |
| | **zone** [zəʊn] | Zone, Gebiet | I'd like a ticket for **~s** 1 and 2, please. |
| | (to) **hike** [haɪk] | wandern | |
| | **hike** | Wanderung, Marsch | |
| | (to) **go on a hike** | wandern gehen | |

| | | | |
|---|---|---|---|
| | **comment (on, about)** ['kɒment] | Kommentar, Bemerkung (zu, über) | ! Betonung: **<u>com</u>ment** ['kɒment] |
| | **Good to have you back.** | Schön, dass du wieder da bist. | |
| p.9 | **middle school** | *(USA) Schule für 11- bis 14-Jährige* | |
| | **grade** [greɪd] *(AE)* | Jahrgangsstufe, Klasse | = *BE* year |
| | (to) **be lucky** ['lʌkɪ] | Glück haben | We **were** ~ and got tickets for a Manchester United match. |
| | (to) **raise money (for)** [reɪz] | Geld sammeln (für) | |
| | (to) **be good/bad at** sth. | gut/schlecht in etwas sein; etwas gut/schlecht können | Paul is **good** ~ Music but **bad** ~ Maths. |
| | (to) **cut the grass** [grɑːs] | Rasen mähen | |
| | **grass** | Gras; Rasen | |
| | **sale** [seɪl] | (Aus-, Schluss-)Verkauf | |
| | **tent** [tent] | Zelt | |
| | **Native American** [ˌneɪtɪv‿ə'merɪkən] | amerikanische(r) Ureinwohner/in, Indianer/in | ! Der Begriff **Native American** wird heute von vielen dem älteren Begriff **Indian** vorgezogen. |
| p.10 | **high school** ['haɪ skuːl] | *(USA) Schule für 14- bis 18-Jährige* | |
| | (to) **begin (-nn-)** [bɪ'gɪn], **began** [bɪ'gæn], **begun** [bɪ'gʌn] | beginnen, anfangen (mit) | It's time to ~. (= to start)<br>(to) **begin** ◄► (to) **stop** |
| | **route** [ruːt] | Strecke, Route | ! In den USA werden wichtige Fernstraßen mit **<u>Route</u>** <u>+ Nummer</u> bezeichnet: **Route 66.** |
| | (to) **dream (of, about)** [driːm] | träumen (von) | verb: (to) **dream** – noun: **dream** |
| | **souvenir** [ˌsuːvə'nɪə] | Souvenir, Mitbringsel | |
| | **license plate** ['laɪsns pleɪt] *(AE)*, **number plate** ['nʌmbə pleɪt] *(BE)* | Nummernschild | |
| | **grand** [grænd] | eindrucksvoll, beeindruckend | The hotel looked ~ from outside, but our room was small and dark. |
| | **foot** [fʊt], *pl* **feet** [fiːt] | Fuß *(Längenmaß; 1 Fuß = 30,48 cm)* | The cabin was quite small, only about 6 **feet** high. |
| | **wing** [wɪŋ] | Flügel | |

(to) **cut the grass**

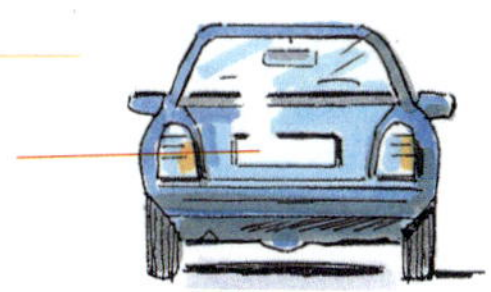


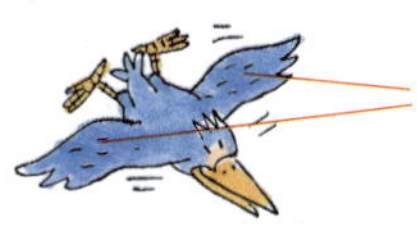

| | | | |
|---|---|---|---|
| | (to) **forgive** [fə'gɪv], **forgave** [fə'geɪv], **forgiven** [fə'gɪvn] | vergeben, verzeihen | I know that she has hurt you, but try and ~ her. |
| p. 11 | **adventure** [əd'ventʃə] | Abenteuer | Our fishing trip in Canada was a great ~. We even saw some bears. |

## Unit 1: New York, New York

| | | | |
|---|---|---|---|
| p. 12 | **avenue** ['ævənjuː] | Allee | We moved to a new house in Park **Avenue.** |
| | **sightseeing trip** ['saɪtsiːɪŋ] | Besichtigungstour | |
| | **deli** ['deli] | Deli *(Lebensmittelgeschäft mit Fastfoodrestaurant)* | If you're hungry, we can get some sandwiches at the ~ on the way home. |
| | **stop** [stɒp] | Halt; *hier:* Anlaufstelle | noun: **stop** – verb: (to) **stop** |
| | **immigrant** ['ɪmɪgrənt] | Einwanderer/Einwanderin | **!** Betonung: **<u>im</u>migrant** ['ɪmɪgrənt] |
| p. 13 | **borough** ['bʌrə, *AE:* 'bɜːrəʊ] | (Stadt-)Bezirk | |

**New York: the five boroughs**

| | | |
|---|---|---|
| **the Bronx** | [brɒŋks] | der nördlichste Bezirk; liegt als einziger auf dem Festland |
| **Manhattan** | [mæn'hætn] | Insel zwischen dem Hudson und dem East River, berühmt für ihre Wolkenkratzer |
| **Queens** | [kwiːnz] | der größte Bezirk; im Südwesten der Insel Long Island gelegen; vor allem Wohngebiet |
| **Brooklyn** | ['brʊklɪn] | wie Queens auf Long Island gelegen; die berühmte Brooklyn Bridge verbindet Brooklyn mit Manhattan |
| **Staten Island** | [ˌstætn‿'aɪlənd] | Insel an der Einfahrt zum Hafen von New York, mit Manhattan durch Fährbetrieb verbunden *(→ Karte auf S. 20)* |

| | | | |
|---|---|---|---|
| p. 14/A 1 | **directions** *(pl)* [də'rekʃnz] | Wegbeschreibung | I didn't know the way so I asked for ~. |
| | **downtown** [ˌdaʊn'taʊn] *(AE)* | (im/in das) Stadtzentrum | Dad works at a bank ~. |
| | **block** [blɒk] | (Häuser-, Wohn-)Block | |
| p. 14/A 2 | **sidewalk** ['saɪdwɔːk] *(AE)*, **pavement** ['peɪvmənt] *(BE)* | Gehweg, Bürgersteig | **sidewalk** *(AE)*, **pavement** *(BE)* |
| | **line** [laɪn] *(AE)*, **queue** [kjuː] *(BE)* | Schlange, Reihe *(wartender Menschen)* | a **line** *(AE)*, a **queue** *(BE)* |

| | | | |
|---|---|---|---|
| p. 15/A 4 | **difference** ['dɪfrəns] | Unterschied | |
| | (to) **wake up** [ˌweɪk‿'ʌp], **woke** [wəʊk], **woken** ['wəʊkən] | aufwachen | Yesterday I only **woke** ~ at 8 o'clock and was late for school. |
| | (to) **wake** sb. **(up)**, **woke, woken** | jn. (auf)wecken | This morning my mother **woke** me ~ at 7. |

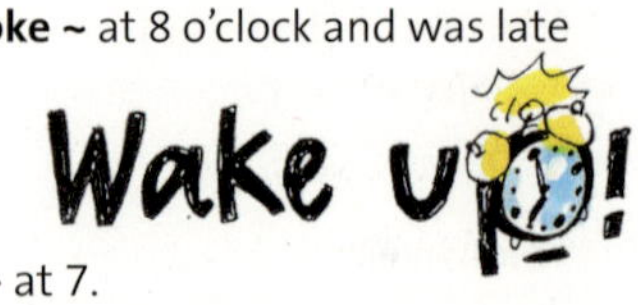

## British English – American English (I)

### Different words

| British English | American English | |
|---|---|---|
| **mobile (phone)** | **cellphone** | Handy |
| **city centre** | **downtown** | Stadtzentrum, Innenstadt |
| **lift** | **elevator** | Fahrstuhl, Aufzug |
| **year** | **grade** | Jahrgangsstufe |
| **queue** | **line** | Schlange, Reihe |
| **pavement** | **sidewalk** | Gehweg, Bürgersteig |
| **underground** | **subway** | U-Bahn |
| **holiday(s)** | **vacation** | Ferien, Urlaub |

### Different spelling

| British English *-tre* | American English: *-ter* |
|---|---|
| cen**tre** | cen**ter** |
| me**tre** | me**ter** |
| thea**tre** | thea**ter** |

| British English: *-our* | American English: *-or* |
|---|---|
| col**our** | col**or** |
| fav**our**ite | fav**or**ite |
| harb**our** | harb**or** |

| British English: | American English: |
|---|---|
| travel**l**ed, travel**l**ing | travel**ed**, travel**ing** |

| | | |
|---|---|---|
| **fire station** ['faɪə steɪʃn] | Feuerwache | |
| **firefighter** ['faɪəfaɪtə] | Feuerwehrmann, -frau | |
| **as** a firefighter/teacher/... | als Feuerwehrmann, -frau/ Lehrer/in/... | He works ~ a firefighter. |
| p.15/A 5 (to) **imagine** sth. [ɪ'mædʒɪn] | sich etwas vorstellen | |
| **anything else** [els] | (irgend)etwas anderes | |

### ... else

**1.** *(anders, unterschiedlich)*

| | |
|---|---|
| I don't like apple juice. Have you got **anything else**? | ... Hast du **irgendetwas anderes**? |
| I'm tired. **Somebody else** will have to tidy up. | ... **Jemand anders** muss aufräumen. |

**2.** *(außerdem, zusätzlich)*

| | |
|---|---|
| **What else** do you know about New York? | **Was** weißt du **(sonst) noch** über New York? |
| I met Susan at the party. – **Who else** did you meet? | **Wen** hast du **(sonst) noch** getroffen? |

| | | |
|---|---|---|
| (to) **put out a fire** | ein Feuer löschen | |
| **shift** [ʃɪft] | Schicht *(bei der Arbeit)* | My dad works 12-hour **~s**. There are eight men and women on his **~**. ! on **my shift** = in meiner Schicht |
| **guy** [gaɪ] *(infml)* | Typ, Kerl | |

| | |
|---|---|
| p.16/A 6 **bagel** ['beɪgl] | Bagel *(ringförmiges Brötchen)* |
| **cream cheese** [ˌkriːm 'tʃiːz] | Frischkäse |
| **cream** [kriːm] | Sahne; Creme |
| **coffee** ['kɒfi] | Kaffee |

| | | | |
|---|---|---|---|
| | (to) **grab** sth. **(-bb-)** [græb] | sich etwas schnappen | He said goodbye, **~bed** his bag and hurried out. |
| | (to) **order** ['ɔːdə] | bestellen | He went into the deli and **~ed** a bagel. |
| | **I'll have ...** | Ich nehme ... *(bei einer Bestellung im Restaurant)* | ! I'**ll have** chips and a cola. (Ich **nehme** Pommes und eine Cola.) |
| | **regular** ['regjələ] | normal *(Größenangabe bei Getränken und Fastfood)* |  regular – large |
| p.17/A 7 | a **must** [mʌst] | ein Muss | Have you been to Brooklyn Bridge? It's a ~. noun: **must** – verb: **must** |
| | **floor** [flɔː] | Stock(werk) | |
| | (to) **cost, cost, cost** [kɒst] | kosten | Was your new computer expensive? – Yes, it ~ £900. |
| | **dollar ($)** ['dɒlə] | Dollar | How much is £900 in **~s**? |
| | **tall** [tɔːl] | hoch *(Bäume, Türme usw.)*; groß *(Person)* |  a **short** woman a **tall** woman |
| | **short** [ʃɔːt] | klein *(Person)* | |
| | **perfect** ['pɜːfɪkt] | perfekt; ideal; vollkommen | ! Betonung: **perfect** ['pɜːfɪkt] |
| | **I'll/You'll/She'll ... be OK.** | Mir/Dir/Ihr ... wird nichts passieren. | Be careful when you climb that tree. – Don't worry. **I'll be ~**. |

## British English – American English (II)

p.20

### Different words

| British English | American English | | British English | American English | |
|---|---|---|---|---|---|
| **rucksack** | **backpack** ['bækpæk] | Rucksack | **rubbish** | **garbage** ['gɑːrbɪdʒ] | Müll, Abfall |
| **biscuit** | **cookie** ['kʊki] | Keks | **trousers** | **pants** [pænts] | Hose |
| **rubber** | **eraser** [ɪ'reɪsər] | Radiergummi | **crisps** | **potato chips** | Kartoffelchips |
| **chips** | **French fries** [fraɪz] | Pommes frites | **timetable** | **schedule** ['skedʒuːl] | Stundenplan; Fahrplan |

| | | | |
|---|---|---|---|
| p.21/P 4 | **hairdresser** ['heədresə] | Friseur/in | |
| p.23/P 9 | **sure** [ʃʊə, ʃɔː] | klar, sicher | Can I have your pencil? – **Sure**, here you are. |
| p.23/P 10 | **zoo** [zuː] | Zoo | |
| | **skyscraper** ['skaɪskreɪpə] | Wolkenkratzer | |
| p.24/P 11 | (to) **be tired of** sth. | genug von etwas haben, etwas satt haben | I'm really **~ of** that CD. / I'm really **~ of** listening to that CD. Can't you play something else? |
| p.24/P 13 | (to) **take a break** | eine Pause machen | We've worked long enough now. Let's **take a ~**. |
| p.25/P 14 | **safety** ['seɪfti] | Sicherheit |  |
| | (to) **work** sth. **out** | etwas herausarbeiten, herausfinden | |

## You can tell me

| | | | |
|---|---|---|---|
| p.26 | **apartment** [ə'pɑːtmənt] *(AE)* | Wohnung | *(BE)* flat |
| | (to) **earn** [ɜːn] | verdienen | |
| | **crowd** [kraʊd] | (Menschen-)Menge, Masse; *(infml auch:)* Clique, Gruppe | |
| | (to) **seem (to be / to do)** [siːm] | (zu sein / zu tun) scheinen | You ~ **(to be)** tired. Did you sleep long enough? |
| | (to) **be on drugs** [drʌgz] | Drogen/Rauschgift nehmen | His eyes look strange. He seems to **be on ~**. |
| | **I feel sick.** [sɪk] | Mir ist schlecht. | |
| | (to) **end** [end] | (be)enden, zu Ende gehen | The road **~s** here. We'll have to walk now.<br>A hot bath is a good way to ~ the day.<br>verb: (to) **end** – noun: **end** |
| | **kiss** [kɪs] | Kuss |  |
| | (to) **kiss** | küssen | |
| | we **should** ... [ʃəd, ʃʊd] | wir sollten ... | I think you ~ ask John before you take his CDs. |
| | (to) **take off** *(infml)* | sich davonmachen, sich aus dem Staub machen | When they saw the police, the thieves **took** ~ in a fast car. |
| | (to) **cry** [kraɪ] | weinen | She's **crying**.  |

### any/anything/anybody – in bejahten Aussagesätzen

p.27 Du kennst **any** bereits in Fragen und verneinten Aussagesätzen:

| | |
|---|---|
| Have we got **any** orange juice? | Haben wir Orangensaft? |
| We haven't got **any** biscuits. | Wir haben keine Kekse. |

Man verwendet **any** auch, wenn „jeder beliebige" gemeint ist.
In dieser Bedeutung kann **any** auch in bejahten Aussagesätzen stehen.

| | |
|---|---|
| You can have **any** bagel with tomato, bacon, ... | ... **jeden (beliebigen)** Bagel ... |
| You can tell me **anything**. | ... **alles (, was es auch sei / egal, was es ist)**. |
| It's easy to dance – **anybody** can do it. | ... **jeder (Beliebige)** ... |

| | | |
|---|---|---|
| **God** [gɒd] | Gott | |
| **beard** [bɪəd] | Bart | |
| **blond** [blɒnd] | blond, hell | |
| **surprised (at** sth.**)** [sə'praɪzd] | überrascht (über/von) | I was ~ **at** the size of their house. It was bigger than I thought. |
| (to) **scream** [skriːm] | schreien, kreischen | The kids **~ed** when they saw the mouse.  |
| (to) **kick** [kɪk] | treten | |

| | | |
|---|---|---|
| **I didn't care.** [keə] | Es war mir egal. | It wasn't cheap, but **I didn't ~**. I bought it anyway. |
| **gun** [gʌn] | Gewehr, Schusswaffe | |
| (to) **get a cab** [kæb] | ein Taxi nehmen |  |
| **brave** [breɪv] | mutig | ! German „brav" = English **good**<br>English **brave** = German „mutig" |
| **hell** [hel] | Hölle | |
| p.28 **false** [fɔ:ls] | falsch, unwahr | What do you think – is this statement true or ~? |

## Unit 2: California, the 'Golden State'?

| | | |
|---|---|---|
| p.34 **golden** ['gəʊldən] | goldene(r,s) | |
| **gold** [gəʊld] | Gold | |
| **earthquake** ['ɜ:θkweɪk] | Erdbeben | |
| **earth** [ɜ:θ] | Erde | What's the hottest country on ~? (= auf der Erde) |

### everybody/everyone, anybody/anyone, ...

Neben den Zusammensetzungen **anybody, everybody, somebody, nobody** gibt es auch – bei gleicher Bedeutung – die Zusammensetzungen auf **-one:**

**anyone, everyone, someone,** ! *(two words:)* **no one**.

| | | |
|---|---|---|
| **anybody / anyone** | ['eniwʌn] | (irgend)jemand |
| **everybody / everyone** | ['evriwʌn] | jeder, alle |
| **somebody / someone** | ['sʌmwʌn] | jemand |
| **nobody / no one** | ['nəʊ_wʌn] | niemand |

| | | |
|---|---|---|
| **homeless** ['həʊmləs] | obdachlos | |
| p.35 **border** ['bɔ:də] | Grenze | The US only has a ~ with Canada and Mexico. |
| p.36/A 1 **business** ['bɪznəs] | Geschäft; Handel | Tina has got a new ~ – a party service. |
| **farmer** ['fɑ:mə] | Bauer/Bäuerin, Landwirt/in | |
| **farming** ['fɑ:mɪŋ] | Landwirtschaft | |
| **wine** [waɪn] | Wein | |
| (to) **have a look at** sth. | sich etwas ansehen, einen Blick werfen auf etwas | |
| **industrial** [ɪn'dʌstriəl] | industriell, Industrie- | |
| **industry** ['ɪndəstri] | Industrie | noun: **<u>in</u>dustry** – adjective: **in<u>dus</u>trial** |
| **company** ['kʌmpəni] | Firma, Gesellschaft | |
| **grape** [greɪp] | Weintraube | some **grapes**  |
| p.37/A 2 **culture** ['kʌltʃə] | Kultur | ! Betonung: **<u>cul</u>ture** ['kʌltʃə] |
| **attitude (to/towards)** ['ætɪtju:d] | Haltung (gegenüber), Einstellung (zu) | What's your ~ **to/towards** clothes? Do you always buy the latest fashion? |

| | | | |
|---|---|---|---|
| | **minority** [maɪ'nɒrəti] | Minderheit | There are 16 girls and 11 boys in my class. The boys are in the **~**. |
| | **majority** [mə'dʒɒrəti] | Mehrheit | The girls are in the **~**. **majority ◄► minority** |
| | **citizen** ['sɪtɪzn] | (Staats-)Bürger/in, Staatsangehörige(r) | |
| | **advantage (over** sb./sth.**)** [əd'vɑːntɪdʒ] | Vorteil (gegenüber jm./etwas) | Cats have an **~ over** dogs: they can climb trees. |
| | **disadvantage** [ˌdɪsəd'vɑːntɪdʒ] | Nachteil | **advantage ◄► disadvantage** |
| | **useful** ['juːsfəl] | nützlich | When you're abroad, it's **~** to speak the language of the country that you're visiting. |
| | **relations** *(pl)* [rɪ'leɪʃnz] | Beziehungen | |
| | **successful** [sək'sesfl] | erfolgreich | |
| | (to) **laugh at** sb. | jn. auslachen, über jn. lachen | The other kids **~ed at** Jenny because she had a funny accent. |
| | **illegal** [ɪ'liːgl] | illegal, ungesetzlich | |
| | **legal** ['liːgl] | legal | **!** Betonung: **legal** ['liːgl] **legal ◄► illegal** |
| | **member (of)** ['membə] | Mitglied (von, in) | |
| | **opinion (of)** [ə'pɪnjən] | Meinung (von) | Manchester United were fantastic. – Do you think so? **In my ~**, Arsenal played better. (= Meiner Meinung nach ...) |
| | **prejudice (against)** ['predʒudɪs] | Voreingenommenheit (gegen), Vorurteil (gegenüber) | |
| p. 38/A 5 | **maid** [meɪd] | Hausangestellte, Zimmermädchen | |
| | (to) **beg (for) (-gg-)** [beg] | betteln (um); (eindringlich) bitten (um) | The old man sat on the street and **~ged** for money. She **~ged** her mum to let her go to the party. |
| p. 38/A 6 | (to) **get married (to** sb.**)** ['mærid] | (jn.) heiraten | They lived together for years before they **got ~**. |
| | **amnesty** ['æmnəsti] | Amnestie, Begnadigung | |
| p. 39/A 7 | (to) **discover** [dɪ'skʌvə] | entdecken; herausfinden | America was **~ed** in 1492. |
| | **during** ['djʊərɪŋ] | während | **~** your holiday = while you were on holiday |

| | | | |
|---|---|---|---|
| p.42/P 1 | **for example** [ˌfər‿ɪg'zɑ:mpl] | zum Beispiel | I like lots of bands, ~ **example** Outkast, ... |
| p.42/P 3 | **sportsman, sportswoman** | Sportler, Sportlerin | |
| | (to) **be called** [kɔ:ld] | heißen, genannt werden | Why **is** California ~ the Golden State? |
| p.43/P 4 | **camp** [kæmp] | Camp, (Ferien-)Lager | |
| | **guidebook** ['gaɪdbʊk] | Reiseführer *(Buch)* | When you go abroad, it's useful to have a ~. |
| | **vegetarian** [ˌvedʒə'teəriən] | vegetarisch; Vegetarier/in | We only eat ~ food (= meals without meat). We're **~s**. |

## Santa Monica – Episode 1 of a TV series

| | | | |
|---|---|---|---|
| p.48 | **cold** [kəʊld] | Kälte | adjective: **cold** – noun: **cold** |
| | **comfortable** ['kʌmftəbl] | bequem, behaglich | a **comfortable** sofa  Come in and make yourself ~. (= ... und machen Sie es sich bequem.) ! Betonung: **<u>com</u>fortable** ['kʌmftəbl] |
| | **uncomfortable** [ʌn'kʌmftəbl] | unbequem, unbehaglich | |
| | **engine** ['endʒɪn] | Motor | |
| p.49 | **guilty** ['gɪlti] | schuldbewusst; schuldig | I felt so ~ because I forgot my mum's birthday. He would never steal anything. He can't be ~. |
| | **jail** [dʒeɪl] | Gefängnis |  |
| | **fight** [faɪt] | Kampf; Schlägerei | verb: (to) **fight** – noun: **fight** |
| | **boyfriend** ['bɔɪfrend] | (fester) Freund | |
| | **girlfriend** ['gɜ:lfrend] | (feste) Freundin | |
| | **serious** ['sɪəriəs] | ernst, ernsthaft | |
| | **drunk** [drʌŋk] | betrunken | |
| | **niece** [ni:s] | Nichte | a daughter of your brother or sister |
| | **nephew** ['nefju:, 'nevju:] | Neffe | a son of your brother or sister |
| p.50 | (to) **believe (in)** [bɪ'li:v] | glauben (an) | Do you ~ **in** God? |
| | (to) **offer** ['ɒfə] | anbieten | |
| | **offer** ['ɒfə] | Angebot | verb: (to) **offer** – noun: **offer** |
| | **argument** ['ɑ:gjumənt] | Argument, Begründung; Streit | ! **argument** = **1.** Argument – There are good ~s for and against this idea. **2.** Streit – Mum and Dad had an ~ last night. Mum shouted a lot. |
| | **social** ['səʊʃl] | sozial, Sozial- | Homelessness is a serious ~ problem in big cities. |
| | **jealousy** ['dʒeləsi] | Eifersucht | noun: **jealousy** – adjective: **jealous** |

## Unit 3: Hermann says 'Willkommen'

| | | | |
|---|---|---|---|
| p.52 | **main** [meɪn] | Haupt-; wichtigste(r, s) | There are so many cars on the ~ road.<br>English and Spanish are two of the world's ~ languages. |
| | (to) **found** [faʊnd] | gründen | (to) **found** a new club = (to) start a new club<br>**!** Nicht verwechseln:<br>(to) **find, found, found** = finden<br>(to) **found, founded, founded** = gründen |
| | **in** 1837 | 1837, im Jahre 1837 | Charlie Chaplin was born ~ 1889. |
| | **tradition** [trə'dɪʃn] | Tradition | **!** Betonung: **tra<u>di</u>tion** [trə'dɪʃn] |
| | **alive** [ə'laɪv] | am Leben, lebendig | Both my grandparents are still ~.<br>**alive** ◄► **dead** |
| p.53 | **countryside** ['kʌntrisaɪd] | Land(schaft), Natur | |
| | **event** [ɪ'vent] | Ereignis; Veranstaltung | |
| | (to) **take place** [ˌteɪk 'pleɪs] | stattfinden | Our next school trip will **take** ~ in two months. |
| p.54/A 1 | **system** ['sɪstəm] | System | **!** Betonung: **<u>sys</u>tem** ['sɪstəm] |
| | **elementary school** [ˌelɪ'mentri skuːl] | *(USA)* Grundschule *(für 6- bis 11-Jährige)* | |
| | **kindergarten** ['kɪndəgɑːtn] | Kindergarten; *(USA)* Vorschule *(für 5- bis 6-Jährige)* | |
| | **semester** [sɪ'mestə] | Semester *(Schulhalbjahr in den USA)* | **!** In Großbritannien ist das Schuljahr in <u>drei</u> **terms** unterteilt, in den USA in <u>zwei</u> **semesters**. |
| | a week/day/month/... **off** | eine Woche/einen Tag/ einen Monat/... frei | |
| | **Easter** ['iːstə] | Ostern; Oster- | an **Easter** egg |
| | **cafeteria** [ˌkæfə'tɪəriə] | Cafeteria; *(USA)* Schulmensa | |
| | **bulletin board** ['bʊlətɪn bɔːd] *(AE)* | schwarzes Brett, Anschlagtafel | = *BE* notice board |
| | **grade** [greɪd] (*BE auch:* **mark** [mɑːk]) | (Schul-)Note, Zensur | |

### US school grades

| | | | |
|---|---|---|---|
| + | A | **excellent** ['eksələnt] | ausgezeichnet, hervorragend |
| ↑ | B | **good** | gut |
| | C | **average** *(n; adj)* ['ævərɪdʒ] | Durchschnitt; durchschnittlich |
| ↓ | D | **below average** | unter Durchschnitt; unterdurchschnittlich |
| – | F | **failure** *(n)* ['feɪljə] | ungenügend |

| | | |
|---|---|---|
| **below** [bɪ'ləʊ] | unten; unter, unterhalb (von) | First look at the pictures ~. ↓ |
| **above** [ə'bʌv] | oben; über, oberhalb (von) | Then look at the chart ~. ↑ |
| **extracurricular activities** (*or:* **extracurriculars**) [ˌekstrəkə'rɪkjələz] | *schulische Angebote außerhalb des regulären Unterrichts, oft als Arbeitsgemeinschaften* | |

| | | | |
|---|---|---|---|
| p.54/A 2 | **period** ['pɪəriəd] | (Unterrichts-/Schul-)Stunde | = *BE* lesson |
| | **health** [helθ] | Gesundheit; Gesundheitslehre | noun: **health** – adjectives: **healthy, unhealthy** |
| | **study hall** ['stʌdi hɔːl] | *Zeit zum selbstständigen Arbeiten/Lernen in der Schule* | At Hermann High students have ~ **hall** every day after lunch. |
| | (to) **study** ['stʌdi] | studieren;<br>sorgfältig durchlesen;<br>lernen | When I finish school, I'm going to ~ history.<br>My dad **studies** the sports page every morning.<br>There's a test tomorrow, so I have to ~ tonight. |
| | **gym** [dʒɪm] | Sporthalle, Turnhalle;<br>Fitnessstudio | ! **gym** = Sport-, Turnhalle (*nicht:* ~~Gymnasium~~) |
| p.55/A 4 | **meeting** ['miːtɪŋ] | Versammlung, Besprechung | The photo club **~s** are on Fridays.<br>verb: (to) **meet** – noun: **meeting** |
| p.56/A 6 | **class** | Unterricht; Kurs | What did you learn in French ~ today?<br>I do an evening ~ in painting on Fridays. |
| | **less** [les] | weniger | |

**little – less – least**

- **little** + uncountable nouns: <u>wenig</u> + nicht zählbare Nomen: — **a <u>little</u> time, money, water, bread, ...** ein <u>wenig</u>/ein <u>bisschen</u> Zeit, Geld, Wasser, Brot, ...

**Comparison** (Steigerung)**:**

**little – less – (the) least**

I've got so **little** hair.
... so wenig Haare

I've got **less** hair.
... weniger Haare

I've got **the least** hair.
... die wenigsten Haare

| | | | |
|---|---|---|---|
| | **rice** [raɪs] | Reis | |
| | **soda** ['səʊdə] *(AE)* | Limonade | |
| | **product** ['prɒdʌkt] | Produkt | |
| | **poultry** ['pəʊltri] | Geflügel | Can you buy a chicken at the ~ shop, please? |
| | **nut** [nʌt] | Nuss | |
| | **bean** [biːn] | Bohne | |
| | **whole-grain** ['həʊlgreɪn] | Vollkorn- | |
| | **whole** [həʊl] | ganze(r, s), gesamte(r, s) | |
| | **exercise** *(no pl)* | (körperliche) Bewegung, Training | ! • **exercise(s)** = Übung(en): Which **exercises** have we got for homework?<br>• **exercise** = Bewegung: The doctors say I need more **exercise**. |
| p.56/A 7 | **muesli** ['mjuːzli] | Müsli | |
| p.57/A 9 | **local** ['ləʊkl] | Lokal-, örtlich; am/vom Ort | Find out what's going on in your hometown! Read your ~ paper and listen to your ~ radio station! |
| | **at first** | zuerst, am Anfang | I didn't like him **at first**, but later we became friends. |
| | **worried (about)** ['wʌrid] | beunruhigt, besorgt (wegen/um) | Sam is ~ **about** his grandfather. He's very ill. |

| | | | |
|---|---|---|---|
| | **strange** ['streɪndʒ] | seltsam, sonderbar;<br>fremd | He looked really ~ with green hair.<br>It was a ~ part of town, so I needed a map. |
| | **soccer** ['sɒkə] | Fußball | ! In Amerika wird „Fußball" als **soccer** bezeichnet (**football** steht dort für **American football**).<br>In Großbritannien wird meist **football** verwendet; **soccer** klingt dort eher förmlich. |
| | (to) **be homesick** ['həʊmsɪk] | Heimweh haben | ! I **am homesick**. = Ich **habe Heimweh**. |
| p. 60/P 2 | **average** *(n; adj)* ['ævərɪdʒ] | Durchschnitt,<br>durchschnittlich,<br>Durchschnitts- | **On** ~ German teenagers get about 35 Euros pocket money a month.<br>! **on** average = **im** Durchschnitt |
| | **population** [ˌpɒpju'leɪʃn] | Bevölkerung,<br>Einwohner(zahl) | |
| | **minus** ['maɪnəs] | minus | ! Aussprache: **minus** ['maɪnəs] |
| | **plus** [plʌs] | plus | |
| | **Celsius (C)** ['selsiəs] | Celsius | 22 °**C** = 22 degrees **Celsius** |

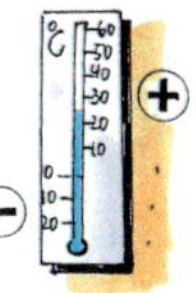

**REVISION: Numbers**

| You write: | You say: | In German: |
|---|---|---|
| 10.35 | ten **point** three five | 10,35 (zehn **Komma** drei fünf) |
| 5.6 % | five **point** six **per cent** | 5,6 % (fünf **Komma** sechs **Prozent**) |
| 10,000 | ten thousand | 10 000 |

**German 'null':**

- phone numbers and dates: **o** [əʊ]
  **340926** = three four **o** nine two six
  **1907** = nineteen **o** seven
- temperatures: **zero**
  **-3°** = three degrees below **zero**
- in most sports: **nil**
  What's the score? – **2–0**. = two **nil**

| | | | |
|---|---|---|---|
| p. 61/P 5 | **Best wishes** ['wɪʃɪz] | *etwa:* Alles Gute / Mit besten Grüßen *(als Briefschluss)* | |
| p. 63/P 9 | **cereal** ['sɪəriəl] | Getreideflocken,<br>Frühstücksflocken | |
| p. 64/P 12 | **soft** [sɒft] | weich | **soft** ◄► **hard** |
| | **soft drink** | alkoholfreies Getränk | Everybody at the party was under 16, so they only had ~ **drinks**. |
| | **machine** [mə'ʃiːn] | *hier:* Automat; *auch:* Maschine | a **soda machine** |

| | | | |
|---|---|---|---|
| p. 65/P 14 | (to) **summarize** sth. ['sʌməraɪz] | etwas zusammenfassen | Try and ~ the story in about 50 words. |
| | **summary** ['sʌməri] | Zusammenfassung | |
| | **guide** [gaɪd] | (Fremden-)Führer/in,<br>Reiseleiter/in | |
| p. 65/P 15 | **platform** ['plætfɔːm] | Bahnsteig, Gleis | Which ~ does the train to St. Louis leave from? |

## Angus Bethune's moment

| | | | |
|---|---|---|---|
| p. 66 | **clumsy** ['klʌmzi] | ungeschickt, tollpatschig | You're so ~ – that's the second plate that you've dropped. |
| | (to) **swap** sth. **(for** sth.**)** **(-pp-)** [swɒp] | etwas (ein)tauschen (für etwas / gegen etwas) | Jake **~ped** his old bike **for** a new skateboard. |
| | (to) **elect** sb. sth. [ɪ'lekt] | jn. zu etwas wählen | They **~ed** her leader of the youth club. ! ... **elected her leader** = ... wählten sie **zur** Leiterin |
| | **election** [ɪ'lekʃn] | Wahl *(von Kandidaten bei einer Abstimmung)* | |
| | (to) **fall in love (with** sb.**)** | sich verlieben (in jn.) | My best friend **has fallen in ~ with** my sister. |
| | **dentist** ['dentɪst] | Zahnarzt, -ärztin | |
| | **fat** [fæt] | fett | |
| | **skinny** ['skɪni] | mager | |
| p. 67 | **I'm embarrassed.** [ɪm'bærəst] | Es ist mir peinlich. | |
| | **heaven** ['hevn] | Himmel *(im religiösen Sinn)* | |
| | **actually** ['æktʃuəli] | nebenbei bemerkt; übrigens | I love Katie Melua. She's a great singer! – And she's a good songwriter, ~. |
| | (to) **clap** **(-pp-)** [klæp] | (Beifall) klatschen | |
| p. 68 | **surprising** [sə'praɪzɪŋ] | überraschend, erstaunlich | |

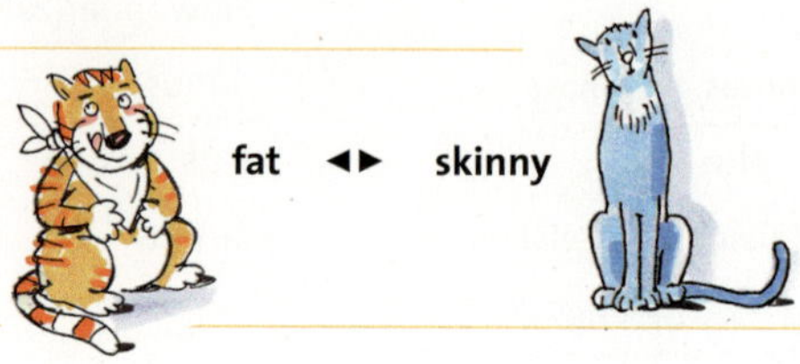


## Unit 4: My life in Atlanta, GA

| | | | |
|---|---|---|---|
| p. 74 | **volunteer** [ˌvɒlən'tɪə] | Freiwillige(r) | **volunteer work** = Arbeit als Freiwillige(r) |
| | **(shopping) mall** ['ʃɒpɪŋ ˌmɔːl] | Einkaufspassage, überdachtes Einkaufszentrum | |
| p. 76/A 1 | **TV listings** *(pl)* ['lɪstɪŋz] | das Fernsehprogramm | |
| | **cable** ['keɪbl] | Kabel *(auch kurz für* Kabelfernsehen) | a piece of **cable**  |
| | **comedy** ['kɒmədi] | Komödie; Comedy | |
| | **documentary** [ˌdɒkju'mentri] | Dokumentarfilm, -beitrag | |
| | **drama** ['drɑːmə] | Fernsehspiel; Drama | |
| | **crime series** ['kraɪm sɪəriːz] | Krimiserie | |
| | **crime** | Kriminalität; Verbrechen | ! *German* **Krimi** = *English* **crime film, crime story** |
| | **reality** [ri'æləti] | Realität, Wirklichkeit | |
| p. 76/A 2 | **programme** ['prəʊgræm] | (Fernseh-)Sendung; Programm | |
| | **channel** ['tʃænl] | (Radio-, Fernseh-)Kanal, (Radio-, Fernseh-)Programm | On which ~ can you watch documentaries? |
| | **viewer** ['vjuːə] | Zuschauer/in | |

| | | | |
|---|---|---|---|
| p.76/A 3 | (to) **be on** | gezeigt werden, laufen *(im Fernsehen / im Kino)* | Please be quiet while the news **is ~**. |
| p.77/A 4 | **anyway** ['eniweɪ] | aber egal; wie auch immer; wie dem auch sei | Sorry, I don't agree with you. **Anyway**, let's talk about something else. |
| | **unbelievable** [ˌʌnbɪ'li:vəbl] | unglaublich | This is ~! (= It's hard to believe.) |
| | **for** two weeks | seit zwei Wochen; zwei Wochen lang | We've lived here **for** five years now. (Wir wohnen jetzt seit fünf Jahren hier.) ! *Nicht:* We ~~live~~ here **for** five years now. |
| | **embarrassing** [ɪm'bærəsɪŋ] | peinlich | |
| | **reporter** [rɪ'pɔ:tə] | Reporter/in |  a **reporter** |
| | **How long ...?** | Seit wann ...? / Wie lange ...? | ~ ~ have Grandma and Grandpa been married? |
| | **explosion** [ɪk'spləʊʒn] | Explosion | ! Betonung: **explosion** [ɪk'spləʊʒn] |
| | **success** [sək'ses] | Erfolg | noun: **success** – adjective: **successful** |
| p.78/A 5 | She **might** be too busy. [maɪt] | Sie könnte zu beschäftigt sein. / Vielleicht ist sie zu beschäftigt. | |

**möglich – wahrscheinlich – sicherlich**

| | | | | |
|---|---|---|---|---|
| My parents | **may** | be at home now. | Meine Eltern | sind jetzt **vielleicht** zu Hause. |
| | **might** | | | **könnten** jetzt **vielleicht** zu Hause sein. |
| | **could** | | | **könnten** jetzt zu Hause sein |
| | **should** | | | **sollten/müssten eigentlich** jetzt zu Hause sein. |
| | **must** | | | **müssen** jetzt zu Hause sein. |

| | | | |
|---|---|---|---|
| p.78/A 6 | **disappointed (about)** [ˌdɪsə'pɔɪntɪd] | enttäuscht (von/über) | I was really ~ that she couldn't come to my party. |
| | **since** 8:30 [sɪns] | seit 8:30 | We've lived here **since** 2003. (Wir wohnen seit 2003 hier.) ! *Nicht:* We ~~live~~ here **since** 2003. |

**German 'seit'**

- **since** mit Zeit**punkt** ● ——► I (wann etwas begonnen hat) — We've been here **since** last Sunday / April / 1998. Wir sind **seit** letztem Sonntag / April / 1998 hier.
- **for** mit Zeit**raum** ⌒ I (wie lange etwas bereits der Fall ist) — We've been here **for** three days / a long time / years. Wir sind **seit** drei Tagen / langem / Jahren hier.

| | | | |
|---|---|---|---|
| | **death** [deθ] | Tod | |
| | **impressed** [ɪm'prest] | beeindruckt | Jo wrote a great essay. His teacher was really ~. |
| p.79/A 7 | **African American** [ˌæfrɪkən‿ə'merɪkən] | Afro-Amerikaner/in; afro-amerikanisch | |
| | **nation** ['neɪʃn] | Nation | |

| | | | |
|---|---|---|---|
| | (to) **judge** sb. **(by)** [dʒʌdʒ] | jn. beurteilen, einschätzen (nach) | Can you ~ people **by** what they wear? |
| | **skin** [skɪn] | Haut | |
| | **but** | sondern | He isn't just good at athletics, ~ at swimming too. |
| | **character** ['kærəktə] | Charakter, Persönlichkeit | ! Betonung: **character** ['kærəktə] |
| | **right** [raɪt] | Recht | ! (to) **be right** = Recht haben, im Recht sein |
| | **speech** [spiːtʃ] | Rede | (to) **make a speech** = eine Rede halten |
| | **research (on)** *(no pl)* [rɪ'sɜːtʃ, 'riːsɜːtʃ] | Recherche; Nachforschung(en) (zu, über) | I have to do some ~ **on** Atlanta for homework. ! (to) **do research** = recherchieren |
| | **holiday** ['hɒlədeɪ] | Feiertag | Christmas Day is a ~ in most countries. |
| p.82/P 3 | (to) **change channels** | umschalten *(Fernsehprogramm)* | |
| | **flat screen** ['flæt skriːn] | Flachbildschirm | |
| | **remote control** [rɪˌməʊt kən'trəʊl] | Fernbedienung | |
| | **satellite** ['sætəlaɪt] | Satellit; Satelliten- | |
| | (to) **receive** [rɪ'siːv] | empfangen | |
| | (to) **turn** sth. **down/up** [tɜːn] | etwas leiser/lauter stellen | Can you ~ **down** that music? It's too loud. |
| | **volume** ['vɒljuːm] | Lautstärke | I can't hear anything. Can you turn up the ~? |
| p.84/P 6 | (to) **draw conclusions** [ˌdrɔː kən'kluːʒnz] | Schlüsse ziehen, schlussfolgern | Don't ~ **conclusions** before you know all the facts. |

## p.87 Melba's story

| | | |
|---|---|---|
| **public** ['pʌblɪk] | öffentlich; Öffentlichkeit | |
| **law** [lɔː] | Gesetz | It's against the ~ to drive a car when you're drunk. |
| (to) **change** [tʃeɪndʒ] | (sich) ändern, (sich) verändern | |

### (to) change – change

| | |
|---|---|
| **(sich) ändern, (sich) verändern** | We had to **change** our holiday plans.<br>The weather was **changing**, so we hurried home. |
| **wechseln** | We **changed** some money at the airport.<br>We were late and didn't have time to **change** clothes.<br>At US schools students **change** rooms for each lesson. |
| **sich umziehen** | I was still wearing my working clothes, so I went upstairs and **changed**. |
| **umsteigen** | Can we go directly to Berlin or do we have to **change** at Hanover? |
| **umschalten** | I check the TV listings before I **change** channels. |
| **(Ver-)Änderung, Wechsel** | It will be a big **change** when you move from London to the country.<br>The **change** from one school to another can be hard for some students. |
| **Wechselgeld; Kleingeld** | Always count your **change**! Shop assistants can make mistakes.<br>Have you got enough **change** for the ticket machine? |

| | | | |
|---|---|---|---|
| p.88 | **president** ['prezɪdənt] | Präsident/in | ! Betonung: **president** ['prezɪdənt] |
| | **soldier** ['səʊldʒə] | Soldat/in | |
| | (to) **protect** [prə'tekt] | schützen | |
| p.89 | (to) **get to know** sb. | jn. kennenlernen | ! • I **got to know** her better during summer camp. (jn. ***im Lauf der Zeit*** kennenlernen)<br>• You don't know him, but you'll **meet** him on Sunday. (jn. ***erstmals*** kennenlernen) |
| | (to) **turn away** | sich abwenden, sich wegdrehen | |
| | (to) **give up** | aufgeben, resignieren | Good footballers never **~ up** – they fight till the last minute. |
| | (to) **return** [rɪ'tɜːn] | zurückkehren | He left the house at 7 and **~ed** 3 hours later.<br>verb: (to) **return** – noun: **return** (= Rückkehr) |
| p.90 | **headline** ['hedlaɪn] | Schlagzeile |   |
| | (to) **come true** [ˌkʌm 'truː] | wahr werden; in Erfüllung gehen | I wanted to become an actor but my dreams didn't **~ true**. |

**Das Dictionary besteht aus zwei alphabetischen Wörterlisten:**

**Englisch – Deutsch** (S. 180–206)
**Deutsch – Englisch** (S. 207–230).

Das **English – German Dictionary** enthält den Wortschatz der Bände 1 bis 3 von *English G 21*.
Wenn du wissen möchtest, was ein Wort bedeutet, wie man es ausspricht oder wie es genau geschrieben wird, kannst du hier nachschlagen.

Im **English – German Dictionary** werden folgende **Abkürzungen** und **Symbole** verwendet:

| | | | |
|---|---|---|---|
| jm. = jemandem | sb. = somebody | *pl* = *plural* (Mehrzahl) | *AE* = *American English* |
| jn. = jemanden | sth. = something | *no pl* = *no plural* | *infml* = *informal* |

° Mit diesem Kringel sind Wörter markiert, die nicht zum Lernwortschatz gehören.
► Der Pfeil verweist auf Kästchen im Vocabulary (S. 164–179), in denen du weitere Informationen zu diesem Wort findest.

Die **Fundstellenangaben** zeigen, wo ein Wort zum ersten Mal vorkommt.
Die Ziffern in Klammern bezeichnen Seitenzahlen:

I = Band 1 • II = Band 2 • III = Band 3 • IV = Band 4
IV Intro (6) = Band 4, Introduction, Seite 6
IV Intro (6/164) = Band 4, Introduction, Seite 164 (im Vocabulary, zu Seite 6)
IV 1 (10) = Band 4, Unit 1, Seite 10
IV 1 (10/165) = Band 4, Unit 1, Seite 165 (im Vocabulary, zu Seite 10)

**Tipps zur Arbeit mit dem Dictionary** findest du im Skills File auf Seite 138.

## A

**a** [ə]
**1.** ein, eine I
**2. once/twice a week** einmal/zweimal pro Woche III • **a bit** ein bisschen, etwas II • **a few** ein paar, einige II • **a little** ein wenig/ein bisschen IV 3 (56/174) **a lot (of)** eine Menge, viel, viele II • **He likes her a lot.** Er mag sie sehr. I
► S. 174 little – less – least
**able** ['eɪbl]: **able to do sth.** etwas tun können; fähig sein / in der Lage sein, etwas zu tun III
**about** [ə'baʊt]
**1.** über I
**2.** ungefähr II
**ask about sth.** nach etwas fragen I • **How about ...?** Wie wär's mit ...? III • **This is about Mr Green.** Es geht um Mr Green. I
**What about ...? 1.** Was ist mit ...? / Und ...? I; **2.** Wie wär's mit ...? I
**What are you talking about?** Wovon redest du? I • **What was the best thing about ...?** Was war das Beste an ...? II
**above** [ə'bʌv] oben; über, oberhalb (von) IV 3 (54)
**accent** ['æksənt] Akzent II
**accident** ['æksɪdənt] Unfall II
**across** [ə'krɒs] (quer) über III
**act** [ækt] aufführen, spielen I
**°Act out ...** Spiele/Spielt ... vor.
**activity** [æk'tɪvəti] Aktivität, Tätigkeit I
**actor** ['æktə] Schauspieler/in II
**actually** ['æktʃuəli] nebenbei bemerkt; übrigens IV 3 (67)
**°adapted** [ə'dæptɪd] adaptiert, bearbeitet
**add (to)** [æd] hinzufügen, ergänzen, addieren (zu) I
**address** [ə'dres] Adresse, Anschrift II
**°admission** [əd'mɪʃn] Eintritt, Eintrittspreis
**adult** ['ædʌlt] Erwachsene(r) III
**advantage** [əd'vɑːntɪdʒ] Vorteil IV 2 (37)
**adventure** [əd'ventʃə] Abenteuer IV Intro (11)
**°advertiser-courier** [ˌædvətaɪzə 'kʊriə] Anzeigenblatt
**advice** *(no pl)* [əd'vaɪs] Rat, Ratschläge III
**afraid** [ə'freɪd]
**1. be afraid (of)** Angst haben (vor) I
**2. I'm afraid** leider II
**African American** [ˌæfrɪkən‿ə'merɪkən] Afro-Amerikaner/in; afroamerikanisch IV 4 (79)
**after** ['ɑːftə] nach *(zeitlich)* I
**°after dark** nach Einbruch der Dunkelheit • **after that** danach I
**after** ['ɑːftə] nachdem II
**afternoon** [ˌɑːftə'nuːn] Nachmittag I • **in the afternoon** nachmittags, am Nachmittag I • **on Friday afternoon** freitagnachmittags, am Freitagnachmittag I
**again** [ə'gen] wieder; noch einmal I
**against** [ə'genst] gegen III
**age** [eɪdʒ]
**1.** Alter III
**°2.** Altersgruppe, Stufe
**ago** [ə'gəʊ]: **a minute ago** vor einer Minute I
**agree (on)** [ə'griː] sich einigen (auf) I • **agree with sb./sth.** jm./etwas zustimmen; mit jm./etwas übereinstimmen II
**airport** ['eəpɔːt] Flughafen III
**°algebra** ['ældʒɪbrə] Algebra
**alive** [ə'laɪv] am Leben, lebendig IV 3 (53)
**all** [ɔːl] alle; alles I • **all day** den ganzen Tag (lang) I • **all over the world** auf der ganzen Welt III
**all right** gut, in Ordnung II • **all the time** die ganze Zeit I • **all the way** den ganzen Weg IV 1 (27)
**from all over the UK/the world/England** aus dem gesamten Vereinigten Königreich/aus der ganzen Welt/aus ganz England III • **This is all wrong.** Das ist ganz falsch. I

**allowed** [ə'laʊd]**: be allowed to do sth.** etwas tun dürfen III
°**almost** ['ɔːlməʊst] fast, beinahe
**alone** [ə'ləʊn] allein I
**along the street** [ə'lɒŋ] entlang der Straße / die Straße entlang II
**alphabet** ['ælfəbet] Alphabet I
°**alphabetical** [ˌælfə'betɪkl] alphabetisch
**already** [ɔːl'redi] schon, bereits II
**also** ['ɔːlsəʊ] auch II
**always** ['ɔːlweɪz] immer I
**am** [ˌeɪ‿'em]**: 7 am** 7 Uhr morgens/vormittags I
**amazing** [ə'meɪzɪŋ] erstaunlich, unglaublich II
**ambulance** ['æmbjələns] Krankenwagen III
**American football** [əˌmerɪkən 'fʊtbɔːl] Football I
°**Americana** [əˌmerɪ'kɑːnə] *Sammelbegriff für alles, was als „typisch amerikanisch" empfunden wird*
**amnesty** ['æmnəsti] Amnestie, Straferlass, Begnadigung IV 2 (38)
**an** [ən] ein, eine I
**and** [ənd, ænd] und I
**angel** ['eɪndʒl] Engel II
**angry (about sth./with sb.)** ['æŋgri] wütend, böse (über etwas/auf jn.) II
**animal** ['ænɪml] Tier II
°**anniversary** [ˌænɪ'vɜːsəri] Jahrestag, Jubiläum, Hochzeitstag
**announcement** [ə'naʊnsmənt] Durchsage, Ansage; Ankündigung, Bekanntgabe III
**anorak** ['ænəræk] Anorak, Windjacke III
**another** [ə'nʌðə] ein(e) andere(r, s); noch ein(e) I • **another 45 p** weitere 45 Pence, noch 45 Pence II
**answer** ['ɑːnsə] antworten; beantworten I
**answer (to)** ['ɑːnsə] Antwort (auf) I
**any** ['eni] irgendein, irgendwelche; jede(r,s) ) IV 1 (27/169) • **any ...?** (irgend)welche ...? I • **not (...) any** kein, keine I • **not (...) any more** nicht mehr III • °**than any other state** als jeder andere Staat
► S.169 any
**anybody** ['enibɒdi] (irgend)jemand II; jede(r) IV 1 (27/169) • **not (...) anybody** niemand II
► S.169 any
**anyone** ['eniwʌn] jede(r) IV 2 (34/170)
► S.169 any
**anything** ['eniθɪŋ] (irgend)etwas II; alles IV 1 (27/169) • **anything else** [els] (irgend)etwas anderes IV 1 (15)
**not (...) anything** nichts II
► S.169 any
► S.167 ... else
**anyway** ['eniweɪ]
**1.** sowieso I
**2.** trotzdem II
**3.** aber egal; wie auch immer; wie dem auch sei IV 4 (77)
**anywhere** ['eniweə] irgendwo(hin) II • **not (...) anywhere** nirgendwo(hin) II
**apartment** [ə'pɑːtmənt] *(AE)* Wohnung IV 1 (26) • °**apartment house** *(AE)* Mehrfamilienhaus; Mietshaus
**appetite** ['æpɪtaɪt] Appetit III
**apple** ['æpl] Apfel I
**appointment** [ə'pɔɪntmənt] Termin, Verabredung I
**April** ['eɪprəl] April I
**are** [ɑː] bist; sind; seid I • **How are you?** Wie geht es dir/Ihnen/euch? II • **The pencils are 35 p.** Die Bleistifte kosten 35 Pence. I • **You're joking, aren't you?** Du machst Witze, nicht wahr? / Das ist nicht dein Ernst, oder? II
**area** ['eəriə] Bereich; Gebiet, Gegend III
**argue** ['ɑːgjuː] sich streiten, sich zanken I
**argument** ['ɑːgjumənt] Streit; Argument IV 2 (50)
**arm** [ɑːm] Arm I
**armchair** ['ɑːmtʃeə] Sessel I
**around** [ə'raʊnd] um ... (herum); in ... umher, durch III • **around six** um sechs herum, gegen sechs III • **around the lake** um den See herum III • **around the town** in der Stadt umher, durch die Stadt III • **run around** herumrennen III
**jump around** herumspringen III
**walk around** herumgehen, umherspazieren III
°**arrest** [ə'rest] verhaften
**arrival (arr)** [ə'raɪvl] Ankunft III
**arrive** [ə'raɪv] ankommen, eintreffen II
**art** [ɑːt] Kunst I
**article** ['ɑːtɪkl] (Zeitungs-)Artikel III
**artificial** [ˌɑːtɪ'fɪʃl] künstlich, Kunst- III
**artist** ['ɑːtɪst] Künstler/in; Grafiker/in III
**as** *(prep)* [əz, æz] als IV 1 (15) • **as a firefighter** als Feuerwehrmann, -frau IV 1 (15)
**as** *(conj)* [əz, æz] als, während II
**as ... as** [əz, æz] so ... wie II • **as old/big as** so alt/groß wie II
**ask (about sth.)** [ɑːsk] fragen (nach etwas) I • **ask questions** Fragen stellen I • **ask sb. for directions** jn. nach dem Weg fragen; jn. um eine Wegbeschreibung bitten IV 1 (14/166) • **ask sb. the way** jn. nach dem Weg fragen II
**asleep** [ə'sliːp]**: be asleep** schlafen I
°**ass** [æs] *(AE, infml)* Arsch
**Assembly** [ə'sembli] Versammlung *(morgendliche Schulversammlung, oft mit Andacht)* III
**at** [ət, æt]**: at 7 Hamilton Street** in der Hamiltonstraße 7 I • **at 8.45** um 8.45 I • **at break** in der Pause *(zwischen Schulstunden)* II • **at first** zuerst, am Anfang IV 3 (57)
**at home** daheim, zu Hause I • **at last** endlich, schließlich I • **at least** zumindest, wenigstens I
**at night** nachts, in der Nacht I
**at school** in der Schule I • **at that table** an dem Tisch (dort) / an den Tisch (dort) I • **at the bottom (of)** unten, am unteren Ende (von) II
**at the butcher's / at the chemist's** beim Metzger/beim Apotheker III
**at the end (of)** am Ende (von) I
**at the Shaws' house** im Haus der Shaws / bei den Shaws zu Hause I • **at the station** am Bahnhof I
**at the top (of)** oben, am oberen Ende, an der Spitze (von) I • **at the weekend** am Wochenende I • **at work** bei der Arbeit / am Arbeitsplatz I
**ate** [et, eɪt] *siehe* **eat**
**athletics** [æθ'letɪks] Leichtathletik III
**attack** [ə'tæk] angreifen III
**attack** [ə'tæk] Angriff III
**attitude (to/towards)** ['ætɪtjuːd] Haltung (gegenüber) Einstellung (zu) IV 2 (37)
**audience** ['ɔːdiəns] Publikum; Zuschauer/innen, Zuhörer/innen II
**August** ['ɔːgəst] August I
**aunt** [ɑːnt] Tante I • **auntie** ['ɑːnti] Tante II
°**auto** ['ɔːtəʊ] *(AE)* Auto, PKW
**autumn** ['ɔːtəm] Herbst I
**avenue** ['ævənjuː] Allee IV 1 (12)
**average** ['ævərɪdʒ] Durchschnitt; durchschnittlich, Durchschnitts- IV 3 (60) • **on average** im Durchschnitt IV 3 (60/175)
► S.173 US school grades
**away** [ə'weɪ] weg, fort I • **turn away** sich abwenden, sich wegdrehen IV 4 (89)
**awesome** *(AE, infml)* ['ɔːsəm] klasse, großartig IV Intro (8)
**awful** ['ɔːfl] furchtbar, schrecklich II

## B

**baby** ['beɪbi] Baby I • **have a baby** ein Baby/Kind bekommen II
**back (to)** [bæk] zurück (nach) I
**back** [bæk]: **back door** Hintertür II
**°in the back** hinten
**background** ['bækgraʊnd] Hintergrund II • **background file** *etwa:* Hintergrundinformation II
**backpack** ['bækpæk] Rucksack IV 1 (20)
**bacon** ['beɪkən] Schinkenspeck II
**bad** [bæd] schlecht, schlimm I
**be bad at sth.** schlecht in etwas sein; etwas schlecht können IV Intro (9) • **do badly (in)** schlecht abschneiden (in) III
**badminton** ['bædmɪntən] Badminton, Federball I • **badminton racket** Badmintonschläger III
**bag** [bæg] Tasche, Beutel, Tüte I
**bagel** ['beɪgl] Bagel (*ringförmiges Gebäck)* IV 1 (16)
**baggy** ['bægi] weit (geschnitten) III
**°bake sale** ['beɪk ˌseɪl] *Verkauf von Backwaren um Geld zu sammeln*
**bakery** ['beɪkəri] Bäckerei III
**ball** [bɔːl]
**1.** Ball *(Sport)* I
**2.** Ball *(Tanzveranstaltung)* IV 3 (66)
**banana** [bəˈnɑːnə] Banane I
**band** [bænd] Band, (Musik-)Gruppe I
**bank** [bæŋk] Bank, Sparkasse I
**bank robber** Bankräuber/in I
**bar** [bɑː] Bar II
**baseball** ['beɪsbɔːl] Baseball I
**baseball cap** Baseballmütze II
**basket** ['bɑːskɪt] Korb I • **a basket of apples** ein Korb Äpfel I
**basketball** ['bɑːskɪtbɔːl] Basketball I
**bat** [bæt]: **table tennis bat** Tischtennisschläger III
**bath** [bɑːθ] Bad, Badewanne II
**have a bath** baden, ein Bad nehmen II
**bathroom** ['bɑːθruːm] Badezimmer I
**be** [biː], **was/were, been** sein I
**be with sb.** mit jemandem zusammen sein IV 3 (66)
**beach** [biːtʃ] Strand II • **on the beach** am Strand II
**bean** [biːn] Bohne IV 3 (56)
**bear** [beə] Bär II
**beard** [bɪəd] Bart IV 1 (27)
**beat** [biːt], **beat, beaten** schlagen; besiegen III
**beaten** ['biːtn] *siehe* **beat**
**beautiful** ['bjuːtɪfl] schön I
**beauty** ['bjuːti] Schönheit III
**became** [bɪ'keɪm] *siehe* **become**
**because** [bɪ'kɒz] weil I
**become** [bɪ'kʌm], **became, become** werden II
**bed** [bed] Bett I • **Bed and Breakfast (B&B)** [ˌbed‿ən 'brekfəst] Frühstückspension (*wörtlich:* Bett und Frühstück) I • **go to bed** ins Bett gehen I
**bedroom** ['bedruːm] Schlafzimmer I
**beef** [biːf] Rindfleisch III
**been** [biːn] *siehe* **be**
**before** [bɪ'fɔː] vor *(zeitlich)* I
**before** [bɪ'fɔː] bevor II
**beg (for) (-gg-)** [beg] betteln (um); eindringlich bitten (um) IV 2 (38)
**began** [bɪ'gæn] *siehe* **begin**
**begin (-nn-)** [bɪ'gɪn], **began, begun** beginnen, anfangen (mit) IV Intro (10)
**beginning** [bɪ'gɪnɪŋ] Beginn, Anfang; Einleitung II
**begun** [bɪ'gʌn] *siehe* **begin**
**behind** [bɪ'haɪnd] hinter II
**believe (in)** [bɪ'liːv] glauben (an) IV 2 (50)
**bell** [bel] Klingel, Glocke III
**The bell rang.** Es klingelte. III
**below** [bɪ'ləʊ] unten; unter, unterhalb (von) IV 3 (54)
**best** [best] am besten II • **the best ...** der/die/das beste ...; die besten ... I • **like sth. best** etwas am meisten mögen III • **Best wishes** *etwa:* Alles Gute / Mit besten Grüßen *(als Briefschluss)* IV 3 (61)
**What was the best thing about ...?** Was war das Beste an ...? II
**bet (-tt-)** [bet], **bet, bet** wetten III
**better** ['betə] besser I • **like sth. better** etwas lieber mögen II
**between** [bɪ'twiːn] zwischen II
**big** [bɪg] groß I • **big wheel** [ˌbɪg 'wiːl] Riesenrad III
**bike** [baɪk] Fahrrad I • **bike ride** (Rad-)Fahrt II • **ride a bike** Rad fahren I
**bill** [bɪl] Rechnung III
**bin** [bɪn] Mülltonne II
**biology** [baɪ'ɒlədʒi] Biologie I
**bird** [bɜːd] Vogel I
**birdcage** ['bɜːdkeɪdʒ] Vogelkäfig III
**birthday** ['bɜːθdeɪ] Geburtstag I
**Happy birthday.** Herzlichen Glückwunsch zum Geburtstag. I • **My birthday is in May.** Ich habe im Mai Geburtstag. I • **My birthday is on 13th June.** Ich habe am 13. Juni Geburtstag. I • **When's your birthday?** Wann hast du Geburtstag? I
**biscuit** ['bɪskɪt] Keks, Plätzchen I
**bit** [bɪt]: **a bit** ein bisschen, etwas II
**°the easy bit** der einfache Teil
**°bitch** [bɪtʃ] *(infml)* Miststück, Schlampe
**black** [blæk] schwarz I
**blame sb. (for)** [bleɪm] jm. die Schuld geben (an); jm. Vorwürfe machen (wegen) III
**bleep** [bliːp] piepsen II
**bleep** [bliːp] Piepton II
**block** [blɒk] (Häuser-, Wohn-)Block IV 1 (14)
**blog** [blɒg] Blog *(Internet-Tagebuch)* IV Intro (8)
**blond** [blɒnd] blond IV 1 (27)
**°blondie** ['blɒndɪ] Blondkopf
**blue** [bluː] blau I
**board** [bɔːd] (Wand-)Tafel I
**on the board** an der/die Tafel I
**notice board** Anschlagtafel, schwarzes Brett I
**boat** [bəʊt] Boot, Schiff I
**°bod** [bɒd] *(infml) Abkürzung für* **body**
**body** ['bɒdi] Körper I • **°student body** Studentenschaft
**book** [bʊk] Buch I
**boot** [buːt] Stiefel I
**border** ['bɔːdə] Grenze IV 2 (35)
**°border patrol** Grenzschutz
**°border guard** Grenzsoldat
**boring** ['bɔːrɪŋ] langweilig I
**born** [bɔːn]: **be born** geboren sein/werden II
**borough** ['bʌrə, *AE:* 'bɜːrəʊ] (Stadt-)Bezirk IV 1 (13)
► S.166 New York: the five boroughs
**boss** [bɒs] Chef/in, Boss III
**both** [bəʊθ] beide I
**bottle** ['bɒtl] Flasche I • **a bottle of milk** eine Flasche Milch I
**bottom** ['bɒtəm] unteres Ende II
**at the bottom (of)** unten, am unteren Ende (von) II
**bought** [bɔːt] *siehe* **buy**
**bowl** [bəʊl] Schüssel I • **a bowl of cornflakes** eine Schale Cornflakes I
**box** [bɒks] Kasten, Kästchen, Kiste I • **sandwich box** Brotdose I
**boy** [bɔɪ] Junge I
**boyfriend** ['bɔɪfrend] (fester) Freund IV 2 (49)
**°bracket** ['brækɪt] Klammer
**brainstorm** ['breɪnstɔːm] brainstormen *(so viele Ideen wie möglich sammeln)* III
**brave** [breɪv] mutig IV 1 (27) • **°as brave as hell** *(infml)* höllisch mutig
**bread** *(no pl)* [bred] Brot I

**break** [breɪk]**, broke, broken**
**1. break a journey** eine Reise unterbrechen III
**°2.** brechen

**break** [breɪk] Pause I • **at break** in der Pause *(zwischen Schulstunden)* II • **take a break** eine Pause machen IV 1 (24)

**breakfast** ['brekfəst] Frühstück I
**have breakfast** frühstücken I

**bridge** [brɪdʒ] Brücke I

**bright** [braɪt] hell, leuchtend II

**brilliant** ['brɪliənt] toll, genial, großartig III

**bring** [brɪŋ]**, brought, brought** (mit-, her)bringen I

**British** ['brɪtɪʃ] britisch; Brite, Britin II

**brochure** ['brəʊʃə] Prospekt, Broschüre II

**broke** [brəʊk] *siehe* **break**

**broken** ['brəʊkən] *siehe* **break**

**broken** *(adj)* ['brəʊkən] gebrochen; zerbrochen, kaputt II

**brother** ['brʌðə] Bruder I

**brought** [brɔːt] *siehe* **bring**

**brown** [braʊn] braun I

**budgie** ['bʌdʒi] Wellensittich I

**build** [bɪld]**, built, built** bauen II

**building** ['bɪldɪŋ] Gebäude II

**built** [bɪlt] *siehe* **build**

°**bulimic** [bu'lɪmɪk] bulimisch, essbrechsüchtig

**bulletin board** ['bʊlətɪn bɔːd] *(AE)* schwarzes Brett, Anschlagtafel IV 3 (54)

**bully** ['bʊli] einschüchtern, tyrannisieren II

**bully** ['bʊli] (Schul-)Tyrann III

**bunk (bed)** [bʌŋk] Etagenbett, Koje II

**burger** ['bɜːgə] Burger IV 2 (36)

°**burn** [bɜːn] brennen; verbrennen

**bus** [bʌs] Bus I • **bus stop** Bushaltestelle III

**business** ['bɪznəs] Geschäft; Handel IV 2 (36) • **Mind your own business.** Das geht dich nichts an! / Kümmere dich um deine eigenen Angelegenheiten! II

**busy** ['bɪzi] belebt, verkehrsreich; hektisch III

**but** [bət, bʌt]
**1.** aber I
**2.** sondern IV 4 (79)

**butcher** ['bʊtʃə] Fleischer/in, Metzger/in III • **at the butcher's** beim Metzger III

**butter** ['bʌtə] Butter III

**button** ['bʌtn] Knopf III

**buy** [baɪ]**, bought, bought** kaufen I

**by** [baɪ]
**1.** von I
**2.** an; (nahe) bei II
**3. by car/train/bike/...** mit dem Auto/Zug/Rad/... II
**4.** bis spätestens, nicht später als III • **by ten o'clock** bis (spätestens) zehn Uhr III
**5. by the way** übrigens II

**Bye.** [baɪ] Tschüs! I

## C

**cab** [kæb] Taxi • **get a cab** ein Taxi nehmen IV 1 (27)

**cabin** ['kæbɪn] Hütte III

**cable** ['keɪbl] Kabel; Kabel- IV 4 (76)
°**cable car** *(USA)* Kabelbahn *(von Drahtseilen gezogene Straßenbahn)*

**café** ['kæfeɪ] *(kleines)* Restaurant, Imbissstube, Café II

**cafeteria** [ˌkæfə'tɪəriə] Cafeteria; *(USA)* Schulmensa IV 3 (54)

**cage** [keɪdʒ] Käfig I

**cake** [keɪk] Kuchen, Torte I

**calendar** ['kælɪndə] Kalender I

**call** [kɔːl] rufen; anrufen; nennen I
**call sb. names** jn. mit Schimpfwörtern hänseln, jm. Schimpfwörter nachrufen III • °**call out** herausrufen

**call** [kɔːl] Anruf, Telefongespräch I

**called** [kɔːld]**: be called** genannt werden, heißen IV 2 (42)

**calm down** [ˌkɑːm 'daʊn] sich beruhigen II

**came** [keɪm] *siehe* **come**

**camel** ['kæml] Kamel II

**camera** ['kæmərə] Kamera, Fotoapparat I

**camp** [kæmp] zelten III

**camp** [kæmp] Camp, (Ferien-)Lager IV 2 (43)

°**campfire** ['kæmpfaɪə] Lagerfeuer

**can** [kən, kæn]
**1.** können I
**2.** dürfen I
**Can I help you?** Kann ich Ihnen helfen?/ Was kann ich für Sie tun? *(im Geschäft)* I

**canal** [kə'næl] Kanal III

**canoe** [kə'nuː] Kanu III

**canoe** [kə'nuː] Kanu fahren III

**canteen** [kæn'tiːn] Kantine, Schulmensa II

**canyon** ['kænjən] Schlucht, Canyon IV Intro (6)

**cap** [kæp] Mütze, Kappe II

**capital** ['kæpɪtl] Hauptstadt III

**captain** ['kæptɪn] Kapitän/in III

°**caption** ['kæpʃn] Bildunterschrift

**car** [kɑː] Auto I • **car park** Parkplatz III

**caravan** ['kærəvæn] Wohnwagen II

**card** [kɑːd] (Spiel-, Post-)Karte I

**care** [keə]**: I don't care.** Es ist mir egal. IV 1 (27)

**career** [kə'rɪə] Karriere III

**careful** ['keəfl]
**1.** vorsichtig II
**2.** sorgfältig II

**caretaker** ['keəteɪkə] Hausmeister/in II

**carrot** ['kærət] Möhre, Karotte I

**cartoon** [kɑː'tuːn] Cartoon (Zeichentrickfilm; Bilderwitz) II

**case** [keɪs] Fall II

**castle** ['kɑːsl] Burg, Schloss II

**cat** [kæt] Katze I

**catch** [kætʃ]**, caught, caught** fangen; erwischen II

**cathedral** [kə'θiːdrəl] Kathedrale, Dom III

**caught** [kɔːt] *siehe* **catch**

**CD** [ˌsiː'diː] CD I • **CD player** CD-Spieler I

**ceilidh** ['keɪli] *Musik- und Tanzveranstaltung, vor allem in Schottland und Irland* III

**cellphone** ['selfəʊn] *(AE)* Handy, Mobiltelefon IV 1 (14)

**Celsius (C)** ['selsiəs] Celsius IV 3 (60)

**cent (c)** [sent] Cent I

**centimetre (cm)** ['sentɪmiːtə] Zentimeter III

**central** ['sentrəl] Zentral-, Mittel- III

**centre** ['sentə] Zentrum, Mitte I
**city centre** Stadtzentrum, Innenstadt I • **sports centre** Sportzentrum I

**century** ['sentʃəri] Jahrhundert II

**cereal** ['sɪəriəl] Getreideflocken, Frühstücksflocken IV 3 (63)

**chair** [tʃeə] Stuhl I

**champion** ['tʃæmpiən] Meister/in, Champion I

**championship** ['tʃæmpiənʃɪp] Meisterschaft III

**change** [tʃeɪndʒ]
**1.** (sich) ändern, (sich) verändern IV 4 (87)
**2.** wechseln IV 4 (82/178)
**3.** umsteigen III
**4.** sich umziehen IV 4 (82/178)
**change channels** umschalten *(Fernsehprogramm)* IV 4 (82)
► S.178 (to) change – change

**change** [tʃeɪndʒ]
**1.** (Ver-)Änderung; Wechsel IV 4 (87/178)
**2.** Wechselgeld I; Kleingeld IV 4 (87/178)
► S.178 (to) change – change

**channel** ['tʃænl] (Radio-, Fernseh-) Kanal, (Radio-, Fernseh-)Programm IV 4 (76) • **change channels** umschalten *(Fernsehprogramm)* IV 4 (82)
**character** ['kærəktə] Charakter, Wesen IV 4 (79)
°**chart** [tʃɑːt] Schaubild, Diagramm, Tabelle
**chat (-tt-)** [tʃæt] plaudern; chatten II
**chat room** ['tʃæt ruːm] Chatroom III
**cheap** [tʃiːp] billig I
**check** [tʃek] (über)prüfen, kontrollieren I
**checkpoint** ['tʃekpɔɪnt] Kontrollpunkt *(hier: zur Selbstüberprüfung)* I
**cheer** [tʃɪə] jubeln, Beifall klatschen II
°**cheerleader** ['tʃɪəliːdə] Cheerleader *(Stimmungsanheizer/innen bei Sportereignissen)*
**cheese** [tʃiːz] Käse I
**chemist** ['kemɪst] Drogerie, Apotheke II • **at the chemist's** beim Apotheker III
**cherry** ['tʃeri] Kirsche II
**chicken** ['tʃɪkɪn] Huhn; (Brat-) Hähnchen I
**child** [tʃaɪld], *pl* **children** ['tʃɪldrən] Kind I
°**chili con carne** [ˌtʃɪli kɒn 'kɑːnɪ] Chili con Carne *(scharfes Gericht aus Fleisch, Chilischoten und anderen Zutaten)*
**chips** *(pl)* [tʃɪps]
**1.** *(BE)* Pommes frites I
**2.** *(AE)* Chips IV 1 (20/168) • **potato chips** *(AE)* Kartoffelchips IV 1 (20/168)
**chocolate** ['tʃɒklət] Schokolade I
°**chocolate milk** Kakao
**choir** ['kwaɪə] Chor I
**choose** [tʃuːz], **chose, chosen** (sich) aussuchen, (aus)wählen I
**chorus** ['kɔːrəs] Refrain III
**chose** [tʃəʊz] *siehe* **choose**
**chosen** ['tʃəʊzn] *siehe* **choose**
**Christmas** ['krɪsməs] Weihnachten I
**church** [tʃɜːtʃ] Kirche I
**cinema** ['sɪnəmə] Kino I • **go to the cinema** ins Kino gehen II
°**circle** ['sɜːkl] Kreis • °**double circle** Doppelkreis, „Kugellager" *(als Kommunikationsform)*
**circus** ['sɜːkəs] (runder) Platz III
**citizen** ['sɪtɪzn] (Staats-)Bürger/in, Staatsangehörige(r) IV 2 (37)
**city** ['sɪti] (Groß-)Stadt I • **city centre** Stadtzentrum, Innenstadt I

°**civil war** [ˌsɪvl 'wɔː] Bürgerkrieg
**clap (-pp-)** [klæp] (Beifall) klatschen IV 3 (67)
**class** [klɑːs]
**1.** (Schul-)Klasse I • **class teacher** Klassenlehrer/in I
**2.** Unterricht; Kurs IV 3 (56)
**classical** ['klæsɪkl] klassisch III
**classmate** ['klɑːsmeɪt] Klassenkamerad/in, Mitschüler/in I
**classroom** ['klɑːsruːm] Klassenzimmer I
**clean** [kliːn] sauber II
**clean** [kliːn] sauber machen, putzen I • **I clean my teeth.** Ich putze mir die Zähne. I
**cleaner** ['kliːnə] Putzfrau, -mann II
**clear** [klɪə] klar, deutlich I
**clever** ['klevə] schlau, klug I
**click on sth.** [klɪk] etwas anklicken II
**climb** [klaɪm] klettern; hinaufklettern (auf) I • **Climb a tree.** Klettere auf einen Baum. I
**clinic** ['klɪnɪk] Klinik II
**clock** [klɒk] (Wand-, Stand-, Turm-) Uhr I
**clone** [kləʊn] Klon III
**close (to)** [kləʊs] nahe (bei, an) IV Intro (8) • **That was close.** Das war knapp. II • °**move closer** näher heranrücken
**close** [kləʊz] schließen, zumachen I
**closed** [kləʊzd] geschlossen II
°**closing phrase** ['kləʊzɪŋ freɪz] Grußformel *(am Briefende)*
**clothes** *(pl)* [kləʊðz, kləʊz] Kleider, Kleidung(sstücke) II
**cloud** [klaʊd] Wolke II
**cloudless** ['klaʊdləs] wolkenlos IV 2 (42)
**cloudy** ['klaʊdi] bewölkt II
**clown** [klaʊn] Clown/in II
**club** [klʌb] Klub; Verein I
**clumsy** ['klʌmzi] ungeschickt, tollpatschig IV 3 (66)
**coach** [kəʊtʃ] Trainer/in III
**coast** [kəʊst] Küste III • **on the coast** an der Küste III
**coffee** ['kɒfi] Kaffee IV 1 (16)
**coffee to go** Kaffee zum Mitnehmen IV 1 (16)
**cola** ['kəʊlə] Cola I
**cold** [kəʊld] kalt I • **be cold** frieren I
**cold** [kəʊld] Kälte IV 2 (48)
**cold** Erkältung II • **have a cold** erkältet sein, eine Erkältung haben II
°**collaps** [kə'læps] zusammenbrechen; einstürzen
**collect** [kə'lekt] sammeln I

**collector** [kə'lektə] Sammler/in II
**colour** ['kʌlə] färben III
**colour** ['kʌlə] Farbe I • **What colour is ...?** Welche Farbe hat ...? I
**colourless** ['kʌlələs] farblos IV 2 (42)
°**combine** [kəm'baɪn] kombinieren, verbinden
**come** [kʌm], **came, come** kommen I • °**come from** kommen/stammen von • **come home** nach Hause kommen I • **come in** hereinkommen I • **Come on. 1.** Na los, komm. II; **2.** Ach komm! / Na hör mal! II • **come true** wahr werden; in Erfüllung gehen IV 4 (90)
**comedy** ['kɒmədi] Komödie; Comedy IV 4 (76)
**comfortable** ['kʌmftəbl] bequem, behaglich, angenehm IV 2 (48)
**Make yourself comfortable.** Machen Sie es sich bequem. / Mach es dir bequem. IV 2 (48)
**comic** ['kɒmɪk] Comic-Heft I
**comment (on, about)** ['kɒment] Kommentar (zu, über) IV Intro (8)
**Commonwealth** ['kɒmənwelθ]**: the Commonwealth** *Gemeinschaft der Länder des ehemaligen Britischen Weltreichs* III
**community** [kə'mjuːnəti]**: community hall** Gemeinschaftshalle, -saal, Gemeindehalle, -saal III
**company** ['kʌmpəni] Firma, Gesellschaft IV 2 (36)
°**compare** [kəm'peə] vergleichen
**comparison** [kəm'pærɪsn] Steigerung; Vergleich II
**competition** [ˌkɒmpə'tɪʃn] Wettbewerb, Wettkampf III
°**complete** [kəm'pliːt] vervollständigen, ergänzen
**computer** [kəm'pjuːtə] Computer I
**concert** ['kɒnsət] Konzert III
**conclusion** [kən'kluːʒn] Schluss(folgerung) IV 4 (84) • **draw conclusions** Schlüsse ziehen, schlussfolgern IV 4 (84)
°**condor** ['kɒndɔː] Kondor
°**content** ['kɒntent] Inhalt; Gehalt
°**the content of sb.'s character** Charakter, Wesen einer Person
°**context** ['kɒntekst]**: from the context** aus dem Zusammenhang, aus dem Kontext
°**continent** ['kɒntɪnənt] Kontinent
**control: remote control** [rɪˌməʊt kən'trəʊl] Fernbedienung IV 4 (82)
**cook** [kʊk] kochen, zubereiten II
**cook** [kʊk] Koch/Köchin III
**cooker** ['kʊkə] Herd I

**cookie** ['kʊkɪ] Keks IV 1 (20)
**cool** [kuːl]
1. kühl II
2. cool I
**copy** ['kɒpi] kopieren; abschreiben II
**copy** ['kɒpi] Kopie II
**corner** ['kɔːnə] Ecke I • **on the corner of Green Street and London Road** Green Street, Ecke London Road II
**cornflakes** ['kɔːnfleɪks] Cornflakes I
**correct** [kə'rekt] berichtigen, korrigieren II
°**correct** [kə'rekt] richtig, korrekt
**cost** [kɒst], **cost, cost** kosten IV 1 (17)
°**cotton** ['kɒtn] Baumwolle
**could** [kəd, kʊd]
1. **he could ...** er konnte ... II
2. **he could ...** er könnte ... IV 4 (78/177)
► S.177 möglich – wahrscheinlich – sicherlich
**count** [kaʊnt] zählen II
**countable** ['kaʊntəbl] zählbar IV 3 (62)
**country** ['kʌntri] Land *(auch als Gegensatz zur Stadt)* II • **in the country** auf dem Land II
**countryside** ['kʌntrisaɪd] Land(schaft), Natur IV 3 (53)
**course** [kɔːs] Kurs, Lehrgang III
**course: of course** [əv 'kɔːs] natürlich, selbstverständlich I
**cousin** ['kʌzn] Cousin, Cousine I
**cover** ['kʌvə]
1. (CD-)Hülle I
°**2. front inside cover** [ˌfrʌnt‿ˌɪnsaɪd 'kʌvə] Umschlaginnenseite
°**cover** ['kʌvə] zudecken, bedecken
**cow** [kaʊ] Kuh II
°**crash into** [kræʃ] zusammenstoßen (mit) / hineinfahren (in)
**cream** [kriːm] Sahne; Creme IV 1 (16/167) • **cream cheese** Frischkäse IV 1 (16)
**crime** [kraɪm] Kriminalität; Verbrechen IV 4 (76) • **crime film** Krimi IV 4 (76/176) • **crime series** Krimiserie IV 4 (76) • **crime story** Krimi IV 4 (76/176)
**crisps** *(pl)* [krɪsps] Kartoffelchips I
**crocodile** ['krɒkədaɪl] Krokodil II
**cross** [krɒs] überqueren II
**cross** [krɒs]: **be cross (with)** böse, sauer sein (auf) I
**crowd** [kraʊd] (Menschen-)Menge, Masse; *(infml auch:)* Clique, Gruppe IV 1 (26)
°**crown** [kraʊn] Krone
**cry** [kraɪ] weinen IV 1 (26)
**culture** ['kʌltʃə] Kultur IV 2 (37)

**cup** [kʌp]
1. Tasse III • **a cup of tea** eine Tasse Tee III
2. Pokal III
**cupboard** ['kʌbəd] Schrank I
**curry** ['kʌri] Curry(gericht) III
°**curtain** ['kɜːtn] Vorhang
**customer** ['kʌstəmə] Kunde, Kundin II
**cut (-tt-)** [kʌt], **cut, cut** schneiden III • **cut sth. off** etwas abtrennen, abschneiden III • **cut the grass** Rasen mähen IV Intro (9)
°**cut** [kʌt] Schnitt
**cycle** ['saɪkl] (mit dem) Rad fahren II • **cycle path** Radweg II

# D

**dad** [dæd] Papa, Vati; Vater I
°**damage** ['dæmɪdʒ] Schaden
**dance** [dɑːns] tanzen I
**dance** [dɑːns] Tanz I • **dance floor** Dancefloor, Tanzfläche IV 3 (66)
**dancer** ['dɑːnsə] Tänzer/in II
**dancing** ['dɑːnsɪŋ] Tanzen I
**dancing lessons** Tanzstunden, Tanzunterricht I
**danger** ['deɪndʒə] Gefahr III
**dangerous** ['deɪndʒərəs] gefährlich II
**dark** [dɑːk] dunkel I
°**dark** [dɑːk]: °**after dark** nach Einbruch der Dunkelheit
**date** [deɪt] Datum I
**daughter** ['dɔːtə] Tochter I
**day** [deɪ] Tag I • **one day** eines Tages I • **days of the week** Wochentage I • °**day out** Tagesausflug • **day trip** Tagesausflug IV Intro (8) • **one-day ticket** Tageskarte III
**dead** [ded] tot I
°**deal** [diːl] Angebot
**dear** [dɪə] Schatz, Liebling I • **Oh dear!** Oje! II
**dear** [dɪə]: **Dear Jay ...** Lieber Jay, ... I
°**Dear Sir or Madam** [sɜː; 'mædəm] Sehr geehrte Damen und Herren
**death** [deθ] Tod IV 4 (78)
°**debate** [dɪ'beɪt] debattieren
**December** [dɪ'sembə] Dezember I
°**decide (on)** [dɪ'saɪd] sich entscheiden (für), beschließen
°**deep** [diːp] tief
**deer**, *pl* **deer** [dɪə] Reh, Hirsch II
**degree** [dɪ'griː] Grad II
**deli** ['deli] *Lebensmittelgeschäft mit Fastfoodrestaurant* IV 1 (13)
**delicious** [dɪ'lɪʃəs] köstlich, lecker II
**dentist** ['dentɪst] Zahnarzt, -ärztin IV 3 (66)

**department store** [dɪ'pɑːtmənt stɔː] Kaufhaus II
**departure (dep)** [dɪ'pɑːtʃə] Abfahrt, Abflug; Abreise III
**describe sth. (to sb.)** [dɪ'skraɪb] (jm.) etwas beschreiben II
**description** [dɪ'skrɪpʃn] Beschreibung II
°**desert** ['dezət] Wüste
**design** [dɪ'zaɪn] entwerfen, gestalten II
**desk** [desk] Schreibtisch I
**detail** ['diːteɪl] Detail, Einzelheit II
°**detailed** ['diːteɪld] genau, ausführlich
**detective** [dɪ'tektɪv] Detektiv/in I
**dialogue** ['daɪəlɒg] Dialog III
**diary** ['daɪəri] Tagebuch; Terminkalender I
**dice**, *pl* **dice** [daɪs] Würfel II
**dictionary** ['dɪkʃənri] Wörterbuch, *(alphabetisches)* Wörterverzeichnis I
**did** [dɪd] *siehe* **do** • **Did you go ...?** Bist du ... gegangen? / Seid ihr ... gegangen? I • **we didn't sing** ['dɪdnt] wir sangen nicht / wir haben nicht gesungen I
**die (of)** *(-ing form:* **dying***)* [daɪ] sterben (an) II
**difference** ['dɪfrəns] Unterschied IV 1 (15)
**different (from)** ['dɪfrənt] verschieden, unterschiedlich; anders (als) I
**difficult** ['dɪfɪkəlt] schwierig, schwer I
**dining room** ['daɪnɪŋ ruːm] Esszimmer I
**dinner** ['dɪnə] Abendessen, Abendbrot I • **have dinner** Abendbrot essen I
**directions** *(pl)* [də'rekʃnz] Wegbeschreibung IV 1 (14) • **ask sb. for directions** jn. nach dem Weg fragen; jn. um eine Wegbeschreibung bitten IV 1 (14/166)
°**director** [də'rektə]: **film director** Regisseur/in
**dirty** ['dɜːti] schmutzig II
**disabled** [dɪs'eɪbld] (körper)behindert III
**disadvantage** [ˌdɪsəd'vɑːntɪdʒ] Nachteil IV 2 (37/171)
°**disagree** [ˌdɪsə'griː] nicht zustimmen; anderer Meinung sein
**disappear** [ˌdɪsə'pɪə] verschwinden II
**disappointed (about)** [ˌdɪsə'pɔɪntɪd] enttäuscht (von/über) IV 4 (78)
**disc jockey (DJ)** ['dɪsk dʒɒki] Diskjockey III
**disco** ['dɪskəʊ] Disko I

**discover** [dɪ'skʌvə] entdecken IV 2 (39)
°**discovery** [dɪ'skʌvəri] Entdeckung
°**discuss** [dɪ'skʌs] besprechen; diskutieren (über)
**discussion** [dɪ'skʌʃn] Diskussion II
**dish** [dɪʃ] Gericht *(Speise)* III
**dishwasher** ['dɪʃwɒʃə] Geschirrspülmaschine I
°**display: °on display** [dɪ'spleɪ] ausgestellt sein, gezeigt werden
°**divide (into)** [dɪ'vaɪd] auf-, einteilen (in)
**divorced** [dɪ'vɔːst] geschieden I
**DJ** ['diː dʒeɪ] (Musik/CDs/Platten) auflegen *(in der Disko)* III
**DJ** ['diː dʒeɪ] Diskjockey III
**do** [duː], **did, done** tun, machen I **Do you like ...?** Magst du ...? I **do a gig** einen Auftritt haben, ein Konzert geben III • **do a good job** gute Arbeit leisten II • **do a project** ein Projekt machen, durchführen II • **do an exercise** eine Übung machen II • **do badly/well (in)** schlecht/gut abschneiden (in) III • °**do songs** Lieder singen/spielen • **do sport** Sport treiben I
**doctor** ['dɒktə] Doktor; Arzt/Ärztin II • **to the doctor's** zum Arzt III
**documentary** [ˌdɒkju'mentri] Dokumentation, Dokumentarfilm IV 4 (76)
**dog** [dɒg] Hund I
**dollar ($)** ['dɒlə] Dollar IV 1 (17)
**done** [dʌn] *siehe* **do** • °**Well done!** [ˌwel 'dʌn] Gut gemacht!
**don't** [dəʊnt]**: Don't listen to Dan.** Hör/Hört nicht auf Dan. I • **I don't know.** Ich weiß es nicht. I • **I don't like ...** Ich mag ... nicht. / Ich mag kein(e) ... I
**door** [dɔː] Tür I
**doorbell** ['dɔːbel] Türklingel I
**dossier** ['dɒsieɪ] Mappe, Dossier *(des Sprachenportfolios)* I
**double** ['dʌbl] zweimal, doppelt, Doppel- I • °**double circle** ['sɜːkl] Doppelkreis, „Kugellager" *(als Gesprächskreis)*
**down** [daʊn] hinunter, herunter, nach unten I • **down there** dort unten II • **fall down** hinfallen II
**download** [ˌdaʊn'ləʊd] runterladen, downloaden III
**downloadable** [ˌdaʊn'ləʊdəbl] herunterladbar, zum Herunterladen IV 4 (85)
**downstairs** [ˌdaʊn'steəz] unten; nach unten I
**downtown** [ˌdaʊn'taʊn] (im/in das) Stadtzentrum IV 1 (14)
**drama** ['drɑːmə]
**1.** Schauspiel, darstellende Kunst I
°**drama group** Theatergruppe
**2.** Spielfilm *(im Fernsehen)* IV 4 (76)
**drank** [dræŋk] *siehe* **drink**
**draw** [drɔː], **drew, drawn**
**1.** zeichnen III
**2. draw conclusions** Schlüsse ziehen, schlussfolgern IV 4 (84)
**drawing** ['drɔːɪŋ] Zeichnung III
**drawn** [drɔːn] *siehe* **draw**
**dream** [driːm] Traum I • **dream house** Traumhaus I
**dream (of, about)** [driːm] träumen (von) IV Intro (10)
**dress** [dres] Kleid I
**dress code** ['dres kəʊd] Kleiderordnung, Bekleidungsvorschrift III
**dressed** [drest]**: get dressed** sich anziehen I
**drew** [druː] *siehe* **draw**
**drink** [drɪŋk] Getränk I
**drink** [drɪŋk], **drank, drunk** trinken I
**drive** [draɪv] Fahrt III
**drive** [draɪv], **drove, driven** *(ein Auto / mit dem Auto)* fahren II
**driven** ['drɪvn] *siehe* **drive**
**driver** ['draɪvə] Fahrer/in II
**drop (-pp-)** [drɒp]
**1.** fallen lassen I
°**2.** sich fallen lassen
**drove** [drəʊv] *siehe* **drive**
**drug** [drʌg] Droge, Rauschgift; Medikament • **be on drugs** Drogen, Rauschgift / Medikamente nehmen IV 1 (26)
**drum** [drʌm] Trommel III
**drums** *(pl)* [drʌmz] Schlagzeug III **play the drums** Schlagzeug spielen III
**drunk** [drʌŋk] *siehe* **drink**
**drunk** [drʌŋk] betrunken IV 2 (49)
°**dumb** [dʌm] dumm
**during** ['djuːrɪŋ] während IV 2 (39)
**dustbin** ['dʌstbɪn] Mülltonne II
**DVD** [ˌdiː viː' diː] DVD I

## E

**each** [iːtʃ] jeder, jede, jedes (einzelne) I
**each other** [iːtʃ_'ʌðə] einander, sich (gegenseitig) III
**ear** [ɪə] Ohr I
**earache** ['ɪəreɪk] Ohrenschmerzen II
**early** ['ɜːli] früh I
**earn** [ɜːn] verdienen IV 1 (26)
**earring** ['ɪərɪŋ] Ohrring I
**earth** [ɜːθ] Erde IV 2 (34/170)
**earthquake** ['ɜːθkweɪk] Erdbeben IV 2 (34)
**east** [iːst] Osten; nach Osten; östlich III
**Easter** ['iːstə] Ostern IV 3 (54)
**easy** ['iːzi] leicht, einfach I
**eat** [iːt], **ate, eaten** essen I
**eaten** ['iːtn] *siehe* **eat**
**editor** ['edɪtə] Redakteur/in III
°**letter to the editor** Leserbrief
**egg** [eg] Ei II
**elect sb. sth.** [ɪ'lekt] jn. zu etwas wählen IV 3 (66)
**election** [ɪ'lekʃn] Wahl *(von Kandidaten bei einer Abstimmung)* IV 3 (66/176)
**electric** [ɪ'lektrɪk] elektrisch, Elektro- III
**electronic** [ɪˌlek'trɒnɪk] elektronisch III
**elementary school** [ˌelɪ'mentri skuːl] *(USA) Grundschule für 6- bis 11-Jährige* IV 3 (54)
**elephant** ['elɪfənt] Elefant I
**elevator** ['elɪveɪtə] *(AE)* Fahrstuhl, Aufzug II
**else** [els]**: anything else** (irgend-) etwas anderes IV 1 (15) • **somebody else** jemand anders IV 1 (15/167) • **What else?** Was (sonst) noch? IV 1 (15/167)
► S.167 ... else
**e-mail** ['iːmeɪl] E-Mail I
**embarrassed** [ɪm'bærəst]**: I'm embarrassed.** Das ist mir peinlich. IV 3 (66)
**embarrassing** [ɪm'bærəsɪŋ] peinlich IV 4 (77)
**empty** ['empti] leer I
°**encyclopedia** [ɪnˌsaɪklə'piːdiə] Enzyklopädie, Lexikon
**end** [end] Ende, Schluss I • **at the end (of)** am Ende (von) I • **in the end** schließlich, zum Schluss III
**end** [end] (be)enden, zu Ende gehen IV 1 (26) • °**end up** enden
**ending** ['endɪŋ] Ende, (Ab-)Schluss *(einer Geschichte, eines Films usw.)* III
**endless** ['endləs] endlos IV 2 (43)
**enemy** ['enəmi] Feind/in II
**engine** ['endʒɪn] Motor IV 2 (48)
°**search engine** Suchmaschine *(im Internet)*
**engineer** [ˌendʒɪ'nɪə] Ingenieur/in II
**English** ['ɪŋglɪʃ] Englisch; englisch I
**enjoy** [ɪn'dʒɔɪ] genießen II • **Enjoy yourself.** Viel Spaß! / Amüsier dich gut! III

**enough** [ɪ'nʌf] genug I
**°Enough's enough.** Jetzt reicht es!
**enter** ['entə] betreten; eintreten (in) III
**°entertainment** [ˌentə'teɪnmənt] Unterhaltung
**°entry** ['entri] Eintrag, Eintragung *(im Wörterbuch, Tagebuch)*
**eraser** [ɪ'reɪsər] *(AE)* Radiergummi IV 1 (20)
**escape (from sb./sth.)** [ɪ'skeɪp] fliehen (vor jm./aus etwas); entkommen III
**essay (about, on)** ['eseɪ] Aufsatz (über) I
**°etc.** [et'setərə] usw.
**euro (€)** ['jʊərəʊ] Euro I
**even** ['i:vn] sogar II
**evening** ['i:vnɪŋ] Abend I • **in the evening** abends, am Abend I
**on Friday evening** freitagabends, am Freitagabend I
**event** [ɪ'vent] Ereignis; Veranstaltung IV 3 (53)
**ever?** ['evə] je? / jemals? / schon mal? II
**every** ['evri] jeder, jede, jedes I
**everybody** ['evribɒdi] jeder, alle II
**everyday** *(adj)* ['evrideɪ] Alltags-; alltägliche(r, s) III
**everyone** ['evriwʌn] jeder, alle IV 2 (34)
**everything** ['evriθɪŋ] alles I
**exactly** [ɪg'zæktli] genau III
**example** [ɪg'zɑ:mpl] Beispiel IV 2 (42)
**for example** zum Beispiel IV 2 (42)
**excellent** ['eksələnt] ausgezeichnet, hervorragend IV 3 (54)
► S.173 US school grades
**°except** [ɪk'sept] außer, bis auf
**exchange student** [ɪks'tʃeɪndʒ ˌstju:dnt] Austauschschüler/in III
**excited** [ɪk'saɪtɪd] begeistert, aufgeregt III
**exciting** [ɪk'saɪtɪŋ] aufregend, spannend I
**Excuse me, ...** [ɪk'skju:z mi:] Entschuldigung, ... / Entschuldigen Sie, ... I
**exercise** ['eksəsaɪz]
**1.** Übung, Aufgabe I
**2.** *(no pl)* (körperliche) Bewegung, Training IV 3 (56)
**exercise book** ['eksəsaɪz bʊk] Schulheft, Übungsheft I
**°exist** [ɪg'zɪst] existieren
**expect** [ɪk'spekt] erwarten III
**expensive** [ɪk'spensɪv] teuer I
**explain sth. to sb.** [ɪk'spleɪn] jm. etwas erklären, erläutern II
**explanation** [ˌeksplə'neɪʃn] Erklärung II
**°explode** [ɪks'pləʊd] explodieren
**explore** [ɪk'splɔ:] erkunden, erforschen I
**explorer** [ɪk'splɔ:rə] Entdecker/in, Forscher/in II
**explosion** [ɪk'spləʊʒn] Explosion IV 4 (77)
**extra** ['ekstrə] zusätzlich I
**extracurricular activities** (*kurz:* **extracurriculars)** [ˌekstrəkə'rɪkjələz] *schulische Angebote außerhalb des regulären Unterrichts, oft als Arbeitsgemeinschaften* IV 3 (54)
**°extraordinaire** [ɪkˌstrɔ:dɪ'neə] unvergleichlich
**eye** [aɪ] Auge I

## F

**face** [feɪs] Gesicht I
**fact** [fækt] Tatsache, Fakt III
**factory** ['fæktri] Fabrik II
**failure** *(n)* ['feɪljə] ungenügend *(USA, Schulnote)* IV 3 (54)
► S.173 US school grades
**fair** [feə] fair, gerecht II
**°faithfully** ['feɪθfəli]: **°Yours faithfully** Mit freundlichen Grüßen *(freundliche, aber formelle Grußformel in Briefen)*
**fall** [fɔ:l], **fell, fallen** fallen, stürzen; hinfallen II • **fall down** hinfallen II • **°fall for sb.** sich in jd. verknallen • **fall in love (with sb.)** sich verlieben (in jn.) IV 3 (66) • **fall off** herunterfallen (von) II
**fallen** ['fɔ:lən] *siehe* **fall**
**false** [fɔ:ls] falsch IV 1 (28)
**family** ['fæməli] Familie I • **family tree** (Familien-)Stammbaum I
**famous (for)** ['feɪməs] berühmt (für, wegen) II
**fan** [fæn] Fan I
**fantastic** [fæn'tæstɪk] fantastisch, toll I
**far** [fɑ:] weit (entfernt) II • **°so far** bis jetzt, bisher
**farm** [fɑ:m] Bauernhof, Farm II
**farmer** ['fɑ:mə] Landwirt/in, Bauer/Bäuerin IV 2 (36)
**farmhouse** ['fɑ:mhaʊs] Farmhaus, Bauernhaus IV 3 (53)
**farming** ['fɑ:mɪŋ] Landwirtschaft IV 2 (36)
**fashion** ['fæʃn] Mode II
**fast** [fɑ:st] schnell II • **fast food** [ˌfɑ:st 'fu:d] Fastfood III
**fat** [fæt] fett IV (66)
**father** ['fɑ:ðə] Vater I
**fault** [fɔ:lt]: **It's not my fault.** Es ist nicht meine Schuld. III
**favourite** ['feɪvərɪt] Lieblings- I
**my favourite colour** meine Lieblingsfarbe I
**February** ['februəri] Februar I
**fed** [fed] *siehe* **feed** • **be fed up (with sth.)** [ˌfed_'ʌp] die Nase voll haben (von etwas) II
**feed** [fi:d], **fed, fed** füttern I
**feel** [fi:l], **felt, felt** sich fühlen; fühlen; sich anfühlen II • **I feel sick.** Mir ist schlecht. IV 1 (26)
**°feeling** ['fi:lɪŋ] Gefühl
**feet** [fi:t] *Plural von „foot"* I
**fell** [fel] *siehe* **fall**
**felt** [felt] *siehe* **feel**
**felt tip** ['felt tɪp] Filzstift I
**female** ['fi:meɪl] weiblich III
**ferry** ['feri] Fähre III
**festival** ['festɪvl] Fest, Festival, Festspiele III
**few** [fju:]: **a few** ein paar, einige II
**fiddle** ['fɪdl] *(infml)* Fiedel, Geige III
**play the fiddle** Geige, Fiedel spielen III
**field** [fi:ld] Feld, Acker, Weide II
**in the field** auf dem Feld II
**fight** [faɪt], **fought, fought** kämpfen III • **fight for** kämpfen (für, um) III
**°fight sth.** etwas bekämpfen
**fight** [faɪt] Kampf; Schlägerei IV 2 (49)
**file** [faɪl]: **background file** *etwa:* Hintergrundinformation(en) II
**grammar file** *Grammatikanhang* I • **skills file** *Anhang mit Lern- und Arbeitstechniken* I • **sound file** Tondatei, Soundfile III
**°fill in** [ˌfɪl_'ɪn]
**1.** einsetzen
**2.** ausfüllen
**film** [fɪlm] Film I • **°film director** Regisseur/in • **film star** Filmstar I
**final** ['faɪnl] Finale, Endspiel III
**final** ['faɪnl] letzte(r, s); End- III
**final score** Endstand *(beim Sport)* III
**find** [faɪnd], **found, found** finden I • **find out (about)** herausfinden (über) I
**finder** ['faɪndə] Finder I
**fine** [faɪn]
**1.** gut, schön; in Ordnung II
**2.** *(gesundheitlich)* gut II
**I'm/He's fine.** Es geht mir/ihm gut. II
**finger** ['fɪŋgə] Finger I
**finish** ['fɪnɪʃ] beenden, zu Ende machen; enden I
**fire** ['faɪə] Feuer, Brand II • **fire safety** Verhalten im Brandfall IV 1 (25) • **fire station** Feuerwache

IV 1 (15) • **put out a fire** ein Feuer löschen IV 1 (15)
**firefighter** ['faɪəfaɪtə] Feuerwehrfrau, -mann IV 1 (15)
**fireman** ['faɪəmən] Feuerwehrmann II
**firewoman** ['faɪə,wʊmən] Feuerwehrfrau II
**first** [fɜːst]
**1.** erste(r, s) I
**2.** zuerst, als Erstes I
**be first** der/die Erste sein I • **the first half** die erste Halbzeit III
**fish** [fɪʃ] fischen, angeln III
**fish**, *pl* **fish** [fɪʃ] Fisch I
**fit (-tt-)** [fɪt] passen I
**fit** [fɪt]: **be fit** fit sein III
**fitness** ['fɪtnəs] Fitness IV 3 (56)
**fitness centre** Fitnesscenter IV 4 (83)
**flash** [flæʃ] Lichtblitz III
**flat** [flæt] Wohnung I
**flat screen** ['flæt skriːn] Flachbildschirm IV 4 (82)
**flew** [fluː] *siehe* **fly**
**flight** [flaɪt] Flug II • **a 14-hour flight** ein 14-stündiger Flug, ein 14-Stunden-Flug III
**floor** [flɔː]
**1.** Fußboden I
**2.** Stockwerk IV 1 (17)
°**flow chart** ['fləʊ tʃɑːt] Flussdiagramm
**flown** [fləʊn] *siehe* **fly**
**flute** [fluːt] Querflöte III
**fly** [flaɪ], **flew, flown** fliegen II
**fog** [fɒg] Nebel II
**foggy** ['fɒgi] neblig II
**folk music** ['fəʊk ˌmjuːzɪk] Folk *(englische, schottische, irische oder nordamerikanische Volksmusik des 20. Jahrhunderts)* III
**follow** ['fɒləʊ] folgen; verfolgen I
°**the following ...** die folgenden ...
**food** [fuːd]
**1.** Essen; Lebensmittel I
**2.** Futter I
**foot** [fʊt], *pl* **feet** [fiːt]
**1.** Fuß I
**2.** Fuß *(Längenmaß; 30,48 cm)* IV Intro (10)
**football** ['fʊtbɔːl] Fußball I
**football boots** Fußballschuhe, -stiefel I
**for** [fə, fɔː] für I • **for breakfast/lunch/dinner** zum Frühstück/Mittagessen/Abendbrot I • **for example** zum Beispiel IV 2 (42)
**for lots of reasons** aus vielen Gründen I • **for miles** meilenweit II • **for three days** drei Tage (lang) I • **for 20 minutes** seit 20 Minuten; 20 Minuten lang IV 4 (77)
**just for fun** nur zum Spaß I
**What for?** Wofür? II • **What's for homework?** Was haben wir als Hausaufgabe auf? I
► S.186 German 'seit'
°**force** [fɔːs] zwingen
**foreground** ['fɔːgraʊnd] Vordergrund II
°**foreign** ['fɒrən] ausländisch, fremd
°**foreign language** Fremdsprache
**forest** ['fɒrɪst] Wald II
**forgave** [fə'geɪv] *siehe* **forgive**
**forget (-tt-)** [fə'get], **forgot, forgotten** vergessen I
**forgive** [fə'gɪv], **forgave, forgiven** vergeben, verzeihen IV Intro (10)
**forgiven** [fə'gɪvn] *siehe* **forgive**
**forgot** [fə'gɒt] *siehe* **forget**
**forgotten** [fə'gɒtn] *siehe* **forget**
**fork** [fɔːk] Gabel III
**form** [fɔːm]
**1.** (Schul-)Klasse I • **form teacher** Klassenlehrer/in I
°**2.** Form
°**form** [fɔːm] bilden
°**formal letter** ['fɔːml] förmlicher Brief
°**forty-niners** *Goldsucher/innen, die 1849 wegen des Goldrausches nach Kalifornien kamen*
**fought** [fɔːt] *siehe* **fight**
**found** [faʊnd] *siehe* **find**
**found** [faʊnd] gründen IV 3 (52)
**fox** [fɒks] Fuchs II
**free** [friː]
**1.** frei I • **free time** Freizeit, freie Zeit I
**2.** kostenlos I
**French** [frentʃ] Französisch I
**French fries** *(AE)* Pommes Frites IV 1 (20)
**Friday** ['fraɪdeɪ, 'fraɪdi] Freitag I
**fridge** [frɪdʒ] Kühlschrank I
**friend** [frend] Freund/in I • °**to be friends with sb.** mit jm. befreundet sein
**friendly** ['frendli] freundlich III
**frog** [frɒg] Frosch II
**from** [frəm, frɒm]
**1.** aus I
**2.** von I
**from all over the UK/the world/England** aus dem gesamten Vereinigten Königreich / aus der ganzen Welt / aus ganz England III
**from Monday to Friday** von Montag bis Freitag III • **I'm from ...** Ich komme aus ... / Ich bin aus ... I
**Where are you from?** Wo kommst du her? I
**front** [frʌnt]: **in front of** vor *(räumlich)* I • **front door** [ˌfrʌnt 'dɔː] Wohnungstür, Haustür I • °**front page** [ˌfrʌnt 'peɪdʒ] Titelseite
°**front inside cover** [ˌfrʌnt‿ˌɪnsaɪd 'kʌvə] vordere Umschlaginnenseite
**fruit** [fruːt] Obst, Früchte; Frucht I
**fruit salad** ['fruːt ˌsæləd] Obstsalat I
**full** [fʊl] voll I
**fun** [fʌn] Spaß I • **have fun** Spaß haben, sich amüsieren I • **Have fun!** Viel Spaß! I • **just for fun** nur zum Spaß I • **Riding is fun.** Reiten macht Spaß. I
**funny** ['fʌni] witzig, komisch I

## G

°**gallery walk** ['gæləri wɔːk] Galerierundgang
**game** [geɪm] Spiel I
°**gap** [gæp] Lücke
**garage** ['gærɑːʒ] *(AE)* Garage II
**garbage** ['gɑːrbɪdʒ] Müll, Abfall IV 1 (20)
**garden** ['gɑːdn] Garten I
**gate** [geɪt] Flugsteig III
°**gateway (to)** ['geɪtweɪ] Tor zu, Zugang zu
**gave** [geɪv] *siehe* **give**
**general** ['dʒenrəl] allgemeine(r, s) III • **in general** im allgemeinen IV 3 (56)
**geography** [dʒi'ɒgrəfi] Geografie, Erdkunde I
**German** ['dʒɜːmən] Deutsch; deutsch; Deutsche(r) I
**Germany** ['dʒɜːməni] Deutschland I
**get (-tt-)** [get], **got, got**
**1.** bekommen, kriegen II
**2.** holen, besorgen II
**3.** gelangen, (hin)kommen I
**4. get angry/hot/...** wütend/heiß/... werden II
**5. get off (the train/bus)** (aus dem Zug/Bus) aussteigen I • **get on (the train/bus)** (in den Zug/Bus) einsteigen I
**6. get up** aufstehen I
**get a cab** ein Taxi nehmen IV 1 (27)
**get dressed** sich anziehen I • **get married (to sb.)** (jn.) heiraten IV 2 (38) • **get ready (for)** sich fertig machen (für), sich vorbereiten (auf) I • **get things ready** Dinge fertig machen, vorbereiten I • **get to know sb.** jn. kennenlernen IV 4 (89)

**getting by in English** [ˌgetɪŋ ˈbaɪ] *etwa:* auf Englisch zurechtkommen I
**ghost** [gəʊst] Geist, Gespenst II
°**giant** [ˈdʒaɪənt] riesig, Riesen-
**gig** [gɪg] *(infml)* Gig, Auftritt III
**do a gig** einen Auftritt haben, ein Konzert geben III
**giraffe** [dʒəˈrɑːf] Giraffe II
**girl** [gɜːl] Mädchen I
**girlfriend** [ˈgɜːlfrend] (feste) Freundin IV 2 (49/172)
**give** [gɪv], **gave, given** geben I
**give up** aufgeben, resignieren IV 4 (89) • °**give up a seat** [siːt] einen Sitzplatz freimachen
**given** [ˈgɪvn] *siehe* **give**
**glad** [glæd] froh, dankbar III
**glass** [glɑːs] Glas I • **a glass of water** ein Glas Wasser I
**glasses** *(pl)* [ˈglɑːsɪz] (eine) Brille I
**glue** [gluː] (auf-, ein)kleben II
**glue** [gluː] Klebstoff I • **glue stick** [ˈgluː stɪk] Klebestift I
**go** [gəʊ], **went, gone** gehen I; fahren II • **go by car/train/bike/...** mit dem Auto/Zug/Rad/... fahren II • **go for a walk** spazieren gehen, einen Spaziergang machen II • **go home** nach Hause gehen I • **go on** weitermachen I • °**How does the story go on?** Wie geht die Geschichte weiter? • **go on a trip** einen Ausflug machen II • **go on holiday** in Urlaub fahren II • **go riding** reiten gehen I • **go shopping** einkaufen gehen I • **go surfing** wellenreiten gehen, surfen gehen II • **go swimming** schwimmen gehen I • **go to bed** ins Bett gehen I • **go to the cinema** ins Kino gehen II • **go together** zusammenpassen, -gehören II • **go well** gut (ver)laufen, gutgehen III
**go with** gehören zu, passen zu III
**coffee to go** Kaffee zum Mitnehmen IV 1 (16) • **Let's go.** Auf geht's! (*wörtlich:* Lass uns gehen.) I
**goal** [gəʊl] Tor *(im Sport)* III
**goalkeeper** [ˈgəʊlkiːpə] Torwart, Torfrau III
**God** [gɒd] Gott IV 1 (27)
°**going west** *Besiedlung des Westens der USA im 19. Jahrhundert*
**go-kart** [ˈgəʊkɑːt] Gokart III
**gold** [gəʊld] Gold IV 2 (34/170)
**golden** [ˈgəʊldən] goldene(r,s) IV 2 (34)
°**gold rush** [ˈgəʊld rʌʃ] Goldrausch
**gone** [gɒn] *siehe* **go**
°**gonna** [ˈgɒnə] *(infml)* (= going to)

**good** [gʊd]
**1.** gut I
**2.** brav II
**Good afternoon.** Guten Tag. *(nachmittags)* I • **Good luck (with ...)!** Viel Glück (bei/mit ...)! I **Good morning.** Guten Morgen. I
**Good to have you back.** Schön, dass du wieder da bist. IV Intro (8)
**be good at sth.** gut in etwas sein; etwas gut können IV Intro (9)
°**The money was good.** Wir haben gut verdient.
► S.173 US school grades
**Goodbye.** [ˌgʊdˈbaɪ] Auf Wiedersehen. I • **say goodbye** sich verabschieden I
**got** [gɒt] *siehe* **get**
**got** [gɒt]: **I've got ...** Ich habe ... I
**I haven't got a chair.** Ich habe keinen Stuhl. I
**grab sth.** (-bb-) [græb] sich etwas schnappen IV 1 (16)
**grade** [greɪd]
**1.** Klasse, Jahrgangsstufe IV Intro (9)
**2.** (Schul-)Note, Zensur IV 3 (54)
► S.173 US school grades
**grammar** [ˈgræmə] Grammatik I
**grammar file** *Grammatikanhang* I
**grand** [grænd] eindrucksvoll, beeindruckend IV Intro (10)
**grandchild** [ˈgræntʃaɪld], *pl* **grandchildren** Enkel/in I
**grandfather** [ˈgrænfɑːðə] Großvater I
**grandma** [ˈgrænmɑː] Oma I
**grandmother** [ˈgrænmʌðə] Großmutter I
**grandpa** [ˈgrænpɑː] Opa I
**grandparents** [ˈgrænpeərənts] Großeltern I
**granny** [ˈgræni] Oma II
**grape** [greɪp] Weintraube IV 2 (36)
**grass** [grɑːs] Gras, Rasen IV Intro (9)
**cut the grass** Rasen mähen IV Intro (9)
**great** [greɪt] großartig, toll I
**green** [griːn] grün I
°**greeting** [ˈgriːtɪŋ] Gruß, Begrüßung
**grew** [gruː] *siehe* **grow**
**grey** [greɪ] grau II
**ground** [graʊnd] (Erd-)Boden III
°**Ground Zero** [ˌgraʊnd ˈzɪərəʊ] Bodennullpunkt *(Bezeichnung für das zerstörte World Trade Center in New York; ursprünglich die Explosionsstelle einer Bombe oder Rakete über dem Boden)*
**grounded** [ˈgraʊndɪd]: **be grounded** Ausgehverbot/Hausarrest haben III

**group** [gruːp] Gruppe I • **group word** Oberbegriff II
°**group** gruppieren
**grow** [grəʊ], **grew, grown**
**1.** *(Getreide usw.)* anbauen, anpflanzen II
**2. grow up** erwachsen werden; aufwachsen III
**grown** [grəʊn] *siehe* **grow**
**grumble** [ˈgrʌmbl] murren, nörgeln I
°**guard** [gɑːd]: °**border guard** Grenzsoldat
**guess** [ges] raten, erraten, schätzen III
**guest** [gest] Gast I
**guide** [gaɪd] (Fremden-)Führer/in, Reiseleiter/in IV 3 (65)
**guidebook** [ˈgaɪdbʊk] Reiseführer IV 2 (43)
**guilty** [ˈgɪlti] schuldig IV 2 (49)
**guinea pig** [ˈgɪni pɪg] Meerschweinchen I
**guitar** [gɪˈtɑː] Gitarre I
**gun** [gʌn] Gewehr, Schusswaffe IV 1 (27)
**guy** [gaɪ] *(infml)* Typ, Kerl IV 1 (15)
**guys** *(pl)* [gaɪz] *(AE, infml)* Leute III
**gym** [dʒɪm] Sport-, Turnhalle; Fitnessstudio IV 3 (54)

## H

**had** [hæd] *siehe* **have** *und* **have got**
**hair** *(no pl)* [heə] Haar, Haare I
**hairdresser** [ˈheədresə] Friseur/Friseurin IV 1 (21)
**hairless** [ˈheələs] haarlos, kahl, unbehaart IV 2 (42)
**half** [hɑːf], *pl* **halves** [hɑːvz]
**1.** Hälfte III
**2.** Halbzeit III
**half** [hɑːf]: **half an hour** eine halbe Stunde III • **half past 11** halb zwölf (11.30/23.30) I • **three and a half days** dreieinhalb Tage IV Intro (8)
**half-time** [ˌhɑːf ˈtaɪm] Halbzeit(pause) III
**hall** [hɔːl] Flur, Diele I • **study hall** *(AE) Zeit zum selbstständigen Arbeiten/Lernen in der Schule* IV 3 (54)
**halves** [hɑːvz] *Plural von „half"*
**hamburger** [ˈhæmbɜːgə] Hamburger I
**hamster** [ˈhæmstə] Hamster I
**hand** [hænd] Hand I
**handball** [ˈhændbɔːl] Handball III
**hang out (with friends)** [ˌhæŋ‿ˈaʊt], *(infml)* **hung, hung** rumhängen, abhängen (mit Freunden/Freundinnen) III

**happen (to)** ['hæpən] geschehen, passieren (mit) I
**happiness** ['hæpinəs] Glück IV 3 (63)
**happy** ['hæpi] glücklich, froh I **Happy birthday.** Herzlichen Glückwunsch zum Geburtstag. I **happy ending** Happyend II
**harbour** ['hɑːbə] Hafen II
**hard** [hɑːd] hart; schwer, schwierig II • **work hard** hart arbeiten II
**hat** [hæt] Hut II
**hate** [heɪt] hassen, gar nicht mögen I
**have** [həv, hæv], **had, had** haben, besitzen II • **have a baby** ein Baby/Kind bekommen II • **have a bath** baden, ein Bad nehmen II **have a cold** erkältet sein, eine Erkältung haben II • **have a look** ansehen, einen Blick werfen auf IV 2 (36) • **have a picnic** ein Picknick machen I • **have a sauna** in die Sauna gehen II • **have a shower** (sich) duschen I • **have a sore throat** Halsschmerzen haben II • **have a temperature** Fieber haben II • **have breakfast/dinner** frühstücken/Abendbrot essen I • **have ... for breakfast** ... zum Frühstück essen/trinken I **have fun** Spaß haben, sich amüsieren I • **have sleepovers** Schlafpartys veranstalten III • **have to do** tun müssen I • **Good to have you back.** Schön, dass du wieder da bist. IV Intro (8) • **I'll have** *(bei einer Bestellung)* Ich nehme ... IV 1 (16)
**have got: I've got ...** [aɪv 'gɒt] Ich habe ... I • **I haven't got a chair.** Ich habe keinen Stuhl. I
**he** [hiː] er I
**head** [hed] Kopf I • **head teacher** Schulleiter/in III • **°price on sb.'s head** Kopfgeld
**headache** ['hedeɪk] Kopfschmerzen II
**°heading** ['hedɪŋ] Überschrift, Titel
**headline** ['hedlaɪn] Schlagzeile IV 4 (90)
**health** [helθ] Gesundheit; Gesundheitslehre IV 3 (54)
**healthy** ['helθi] gesund II
**hear** [hɪə], **heard, heard** hören I
**heard** [hɜːd] *siehe* **hear**
**heart** [hɑːt] Herz II
**heaven** ['hevn] Himmel IV 3 (67)
**°heavy** ['hevi] schwer *(von Gewicht)*
**hedgehog** ['hedʒhɒg] Igel II
**held** [held] *siehe* **hold**
**helicopter** ['helɪkɒptə] Hubschrauber, Helikopter II
**hell** [hel] Hölle IV 1 (27) • **°as brave as hell** *(infml)* höllisch mutig
**Hello.** [hə'ləʊ] Hallo. / Guten Tag. I
**helmet** ['helmɪt] Helm III
**help** [help] helfen I • **Help yourself!** Bedien dich! / Greif zu! III **Can I help you?** Kann ich Ihnen helfen? / Was kann ich für Sie tun? *(im Geschäft)* I
**help** [help] Hilfe I
**her** [hə, hɜː]
**1.** ihr, ihre I
**2.** sie; ihr I
**here** [hɪə]
**1.** hier I
**2.** hierher I
**Here you are.** Bitte sehr. / Hier bitte. I
**hers** [hɜːz] ihrer, ihre, ihrs II
**herself** [hə'self, hɜː'self] sich (selbst) III
**Hey.** [heɪ] Hallo! III
**Hi!** [haɪ] Hallo! I • **Say hi to Dilip for me.** Grüß Dilip von mir. I
**hid** [hɪd] *siehe* **hide**
**hidden** ['hɪdn] *siehe* **hide**
**hide** [haɪd], **hid, hidden** sich verstecken; *(etwas)* verstecken I
**high** [haɪ] hoch III • **high school** *(USA) Schule für 14-18-Jährige* IV Intro (10)
**°highlighted** ['haɪlaɪtɪd] hervorgehoben
**°hijacker** ['haɪdʒækə] (Flugzeug-)Entführer/in
**hike** [haɪk] wandern IV Intro (8)
**hike** [haɪk] Wanderung IV Intro (8/164) • **go on a hike** wandern gehen IV Intro (8/164)
**hill** [hɪl] Hügel II
**hilly** ['hɪli] hügelig III
**him** [hɪm] ihn; ihm I
**himself** [hɪm'self] sich (selbst) III
**hip hop** ['hɪp hɒp] Hip Hop III
**hippo** ['hɪpəʊ] Flusspferd II
**his** [hɪz]
**1.** sein, seine I
**2.** seiner, seine, seins II
**°Hispanic** [hɪs'pænɪk] *US-amerikanischer Ausdruck für Menschen mit Wurzeln in spanischsprachigen Ländern, besonders in Mittelamerika*
**°historic** [hɪ'stɒrɪk] historisch
**history** ['hɪstri] Geschichte I
**hit (-tt-)** [hɪt], **hit, hit**
**1.** schlagen II
**°2.** treffen
**°hi-tech** [ˌhaɪ'tek] Hightech- *(Verfahren, Produkt auf dem neuesten Stand der Technik)*
**hobby** ['hɒbi] Hobby I
**hockey** ['hɒki] Hockey I • **hockey shoes** Hockeyschuhe I
**°hog** [hɒg] (männliches) Mastschwein
**hold** [həʊld], **held, held** halten II **°hold on to sth.** sich an etwas festhalten • **°hold up** hochhalten
**°hole** [həʊl] Loch
**holiday** ['hɒlədeɪ]
**1.** Feiertag IV 4 (79)
**2.** Ferien I
**holiday flat** Ferienwohnung II **go on holiday** in Urlaub fahren II **a two-week holiday** ein zweiwöchiger Urlaub III
**home** [həʊm] Heim, Zuhause I **at home** daheim, zu Hause I **come home** nach Hause kommen I • **get home** nach Hause kommen I • **go home** nach Hause gehen I
**homeless** ['həʊmləs] obdachlos IV 2 (34)
**homesick** ['həʊmsɪk]**: be homesick** Heimweh haben IV 3 (57)
**hometown** ['həʊmtaʊn] Heimatstadt IV Intro (8)
**homework** *(no pl)* ['həʊmwɜːk] Hausaufgabe(n) I • **do homework** die Hausaufgabe(n) machen I **What's for homework?** Was haben wir als Hausaufgabe auf? I
**Hooray!** [hu'reɪ] Hurra! II
**hope** [həʊp] hoffen II • **°hope for** hoffen auf
**hope** [həʊp] Hoffnung III
**horrible** ['hɒrəbl] scheußlich, grauenhaft II
**horse** [hɔːs] Pferd I
**hospital** ['hɒspɪtl] Krankenhaus II
**hostel** ['hɒstl] Herberge, Wohnheim III • **youth hostel** Jugendherberge III
**hot** [hɒt] heiß I • **hot chocolate** heiße Schokolade I
**hotel** [həʊ'tel] Hotel II
**hotline** ['hɒtlaɪn] Hotline II
**hour** ['aʊə] Stunde II • **half an hour** [ˌhɑːf‿ən‿'aʊə] eine halbe Stunde III • **a 14-hour flight** ein 14-stündiger Flug, ein 14-Stunden-Flug III • **a 24-hour supermarket** ein Supermarkt, der 24 Stunden geöffnet ist III
**°hours** [aʊəz]**: °(opening) hours** *(pl)* Öffnungszeiten
**house** [haʊs] Haus I • **at the Shaws' house** im Haus der Shaws / bei den Shaws zu Hause I
**how** [haʊ] wie I • **How about ...?** Wie wär's mit ...? III • **How am I**

**doing?** Wie komme ich voran? *(Wie sind meine Fortschritte?)* III
**How are you?** Wie geht es dir/ Ihnen/euch? II • **How do you know ...?** Woher weißt/kennst du ...? I • **how long?** seit wann? IV 4 (77) • **how many?** wie viele? I **how much?** wie viel? I • **How much is/are ...?** Was kostet/kosten ...? / Wie viel kostet/kosten ...? I • **How old are you?** Wie alt bist du? I • **How was ...?** Wie war ...? I
**huge** [hju:dʒ] riesig, sehr groß III
°**human history** [ˌhju:mən ˈhɪstri] Menschheitsgeschichte
**hundred** [ˈhʌndrəd] hundert I
**hung out** [ˌhʌŋ‿ˈaʊt] *siehe* **hang out**
**hungry** [ˈhʌŋgri] hungrig III • **be hungry** Hunger haben, hungrig sein III
**hunt** [hʌnt] jagen III
**hunt** [hʌnt] Jagd III
**hurry** [ˈhʌri] eilen; sich beeilen II **hurry up** sich beeilen I
**hurry** [ˈhʌri]**: be in a hurry** in Eile sein, es eilig haben I
**hurt** [hɜ:t]**, hurt, hurt** wehtun; verletzen I
**hurt** [hɜ:t] verletzt II
**husband** [ˈhʌzbənd] Ehemann II
**hutch** [hʌtʃ] (Kaninchen-)Stall I

## I

**I** [aɪ] ich I • **I'm** [aɪm] ich bin I **I'm from ...** Ich komme aus ... / Ich bin aus ... I • **I'm ... years old.** Ich bin ... Jahre alt. I • **I'm sorry.** Entschuldigung. / Tut mir leid. I
**ice** [aɪs]**: ice cream** (Speise-)Eis I **ice hockey** Eishockey • **ice rink** Schlittschuhbahn II
**idea** [aɪˈdɪə] Idee, Einfall I
**if** [ɪf]
1. falls, wenn II
2. ob II
**ill** [ɪl] krank II
**illegal** [ɪˈli:gl] illegal, ungesetzlich IV 2 (37)
**illness** [ˈɪlnəs] Krankheit IV 3 (63)
°**imaginary** [ɪˈmædʒɪnəri] imaginär, *(nur in der Vorstellung vorhanden, nicht wirklich)*
**imagine sth.** [ɪˈmædʒɪn] sich etwas vorstellen IV 1 (15)
**immigrant** [ˈɪmɪgrənt] Einwanderer/Einwanderin IV 1 (12)
°**immigration** [ˌɪmɪˈgreɪʃn] Einwanderung
**important** [ɪmˈpɔ:tnt] wichtig II
**impossible** [ɪmˈpɒsəbl] unmöglich II
**impressed** [ɪmˈprest] beeindruckt IV 4 (78)
°**improve** [ɪmˈpru:v] verbessern
**in** [ɪn] in I • **in ... Street** in der ...straße I • **in English** auf Englisch I • **in front of** vor *(räumlich)* I **in here** hier drinnen I • **in my opinion** meiner Meinung nach IV 2 (37) • **in the afternoon** nachmittags, am Nachmittag I • **in the country** auf dem Land II • **in the end** schließlich, zum Schluss III **in the evening** abends, am Abend I • **in the field** auf dem Feld II **in the morning** am Morgen, morgens I • **in the photo** auf dem Foto I • **in the picture** auf dem Bild I • °**in the world** auf der Welt **in the yard** auf dem Hof II • **in time** rechtzeitig II • **in 1837** 1837, im Jahre 1837 IV 3 (52) • °**in the 1850s** in den 50er Jahren des 19. Jahrhunderts
°**independence** [ˌɪndɪˈpendəns] Unabhängigkeit
**industrial** [ɪnˈdʌstriəl] industriell, Industrie IV 2 (36)
**industry** [ˈɪndəstri] Industrie IV 2 (36/170)
**infinitive** [ɪnˈfɪnətɪv] Infinitiv *(Grundform des Verbs)* I
°**informal letter** [ɪnˈfɔ:ml] informeller, nicht förmlicher Brief
**information (about/on)** *(no pl)* [ˌɪnfəˈmeɪʃn] Information(en) (über) II
**inline skating** [ˈɪnlaɪn ˌskeɪtɪŋ] Inlineskaten III
**inside** [ˌɪnˈsaɪd]
1. innen (drin), drinnen I
2. nach drinnen II
3. **inside the car** ins Auto (hinein), ins Innere des Autos II
°**front inside cover** [ˌfrʌnt‿ˌɪnsaɪd ˈkʌvə] Umschlaginnenseite
**install** [ɪnˈstɔ:l] installieren, einrichten II
**instant messages** *(pl)* [ˌɪnstənt ˈmesɪdʒɪz] *Nachrichten, die man im Internet austauscht (in Echtzeit)* III
**instructions** *(pl)* [ɪnˈstrʌkʃnz] (Gebrauchs-)Anweisung(en), Anleitung(en) II
**instrument** [ˈɪnstrəmənt] Instrument III
°**integration** [ɪntəgreɪʃn] Integration
**interest** [ˈɪntrəst] Interesse III
**interested** [ˈɪntrəstɪd]**: be interested (in)** interessiert sein (an), sich interessieren (für) III
**interesting** [ˈɪntrəstɪŋ] interessant I
**international** [ˌɪntəˈnæʃnəl] international III
**internet** [ˈɪntənet] Internet III **surf the internet** im Internet surfen III
°**interstate** [ˌɪntəˈsteɪt] *(AE)* Autobahn
**interview** [ˈɪntəvju:] Interview I
**interview** [ˈɪntəvju:] interviewen, befragen II
**into** [ˈɪntə, ˈɪntʊ] in ... (hinein) I
**introduction (to)** [ˌɪntrəˈdʌkʃn] Einführung (in) III
**invitation (to)** [ˌɪnvɪˈteɪʃn] Einladung (zu) I
**invite (to)** [ɪnˈvaɪt] einladen (zu) I
°**irregular** [ɪˈregjələ] unregelmäßig
**is** [ɪz] ist I
**island** [ˈaɪlənd] Insel II
°**issue** [ˈɪʃu:] (Streit-)Frage, Thema, Angelegenheit
**it** [ɪt] er/sie/es I • **It's £1.** Er/Sie/ Es kostet 1 Pfund. I • **It says here: ...** Hier steht: ... / Es heißt hier: ... II
**its** [ɪts] sein/seine; ihr/ihre I
**itself** [ɪtˈself] sich (selbst) III

## J

**jacket** [ˈdʒækɪt] Jacke, Jackett II
**jail** [dʒeɪl] Gefängnis IV 2 (49)
**January** [ˈdʒænjuəri] Januar I
**jazz** [dʒæz] Jazz III
**jealous (of)** [ˈdʒeləs] neidisch (auf); eifersüchtig (auf) III
**jealousy** [ˈdʒeləsi] Eifersucht IV 2 (50)
**jeans** *(pl)* [dʒi:nz] Jeans I
°**jerk** [dʒɜ:k] Dummkopf
**jewellery** [ˈdʒu:əlri] Schmuck III
°**Jewish** [ˈdʒu:ɪʃ] jüdisch
**job** [dʒɒb] Aufgabe, Job I
**join sb.** [dʒɔɪn] sich jm. anschließen; bei jm. mitmachen II
**joke** [dʒəʊk] Witz I
**joke** [dʒəʊk] scherzen, Witze machen II
**journey** [ˈdʒɜ:ni] Fahrt, Reise III
°**Jr. (junior)** [ˈdʒu:niə] der Jüngere *(bes. in den USA: unterscheidet den Sohn vom gleichnamigen Vater)*
**judge sb. (by)** [dʒʌdʒ] jn. beurteilen (nach) IV 4 (79)
**judo** [ˈdʒu:dəʊ] Judo I • **do judo** Judo machen I
**jug** [dʒʌg] Krug I • **a jug of milk** ein Krug Milch I
**juice** [dʒu:s] Saft I
**July** [dʒuˈlaɪ] Juli I

**jumble sale** ['dʒʌmbl seɪl] Wohltätigkeitsbasar I
**jump** [dʒʌmp] springen II • **jump around** herumspringen III
**June** [dʒu:n] Juni I
**junior** ['dʒu:niə] Junioren-, Jugend- I
**just** [dʒʌst]
**1.** (einfach) nur, bloß I
**2.** gerade (eben), soeben II

## K

**kangaroo** [ˌkæŋgə'ru:] Känguru II
**keep** [ki:p], **kept, kept:**
**keep fit** fit bleiben • **keep in touch** in Verbindung bleiben, Kontakt halten III • **keep sth. warm/cool/open/...** etwas warm/kühl/offen/... halten II
**kept** [kept] *siehe* **keep**
**key** [ki:] Schlüssel • **key ring** Schlüsselring II • **key word** Stichwort, Schlüsselwort I
**keyboard** ['ki:bɔ:d] Keyboard *(elektronisches Tasteninstrument)* III
**kick** [kɪk] treten IV 1 (27)
**kid** [kɪd] Kind, Jugendliche(r) I
**kidney** ['kɪdni] Niere III
**kill** [kɪl] töten I
**kilogram (kg)** ['kɪləgræm], **kilo** ['ki:ləʊ] Kilogramm, Kilo (kg) III
**two kilos of oranges** zwei Kilo Orangen III • **a 150-kilogram bear** ein 150 Kilogramm schwerer Bär III
**kilometre (km)** ['kɪləmi:tə] Kilometer III • **a ten-kilometre walk** eine Zehn-Kilometer-Wanderung III
**kind (of)** [kaɪnd] Art III • **What kind of car...?** Was für ein Auto III
**kindergarten** ['kɪndəgɑ:tn] Kindergarten; *(USA)* Vorschule *(für 5- bis 6-jährige)* IV 3 (54)
**king** [kɪŋ] König I
**kiss** [kɪs] küssen IV 1 (26/169)
**kiss** [kɪs] Kuss IV 1 (26)
**kitchen** ['kɪtʃɪn] Küche I
**kite** [kaɪt] Drachen I
**kiwi** ['ki:wi:] Kiwi II
**knee** [ni:] Knie I
**knew** [nju:] *siehe* **know**
**knife** [naɪf], *pl* **knives** [naɪvz] Messer III
**know** [nəʊ], **knew, known**
**1.** wissen I
**2.** kennen I
**know about sth.** von etwas wissen; über etwas Bescheid wissen II
**get to know sb.** jn. kennenlernen IV 4 (89) • **How do you know ...?** Woher weißt du ...? / Woher kennst du ...? I • **I don't know.** Ich weiß es nicht. I • **..., you know.** ..., wissen Sie. / ..., weißt du. I • **You know what, Sophie?** Weißt du was, Sophie? I
**known** [nəʊn] *siehe* **know**

## L

°**label** ['leɪbl] beschriften, etikettieren
**laid** [leɪd] *siehe* **lay**
**lake** [leɪk] (Binnen-)See II
**lamb** [læm] Lamm(fleisch) III
**lamp** [læmp] Lampe I
**land** [lænd] landen II
**land** [lænd] Land, Grund und Boden II
**lane** [leɪn] Gasse, Weg III
**language** ['læŋgwɪdʒ] Sprache I
°**foreign language** Fremdsprache
**large** [lɑ:dʒ] groß II
**lasagne** [lə'zænjə] Lasagne I
**last** [lɑ:st] letzte(r, s) I • **the last day** der letzte Tag I • **at last** endlich, schließlich I
**late** [leɪt] spät; zu spät I • **be late** zu spät sein/kommen I • **Sorry, I'm late.** Entschuldigung, dass ich zu spät bin/komme. I
**later** ['leɪtə] später I
**latest** ['leɪtɪst] neueste(r, s) III
°**Latino** [læ'ti:nəʊ] *Amerikaner/in lateinamerikanischer Herkunft*
**laugh** [lɑ:f] lachen I • **laugh at sb.** jn. auslachen IV 2 (37)
**laughter** ['lɑ:ftə] Gelächter II
**law** [lɔ:] Gesetz IV 4 (87)
**lay** [leɪ], **laid, laid: lay the table** den Tisch decken I
**leader** ['li:də] (An-)Führer/in, Leiter/in, III
°**lean over** [ˌli:n‿'əʊvə] herüberbeugen, -lehnen
**learn** [lɜ:n] lernen I • **learn sth. about sth.** etwas über etwas erfahren, etwas über etwas herausfinden II
**least** [li:st] am wenigsten IV 3 (56)
**like sth. least** etwas am wenigsten mögen III • **at least** zumindest, wenigstens I
► S.174 little – less – least
**leave** [li:v], **left, left**
**1.** (weg)gehen; abfahren II
**2.** verlassen II
**3.** zurücklassen II
°**4. leave sb. alone** jn. in Ruhe lassen
**left** [left] *siehe* **leave**
**left** [left] linke(r, s) II • **look left** nach links schauen II • **on the left** links, auf der linken Seite II • **turn left** (nach) links abbiegen II
**leg** [leg] Bein I
**legal** ['li:gl] legal, gesetzlich IV 2 (37/171)
°**legend** ['ledʒənd] Legende
**leisure centre** ['leʒə sentə] Freizeitzentrum, -park II
**lemonade** [ˌlemə'neɪd] Limonade I
**less** [les] weniger IV 3 (56)
► S.174 little – less – least
**lesson** ['lesn] (Unterrichts-)Stunde I • **lessons** *(pl)* Unterricht I
**let** [let], **let, let** lassen II • **Let's ...** Lass uns ... / Lasst uns ... I • **Let's go.** Auf geht's! (*wörtlich:* Lass uns gehen.) I • **Let's look at the list.** Sehen wir uns die Liste an. / Lasst uns die Liste ansehen. I
**letter** ['letə]
**1.** Buchstabe I
**2. letter (to)** Brief (an) II
°**letter to the editor** Leserbrief
**lettuce** ['letɪs] (Kopf-)Salat II
°**liberty** ['lɪbəti] Freiheit
**library** ['laɪbrəri] Bibliothek, Bücherei I
**license plate** ['laɪsns pleɪt] *(AE)* Nummernschild IV Intro (10)
**life** [laɪf], *pl* **lives** [laɪvz] Leben I
**lift** [lɪft] Fahrstuhl, Aufzug II
**light** [laɪt] Licht III
**like** [laɪk] wie I • **What was the weather like?** Wie war das Wetter? II
**like** [laɪk] mögen, gernhaben I
**like sth. best/least** etwas am meisten/wenigsten mögen III
**like sth. better** etwas lieber mögen II • **I like swimming/dancing.** Ich schwimme/tanze gern. I • **I'd like ... (= I would like ...)** Ich hätte gern ... / Ich möchte gern ... I • **I'd like to talk about ... (= I would like to talk about ...)** Ich möchte/würde gern über ... reden I • **Would you like ...?** Möchtest du ...? / Möchten Sie ...? I • **Would you like some?** Möchtest du etwas/ein paar? / Möchten Sie etwas/ein paar? I
**likeable** ['laɪkəbl] liebenswert, nett, sympathisch IV 4 (85)
**line** [laɪn]
**1.** Zeile II
**2.** (U-Bahn-)Linie III
**3.** *(AE)* Schlange, Reihe *(wartender Menschen)* IV 1 (14)
**link** [lɪŋk] verbinden, verknüpfen I

**link** [lɪŋk] Verbindung, Verknüpfung III
**linking word** ['lɪŋkɪŋ wɜːd] Bindewort II
**lion** ['laɪən] Löwe II
**list** [lɪst] Liste I
**list** [lɪst] auflisten, aufzählen II
**listen (to)** ['lɪsn] zuhören; sich etwas anhören I
**listener** ['lɪsnə] Zuhörer/in II
**listing** ['lɪstɪŋ]: **TV listings** *(pl)* Fernsehprogramm IV 4 (76)
**little** ['lɪtl]
1. klein I
2. wenig IV 3 (56) • **a little** ein wenig/ein bisschen
► S.174 little – less – least
**live** [lɪv] leben, wohnen I
**live music** [laɪv] Livemusik II
**liver** ['lɪvə] Leber III
**lives** [laɪvz] *Plural von „life"* I
**living room** ['lɪvɪŋ ruːm] Wohnzimmer I
**local** ['ləʊkl] Orts-, örtlich II
**location** [ləʊ'keɪʃn]
1. Wohn-/Standort, Lage III
°2. Drehort
**lock** [lɒk] abschließen; sperren III
**long** [lɒŋ] lang I
**look** [lʊk]
1. schauen, gucken I
2. **look different/great/old** anders/toll/alt aussehen I
**look after sth./sb.** auf etwas/jn. aufpassen; sich um etwas/jn. kümmern II • **look at** ansehen, anschauen I • **look for** suchen II
**look left/right** nach links/rechts schauen II • **look round** sich umsehen I • **look sth. up** etwas nachschlagen III • **look up (from)** hochsehen, aufschauen (von) II
**look** [lʊk] Blick IV 2 (36) • **have a look at sth.** sich etwas ansehen, einen Blick werfen auf etwas IV 2 (36)
**lorry** ['lɒri] Lastwagen III
**lose** [luːz], **lost, lost** verlieren II
**lost** [lɒst] *siehe* **lose**
**lot** [lɒt]: **a lot (of)** eine Menge, viel, viele II • **Thanks a lot!** Vielen Dank! I • **He likes her a lot.** Er mag sie sehr. I • **lots more** viel mehr I • **lots of** eine Menge, viele, viel I
**loud** [laʊd] laut I
**love** [lʌv] lieben, sehr mögen II
**love** [lʌv] Liebe II • **Love ...** Liebe Grüße, ... *(Briefschluss)* I • **love story** Liebesgeschichte IV 2 (50)
**fall in love (with sb.)** sich verlieben (in jn.) IV 3 (66)
°**lox** [lɑːks] *Jiddisch:* (gepökelter) Lachs
**luck** [lʌk]: **Good luck (with ...)!** Viel Glück (bei/mit ...)! I
**luckily** ['lʌkɪli] zum Glück, glücklicherweise II
**lucky** ['lʌki]: **be lucky (with)** Glück haben (mit) IV Intro (9)
**lunch** [lʌntʃ] Mittagessen I
**lunch break** Mittagspause I

## M

**machine** [mə'ʃiːn]
1. Automat IV 3 (64)
2. Maschine I
**mad** [mæd] verrückt I • **be mad about sth.** verrückt nach/auf etwas sein III
°**madam** ['mædəm]: °**Dear Sir or Madam** Sehr geehrte Damen und Herren
**made** [meɪd] *siehe* **make**
**madness** ['mædnəs] Verrücktheit IV 3 (63)
**magazine** [ˌmægə'ziːn] Zeitschrift, Magazin I
**maid** [meɪd] Dienstmädchen IV 2 (38)
**mail** [meɪl] schicken, senden *(per Post oder E-Mail)* III • **mail sb.** jn. anmailen II
**mail** [meɪl] Mail III
**main** [meɪn] Haupt-; wichtigste(r,s) IV 3 (52)
**majority** [mə'dʒɒrəti] Mehrheit IV 2 (37/171)
**make** [meɪk], **made, made** machen; bauen I • **make a mess** alles durcheinanderbringen, alles in Unordnung bringen I • **make a speech** eine Rede halten IV 4 (79/177) • °**make it to the end** bis zum Schluss durchhalten / es bis zum Ende schaffen • **Make yourself comfortable.** Machen Sie es sich bequem. / Mach es dir bequem. IV 2 (48) • °**They didn't make it.** Sie haben es nicht geschafft. / Sie haben es nicht überlebt. • °**make notes** sich Notizen machen • °**What makes a game a good game?** Was macht ein Spiel zu einem guten Spiel?
**make-up** ['meɪkʌp] Make-up II
**male** [meɪl] männlich III
**mall** [mɔːl]: **shopping mall** Einkaufspassage, überdachtes Einkaufszentrum IV 4 (74)
**man** [mæn], *pl* **men** [men] Mann I
**many** ['meni] viele I • **how many?** wie viele? I
**map** [mæp] Landkarte, Stadtplan II
**March** [mɑːtʃ] März I
**mark** [mɑːk] *(BE)* (Schul-)Note, Zensur IV 3 (54/173)
**mark sth. up** [ˌmɑːk‿'ʌp] etwas markieren, kennzeichnen II
**market** ['mɑːkɪt] Markt II
**marmalade** ['mɑːməleɪd] (Orangen-)Marmelade I
**married (to)** ['mærɪd] verheiratet (mit) I
**mashed potatoes** [ˌmæʃt pə'teɪtəʊz] Kartoffelbrei, Kartoffelpüree III
**match** [mætʃ] Spiel, Wettkampf I
°**match** [mætʃ]
1. passen zu
2. zuordnen
°**Match the letters and numbers.** Ordne die Buchstaben den Zahlen zu.
**mate** [meɪt] *(infml)* Freund/in, Kumpel III
°**material** [mə'tɪəriəl] Material
**maths** [mæθs] Mathematik I
**matter** ['mætə]: **What's the matter?** Was ist los? / Was ist denn? II
**May** [meɪ] Mai I
**may** [meɪ] dürfen III
► S.177 möglich – wahrscheinlich – sicherlich
**maybe** ['meɪbi] vielleicht I
°**mayor** ['meə] Bürgermeister
**me** [miː] mir; mich I • **Me too.** Ich auch. I • **more than me** mehr als ich II • **That's me.** Das bin ich. I
**Why me?** Warum ich? I
**meal** [miːl] Mahlzeit, Essen III
**mean** [miːn], **meant, meant**
1. bedeuten III • **What does 'forest' mean?** Was bedeutet „forest"? III
2. meinen *(sagen wollen)* II
**meaning** ['miːnɪŋ] Bedeutung III
**meant** [ment] *siehe* **mean**
**meat** [miːt] Fleisch I
**medal** ['medl] Medaille III
**media** *(pl)* ['miːdiə] Medien III
**mediation** [ˌmiːdi'eɪʃn] Vermittlung, Sprachmittlung, Mediation II
**medium** ['miːdiəm] mittel(groß) II
**meet** [miːt], **met, met**
1. treffen; kennenlernen I
2. sich treffen I
**Nice to meet you.** Nett, dich kennenzulernen. III
**meeting** ['miːtɪŋ] Versammlung, Besprechung IV 3 (55)
**member** ['membə] Mitglied IV 2 (37)
**men** [men] *Plural von „man"* I
**menu** ['menjuː] Speisekarte II

**mess** [mes]**: be a mess** sehr unordentlich sein; fürchterlich aussehen II • **make a mess** alles durcheinanderbringen, alles in Unordnung bringen I
**message** ['mesɪdʒ] Nachricht III
**text message** ['tekst ˌmesɪdʒ] SMS III
**met** [met] *siehe* **meet**
**metre** ['miːtə] Meter II
**mice** [maɪs] *Plural von „mouse"* I
**microphone** ['maɪkrəfəʊn] Mikrofon III
**middle (of)** ['mɪdl] Mitte I; Mittelteil II • **middle school** *(USA) Schule für 11- bis 14-Jährige* IV Intro (9)
°**midtown** ['mɪdtaʊn] *Teil Manhattans, New York City, Geschäftsviertel, bekannt für das Empire State Building und das Chrysler Building*
**might** [maɪt]**: She might be too busy.** Sie könnte zu beschäftigt sein. / Vielleicht ist sie zu beschäftigt. IV 4 (78)
► S.177 möglich – wahrscheinlich – sicherlich
**mild** [maɪld] mild III
**mile** [maɪl] Meile *(= ca. 1,6 km)* II
**for miles** meilenweit II
**milk** [mɪlk] Milch I
**million** ['mɪljən] Million III
**mime** [maɪm] pantomimisch darstellen, vorspielen II
°**mime** [maɪm] Pantomime
**mind** [maɪnd]**: Mind your own business.** Das geht dich nichts an! / Kümmere dich um deine eigenen Angelegenheiten! II • °**Never mind.** *etwa:* Nicht so wichtig. / Ist (doch) egal. / Das willst du gar nicht wissen.
**mind map** ['maɪnd mæp] Mindmap („Gedankenkarte", „Wissensnetz") I
**mine** [maɪn] meiner, meine, meins II
**minority** [maɪ'nɒrəti] Minderheit IV 2 (37)
**mints** *(pl)* [mɪnts] Pfefferminzbonbons I
**minus** ['maɪnəs] minus IV 3 (60)
**minute** ['mɪnɪt] Minute I • **Wait a minute.** Warte mal! / Moment mal! II
**mirror** ['mɪrə] Spiegel II
**miss** [mɪs]
**1.** vermissen II
**2. Miss a turn.** Einmal aussetzen. II
**Miss White** [mɪs] Frau White *(unverheiratet)* I
**missing** ['mɪsɪŋ]**: be missing** fehlen II • °**the missing information/words** die fehlenden Informationen/Wörter
**mistake** [mɪ'steɪk] Fehler I
**mix** [mɪks] mischen, mixen III
**mix** [mɪks] Mix, Mischung III
**mixture** ['mɪkstʃə] Mischung III
°**mix up** [ˌmɪks_'ʌp] durcheinanderbringen
**mobile (phone)** ['məʊbaɪl] Mobiltelefon, Handy I
**model** ['mɒdl] Modell*(-flugzeug, -schiff usw.)* I; (Foto-)Modell II
**modern** ['mɒdən] modern III
**mole** [məʊl] Maulwurf II
**mom** [mɒm, *AE* mɑm] *(AE)* Mama, Mutti; Mutter III
**moment** ['məʊmənt] Moment III
**Monday** ['mʌndeɪ, 'mʌndi] Montag I • **Monday morning** Montagmorgen I
**money** ['mʌni] Geld I • °**make money** Geld verdienen • **raise money (for)** Geld sammeln (für) IV Intro (9) • °**The money was good.** Wir haben gut verdient.
**monitor** ['mɒnɪtə] Monitor, Bildschirm III
**monkey** ['mʌŋki] Affe II
**monster** ['mɒnstə] Ungeheuer, Monster II
**month** [mʌnθ] Monat I
°**monument** ['mɒnjumənt] Denkmal, Monument
**moon** [muːn] Mond II
**more** [mɔː] mehr I • **lots more** viel mehr I • **more than** mehr als II • **more than me** mehr als ich II
**more boring (than)** langweiliger (als) II • **no more music** keine Musik mehr I • **not (...) any more** nicht mehr III
**morning** ['mɔːnɪŋ] Morgen, Vormittag I • **in the morning** morgens, am Morgen I • **Monday morning** Montagmorgen I • **on Friday morning** freitagmorgens, am Freitagmorgen I
**most** [məʊst] (der/die/das) meiste ...; am meisten II • **most people** die meisten Leute I • **(the) most boring** der/die/das langweiligste ...; am langweiligsten II
**motel** [məʊ'tel] Motel IV Intro (10)
**mother** ['mʌðə] Mutter I
**mountain** ['maʊntən] Berg II
**mouse** [maʊs]**,** *pl* **mice** [maɪs] Maus I
**mouth** [maʊθ] Mund I
**move** [muːv]
**1.** bewegen; sich bewegen II
**Move back one space.** Geh ein Feld zurück. II • °**move closer** näher heranrücken • **Move on one space.** Geh ein Feld vor. II
**2. move (to)** umziehen (nach, in) II • **move in** einziehen II • **move out** ausziehen II
**movement** ['muːvmənt] Bewegung II
**movie** ['muːvi] Film III
**MP3 player** [ˌempiː'θriː ˌpleɪə] MP3-Spieler I
**Mr ...** ['mɪstə] Herr ... I
**Mrs ...** ['mɪsɪz] Frau ... I
**Ms ...** [mɪz, məz] Frau ... II
**much** [mʌtʃ] viel I • **how much?** wie viel? I • **How much is/are ...?** Was kostet/kosten ...? / Wie viel kostet/kosten ...? I • **like/love sth. very much** etwas sehr mögen/sehr lieben II
**muesli** ['mjuːzli] Müsli IV 3 (56)
°**mule** [mjuːl] Maultier
**multiple choice** [ˌmʌltɪpl 'tʃɔɪs] Multiple-Choice II
**mum** [mʌm] Mama, Mutti; Mutter I
**museum** [mju'ziːəm] Museum I
**mushroom** ['mʌʃrʊm] Pilz III
**music** ['mjuːzɪk] Musik I • °**put on music** Musik auflegen
**musical** ['mjuːzɪkl] Musical I
**must** [mʌst] müssen I
► S.177 möglich – wahrscheinlich – sicherlich
**must** [mʌst]**: a must** ein Muss IV 1 (17)
°**mustache** [məs'tɑːʃ] *(AE)* Schnurrbart
**mustn't do** ['mʌsnt] nicht tun dürfen II
**my** [maɪ] mein/e I
**myself** [maɪ'self] mir/mich (selbst) III

## N

**name** [neɪm] Name I • **My name is ...** Ich heiße ... / Mein Name ist ... I • **What's your name?** Wie heißt du? I
**name** [neɪm] nennen; benennen II
**nation** ['neɪʃn] Nation IV 4 (79)
**national** ['næʃnəl] national III
**national park** Nationalpark IV Intro (8)
**Native American** [ˌneɪtɪv_ə'merɪkən] amerikanische(r) Ureinwohner/in, Indianer/in IV Intro (9)
°**natural history** [ˌnætʃrəl 'hɪstri] Naturkunde

**near** [nɪə] in der Nähe von, nahe (bei) I
**neat** [ni:t] gepflegt II • **neat and tidy** schön ordentlich II
**need** [ni:d] brauchen, benötigen I
°**need to do sth.** etwas tun müssen
**needn't do** ['ni:dnt] nicht tun müssen, nicht zu tun brauchen II
**neighbour** ['neɪbə] Nachbar/in I
**nephew** ['nefju:] Neffe IV 2 (49/172)
**nervous** ['nɜ:vəs] nervös, aufgeregt I
**nervousness** ['nɜ:vəsnəs] Nervosität IV 3 (63)
°**network** ['netwɜ:k] (Wörter-)Netz
**never** ['nevə] nie, niemals I
°**Never mind.** *etwa:* Nicht so wichtig. / Ist (doch) egal. / Das willst du gar nicht wissen.
**new** [nju:] neu I
**news** *(no pl)* [nju:z] Nachrichten, Neuigkeiten III • **That's good news.** Das sind gute Nachrichten. III
**newspaper** ['nju:speɪpə] Zeitung I
**next** [nekst]: **be next** der/die Nächste sein I • **the next morning/day** am nächsten Morgen/Tag I • **What have we got next?** Was haben wir als Nächstes? I
**next to** [nekst] neben II
**nice** [naɪs] schön, nett I • **Nice to meet you.** Nett, dich kennenzulernen. III
**niece** [ni:s] Nichte IV 2 (49)
**night** [naɪt] Nacht, später Abend I
**at night** nachts, in der Nacht I
**on Friday night** freitagnachts, Freitagnacht I
**nil** [nɪl] null III
**no** [nəʊ] nein I
**no** [nəʊ] kein, keine I • **no more music** keine Musik mehr I • **no one** ['nəʊ wʌn] niemand IV 2 (34/170) • **No smoking.** Rauchen verboten. III • **No way!** Auf keinen Fall! / Kommt nicht in Frage! II
**nobody** ['nəʊbədi] niemand II
**nod (-dd-)** [nɒd] nicken (mit) II
**noise** [nɔɪz] Geräusch; Lärm I
**noisy** ['nɔɪzi] laut, lärmend II
°**normal** ['nɔ:ml] normal
**north** [nɔ:θ] Norden; nach Norden; nördlich III
**north-east** [ˌnɔ:θ'i:st] Nordosten; nach Nordosten; nordöstlich III
**north-west** [ˌnɔ:θ'west] Nordwesten; nach Nordwesten; nordwestlich III
**nose** [nəʊz] Nase I
**not** [nɒt] nicht I • **not (...) any** kein, keine I • **not (...) any more** nicht mehr III • **not (...) anybody** niemand II • **not (...) anything** nichts II • **not (...) anywhere** nirgendwo(hin) II • **not (...) yet** noch nicht II
**note** [nəʊt] Mitteilung, Notiz I
°**make notes** sich Notizen machen
**take notes** sich Notizen machen I
**nothing** ['nʌθɪŋ] nichts II
°**notice** ['nəʊtɪs] Notiz, Mitteilung
**notice board** Anschlagtafel, schwarzes Brett I
**November** [nəʊ'vembə] November I
**now** [naʊ] nun, jetzt I • °**now and then** damals und heute
**number** ['nʌmbə] Zahl, Ziffer, Nummer I • **number plate** Nummernschild IV Intro (10/165)
**nut** [nʌt] Nuss IV 3 (56)

## O

**o** [əʊ] null I
°**observatory** [əb'zɜ:vətri] Aussichtsplattform
°**ocean: the Pacific Ocean** [pəˌsɪfɪk 'əʊʃn] der Pazifischer Ozean, der Pazifik
**o'clock** [ə'klɒk]: **eleven o'clock** elf Uhr I
**October** [ɒk'təʊbə] Oktober I
°**odd** [ɒd]: **What word is the odd one out?** Welches Wort passt nicht dazu / gehört nicht dazu?
**of** [əv, ɒv] von I • **two kilos of oranges** zwei Kilo Orangen III
**of course** [əv 'kɔ:s] natürlich, selbstverständlich I
**off** [ɒf]: **a week/day/month ... off** eine Woche / einen Tag / einen Monat ... frei IV 3 (54) • **cut sth. off** etwas abtrennen, abschneiden III
**fall off** herunterfallen (von) II
**get off (the train/bus)** (aus dem Zug/Bus) aussteigen I • **take sth. off** etwas ausziehen *(Kleidung)* II
**take 10 c off** 10 Cent abziehen I
**turn on/off** ein-/ausschalten III
**offer** ['ɒfə] anbieten IV 2 (50)
**offer** ['ɒfə] Angebot IV 2 (50/172)
**often** ['ɒfn] oft, häufig I
**Oh dear!** [əʊ 'dɪə] Oje! II
**Oh well ...** [əʊ 'wel] Na ja ... / Na gut ... I
**oil** [ɔɪl] Öl III • **oil rig** ['ɔɪl rɪg] (Öl-)Bohrinsel III
**OK** [əʊ'keɪ] okay, gut, in Ordnung I
**I'll/You'll/She'll/ ... be OK.** Mir/Dir/Ihr/...wird nichts passieren. IV 1 (17)
**okay** [əʊ'keɪ] okay IV 1 (26)
**old** [əʊld] alt I • **a sixteen-year-old** ein/e Sechzehnjährige/r III
**a sixteen-year-old girl** ein sechzehnjähriges Mädchen III
**old-fashioned** [ˌəʊld'fæʃnd] altmodisch III
°**Olympic Games** [əˌlɪmpɪk 'geɪmz]: °**the Olympic Games** die Olympischen Spiele; die Olympiade
**on** [ɒn]
**1.** auf I
**2.** eingeschaltet sein, an sein *(Radio, Licht usw.)* II
**on 13th June** am 13. Juni I • °**on display** [dɪ'spleɪ] ausgestellt sein, gezeigt werden • **on Friday** am Freitag I • **on Friday afternoon** freitagnachmittags, am Freitagnachmittag I • **on Friday evening** freitagabends, am Freitagabend I • **on Friday morning** freitagmorgens, am Freitagmorgen I • **on Friday night** freitagnachts, Freitagnacht I • **on my shift** in meiner Schicht IV 1 (15) • **on the beach** am Strand II • **on the board** an die Tafel I • **on the bus** im Bus III • **on the coast** an der Küste III • **on the corner of Green Street and London Road** Green Street, Ecke London Road II • **on the left** links, auf der linken Seite II • **on the phone** am Telefon I • **on the plane** im Flugzeug II • **on the radio** im Radio I • **on the right** rechts, auf der rechten Seite II
**on the train** im Zug I • **on TV** im Fernsehen I • **be on** gezeigt werden, laufen *(im Fernsehen/Kino)* IV 4 (76) • **What page are we on?** Auf welcher Seite sind wir? I
**straight on** geradeaus weiter II
**once** [wʌns] einmal III • **once a week** einmal pro Woche III
**one** [wʌn] eins, ein, eine I • **one day** eines Tages I • **one-day ticket** Tageskarte III • **a new one** ein neuer / eine neue / ein neues II • **my old ones** meine alten II • **no one** niemand IV 2 (34/170)
**onion** ['ʌnjən] Zwiebel III
**online** [ˌɒn'laɪn] online, Online- III
**only** ['əʊnli]
**1.** nur, bloß I
**2. the only guest** der einzige Gast I
°**3.** erst
**onto** ['ɒntə, 'ɒntu] auf (... hinauf) III

**open** ['əʊpən] öffnen, aufmachen I
**open** ['əʊpən] offen, geöffnet II
°**opening sentence** [ˌəʊpənɪŋ 'sentəns] Einleitungssatz • °**(opening) hours** *(pl)* ['əʊpənɪŋ haʊz] Öffnungszeiten
**opera: soap opera** ['səʊp_ɒprə] Seifenoper IV 2 (50)
**operation (on)** [ˌɒpə'reɪʃn] Operation (an) III
**opinion** [ə'pɪnjən] Meinung IV 2 (37)
**opposite** ['ɒpəzɪt] Gegenteil I
**or** [ɔː] oder I
**orange** ['ɒrɪndʒ] orange(farben) I
**orange** ['ɒrɪndʒ] Orange, Apfelsine I • **orange juice** ['ɒrɪndʒ dʒuːs] Orangensaft I
**order** ['ɔːdə] bestellen IV 1 (16)
°**order** ['ɔːdə]
1. Reihenfolge • **in the right order** in der richtigen Reihenfolge • **word order** Wortstellung
2. Befehl
**organize** ['ɔːgənaɪz] ordnen, organisieren III
°**original** [ə'rɪdʒənl] urpsrünglich
**other** ['ʌðə] andere(r, s) I • **the others** die anderen I • **the other way round** anders herum II
**Ouch!** [aʊtʃ] Autsch! I
**our** ['aʊə] unser, unsere I
**ours** ['aʊəz] unserer, unsere, unseres II
**ourselves** [aʊə'selvz] uns (selbst) III
**out** [aʊt] heraus, hinaus; draußen II
**out of ...** aus ... (heraus/hinaus) I
**outfit** ['aʊtfɪt] Outfit *(Kleidung; Ausrüstung)* II
**outside** [ˌaʊt'saɪd]
1. draußen I
2. nach draußen II
3. **outside his room** vor seinem Zimmer; außerhalb seines Zimmers I
**over** ['əʊvə]
1. über, oberhalb von I
2. **be over** vorbei/zu Ende sein I
**all over the world** auf der ganzen Welt III • **from all over the UK/the world/England** aus dem gesamten Vereinigten Königreich / aus der ganzen Welt / aus ganz England III • **over there** da drüben, dort drüben I • **over to ...** hinüber zu/nach ... II
**own** [əʊn]: **our own pool** unser eigenes Schwimmbad II

## P

°**Pacific: the Pacific Ocean** [pəˌsɪfɪk 'əʊʃn] der Pazifische Ozean, der Pazifik
**pack** [pæk] packen, einpacken II
**packet** ['pækɪt] Päckchen, Packung, Schachtel I • **a packet of mints** ein Päckchen/eine Packung Pfefferminzbonbons I
**pads** *(pl)* [pædz] *(Knie- usw.)*Schützer *(für Inlineskater)*; Schulterpolster *(beim American Football)* III
**page** [peɪdʒ] (Buch-, Heft-)Seite I
**What page are we on?** Auf welcher Seite sind wir? I
**paid** [peɪd] *siehe* **pay**
**paint** [peɪnt] (an)malen I
**painter** ['peɪntə] Maler/in II
**pair** [peə]: **a pair (of)** ein Paar II
**palace** ['pæləs] Palast, Schloss III
°**pan** [pæn] Pfanne
**pants** *(pl)* [pænts] *(AE)* Hose IV 1 (20)
**paper** ['peɪpə]
1. Papier I
2. Zeitung II
**paragraph** ['pærəgrɑːf] Absatz *(in einem Text)* II
**Paralympics** [ˌpærə'lɪmpɪks] Paralympische Spiele *(Olympische Spiele für Sportler/innen mit körperlicher Behinderung)* III
**paramedic** [ˌpærə'medɪk] Sanitäter/in II
**paraphrase** ['pærəfreɪz] umschreiben, anders ausdrücken III
**parcel** ['pɑːsl] Paket I
**parents** ['peərənts] Eltern I
**park** [pɑːk] Park I • **(park) ranger** *Ranger sind eine Art Aufseher/in in Nationalparks, die auch Führungen machen und als Wald- und Wildhüter/innen arbeiten* IV Intro (9)
**parliament** ['pɑːləmənt] Parlament III
**parrot** ['pærət] Papagei I
**part** [pɑːt] Teil I • °**take part** [ˌteɪk 'pɑːt] teilnehmen
**partner** ['pɑːtnə] Partner/in I
**party** ['pɑːti] Party I
**pass** [pɑːs] (herüber)reichen, weitergeben I • **pass round** herumgeben I
**past** [pɑːst] Vergangenheit I
**past** [pɑːst] vorbei (an), vorüber (an) II • **half past 11** halb zwölf (11.30/23.30) I • **quarter past 11** Viertel nach elf (11.15/23.15) I
**pasta** *(no pl)* ['pæstə] Pasta, Nudeln, Teigwaren IV 3 (56)
**path** [pɑːθ] Pfad, Weg II

°**patrol** [pə'trəʊl]: °**border patrol** Grenzschutz
**pavement** ['peɪvmənt] Gehweg, Bürgersteig IV 1 (14/166)
**pay (for)** [peɪ], **paid, paid** bezahlen II
**PE** [ˌpiː_'iː], **Physical Education** [ˌfɪzɪkəl_edʒu'keɪʃn] Turnen, Sportunterricht I
**pea** [piː] Erbse III
**pen** [pen] Kugelschreiber, Füller I
**pence (p)** *(pl)* [pens] Pence *(Plural von „penny")* I
**pencil** ['pensl] Bleistift I • **pencil case** Federmäppchen I • **pencil sharpener** Bleistiftanspitzer I
**penny** ['peni] *kleinste britische Münze* I
**people** ['piːpl] Menschen, Leute I
**per** [pɜː, pə] pro III
**per cent (%)** [pə' sent] Prozent III
**perfect** ['pɜːfɪkt] perfekt; ideal; vollkommen IV 1 (17)
**period** ['pɪərɪəd] (Unterrichts-/Schul-)Stunde IV 3 (54)
**person** ['pɜːsn] Person II
**personal** ['pɜːsənl] persönliche(r, s) III
**pet** [pet] Haustier I • **pet shop** Tierhandlung I
**phone** [fəʊn] Telefon I • **on the phone** am Telefon I • **phone call** Anruf, Telefongespräch I • **phone number** Telefonnummer I
**phone** [fəʊn] telefonieren, anrufen I
**photo** ['fəʊtəʊ] Foto I • **in the photo** auf dem Foto I • **take photos** Fotos machen, fotografieren I
**photographer** [fə'tɒgrəfə] Fotograf/in III
°**phrase** [freɪz] Ausdruck, (Rede-)Wendung
**piano** [pi'ænəʊ] Klavier, Piano I
**play the piano** Klavier spielen I
**pick up** [ˌpɪk_'ʌp]: **pick sb. up** jn. abholen III • **pick sth. up** etwas hochheben, aufheben II
**picnic** ['pɪknɪk] Picknick I • **have a picnic** ein Picknick machen I
**picture** ['pɪktʃə] Bild I • **in the picture** auf dem Bild I • **picture story** Bildergeschichte IV 2 (45)
**pie** [paɪ] Obstkuchen; Pastete II
**piece** [piːs]: **a piece of** ein Stück I • **a piece of paper** ein Stück Papier I
**piercing** ['pɪəsɪŋ] Piercing III
**pig** [pɪg] Schwein III
**pink** [pɪŋk] pink(farben), rosa I
°**pioneer** [ˌpaɪə'nɪə] Pionier

**pirate** ['paɪrət] Pirat, Piratin I
**pitch** [pɪtʃ] Fußball-/Hockeyplatz III
**pizza** ['piːtsə] Pizza I
**place** [pleɪs] Ort, Platz I
°**placemat** ['pleɪsmæt] Set, Platzdeckchen
**plan** [plæn] Plan I
**plan (-nn-)** [plæn] planen I
**plane** [pleɪn] Flugzeug II • **on the plane** im Flugzeug II
**planet** ['plænɪt] Planet II
°**plantation** [plæn'teɪʃn] Plantage
**plate** [pleɪt]
1. Teller I • **a plate of chips** ein Teller Pommes frites I
2. **license plate** *(AE)* Nummernschild IV Intro (10) • **number plate** *(BE)* Nummernschild IV Intro (10/165)
**platform** ['plætfɔːm] Bahnsteig, Gleis IV 3 (65)
**play** [pleɪ] spielen I • **play football** Fußball spielen I • °**play music** musizieren • °**play sports** *(AE)* Sport treiben • **play the drums** *(pl)* Schlagzeug spielen III • **play the fiddle** Geige, Fiedel spielen III **play the guitar** Gitarre spielen I • **play the piano** Klavier spielen I
**play** [pleɪ] Theaterstück I
**player** ['pleɪə] Spieler/in I
**please** [pliːz] bitte *(in Fragen und Aufforderungen)* I
**plug** [plʌg] Stecker III
**plus** [plʌs] plus IV 3 (60/175)
**pm** [ˌpiː‿'em]: **7 pm** 7 Uhr abends/19 Uhr I
**pocket** ['pɒkɪt] Tasche *(an Kleidungsstück)* II • **pocket money** Taschengeld II
**poem** ['pəʊɪm] Gedicht I
**point** [pɔɪnt] Punkt II • **10.4 (ten point four)** 10,4 (zehn Komma vier) III
**point (at/to sth.)** [pɔɪnt] zeigen, deuten (auf etwas) II
**police** *(pl)* [pə'liːs] Polizei I
**police station** Polizeiwache, Polizeirevier II
**policeman** [pə'liːsmən] Polizist II
**policewoman** [pə'liːswʊmən] Polizistin II
°**politics** ['pɒlɪtɪks] Politik
**poltergeist** ['pəʊltəgaɪst] Poltergeist I
**poor** [pɔː, pʊə]
1. arm I
°2. armselig
**poor Sophie** (die) arme Sophie I
**pop** [pɒp] Pop(musik) III
**popcorn** ['pɒpkɔːn] Popcorn II
**popular** ['pɒpjələ] beliebt, populär III
**population** [ˌpɒpju'leɪʃn] Bevölkerung, Einwohner(zahl) IV 3 (60)
**pork** [pɔːk] Schweinefleisch III
**possible** ['pɒsəbl] möglich II
**postcard** ['pəʊstkɑːd] Postkarte II
**poster** ['pəʊstə] Poster I
**post office** ['pəʊst‿ɒfɪs] Postamt II
**postscript (PS)** ['pəʊstskrɪpt] Postskript *(Nachschrift unter Briefen)* III
**potato** [pə'teɪtəʊ], *pl* **potatoes** Kartoffel I • **potato chips** *(AE)* Kartoffelchips IV 1 (20)
**poultry** ['pəʊltri] Geflügel IV 3 (56)
**pound (£)** [paʊnd] Pfund *(britische Währung)* I
**practice** ['præktɪs] *hier:* Übungsteil I
**practise** ['præktɪs]
1. üben; trainieren I
°2. ausüben, praktizieren
**prejudice (against)** ['predʒudɪs] Voreingenommenheit (gegen), Vorurteil (gegenüber) IV 2 (37)
**prepare (for)** [prɪ'peə] vorbereiten; sich vorbereiten (auf)
**present** ['preznt]
1. Gegenwart I
2. Geschenk I
°**present sth. (to sb.)** [prɪ'zent] (jm.) etwas präsentieren, vorstellen
**presentation** [ˌprezn'teɪʃn] Präsentation, Vorstellung I
**presenter** [prɪ'zentə] Moderator/in II
**president** ['prezɪdənt] Präsident/in IV 4 (88)
**press** [pres] drücken III
**pretty** ['prɪti] hübsch I
**pretty healthy/good/...** ['prɪti] ziemlich gesund/gut/... II
**price** [praɪs] (Kauf-)Preis I • °**price on sb.'s head** Kopfgeld
°**private spot** [ˌpraɪvət 'spɒt] abgelegener, ungestörter Platz
**prize** [praɪz] Preis, Gewinn I
**probably** ['prɒbəbli] wahrscheinlich II
**problem** ['prɒbləm] Problem II
**produce** [prə'djuːs] produzieren, herstellen III
**product** ['prɒdʌkt] Produkt IV 3 (56)
**profile** ['prəʊfaɪl] Porträt, Steckbrief III
**programme** ['prəʊgræm]
1. Programm I
2. (Fernseh-)Sendung IV 4 (76)
**project (about, on)** ['prɒdʒekt] Projekt (über, zu) I • **do a project** ein Projekt machen, durchführen II
**promise** ['prɒmɪs] versprechen II
°**pronounce** [prə'naʊns] aussprechen
**pronunciation** [prəˌnʌnsi'eɪʃn] Aussprache I
**proof** *(no pl)* [pruːf] Beweis(e) II
**protect** [prə'tekt] schützen IV 4 (88)
**proud (of sb./sth.)** [praʊd] stolz (auf jn./etwas) II
**PS** [ˌpiː‿'es] **(postscript** ['pəʊstskrɪpt]**)** PS (Postskript; *Nachschrift unter Briefen*) III
**pub** [pʌb] Kneipe, Lokal II
**public** ['pʌblɪk] öffentlich; Öffentlichkeit IV 4 (87)
**publish** ['pʌblɪʃ] veröffentlichen III
**pull** [pʊl] ziehen I
**pullover** ['pʊləʊvə] Pullover II
**purple** ['pɜːpl] violett; lila I
**purse** [pɜːs] Geldbörse II
**push** [pʊʃ] drücken, schieben, stoßen I
**put (-tt-)** [pʊt], **put, put** legen, stellen, *(etwas wohin)* tun I • °**put on music** Musik auflegen • **put out a fire** ein Feuer löschen IV 1 (15)
**put sth. on** etwas anziehen *(Kleidung)* II • °**Put up your hand.** Heb deine Hand. / Hebt eure Hand.
**puzzled** ['pʌzld] verwirrt II
**pyjamas** *(pl)* [pə'dʒɑːməz] Schlafanzug II
°**pyramid** ['pɪrəmɪd] Pyramide

## Q

**quarter** ['kwɔːtə]: **quarter past 11** Viertel nach 11 (11.15/23.15) I
**quarter to 12** Viertel vor 12 (11.45/23.45) I
**quay** [kiː] Kai, Kaimauer III
**queen** [kwiːn] Königin III
**question** ['kwestʃn] Frage I • **ask questions** Fragen stellen I
°**question word** Fragewort
**queue** [kjuː] Schlange, Reihe *(wartender Menschen)* IV 1 (14/166)
**quick** [kwɪk] schnell I
**quiet** ['kwaɪət] leise, still, ruhig I
°**quit** [kwɪt] aufhören, aufgeben
**quite bad/quick/good ...** [kwaɪt] ziemlich schlimm/schnell/gut/... II
**quiz** [kwɪz], *pl* **quizzes** ['kwɪzɪz] Quiz, Ratespiel I

## R

**rabbit** ['ræbɪt] Kaninchen I
**racket** ['rækɪt]: **badminton racket** Badmintonschläger III
**radio** ['reɪdiəʊ] Radio I • **on the radio** im Radio I

°**raft** [rɑːft] Schlauchboot *(wildwassertauglich)*
**rafting** ['rɑːftɪŋ] Rafting IV 3 (65)
**railway** ['reɪlweɪ] Eisenbahn II
**rain** [reɪn] Regen II
**rain** [reɪn] regnen II
**rainy** ['reɪni] regnerisch II
**raise money (for)** [reɪz] Geld sammeln (für) IV Intro (9)
**ran** [ræn] *siehe* **run**
**rang** [ræŋ] *siehe* **ring**
**ranger** ['reɪndʒə]: **(park) ranger** *Ranger sind eine Art Aufseher/in in Nationalparks, die auch Führungen machen und als Wald- und Wildhüter/innen arbeiten* IV Intro (9)
**rap** [ræp] Rap *(rhythmischer Sprechgesang)* I
**rapper** ['ræpə] Rapper/in IV 1 (24)
**RE** [ˌɑːr‿'iː], **Religious Education** [rɪˌlɪdʒəs‿edʒu'keɪʃn] Religion, Religionsunterricht I
°**reaction (to)** [ri'ækʃn] Reaktion (to)
**read** [riːd], **read, read** lesen I
°**read out** vorlesen • °**Read out loud.** Lies laut vor. • °**Read the poem to a partner.** Lies das Gedicht einem Partner/einer Partnerin vor.
**read** [red] *siehe* **read**
**reader** ['riːdə] Leser/in II
**ready** ['redi] bereit, fertig I • **get ready (for)** sich fertig machen (für), sich vorbereiten (auf) I • **get things ready** Dinge fertig machen, vorbereiten I
**real** [rɪəl] echt, wirklich I
**realistic** [ˌriːə'lɪstɪk] realistisch, wirklichkeitsnah III
**reality** [ri'æləti] Realität, Wirklichkeit IV 4 (76) • **reality show** Realityshow IV 4 (76)
**really** ['rɪəli] wirklich I
**reason** ['riːzn] Grund, Begründung I • **for lots of reasons** aus vielen Gründen I
**receive** [rɪ'siːv] empfangen IV 4 (82)
**record** [rɪ'kɔːd] *(Musik / einen Film)* aufnehmen III
**recorder** [rɪ'kɔːdə] Blockflöte III
**recording** [rɪ'kɔːdɪŋ] Aufnahme, Aufzeichnung III
**recycled** [ˌriː'saɪkld] wiederverwertet, wiederverwendet, recycelt II
**recycling** [ˌriː'saɪklɪŋ] Wiederverwertung, Recycling II
**red** [red] rot I
°**reflex** ['riːfleks] Reflex
**reggae** ['regeɪ] Reggae III
**regular** ['regjələ] normal *(Größenangabe bei Getränken und Fastfood)* IV 1 (16)
**rehearsal** [rɪ'hɜːsl] Probe *(am Theater)* I
**rehearse** [rɪ'hɜːs] proben *(am Theater)* I
**relations** *(pl)* [rɪ'leɪʃnz] Beziehungen IV 2 (37)
**relax** [rɪ'læks] (sich) entspannen, sich ausruhen II
°**religion** [rɪ'lɪdʒən] Religion
**remember sth.** [rɪ'membə]
**1.** sich erinnern (an etwas) I
**2.** sich etwas merken I
°**3. remember sb.** jemandes gedenken
°**Remember ...** Denk dran, ...
**remote control** [rɪˌməʊt kən'trəʊl] Fernbedienung IV 4 (82)
°**repeat** [rɪ'piːt] wiederholen
**report (on)** [rɪ'pɔːt] Bericht, Reportage (über) I
**report (to sb.)** [rɪ'pɔːt] (jm.) berichten II
**reporter** [rɪ'pɔːtə] Reporter/in IV 4 (77)
**represent** [ˌreprɪ'zent] repräsentieren, vertreten III
**rescue helicopter** ['reskjuː ˌhelɪkɒptə] Rettungshubschrauber II
**research (on)** *(no pl)* [rɪ'sɜːtʃ, 'riːsɜːtʃ] Recherche (zu, über); Nachforschungen (zu, über) IV 4 (79)
**do research** recherchieren IV 4 (79/178)
°**reservation** [ˌrezə'veɪʃn] Reservat *(Schutzgebiet für Volksgruppen, besonders für Indianer in Nordamerika)*
**rest** [rest] Rest II
**restaurant** ['restrɒnt] Restaurant II
**result** [rɪ'zʌlt] Ergebnis, Resultat I
**return** [rɪ'tɜːn] zurückkehren IV 4 (89)
**return ticket** Rückfahrkarte II
**return** [rɪ'tɜːn] Rückkehr IV 4 (89/179)
**revise** [rɪ'vaɪz]
**1.** überarbeiten III
**2.** wiederholen III
**revision** [rɪ'vɪʒn] Wiederholung *(des Lernstoffs)* I
**rhino** ['raɪnəʊ] Nashorn II
**rice** [raɪs] Reis IV 3 (56)
**rich** [rɪtʃ] reich II
**ridden** ['rɪdn] *siehe* **ride**
**ride** [raɪd], **rode, ridden** reiten I
**go riding** ['raɪdɪŋ] reiten gehen I
**ride a bike** Rad fahren I
**ride** [raɪd]: **(bike) ride** (Rad-)Fahrt II
**right** [raɪt] Recht IV 4 (79)
**right** [raɪt] richtig I • **all right** [ɔːl 'raɪt] gut, in Ordnung II • **be right** Recht haben I • **That's right.** Das ist richtig. / Das stimmt. I • **You need a school bag, right?** Du brauchst eine Schultasche, stimmt's? / nicht wahr? I
**right** [raɪt] rechte(r, s) II • **look right** nach rechts schauen II • **on the right** rechts, auf der rechten Seite II • **turn right** (nach) rechts abbiegen II
**right** [raɪt]: **right now** jetzt sofort; jetzt gerade I
**ring** [rɪŋ] Ring II
**ring** [rɪŋ], **rang, rung** klingeln, läuten II • **The bell rang.** Es klingelte. III
**ringtone** ['rɪŋtəʊn] Klingelton III
**river** ['rɪvə] Fluss II
°**rm** *Abkürzung für* **room**
**RnB** [ˌɑːr‿ən'biː] RnB *(Rhythm and Blues; Form des Blues, in der Rhythmus eine große Rolle spielt)* III
**road** [rəʊd] Straße I • **Park Road** [ˌpɑːk 'rəʊd] Parkstraße I
°**rob (-bb-)** [rɒb] be-, ausrauben
**rock** [rɒk] Fels, Felsen III
**rock (music)** [rɒk] Rock(musik) III
**rode** [rəʊd] *siehe* **ride**
**role** [rəʊl] Rolle III • **role play** Rollenspiel II
**roll** [rəʊl] Brötchen I
**rollerblades** ['rəʊləbleɪdz] Rollerblades IV 1 (14)
**rollerskating** ['rəʊləskeɪtɪŋ] Rollerskaten IV 1 (14)
**Roman** ['rəʊmən] römisch; Römer, Römerin II
**room** [ruːm] Raum, Zimmer I
°**root** [ruːt] Wurzel
**round** [raʊnd] rund II
**round** [raʊnd] um ... (herum); in ... umher II • **the other way round** anders herum II
**route** [ruːt] Strecke, Route IV Intro (10)
**rubber** ['rʌbə] Radiergummi I
**rubbish** ['rʌbɪʃ] (Haus-)Müll, Abfall II
**rucksack** ['rʌksæk] Rucksack III
**rude** [ruːd] unhöflich, unverschämt II
**rule** [ruːl] Regel, Vorschrift III
**ruler** ['ruːlə] Lineal I
**run** [rʌn] (Wett-)Lauf II
**run (-nn-)** [rʌn], **ran, run** laufen, rennen I • **run around** herumrennen III
**rung** [rʌŋ] *siehe* **ring**
**runner** ['rʌnə] Läufer/in II
**running shoes** ['rʌnɪŋ ʃuːz] Laufschuhe III
°**rush to** [rʌʃ] stürzen nach, stürmen nach
°**rush:** °**gold rush** ['gəʊld rʌʃ] Goldrausch

# S

**sad** [sæd]
**1.** traurig II
°**2.** *Jugendsprache:* peinlich
**saddle** ['sædl] Sattel III
**safe (from)** [seɪf] sicher, in Sicherheit (vor) II
**safety** ['seɪfti] Sicherheit IV 1 (25)
**fire safety** Verhalten im Brandfall IV 1 (25)
**said** [sed] *siehe* **say**
**sailor** ['seɪlə] Seemann, Matrose II
**salad** ['sæləd] Salat *(als Gericht oder Beilage)* I
**sale** [seɪl] (Aus-, Schluss-)Verkauf IV Intro (9) • **for sale** *(auf Schild)* zu verkaufen IV Intro (9)
°**salmon** ['sæmən] Lachs
**same** [seɪm]**: the same ...** der-/die-/dasselbe ...; dieselben ... I • **be/look the same** gleich sein/aussehen I
**sandwich** ['sænwɪtʃ] Sandwich, *(zusammengeklapptes)* belegtes Brot I • **sandwich box** Brotdose I
**sang** [sæŋ] *siehe* **sing**
°**sank down** [sæŋk] *siehe* **sink down**
**sat** [sæt] *siehe* **sit**
**satellite** ['sætəlaɪt] Satellit IV 4 (82)
**Saturday** ['sætədeɪ, 'sætədi] Samstag, Sonnabend I
**sauna** ['sɔːnə] Sauna II • **have a sauna** in die Sauna gehen II
**sausage** ['sɒsɪdʒ] (Brat-, Bock-) Würstchen, Wurst I
**save** [seɪv]
**1.** retten II
**2.** sparen II
**saw** [sɔː] *siehe* **see**
**saxophone** ['sæksəfəʊn] Saxophon III
**say** [seɪ]**, said, said** sagen I • **It says here: ...** Hier steht: ... / Es heißt hier: ... II • **say goodbye** sich verabschieden I • **Say hi to Dilip for me.** Grüß Dilip von mir. I
**say sorry** sich entschuldigen II
**scan a text (-nn-)** [skæn] einen Text schnell nach bestimmten Wörtern/ Informationen absuchen II
**scared** [skeəd] verängstigt II • **be scared (of)** Angst haben (vor) I
**scarf** [skɑːf]**,** *pl* **scarves** [skɑːvz] Schal III
**scary** ['skeəri] unheimlich; gruselig I
**scene** [siːn] Szene I
**schedule** ['skedʒuːl] *(AE)*
**1.** Fahrplan IV 1 (20
**2.** Stundenplan IV 1 (20)

**school** [skuːl] Schule I • **at school** in der Schule I • **school bag** Schultasche I • **school subject** Schulfach I
**science** ['saɪəns] Naturwissenschaft I
**score (a goal)** [skɔː], [gəʊl] ein Tor schießen, einen Treffer erzielen III
**score** [skɔː] Spielstand; Punktestand III • **final score** Endstand *(beim Sport)* III • **What's the score? – 2–0 (two nil)** Wie steht es? *(beim Sport)* – 2:0. III
**scoreless** ['skɔːləs] torlos IV 2 (42)
°**scrapbook** ['skræpbʊk] Sammelalbum
**scream** [skriːm] schreien, kreischen IV 1 (27)
**screen** [skriːn] Bildschirm IV 4 (77)
**flat screen** Flachbildschirm IV 4 (82)
°**script** [skrɪpt] Drehbuch
**sea** [siː] Meer, *(die)* See I
°**search engine** ['sɜːtʃ‿endʒɪn] Suchmaschine *(im Internet)*
°**seat** [siːt] Sitzplatz • °**give up a seat** einen Sitzplatz freimachen
**second** ['sekənd] zweite(r, s) I
**second-hand** [ˌsekənd 'hænd] gebraucht; aus zweiter Hand III
**section** ['sekʃn] Abschnitt, Teil, (Themen-)Bereich III
**see** [siː]**, saw, seen**
**1.** sehen I
**2. see sb.** jn. besuchen, jn. aufsuchen II
**See?** Siehst du? I • **See you.** Tschüs. / Bis bald. I • °**You see, ...** Wissen Sie, ... • **Wait and see!** Wart's ab! III
**seem (to be/do)** [siːm] (zu sein / zu tun) scheinen IV 1 (26)
**seen** [siːn] *siehe* **see**
**sell** [sel]**, sold, sold** verkaufen II
**semester** [sɪ'mestə] Semester *(Schulhalbjahr in den USA)* IV 3 (54)
**semi-final** [ˌsemi'faɪnl] Halbfinale III
**send (to)** [send]**, sent, sent** schicken, senden (an) II
**sent** [sent] *siehe* **send**
**sentence** ['sentəns] Satz I
**September** [sep'tembə] September I
°**sequoia** [ sɪ'kwɔɪə] Sequoia, Mammutbaum
**series,** *pl* **series** ['sɪəriːz] (Sende-) Reihe, Serie II
**serious** ['sɪəriəs] ernst, ernsthaft IV 2 (49)
°**settler** ['setlə] Siedler/in

**setup** ['setʌp] Setup II
**sex** [seks] Geschlecht III
**share sth. (with sb.)** [ʃeə] sich etwas teilen (mit jm.) I
**she** [ʃiː] sie I
**sheep,** *pl* **sheep** [ʃiːp] Schaf II
**shelf** [ʃelf]**,** *pl* **shelves** [ʃelvz] Regal(brett) I
**shift** [ʃɪft] Schicht IV 1 (15)
**shine** [ʃaɪn]**, shone, shone** scheinen *(Sonne)* II
**ship** [ʃɪp] Schiff I
**shirt** [ʃɜːt] Hemd I
°**shiver** ['ʃɪvə] zittern
**shocked** [ʃɒkt] schockiert III
**shoe** [ʃuː] Schuh I
**shone** [ʃɒn] *siehe* **shine**
**shoot** [ʃuːt]**, shot, shot** schießen, erschießen III
**shop** [ʃɒp] Laden, Geschäft I
**shop assistant** ['ʃɒp‿əˌsɪstənt] Verkäufer/in I • **shop window** Schaufenster II
**shop (-pp-)** [ʃɒp] einkaufen (gehen) I
**shopping** ['ʃɒpɪŋ] (das) Einkaufen I
**shopping mall** Einkaufspassage, überdachtes Einkaufszentrum IV 4 (74) • **go shopping** einkaufen gehen I • **shopping list** Einkaufsliste I
**short** [ʃɔːt]
**1.** kurz I
**2.** klein *(Person)* IV 1 (17/168)
**shorts** *(pl)* [ʃɔːts] Shorts, kurze Hose I
**shot** [ʃɒt] *siehe* **shoot**
**should** [ʃəd, ʃʊd]**: we should ...** wir sollten ... IV 1 (26)
► S.177 möglich – wahrscheinlich – sicherlich
**shoulder** ['ʃəʊldə] Schulter I
**shout** [ʃaʊt] schreien, rufen I
**show** [ʃəʊ] Show, Vorstellung I
**show** [ʃəʊ]**, showed, shown** zeigen I
**shower** ['ʃaʊə] Dusche I • **have a shower** (sich) duschen I
**shown** [ʃəʊn] *siehe* **show**
**shut up** [ˌʃʌt‿'ʌp]**, shut, shut** den Mund halten II
**shy** [ʃaɪ] schüchtern, scheu II
**sick** [sɪk]**: I feel sick.** Mir ist schlecht. IV 1 (26)
**side** [saɪd] Seite II
**sidewalk** ['saɪdwɔːk] *(AE)* Gehweg, Bürgersteig IV 1 (14)
**sights** *(pl)* [saɪts] Sehenswürdigkeiten II
**sightseeing trip** ['saɪtsiːɪŋ trɪp] Besichtigungstour IV 1 (13)
**sign** [saɪn] Schild; Zeichen III

**silent letter** [ˌsaɪlənt 'letə] „stummer" Buchstabe *(nicht gesprochener Buchstabe)* II
**silly** ['sɪli] albern, dumm I
**since** [sɪns]**: since April 4th** seit dem 4. April IV 4 (78)
► S.177 German 'seit'
°**sincerely** [sɪn'sɪəli]**: Yours sincerely** Mit freundlichen Grüßen / Herzliche Grüße *(freundliche Grußformel in Briefen)*
**sing** [sɪŋ]**, sang, sung** singen I
**singer** ['sɪŋə] Sänger/in II
**single** ['sɪŋgl] ledig, alleinstehend I
**single (ticket)** ['sɪŋgl] einfache Fahrkarte *(nur Hinfahrt)* III
**sink** [sɪŋk] Spüle, Spülbecken I
°**sink down** [sɪŋk]**, sank, sunk** niedersinken/zusammensinken
°**sir** [sɜː]**: °Dear Sir or Madam** Sehr geehrte Damen und Herren
**sister** ['sɪstə] Schwester I
**sit (-tt-)** [sɪt]**, sat, sat** sitzen; sich setzen I • **sit down** sich hinsetzen II • **Sit with me.** Setz dich zu mir. / Setzt euch zu mir. I
**size** [saɪz] Größe I
**skate** ['skeɪt] Inliner fahren I
**skateboard** ['skeɪtbɔːd] Skateboard I
**skates** *(pl)* [skeɪts] Inliner I
**sketch** [sketʃ] Sketch I
**ski** [skiː] Ski fahren/laufen III
**ski** [skiː] Ski III
**skills file** ['skɪlz faɪl] *Anhang mit Lern- und Arbeitstechniken* I
**skim a text (-mm-)** [skɪm] einen Text überfliegen *(um den Inhalt grob zu erfassen)* III
**skin** [skɪn] Haut IV 4 (79)
**skinny** ['skɪni] mager IV 3 (66/176)
**skirt** [skɜːt] Rock II
**sky** [skaɪ] Himmel II
°**skyline** ['skaɪˌlaɪn] Skyline *(Horizont; Silhouette)*
**skyscraper** ['skaɪskreɪpə] Wolkenkratzer IV 1 (23)
°**skywalk** ['skaɪwɔːk] *oberirdische, wettergeschützte Fußgängerverbindung*
**slave** [sleɪv] Sklave, Sklavin II
**sledge** [sledʒ] Schlitten III
**sleep** [sliːp]**, slept, slept** schlafen I
**sleep** [sliːp] Schlaf III
**sleepless** ['sliːpləs] schlaflos IV 2 (42)
**sleepover** ['sliːpəʊvə] Schlafparty III
**slept** [slept] *siehe* **sleep**
**slow** [sləʊ] langsam II
**small** [smɔːl] klein I
**smart** [smɑːt] clever, schlau II
**smell** [smel] riechen II
**smell** [smel] Geruch II
**smile** [smaɪl] lächeln I • **smile at sb.** jn. anlächeln II
**smile** [smaɪl] Lächeln II
**smoke** [sməʊk] rauchen III • **no smoking** Rauchen verboten III
**smoke** [sməʊk] Rauch III
**snack** [snæk] Snack, Imbiss II
**snake** [sneɪk] Schlange I
**snow** [snəʊ] Schnee II
**snowball** ['snəʊbɔːl] Schneeball IV 3 (66)
**snowshoe** ['snəʊʃuː] Schneeschuh III
**snowshoeing** ['snəʊʃuːɪŋ] Schneeschuhwandern III
**so** [səʊ]
**1.** also; deshalb, daher I • **So?** Und? / Na und? II
**2. so sweet** so süß I • °**so far** bis jetzt, bisher
**3. Do you really think so?** Meinst du wirklich? / Glaubst du das wirklich? II
**soap** [səʊp] Seife I • **soap opera** *(kurz:* **soap***)* Seifenoper IV 2 (50)
**soccer** ['sɒkə] Fußball IV 3 (57)
**social** ['səʊʃl] sozial, Sozial- IV 2 (50)
**sock** [sɒk] Socke, Strumpf I
**soda** ['səʊdə] *(AE)* Limonade IV 3 (56) • **soda machine** *(AE)* Getränkeautomat IV 3 (64)
**sofa** ['səʊfə] Sofa I
**soft** [sɒft] weich IV 3 (64/175) • **soft drink** alkoholfreies Getränk IV 3 (64)
**software** ['sɒftweə] Software II
**sold** [səʊld] *siehe* **sell**
**soldier** ['səʊldʒə] Soldat/in IV 4 (88)
**some** [səm, sʌm] einige, ein paar I **some cheese/juice** etwas Käse/ Saft I
**somebody** ['sʌmbədi] jemand I **Find/Ask somebody who ...** Finde/Frage jemanden, der ... II **somebody else** jemand anders IV 1 (15/167)
► S.167 ... else
**someone** ['sʌmwʌn] jemand IV 2 (34/170)
**something** ['sʌmθɪŋ] etwas II
**sometimes** ['sʌmtaɪmz] manchmal I
**somewhere** ['sʌmweə] irgendwo(hin) II
**son** [sʌn] Sohn I
**song** [sɒŋ] Lied, Song I
**soon** [suːn] bald I
**sore** [sɔː]**: have a sore throat** Halsschmerzen haben II
**sorry** ['sɒri]**: (I'm) sorry.** Entschuldigung. / Tut mir leid. I • °**I'm sorry about your guitar.** Es tut mir leid wegen deiner Gitarre. • **Sorry, I'm late.** Entschuldigung, dass ich zu spät bin/komme. I • **Sorry?** Wie bitte? I • **say sorry** sich entschuldigen II
**sort** [sɔːt] Art, Sorte II
**sound** [saʊnd] klingen, sich *(gut usw.)* anhören I
**sound** [saʊnd] Laut; Klang I **sound file** ['saʊnd faɪl] Tondatei, Soundfile III
**soup** [suːp] Suppe II
°**source** [sɔːs] (Informations-)Quelle
**south** [saʊθ] Süden; nach Süden; südlich III
**south-east** [ˌsaʊθ'iːst] Südosten; nach Südosten, südöstlich III
**south-west** [ˌsaʊθ'west] Südwesten; nach Südwesten; südwestlich III
**souvenir** [ˌsuːvə'nɪə] Souvenir, Mitbringsel IV Intro (10)
**space** [speɪs]**: Move back one space.** Geh ein Feld zurück. II • **Move on one space.** Geh ein Feld vor. II
**spaghetti** [spə'geti] Spaghetti II
°**Spanish-speaking** ['spænɪʃ] spanischsprachig; Spanisch sprechend
**speak (to)** [spiːk]**, spoke, spoken** sprechen (mit), reden (mit) II
**special** ['speʃl] besondere(r,s) I • **a special day** ein besonderer Tag I
**speech** [spiːtʃ] Rede IV 4 (79) **make a speech** eine Rede halten IV 4 (79/177) • °**speech bubble** Sprechblase
**spell** [spel] buchstabieren I
**spelling** ['spelɪŋ] (Recht-)Schreibung, Schreibweise III
**spend** [spend]**, spent, spent: spend money (on)** Geld ausgeben (für) II • **spend time (on)** Zeit verbringen (mit) II
**spent** [spent] *siehe* **spend**
**spicy** ['spaɪsi] würzig, scharf gewürzt III
**spoke** [spəʊk] *siehe* **speak**
**spoken** ['spəʊkən] *siehe* **speak**
**spoon** [spuːn] Löffel III
**sport** [spɔːt] Sport; Sportart I **do sport** *(BE)* Sport treiben °**play sports** *(AE)* Sport treiben I **sports centre** Sportzentrum I
**sportsman** ['spɔːtsmən] Sportler IV 2 (42)
**sportswoman** ['spɔːtswʊmən] Sportlerin IV 2 (42)
**sporty** ['spɔːti] sportlich III
°**spot: private spot** [ˌpraɪvət 'spɒt] abgelegener, ungestörter Platz
**spotlight** ['spɒtlaɪt] Spotlight IV 3 (67)

**spring** [sprɪŋ] Frühling I
**spy** [spaɪ] Spion/in I
**square** [skweə] Platz III
**squirrel** ['skwɪrəl] Eichhörnchen II
**stadium** ['steɪdiəm] Stadion III
**stage** [steɪdʒ] Bühne III
**stairs** *(pl)* [steəz] Treppe; Treppenstufen I
**stamp** [stæmp] Briefmarke I
**stand** [stænd], **stood, stood** stehen; sich (hin)stellen II
**star** [stɑː]
**1.** Stern II
**2.** (Film-, Pop-)Star I
**start** [stɑːt] starten, anfangen, beginnen (mit) I
**state** [steɪt] Staat III
**statement** ['steɪtmənt] Aussage, Feststellung III
**station** ['steɪʃn] Bahnhof I • **at the station** am Bahnhof I
**statue** ['stætʃuː] Statue II
**stay** [steɪ]
**1.** bleiben I
**2.** wohnen, übernachten II
**steak** [steɪk] Steak III
**steal** [stiːl], **stole, stolen** stehlen II
**steel** [stiːl] Stahl III • **steel drum** [ˌstiːl 'drʌm] Steeldrum III
**step** [step] Schritt I
**stereo** ['steriəʊ] Stereoanlage I
**still** [stɪl] (immer) noch I
**stole** [stəʊl] *siehe* **steal**
**stolen** ['stəʊlən] *siehe* **steal**
**stomach** ['stʌmək]
**1.** Magen II
**2.** Bauch III
**stomach ache** Magenschmerzen, Bauchweh II
**stone** [stəʊn] Stein II
**stood** [stʊd] *siehe* **stand**
**stop** [stɒp] Halt IV 1 (12)
**stop (-pp-)** [stɒp]
**1.** aufhören I
**2.** anhalten I
**Stop that!** Hör auf damit! / Lass das! I
**storm** [stɔːm] Sturm; Gewitter II
**stormy** ['stɔːmi] stürmisch II
**story** ['stɔːri] Geschichte, Erzählung I
**straight on** [streɪt‿'ɒn] geradeaus weiter II
**strange** [streɪndʒ] seltsam, sonderbar; fremd IV 3 (57)
**strawberry** ['strɔːbəri] Erdbeere II
**street** [striːt] Straße I • **at 7 Hamilton Street** in der Hamiltonstraße 7 I
**stress** [stres] Betonung III
°**stressed** [strest] betont
**strict** [strɪkt] streng III
**strike** [straɪk] Streik III • **be on strike** streiken, sich im Streik befinden III • **go on strike** streiken, in den Streik treten III
**strong** [strɒŋ] stark II
**structure** ['strʌktʃə] strukturieren, aufbauen II
**student** ['stjuːdənt] Schüler/in; Student/in I • °**student body** Studentenschaft
**study** ['stʌdɪ] studieren; sorgfältig durchlesen; lernen IV 3 (54/174)
**study hall** *Zeit zum selbstständigen Arbeiten/Lernen in der Schule* IV 3 (54) • **study skills** *(pl)* Lern- und Arbeitstechniken I
**stuff** [stʌf] Zeug, Kram II
**stupid** ['stjuːpɪd] blöd, dämlich II
**subject** ['sʌbdʒɪkt]
**1.** Schulfach I
°**2.** *Betreff in einer E-Mail*
°**suburb** ['sʌbɜːb] Vorort
**subway** ['sʌbweɪ]: **the subway** *(AE)* die U-Bahn II
**successful** [sək'sesfl] erfolgreich IV 2 (37)
°**such** [sʌtʃ] so, solch
**suddenly** ['sʌdnli] plötzlich, auf einmal I
**sugar** ['ʃʊgə] Zucker II
**suitcase** ['suːtkeɪs] Koffer II
**summarize sth.** ['sʌməraɪz] etwas zusammenfassen IV 3 (65)
**summary** ['sʌməri] Zusammenfassung IV 3 (65/175)
**summer** ['sʌmə] Sommer I
**sun** [sʌn] Sonne II
**Sunday** ['sʌndeɪ, 'sʌndi] Sonntag I
**sung** [sʌŋ] *siehe* **sing**
**sunglasses** *(pl)* ['sʌnglɑːsɪz] (eine) Sonnenbrille I
**sunny** ['sʌni] sonnig II
°**sunshine** ['sʌnʃaɪn] Sonnenschein
**super** ['suːpə] super IV 2 (45)
**supermarket** ['suːpəmɑːkɪt] Supermarkt II • **a 24-hour supermarket** ein Supermarkt, der 24 Stunden geöffnet ist III
**sure** [ʃʊə, ʃɔː] klar, sicher IV 1 (23)
**be sure** sicher sein II
**surf the internet** [sɜːf] im Internet surfen III
**surfboard** ['sɜːfbɔːd] Surfbrett II
**surfing** ['sɜːfɪŋ]: **go surfing** wellenreiten gehen, surfen gehen II
°**surname** ['sɜːneɪm] Familienname
**surprise** [sə'praɪz] Überraschung III
**surprised (at sth.)** [sə'praɪzd] überrascht (über etwas) IV 1 (27)
**surprising** [sə'praɪzɪŋ] überraschend, erstaunlich IV 3 (68)
**survey (on)** ['sɜːveɪ] Umfrage, Untersuchung (über) II
**survive** [sə'vaɪv] überleben II
**swam** [swæm] *siehe* **swim**
**swap sth. (for sth.) (-pp-)** [swɒp] etwas (ein)tauschen (für etwas/gegen etwas) IV 3 (66)
°**sweat** [swet] schwitzen
**sweatshirt** ['swetʃɜːt] Sweatshirt I
**sweet** [swiːt] süß I
**sweetheart** ['swiːthɑːt] Liebling, Schatz II
**sweets** *(pl)* [swiːts] Süßigkeiten I
**swim (-mm-)** [swɪm], **swam, swum** schwimmen I • **go swimming** schwimmen gehen I
**swimmer** ['swɪmə] Schwimmer/in II
**swimming** ['swɪmɪŋ]: **swimming pool** Schwimmbad, Schwimmbecken I • **swimming trunks** *(pl)* ['swɪmɪŋ trʌŋks] Badehose III
**swimsuit** ['swɪmsuːt] Badeanzug III
**swum** [swʌm] *siehe* **swim**
**syllable** ['sɪləbl] Silbe I
**system** ['sɪstəm] System IV 3 (54)

# T

**table** ['teɪbl] Tisch I
**table tennis** ['teɪbl tenɪs] Tischtennis I • **table tennis bat** Tischtennisschläger III
**take** [teɪk], **took, taken**
**1.** nehmen I
**2.** (weg-, hin)bringen I
**3.** dauern, *(Zeit)* brauchen III
**take a break** eine Pause machen IV 1 (24) • °**take a ride** eine Fahrt machen • **take notes** sich Notizen machen I • **take off** *(infml)* sich davonmachen, sich aus dem Staub machen IV 1 (26) • **take out** herausnehmen I • °**take over a plane** die Kontrolle über ein Flugzeug übernehmen • °**take part** teilnehmen • **take photos** Fotos machen, fotografieren I • **take place** stattfinden IV 3 (53) • **take sth. off** etwas ausziehen *(Kleidung)* II • **take 10 c off** 10 Cent abziehen I • °**Take turns.** Wechselt euch ab. • **We'll take them.** *(beim Einkaufen)* Wir nehmen sie. I
**taken** ['teɪkən] *siehe* **take**
**talk** [tɔːk]: **talk (about)** reden (über), sich unterhalten (über) I • **talk (to)** reden (mit), sich unterhalten (mit) I

**tall** [tɔ:l] hoch *(Bäume, Türme usw.)*; groß *(Person)* IV 1 (17)
**taught** [tɔ:t] *siehe* **teach**
**taxi** ['tæksi] Taxi III
**tea** [ti:] Tee; *(auch:) leichte Nachmittags- oder Abendmahlzeit* I
**teach** [ti:tʃ], **taught, taught** unterrichten, lehren I
**teacher** ['ti:tʃə] Lehrer/in I • **head teacher** Schulleiter/in III
**team** [ti:m] Team, Mannschaft I
**teaspoon** ['ti:spu:n] Teelöffel III
**teddy** ['tedi] Teddy III
**teen** [ti:n] Teenager-, Jugend- III
**teenager** ['ti:neɪdʒə] Teenager, Jugendliche(r) II
**teeth** [ti:θ] *Plural von „tooth"* I
**telephone** ['telɪfəʊn] Telefon I
**telephone number** Telefonnummer I • **What's your telephone number?** Was ist deine Telefonnummer? I
**television (TV)** ['telɪvɪʒn] Fernsehen I
**tell (about)** [tel], **told, told** erzählen (von), berichten (über) I • **Tell me your names.** Sagt mir eure Namen. I • **tell sb. the way** jm. den Weg beschreiben II
**temperature** ['temprətʃə] Temperatur II • **have a temperature** Fieber haben II
**tennis** ['tenɪs] Tennis I
**tent** [tent] Zelt IV Intro (9)
**term** [tɜ:m] Trimester II
**terrible** ['terəbl] schrecklich, furchtbar I
**test** [test] Test, Prüfung II
**text** [tekst] Text I
**text sb.** [tekst] jm. eine SMS schicken III
**text message** ['tekst ˌmesɪdʒ] SMS III
**than** [ðæn, ðən] als II • **more than** mehr als II • **more than me** mehr als ich II
**thank** [θæŋk]: **Thank you.** Danke (schön). I • **Thanks.** Danke. I
**Thanks a lot!** Vielen Dank! I
**Thanks very much!** Danke sehr! / Vielen Dank! II
**that** [ðət, ðæt]
**1.** das (dort) I
**2.** jene(r, s) I
**That's me.** Das bin ich. I • **That's right.** Das ist richtig. / Das stimmt. I • **That's up to you.** Das liegt bei dir. / Das kannst/musst du (selbst) entscheiden. III • **That was close.** Das war knapp. II
**that** [ðət, ðæt] der, die, das; die *(Relativpronomen)* III
**that** [ðət, ðæt] dass I
**that far/good/bad/...** [ðæt] so weit/gut/schlecht/... III
**the** [ðə, ði] der, die, das; die I
**°the 1960s** die sechziger Jahre *(des 20. Jahrhunderts)*
**theatre** ['θɪətə] Theater II
**their** [ðeə] ihr, ihre *(Plural)* I
**theirs** [ðeəz] ihrer, ihre, ihrs II
**them** [ðəm, ðem] sie; ihnen I
**°theme** [θi:m]: **°theme park** Themenpark *(Freizeitpark mit Attraktionen zum einem bestimmten Thema)*
**°theme song** Titelsong
**themselves** [ðəm'selvz] sich (selbst) III
**then** [ðen] dann, danach I • **°now and then** damals und heute
**°therapy** ['θerəpi] (Psycho-)Therapie
**there** [ðeə]
**1.** da, dort I
**2.** dahin, dorthin I
**down there** dort unten II • **over there** da drüben, dort drüben I
**there are** es sind (vorhanden); es gibt I • **there's** es ist (vorhanden); es gibt I • **there isn't a ...** es ist kein/e ...; es gibt kein/e ... I
**thermometer** [θə'mɒmɪtə] Thermometer II
**these** [ði:z] diese, die (hier) I
**they** [ðeɪ] sie *(Plural)* I
**thief** [θi:f], *pl* **thieves** [θi:vz] Dieb/in II
**thing** [θɪŋ] Ding, Sache I • **What was the best thing about ...?** Was war das Beste an ...? II
**think** [θɪŋk], **thought, thought** glauben, meinen, denken I
**think about 1.** nachdenken über II; **2.** denken über, halten von II
**think of 1.** denken über, halten von II; **2.** denken an; sich ausdenken II
**third** [θɜ:d] dritte(r, s) I
**this** [ðɪs]
**1.** dies (hier) I
**2.** diese(r, s) I
**This is Isabel.** Hier spricht Isabel. / Hier ist Isabel. *(am Telefon)* II
**this morning/afternoon/evening** heute Morgen/Nachmittag/Abend I • **this way** hier entlang, in diese Richtung II
**those** [ðəʊz] die (da), jene (dort) I
**thought** [θɔ:t] *siehe* **think**
**thought** [θɔ:t] Gedanke III
**thousand** ['θaʊznd] tausend I
**threw** [θru:] *siehe* **throw**
**throat** [θrəʊt] Hals, Kehle II
**through** [θru:] durch II
**throw** [θrəʊ], **threw, thrown**
**1.** werfen I
**°2. throw up** sich übergeben, erbrechen
**thrown** [θrəʊn] *siehe* **throw**
**Thursday** ['θɜ:zdeɪ, 'θɜ:zdi] Donnerstag I
**°tick** [tɪk] Häkchen
**°tick** [tɪk] ankreuzen, ein Häkchen machen
**ticket** ['tɪkɪt]
**1.** Eintrittskarte I
**2.** Fahrkarte II • **return ticket** Rückfahrkarte II • **single ticket** einfache Fahrkarte *(nur Hinfahrt)* III
**tidy** ['taɪdi] aufräumen I
**tidy** ['taɪdi] ordentlich, aufgeräumt II
**tiger** ['taɪgə] Tiger II
**tight** [taɪt] eng III
**till** [tɪl] bis *(zeitlich)* I
**time** [taɪm]
**1.** Zeit; Uhrzeit I
**2. time(s)** Mal(e); -mal II
**in time** rechtzeitig III • **three times** dreimal III • **What's the time?** Wie spät ist es? I • **°What time?** Um welche Uhrzeit?
**°timeline** ['taɪmlaɪn] Zeitleiste
**timetable** ['taɪmteɪbl]
**1.** Stundenplan I
**2.** Fahrplan II
**timing** ['taɪmɪŋ] Timing IV 4 (78)
**tip** [tɪp] Tipp II
**tired** ['taɪəd] müde I • **be tired of sth.** genug von etwas haben, etwas satt haben IV 1 (24)
**title** ['taɪtl] Titel, Überschrift I
**to** [tə, tu]
**1.** zu, nach I • **to Jenny's** zu Jenny I • **to the doctor's** zum Arzt III
**°to the front** nach vorn
**2. an e-mail to** eine E-Mail an I
**write to** schreiben an I
**3. quarter to 12** Viertel vor 12 (11.45/23.45) I • **from Monday to Friday** von Montag bis Freitag III
**4. try to help/to play/...** versuchen, zu helfen/zu spielen/... I
**5.** um zu II
**toast** [təʊst] Toast(brot) I
**tobacco** [tə'bækəʊ] Tabak II
**today** [tə'deɪ] heute I
**toe** [təʊ] Zeh I
**together** [tə'geðə] zusammen I
**toilet** ['tɔɪlət] Toilette I
**told** [təʊld] *siehe* **tell**
**tomato** [tə'mɑ:təʊ], *pl* **tomatoes** Tomate II
**tomorrow** [tə'mɒrəʊ] morgen I
**tomorrow's weather** das Wetter von morgen II

**tonight** [tə'naɪt] heute Nacht, heute Abend I • **tonight's programme** das Programm von heute Abend; das heutige Abendprogramm II
**too** [tu:]**: from Bristol too** auch aus Bristol I • **Me too.** Ich auch. I
**too much/big/...** [tu:] zu viel/ groß/... I
**took** [tʊk] *siehe* **take**
**tooth** [tu:θ], *pl* **teeth** [ti:θ] Zahn I
**toothache** ['tu:θeɪk] Zahnschmerzen II
**top** [tɒp]
**1.** Spitze, oberes Ende I • **at the top (of)** oben, am oberen Ende, an der Spitze (von) I
**2.** Top, Oberteil I
**topic** ['tɒpɪk] Thema, Themenbereich I • **topic sentence** *Satz, der in das Thema eines Absatzes einführt* II
**tornado** [tɔ:'neɪdəʊ] Tornado, Wirbelsturm II
**tortoise** ['tɔ:təs] Schildkröte I
**touch** [tʌtʃ] berühren, anfassen II
**keep in touch** in Verbindung bleiben, Kontakt halten III
**tour (of the house)** [tʊə] Rundgang, Tour (durch das Haus) I
°**tourism** ['tʊərɪzəm] Tourismus, Fremdenverkehr
**tourist** ['tʊərɪst] Tourist/in II
**tourist information** Fremdenverkehrsamt II
**towards sb./sth.** [tə'wɔ:dz] auf jn./ etwas zu II
**tower** ['taʊə] Turm I
**town** [taʊn] (Klein-)Stadt I
**tradition** [trə'dɪʃn] Tradition IV 3 (53)
**traffic** ['træfɪk] Verkehr II
°**trail** [treɪl] Pfad
**train** [treɪn] Zug I • **on the train** im Zug I
**train** [treɪn] trainieren III
**trainers** *(pl)* ['treɪnəz] Turnschuhe II
**training session** ['seʃn] Trainingsstunde, -einheit III
**tram** [træm] Straßenbahn III
**translate (from ... into)** [træns'leɪt] übersetzen (aus ... ins) III
**translation** [træns'leɪʃn] Übersetzung III
**transport** ['trænspɔ:t] Beförderung, Transport III
**travel (-ll-)** ['trævl] reisen II
**Travelcard** ['trævlkɑ:d] Tagesfahrkarte *(der Londoner Verkehrsbetriebe)* III
**tree** [tri:] Baum I
**trendy** ['trendi] modisch, schick III
°**tribute** ['trɪbju:t] Ehrung; Würdigung

**trick** [trɪk]
**1.** (Zauber-)Kunststück, Trick I
**do tricks** (Zauber-)Kunststücke machen I
**2.** Streich II
**trip** [trɪp] Reise; Ausflug I • **day trip** Tagesausflug IV Intro (8) • **go on a trip** einen Ausflug machen II
**trouble** ['trʌbl] Schwierigkeiten, Ärger II • **be in trouble** in Schwierigkeiten sein; Ärger kriegen II
**trousers** *(pl)* ['traʊzəz] Hose II
**true** [tru:] wahr II • **come true** wahr werden; in Erfüllung gehen IV 4 (90)
**trumpet** ['trʌmpɪt] Trompete III
**try** [traɪ]
**1.** versuchen I
**2.** probieren, kosten I
**try and do sth. / try to do sth.** versuchen, etwas zu tun I • **try on** anprobieren *(Kleidung)* I
**T-shirt** ['ti:ʃɜ:t] T-Shirt I
**tsunami** [tsu:'nɑ:mi] Tsunami IV 2 (34)
**tube** [tju:b]**: the Tube** *(no pl)* die Londoner U-Bahn III
**Tuesday** ['tju:zdeɪ, 'tju:zdi] Dienstag I
**tunnel** ['tʌnl] Tunnel II
**turkey** ['tɜ:ki] Truthahn III
**turn** [tɜ:n]
**1.** sich umdrehen II • **turn away** sich abwenden, sich wegdrehen IV 4 (89) • **turn left/right** (nach) links/rechts abbiegen II • **turn to sb.** sich jm. zuwenden; sich an jn. wenden II
**2. turn on/off** ein-/ausschalten III
**3. turn sth. down/up** etwas leiser/ lauter stellen IV 4 (82)
**turn** [tɜ:n]**: It's your turn.** Du bist dran / an der Reihe. I • **Miss a turn.** Einmal aussetzen. II • °**Take turns.** Wechselt euch ab. • **Whose turn is it?** Wer ist dran / an der Reihe? II
**TV** [ti:'vi:]
**1.** Fernsehgerät IV 4 (77)
**2.** Fernsehen I • **on TV** im Fernsehen I • **watch TV** fernsehen I
**TV listings** *(pl)* Fernsehprogramm IV 4 (76)
**twice** [twaɪs] zweimal III • **twice a week** zweimal pro Woche III
**twin** [twɪn]**: twin brother** Zwillingsbruder I • **twins** *(pl)* Zwillinge I
**type** [taɪp] *(infml)* Typ III

## U

**unbelievable** [ˌʌnbɪ'li:vəbl] unglaublich IV 4 (77)
**unbreakable** [ʌn'breɪkəbl] unzerbrechlich IV 4 (85)
**uncle** ['ʌŋkl] Onkel I
**uncomfortable** [ʌn'kʌmftəbl] unbequem, unbehaglich, unangenehm IV 2 (48/172)
**uncool** [ˌʌn'ku:l] *(infml)* uncool III
**uncountable** [ʌn'kaʊntəbl] unzählbar IV 3 (62)
**under** ['ʌndə] unter I
**underground** ['ʌndəgraʊnd]**: the underground** die U-Bahn II
°**underline** [ˌʌndə'laɪn] unterstreichen
°**underlined** [ˌʌndə'laɪnd] unterstrichen
**understand** [ˌʌndə'stænd]**, understood, understood** verstehen, begreifen I
**understood** [ˌʌndə'stʊd] *siehe* **understand**
**underwear** ['ʌndəweə] Unterwäsche III
**unfair** [ˌʌn'feə] unfair III
**unfriendly** [ʌn'frendli] unfreundlich III
**unhappy** [ʌn'hæpi] unglücklich III
**unhealthy** [ʌn'helθi] ungesund III
**uniform** ['ju:nɪfɔ:m] Uniform I
**unit** ['ju:nɪt] Lektion, Kapitel I
**united: the United Kingdom (UK)** [juˌnaɪtɪd 'kɪŋdəm], [ˌju: 'keɪ] das Vereinigte Königreich *(Großbritannien und Nordirland)* III • **United States (US)** [juˌnaɪtɪd 'steɪts], [ˌju:‿'es] die Vereinigten Staaten *(von Amerika)* III
**unlock** [ˌʌn'lɒk] aufschließen; entsperren III
**unreadable** [ʌn'ri:dəbl] unleserlich IV 4 (85)
**unrealistic** [ˌʌnrɪə'lɪstɪk] unrealistisch IV 3 (68)
**unsafe** [ʌn'seɪf] nicht sicher, gefährlich III
**untidy** [ʌn'taɪdi] unordentlich III
**until** [ən'tɪl] bis III
**up** [ʌp] hinauf, herauf, nach oben I
**up the hill** den Hügel hinauf II
**That's up to you.** Das liegt bei dir. / Das kannst/musst du (selbst) entscheiden. III
**upset** [ˌʌp'set] aufgebracht, gekränkt, mitgenommen III
**upset sb. (-tt-)** [ʌp'set]**, upset, upset** jn. ärgern, kränken, aus der Fassung bringen III

**upstairs** [ˌʌpˈsteəz] oben; nach oben I
**us** [əs, ʌs] uns I
**use** [juːz] benutzen, verwenden I
**useful** [ˈjuːsfəl] nützlich IV 2 (37)
**useless** [ˈjuːsləs] nutzlos IV 2 (42)
**usually** [ˈjuːʒuəli] meistens, gewöhnlich, normalerweise I

## V

**vacation** [vəˈkeɪʃn, *AE:* veɪˈkeɪʃn] *(AE)* Urlaub, Ferien III
**valley** [ˈvæli] Tal II
**vegetable** [ˈvedʒtəbl] *(ein)* Gemüse III • **°vegetable oil** Pflanzenöl
**vegetarian** [ˌvedʒəˈteəriən] vegetarisch IV 2 (43); Vegetarier/in IV 2 (43/171)
**very** [ˈveri] sehr I • **like/love sth. very much** etwas sehr mögen/sehr lieben II • **Thanks very much!** Danke sehr! / Vielen Dank! II
**victim** [ˈvɪktɪm] Opfer III
**video** [ˈvɪdiəʊ] Video III
**view** [vjuː] Aussicht, Blick II
**viewer** [ˈvjuːə] Zuschauer/in IV 4 (76)
**village** [ˈvɪlɪdʒ] Dorf I
**violin** [ˌvaɪəˈlɪn] Violine, Geige III
**visit** [ˈvɪzɪt] besuchen II
**visit** [ˈvɪzɪt] Besuch II
**visitor** [ˈvɪzɪtə] Besucher/in, Gast I
**vocabulary** [vəˈkæbjələri] Vokabelverzeichnis, Wörterverzeichnis I
**voicemail** [ˈvɔɪsmeɪl] Voicemail III
**volleyball** [ˈvɒlibɔːl] Volleyball I
**volume** [ˈvɒljuːm] Lautstärke IV 4 (82)
**volunteer** [ˌvɒlənˈtɪə] Freiwillige(r) IV 4 (74) • **volunteer work** Arbeit als Freiwillige(r) IV 4 (74)

## W

**°wagon train** [ˈwægən treɪn] Planwagenkolonne, -zug
**wait (for)** [weɪt] warten (auf) I
**Wait a minute.** Warte mal! / Moment mal! II • **Wait and see!** Wart's ab! III • **I can't wait to see ...** ich kann es kaum erwarten, ... zu sehen I
**waiter** [ˈweɪtə] Kellner II
**waiting room** [ˈweɪtɪŋ ruːm] Wartezimmer IV 4 (87)
**waitress** [ˈweɪtrəs] Kellnerin II
**wake** [weɪk]**, woke, woken:**
**1. wake sb. (up)** jn. (auf)wecken IV 1 (15/166)
**2. wake up** aufwachen IV 1 (15)
**walk** [wɔːk] (zu Fuß) gehen I
**walk around** herumlaufen, umherspazieren III • **walk around the town** in der Stadt umhergehen, durch die Stadt gehen III
**walk** [wɔːk] Spaziergang II • **go for a walk** spazieren gehen, einen Spaziergang machen II **a ten-kilometre walk** eine Zehn-Kilometer-Wanderung III
**wall** [wɔːl] Wand; Mauer II
**°wander** [ˈwɒndə] wandern; schlendern
**want** [wɒnt] (haben) wollen I
**°want sb. to do sth.** wollen, dass jemand etwas tut • **want to do** tun wollen I
**°war** [wɔː] Krieg
**wardrobe** [ˈwɔːdrəʊb] Kleiderschrank I
**warm** [wɔːm] warm II
**was** [wəz, wɒz]**: (I/he/she/it) was** *siehe* **be**
**wash** [wɒʃ] waschen I • **I wash my face.** Ich wasche mir das Gesicht. I
**washing machine** [ˈwɒʃɪŋ məˌʃiːn] Waschmaschine I
**watch** [wɒtʃ] beobachten, sich etwas ansehen; zusehen I
**watch TV** fernsehen I
**watch** [wɒtʃ] Armbanduhr I
**water** [ˈwɔːtə] Wasser I; Mineralwasser IV 1 (16)
**wave** [weɪv] winken II
**way** [weɪ]
**1.** Weg II • **all the way** den ganzen Weg IV 1 (27) • **ask sb. the way** jn. nach dem Weg fragen II • **on the way (to)** auf dem Weg (zu/nach) II • **tell sb. the way** jm. den Weg beschreiben II
**2.** Richtung II • **the other way round** anders herum II • **the wrong way** in die falsche Richtung II • **this way** hier entlang, in diese Richtung II • **which way?** in welche Richtung? / wohin? II
**3. by the way** übrigens II
**4. No way!** Auf keinen Fall! / Kommt nicht in Frage! II
**we** [wiː] wir I
**weak** [wiːk] schwach II
**weakness** [ˈwiːknəs] Schwäche IV 3 (63)
**wear** [weə]**, wore, worn** tragen, anhaben *(Kleidung)* I
**weather** [ˈweðə] Wetter II
**webcam** [ˈwebkæm] Webcam, Internetkamera III
**website** [ˈwebsaɪt] Website II
**Wednesday** [ˈwenzdeɪ, ˈwenzdi] Mittwoch I
**week** [wiːk] Woche I • **days of the week** Wochentage I • **a two-week holiday** ein zweiwöchiger Urlaub III
**weekend** [ˌwiːkˈend] Wochenende I **at the weekend** am Wochenende I
**welcome** [ˈwelkəm]
**1. Welcome (to Bristol).** Willkommen (in Bristol). I
**2. You're welcome.** Gern geschehen. / Nichts zu danken. I
**welcome sb. (to)** [ˈwelkəm] jn. begrüßen, willkommen heißen (in) I
**They welcome you to ...** Sie heißen dich in ... willkommen I
**well** [wel]
**1.** gut II • **go well** gut (ver)laufen, gutgehen III • **do well (in)** gut abschneiden (in) III • **You did well.** Das hast du gut gemacht. II • **Oh well ...** Na ja ... / Na gut ... I • **Well, ...** Nun, ... / Also, ... I
**°Well done!** [ˌwel ˈdʌn] Gut gemacht!
**2.** *(gesundheitlich)* gut; gesund, wohlauf II
**Welsh** [welʃ] walisisch; Walisisch II
**went** [went] *siehe* **go**
**were** [wə, wɜː]**: (we/you/they) were** *siehe* **be**
**west** [west] Westen; nach Westen; westlich III • **°going west** *Besiedlung des Westens der USA im 19. Jahrhundert*
**western** [ˈwestən] westlich, West- III
**wet** [wet] feucht, nass III
**what** [wɒt]
**1.** was I
**2.** welche(r, s) I
**°What a ...!** Was für ein ...! • **What about ...? 1.** Was ist mit ...? / Und ...? I; **2.** Wie wär's mit ...? I • **What are you talking about?** Wovon redest du? I • **What colour is ...?** Welche Farbe hat ...? I • **°What else can you do?** Was kannst du sonst noch machen? • **What for?** Wofür? II • **What have we got next?** Was haben wir als Nächstes? I • **What kind of car ...?** Was für ein Auto...? III • **What page are we on?** Auf welcher Seite sind wir? I • **What's for homework?** Was haben wir als Hausaufgabe auf? I • **°What time?** Um wie viel Uhr? / Wann? • **What's the matter?** Was ist los? / Was ist

denn? II • **What's the time?** Wie spät ist es? I • **What's your name?** Wie heißt du? I • **What's your telephone number?** Was ist deine Telefonnummer? I • **What was the weather like?** Wie war das Wetter? II
**wheel** [wi:l] Rad III • **big wheel** Riesenrad III
**wheelchair** ['wi:ltʃeə] Rollstuhl I
**when** [wen] wann I • **When's your birthday?** Wann hast du Geburtstag? I
**when** [wen]
**1.** wenn I
**2.** als I
**where** [weə]
**1.** wo I
**2.** wohin I
**Where are you from?** Wo kommst du her? I
**which** [wɪtʃ]: **Which picture ...?** Welches Bild ...? I • **which way?** in welche Richtung? / wohin? II
**which** [wɪtʃ] der, die, das; die *(Relativpronomen)* III
**while** [waɪl] während III
**whisky** ['wɪski] Whisky II
**whisper** ['wɪspə] flüstern I
**whistle** ['wɪsl] pfeifen II
**white** [waɪt] weiß I
**who** [hu:]
**1.** wer I
**2.** wen / wem II
**Who else?** Wen (sonst) noch? IV 1 (15/167)
**who** [hu:] der, die, das; die *(Relativpronomen)* III • **Find/Ask somebody who ...** Finde/Frage jemanden, der ... II
▸ S.167 ... else
°**whoever** [hu:'evə] wer auch immer
**whole** [həʊl] ganze(r,s), gesamte(r,s) IV 3 (56)
**whole-grain** ['həʊlgreɪn] Vollkorn- IV 3 (56)
**whose?** [hu:z] wessen? II • **Whose are these?** Wem gehören diese? II
**Whose turn is it?** Wer ist dran / an der Reihe? II
**why** [waɪ] warum I • **Why me?** Warum ich? I
°**wide** [waɪd] breit, weit
**wife** [waɪf], *pl* **wives** [waɪvz] Ehefrau II
**wild** [waɪld] wild II
**will** [wɪl]: **you'll be cold (= you will be cold)** du wirst frieren; ihr werdet frieren II • **you won't be cold** [wəʊnt] **(= you will not be cold)** du wirst nicht frieren; ihr werdet nicht frieren II
**win (-nn-)** [wɪn], **won, won** gewinnen I
**wind** [wɪnd] Wind I
**window** ['wɪndəʊ] Fenster I
**windsurfing** ['wɪndsɜ:fɪŋ] Windsurfen III
**windy** ['wɪndi] windig I
**wine** [waɪn] Wein IV 2 (36)
°**winery** ['waɪnəri] Weingut
**wing** [wɪŋ] Flügel IV Intro (10)
**winner** ['wɪnə] Gewinner/in, Sieger/in II
**winter** ['wɪntə] Winter I
**wishes** ['wɪʃɪz]: **Best wishes** *etwa:* Alles Gute / Mit besten Grüßen *(als Briefschluss)* IV 3 (61)
**with** [wɪð]
**1.** mit I
**2.** bei I
**be with sb.** mit jemandem zusammen sein IV 3 (66) • **go with** gehören zu, passen zu III • **Sit with me.** Setz dich zu mir. / Setzt euch zu mir. I
**without** [wɪ'ðaʊt] ohne I
**wives** [waɪvz] *Plural von „wife“* II
**woke** [wəʊk] *siehe* **wake**
**woken** [wəʊkən] *siehe* **wake**
**wolf** [wʊlf], *pl* **wolves** [wʊlvz] Wolf II
**woman** ['wʊmən], *pl* **women** ['wɪmɪn] Frau I
**won** [wʌn] *siehe* **win**
**won't** [wəʊnt]: **you won't be cold (= you will not be cold)** du wirst nicht frieren; ihr werdet nicht frieren II
**wonder** ['wʌndə] sich fragen, gern wissen wollen II
**woodpecker** ['wʊdpekə] Specht II
**word** [wɜ:d] Wort I • **word building** Wortbildung II
°**word order** Wortstellung
**wore** [wɔ:] *siehe* **wear**
**work** [wɜ:k]
**1.** arbeiten I
°**2.** funktionieren
**work hard** hart arbeiten II
**work on sth.** an etwas arbeiten I
°**work out** gut ausgehen • **work sth. out** etwas herausarbeiten, herausfinden IV 1 (25) • °**work sth. through** etwas durcharbeiten
**work** [wɜ:k] Arbeit I • **at work** bei der Arbeit/am Arbeitsplatz I
**worker** ['wɜ:kə] Arbeiter/in II
**worksheet** ['wɜ:kʃi:t] Arbeitsblatt I
**workshop** ['wɜ:kʃɒp] Workshop, Lehrgang III
**world** [wɜ:ld] Welt I • **all over the world** auf der ganzen Welt III • **from all over the UK/the world/England** aus dem gesamten Vereinigten Königreich / aus der ganzen Welt / aus ganz England II • °**in the world** auf der Welt
**worn** [wɔ:n] *siehe* **wear**
**worried** ['wʌrid] besorgt, beunruhigt (wegen, um) IV 3 (57)
**worry** ['wʌri] Sorge, Kummer II
**worry (about)** ['wʌri] sich Sorgen machen (wegen, um) I • **Don't worry.** Mach dir keine Sorgen. I
**worse** [wɜ:s] schlechter, schlimmer II
**worst** [wɜ:st]: **(the) worst** am schlechtesten, schlimmsten; der/die/das schlechteste, schlimmste ... II
**would** [wəd, wʊd]: **I/you/... would ...** ich würde/du würdest ... III • **I'd like ... (= I would like ...)** Ich hätte/möchte gern ... I • **Would you like ...?** Möchtest du ...? /Möchten Sie ...? I • **Would you like some?** Möchtest du etwas/ein paar? / Möchten Sie etwas/ein paar? I
**I'd like to talk about ... (= I would like to talk about ...)** Ich möchte über ... reden / Ich würde gern über ... reden I • °**She would not give up her seat.** Sie wollte ihren Sitzplatz nicht freigeben.
**write** [raɪt], **wrote, written** schreiben I • **write down** aufschreiben I • **write to** schreiben an I
**writer** ['raɪtə] Schreiber/in; Schriftsteller/in II
**written** ['rɪtn] *siehe* **write**
**wrong** [rɒŋ] falsch, verkehrt I
**be wrong** **1.** falsch sein I; **2.** sich irren, Unrecht haben II • **the wrong way** in die falsche Richtung II
**wrote** [rəʊt] *siehe* **write**

## Y

**yard** [jɑ:d] Hof II • **in the yard** auf dem Hof II
**yawn** [jɔ:n] gähnen II
**year** [jɪə]
**1.** Jahr I
**2.** Jahrgangsstufe I
**a sixteen-year-old** ein/e Sechzehnjährige/r III • **a sixteen-year-old girl** ein sechzehnjähriges Mädchen III
**yellow** ['jeləʊ] gelb I
**yes** [jes] ja I
**yesterday** ['jestədeɪ, 'jestədi] gestern I • **yesterday morning/afternoon/**

**evening** gestern Morgen/Nachmittag/Abend I • **yesterday's homework** die Hausaufgaben von gestern II
**yet** [jet]: **not (...) yet** noch nicht II
**yet?** schon? II
°**Yiddish** ['jɪdɪʃ] Jiddisch; jiddisch
°**yo** [jəʊ] *(infml)* hey
**yoga** ['jəʊgə] Yoga I
**you** [juː]
**1.** du; Sie I
**2.** ihr I • **you two** ihr zwei I
**3.** dir; dich; euch I
**young** [jʌŋ] jung I
**your** [jɔː]
**1.** dein/e I
**2.** Ihr I
**3.** euer/eure I
**yours** [jɔːz]
**1.** deiner, deine, deins II
**2.** Ihrer, Ihre, Ihrs II
**3.** eurer, eure, eures II
**yourself** [jɔː'self] dir/dich (selbst) III
**yourselves** [jɔː'selvz] euch (selbst) III
**youth** [juːθ] Jugend, Jugend- III
**youth club** Jugendclub III • **youth group** Jugendgruppe IV Intro (9)
**youth hostel** Jugendherberge III
**yuck** [jʌk] igitt III
°**yummy** ['jʌmi] *(infml)* lecker

## Z

**zebra** ['zebrə] Zebra II
**zero** ['zɪərəʊ] null I • °**Ground Zero** [ˌgraʊnd 'zɪərəʊ] Bodennullpunkt *(Bezeichnung für das zerstörte World Trade Center in New York; ursprünglich die Explosionsstelle einer Bombe oder Rakete über dem Boden)*
**zone** [zəʊn] Zone, Gebiet IV Intro (8)
**zoo** [zuː] Zoo IV 1 23

## English sounds (Englische Laute)

Die Lautschrift in den eckigen Klammern zeigt dir, wie ein Wort ausgesprochen wird.
In der folgenden Übersicht findest du alle Lautzeichen.

| Vokale (Selbstlaute) | | | | Konsonanten (Mitlaute) | | | |
|---|---|---|---|---|---|---|---|
| [iː] | green | [eɪ] | skate | [b] | box | [f] | full |
| [i] | happy | [aɪ] | time | [p] | play | [v] | very |
| [ɪ] | in | [ɔɪ] | boy | [d] | dad | [s] | sister |
| [e] | yes | [əʊ] | old | [t] | ten | [z] | please |
| [æ] | black | [aʊ] | now | [g] | good | [ʃ] | shop |
| [ɑː] | park | [ɪə] | here | [k] | cat | [ʒ] | television |
| [ɒ] | song | [eə] | where | [m] | mum | [tʃ] | teacher |
| [ɔː] | morning | [ʊə] | tour | [n] | no | [dʒ] | Germany |
| [uː] | blue | | | [ŋ] | sing | [θ] | thanks |
| [ʊ] | book | | | [l] | hello | [ð] | this |
| [ʌ] | mum | | | [r] | red | [h] | he |
| [ɜː] | T-shirt | | | [w] | we | | |
| [ə] | a partner | | | [j] | you | | |

## The English alphabet (Das englische Alphabet)

| | | | | | | | |
|---|---|---|---|---|---|---|---|
| **a** | [eɪ] | **h** | [eɪtʃ] | **o** | [əʊ] | **v** | [viː] |
| **b** | [biː] | **i** | [aɪ] | **p** | [piː] | **w** | ['dʌbljuː] |
| **c** | [siː] | **j** | [dʒeɪ] | **q** | [kjuː] | **x** | [eks] |
| **d** | [diː] | **k** | [keɪ] | **r** | [ɑː] | **y** | [waɪ] |
| **e** | [iː] | **l** | [el] | **s** | [es] | **z** | [zed] |
| **f** | [ef] | **m** | [em] | **t** | [tiː] | | |
| **g** | [dʒiː] | **n** | [en] | **u** | [juː] | | |

Das **German – English Dictionary** enthält den **Lernwortschatz** der Bände 1 bis 4 von *English G 21*. Es kann dir eine erste Hilfe sein, wenn du vergessen hast, wie etwas auf Englisch heißt.

Wenn du wissen möchtest, wo das englische Wort zum ersten Mal in *English G 21* vorkommt, dann kannst du im **English – German Dictionary** (S.180–206) nachschlagen.

Im **German – English Dictionary** werden folgende **Abkürzungen** und **Symbole** verwendet:

| | | | | |
|---|---|---|---|---|
| jm. = jemandem | sb. = somebody | *pl = plural* | *BE = British English* | *infml = informal* |
| jn. = jemanden | sth. = something | *no pl = no plural* | *AE = American English* | |

► Der Pfeil verweist auf Kästchen im Vocabulary (S.164–179), in denen du weitere Informationen findest.

## A

**abbiegen: (nach) links/rechts abbiegen** turn left/right [tɜːn]
**Abend** evening ['iːvnɪŋ]; *(später Abend)* night [naɪt] • **am Abend, abends** in the evening
**Abendbrot, -essen** dinner ['dɪnə] **Abendbrot essen** have dinner **zum Abendbrot** for dinner
**aber** but [bət, bʌt]
**abfahren** *(wegfahren)* leave [liːv]
**Abfahrt** *(Abreise)* departure (dep) [dɪ'pɑːtʃə]
**Abfall** rubbish ['rʌbɪʃ] *(BE)*; garbage ['gɑːbɪdʒ] *(AE)*
**Abflug** departure (dep) [dɪ'pɑːtʃə]
**abhängen (mit Freunden/Freundinnen)** *(rumhängen)* hang out (with friends) [,hæŋ_'aʊt]
**abholen: jn. abholen** pick sb. up [,pɪk_'ʌp]
**Abreise** departure (dep) [dɪ'pɑːtʃə]
**Absatz** *(in einem Text)* paragraph ['pærəgrɑːf]
**abschließen** lock [lɒk]
**Abschluss** *(einer Geschichte, eines Films usw.)* ending ['endɪŋ]
**abschneiden: etwas abschneiden** cut sth. off [,kʌt_'ɒf]
**Abschnitt** section ['sekʃn]
**abschreiben** *(kopieren)* copy ['kɒpi]
**abtrennen: etwas abtrennen** *(abschneiden)* cut sth. off [,kʌt_'ɒf]
**abwenden: sich abwenden** turn away [,tɜːn_ə'weɪ]
**abziehen: 10 Cent abziehen** take 10 c off [,teɪk_'ɒf]
**Acker** field [fiːld]
**addieren (zu)** add (to) [æd]
**Adresse** address [ə'dres]
**Affe** monkey ['mʌŋki]
**Afro-Amerikaner** African American [,æfrɪkən_ə'merɪkən]
**afro-amerikanisch** African American [,æfrɪkən_ə'merɪkən]
**Aktivität** activity [æk'tɪvəti]
**Akzent** accent ['æksənt]
**albern** silly ['sɪli]
**alkoholfreies Getränk** soft drink
**alle** *(die ganze Gruppe)* all [ɔːl]; *(jeder)* everyone ['evrɪwʌn], everybody ['evribɒdi]
**Allee** avenue ['ævənjuː]
**allein** alone [ə'ləʊn]
**alleinstehend** single ['sɪŋgl]
**alles** everything ['evriθɪŋ]; anything ['eniθɪŋ]; all [ɔːl] • **Alles Gute** *(als Briefschluss)* Best wishes ['wɪʃɪz]
**allgemeine (r, s)** general ['dʒenrəl] **im allgemeinen** in general
**alltägliche(r, s), Alltags-** everyday ['evrideɪ]
**Alphabet** alphabet ['ælfəbet]
**als 1.** *(zeitlich)* when [wen]; *(während)* as [əz, æz]
**2. als Feuerwehrmann/als Lehrer/ als ...** as a firefighter / a teacher/ ...
**3. größer/teurer als** bigger/more expensive than [ðæn, ðən]
**also** *(daher, deshalb)* so [səʊ]
**Also, ...** Well, ... [wel]
**alt** old [əʊld]
**Alter** age [eɪdʒ]
**altmodisch** old-fashioned [,əʊld'fæʃnd]
**am 1. am Bahnhof** at the station **am oberen Ende (von)** at the top (of) • **am Strand** on the beach **am Telefon** on the phone • **am unteren Ende (von)** at the bottom (of) ['bɒtəm]
**2.** *(nahe bei)* **am Meer** by the sea
**3.** *(zeitlich)* **am 13. Juni** on 13th June • **am Morgen/Nachmittag/ Abend** in the morning/afternoon/ evening • **am Ende (von)** at the end (of) • **am Freitag** on Friday **am Freitagmorgen** on Friday morning • **am nächsten Morgen/ Tag** the next morning/day • **am Wochenende** at the weekend
**Amnestie** amnesty ['æmnəsti]
**amüsieren: sich amüsieren** have fun [hæv 'fʌn] • **Amüsier dich gut!** Enjoy yourself.
**an 1. an dem/den Tisch (dort)** at that table • **an der Spitze** at the top (of) • **an der/die Tafel** on the board • **an jn. schreiben** write to sb.
**2.** *(nahe bei)* **an der See** by the sea
**3. Was war das Beste an ...?** What was the best thing about ...?
**4. an sein** *(Radio, Licht usw.)* be on
**anbauen** *(Getreide usw.)* grow [grəʊ]
**anbieten** offer ['ɒfə]
**andere(r, s)** other ['ʌðə] • **die anderen** the others • **(irgend)etwas anderes** anything else [els]
► S.167 ... else
**ändern: sich ändern** change [tʃeɪndʒ]
► S.178 (to) change – change
**anders (als)** different (from) ['dɪfrənt] **anders ausdrücken** *(umschreiben)* paraphrase ['pærəfreɪz] • **anders herum** the other way round **jemand anders** somebody else [els]
► S.167 ... else
**Änderung** change [tʃeɪndʒ]
► S.178 (to) change – change
**Anfang** beginning [bɪ'gɪnɪŋ] • **am Anfang** at first
**anfangen (mit)** start [stɑːt]; begin [bɪ'gɪn]
**anfassen** touch [tʌtʃ]
**anfühlen: sich gut anfühlen** feel good [fiːl]
**Anführer/in** leader ['liːdə]
**Angebot** offer ['ɒfə]
**angeln** fish [fɪʃ]
**angenehm** *(bequem, behaglich)* comfortable ['kʌmftəbl]
**angreifen** attack [ə'tæk]
**Angriff** attack [ə'tæk]
**Angst haben (vor)** be afraid (of) [ə'freɪd]; be scared (of) [skeəd]
**anhaben** *(Kleidung)* wear [weə]
**anhalten** stop [stɒp]
**Anhänger/in** *(Fan)* supporter [sə'pɔːtə]
**anhören 1. sich etwas anhören** listen to sth. ['lɪsn]

**2. sich gut anhören** sound good [saʊnd]
**anklicken: etwas anklicken** click on sth. [klɪk]
**ankommen** arrive [ə'raɪv]
**Ankündigung** announcement [ə'naʊnsmənt]
**Ankunft** arrival (arr) [ə'raɪvl]
**anlächeln: jn. anlächeln** smile at sb. [smaɪl]
**Anleitung(en)** *(Gebrauchsanweisungen)* instructions *(pl)* [ɪn'strʌkʃnz]
**anmailen: jn. anmailen** mail sb. [meɪl]
**anmalen** paint [peɪnt]; *(bunt ausmalen)* colour ['kʌlə]
**Anorak** anorak ['ænəræk]
**anpflanzen** *(Getreide usw.)* grow [grəʊ]
**anprobieren** *(Kleidung)* try on [ˌtraɪ_'ɒn]
**Anruf** call; phone call ['fəʊn kɔːl]
**anrufen** call [kɔːl]; phone [fəʊn]
**Ansage** *(Durchsage)* announcement [ə'naʊnsmənt]
**anschauen** look at [lʊk]
**Anschlagtafel** notice board ['nəʊtɪs bɔːd] *(BE)*; bulletin board ['bʊlətɪn bɔːd] *(AE)*
**anschließen: sich jm. anschließen** join sb. [dʒɔɪn]
**Anschrift** address [ə'dres]
**ansehen: sich etwas ansehen** look at sth. [lʊk]; watch sth. [wɒtʃ]; have a look at sth.
**Antwort (auf)** answer (to) ['ɑːnsə]
**antworten** answer ['ɑːnsə]
**Anweisung(en)** *(Gebrauchsanweisungen)* instructions *(pl)* [ɪn'strʌkʃnz]
**anziehen: etwas anziehen** *(Kleidung)* put sth. on [ˌpʊt_'ɒn] • **sich anziehen** get dressed [get 'drest]
**Apfel** apple ['æpl]
**Apfelsine** orange ['ɒrɪndʒ]
**Apotheke** chemist ['kemɪst]
**Apotheker: beim Apotheker** at the chemist's
**Appetit** appetite ['æpɪtaɪt] • **Guten Appetit** Enjoy! [ɪn'dʒɔɪ]
**April** April ['eɪprəl]
**Arbeit** work [wɜːk] • **bei der Arbeit / am Arbeitsplatz** at work • **gute Arbeit leisten** do a good job
**arbeiten (an)** work (on) [wɜːk]
**Arbeiter/in** worker ['wɜːkə]
**Arbeitsblatt** worksheet ['wɜːkʃiːt]
**Arbeits- und Lerntechniken** study skills ['stʌdi skɪlz]
**Ärger** *(Schwierigkeiten)* trouble ['trʌbl] • **Ärger kriegen** be in trouble
**ärgern: jn. ärgern** *(kränken)* upset sb. [ʌp'set]
**Argument** argument ['ɑːgjumənt]
**arm** poor [pɔː, pʊə]
**Arm** arm [ɑːm]
**Armbanduhr** watch [wɒtʃ]
**Art 1.** *(Sorte)* sort (of) [sɔːt]; kind (of) [kaɪnd]
**2. Art und Weise** way [weɪ]
**Artikel** article ['ɑːtɪkl]
**Arzt/Ärztin** doctor ['dɒktə] • **zum Arzt** to the doctor's
**auch: auch aus Bristol** from Bristol too [tuː]; also from Bristol ['ɔːlsəʊ]
**Ich auch.** Me too.
**auf** on [ɒn] • **auf (... hinauf)** onto ['ɒntə, 'ɒntʊ] • **auf dem Bild/Foto** in the picture/photo • **auf dem Feld** in the field • **auf dem Hof** in the yard • **auf dem Land** *(im Gegensatz zur Stadt)* in the country; *(nicht auf dem Wasser)* on land
**auf dem Weg (zu/nach)** on the way (to) • **auf der ganzen Welt** all over the world • **auf einmal** suddenly ['sʌdnli] • **auf Englisch** in English • **Auf geht's!** Let's go.
**auf jn./etwas zu** towards sb./sth. [tə'wɔːdz] • **Auf keinen Fall!** No way! • **Auf welcher Seite sind wir?** What page are we on?
**Auf Wiedersehen.** Goodbye. [ˌgʊd-'baɪ]
**aufbewahren** keep [kiːp]
**aufführen** *(Szene, Dialog)* act [ækt]
**Aufgabe** *(im Schulbuch)* exercise ['eksəsaɪz]; *(Job)* job [dʒɒb]
**aufgeben** *(resignieren)* give up
**aufgebracht (wegen)** upset [ˌʌp'set]
**aufgeräumt** *(ordentlich)* tidy ['taɪdi]
**aufgeregt** *(nervös)* nervous ['nɜːvəs]; *(begeistert)* excited [ɪk'saɪtɪd]
**aufheben: etwas aufheben** *(hochheben)* pick sth. up [ˌpɪk_'ʌp]
**aufhören** stop [stɒp]
**auflegen** *(Musik/CDs/Platten; in der Disko)* DJ ['diːdʒeɪ]
**auflisten** list [lɪst]
**aufmachen** open ['əʊpən]
**Aufnahme** *(Aufzeichnung)* recording [rɪ'kɔːdɪŋ]
**aufnehmen** *(Musik / einen Film)* record [rɪ'kɔːd]
**aufpassen: auf etwas/jn. aufpassen** look after sth./sb. [ˌlʊk_'ɑːftə]
**aufräumen** tidy ['taɪdi]
**aufregend** exciting [ɪk'saɪtɪŋ]
**Aufsatz** essay ['eseɪ]
**aufschauen (von)** look up (from) [ˌlʊk_'ʌp]
**aufschließen** unlock [ˌʌn'lɒk]
**aufschreiben** write down [ˌraɪt 'daʊn]
**Aufseher/in** *(Parkaufseher/innen in Nationalparks, die auch Führungen machen und als Wald- und Wildhüterinnen arbeiten)* park ranger ['pɑːk reɪndʒə]
**aufstehen** get up [ˌget_'ʌp]
**aufsuchen: jn. aufsuchen** see sb. [siː]
**Auftritt** *(Konzert)* gig [gɪg] *(infml)*
**einen Auftritt haben** *(ein Konzert geben)* do a gig
**aufwachsen** grow up [ˌgrəʊ_'ʌp]
**aufzählen** *(auflisten)* list [lɪst]
**Aufzeichnung** *(Aufnahme)* recording [rɪ'kɔːdɪŋ]
**Aufzug** lift [lɪft] *(BE)*; elevator ['elɪveɪtə] *(AE)*
**aufwachen** wake up [weɪk]
**aufwecken: jd. aufwecken** wake sb. up [weɪk]
**Auge** eye [aɪ]
**August** August ['ɔːgəst]
**aus: Ich komme/bin aus ...** I'm from ... [frəm, frɒm] • **aus ... (heraus/hinaus)** out of ... ['aʊt_əv] • **aus der ganzen Welt** from all over the world • **aus dem Zug/Bus aussteigen** get off the train/bus
**aus vielen Gründen** for lots of reasons • **aus zweiter Hand** *(gebraucht)* second-hand [ˌsekənd 'hænd]
**ausdenken: sich etwas ausdenken** think of sth. [θɪŋk]
**ausdrücken: anders ausdrücken** *(umschreiben)* paraphrase ['pærəfreɪz]
**Ausflug** trip [trɪp] • **einen Ausflug machen** go on a trip
**ausgeben: Geld ausgeben (für)** spend money (on) [spend]
**Ausgehverbot haben** be grounded ['graʊndɪd]
**ausgezeichnet** *(hervorragend)* excellent ['eksələnt]
► S.173 US school grades
**auslachen: jn. auslachen** laugh at sb. [lɑːf]
**ausmalen** *(bunt anmalen, kolorieren)* colour ['kʌlə]
**ausruhen: sich ausruhen** relax [rɪ'læks]
**Aussage** statement ['steɪtmənt]
**ausschalten** turn off [tɜːn]
**aussehen: anders/toll/alt aussehen** look different/great/old [lʊk]
**fürchterlich aussehen** be a mess [mes]
**außerhalb seines Zimmers** outside his room [ˌaʊt'saɪd]
**aussetzen: Einmal aussetzen.** Miss a turn. [tɜːn]
**Aussicht (auf)** *(Blick)* view (of) [vjuː]

**Aussprache** pronunciation [prəˌnʌnsiˈeɪʃn]
**aussteigen (aus dem Zug/Bus)** get off (the train/bus) [ˌget‿ˈɒf]
**aussuchen: (sich) etwas aussuchen** choose sth. [tʃuːz]
**Austauschschüler/in** exchange student [ɪksˈtʃeɪndʒ ˌstjuːdnt]
**Ausverkauf** sale [seɪl]
**auswählen** choose [tʃuːz]
**ausziehen 1.** *(aus Wohnung)* move out [ˌmuːv‿ˈaʊt]
**2. etwas ausziehen** *(Kleidung)* take sth. off [ˌteɪk‿ˈɒf]
**Auto** car [kɑː]
**Autofahrt** drive [draɪv]
**Automat** machine [məˈʃiːn]
**Autsch!** Ouch! [aʊtʃ]

## B

**Baby** baby [ˈbeɪbi] • **ein Baby bekommen** have a baby
**Bäckerei** bakery [ˈbeɪkəri]
**Badeanzug** swimsuit [ˈswɪmsuːt]
**Badehose** swimming trunks *(pl)* [trʌŋks]
**baden** *(ein Bad nehmen)* have a bath [bɑːθ]
**Badewanne** bath [bɑːθ]
**Badezimmer** bathroom [ˈbɑːθruːm]
**Badminton** badminton [ˈbædmɪntən]
**Badmintonschläger** badminton racket [ˈrækɪt]
**Bagel** *(ringförmiges Gebäck)* bagel [ˈbeɪgl]
**Bahnhof** station [ˈsteɪʃn] • **am Bahnhof** at the station
**Bahnsteig** platform [ˈplætfɔːm]
**bald** soon [suːn] • **Bis bald.** See you. [ˈsiː juː]
**Ball 1.** ball [bɔːl]
**2.** *(Tanzveranstaltung)* ball [bɔːl]
**Banane** banana [bəˈnɑːnə]
**Band** *(Musikgruppe)* band [bænd]
**Bank** *(Sparkasse)* bank [bæŋk]
**Bankräuber/in** bank robber [ˈrɒbə]
**Bar** bar [bɑː]
**Bär** bear [beə]
**Bart** beard [bɪəd]
**Baseball** baseball [ˈbeɪsbɔːl]
**Baseballmütze** baseball cap [kæp]
**Basketball** basketball [ˈbɑːskɪtbɔːl]
**Bauchweh** stomach ache [ˈstʌmək‿eɪk]
**bauen** build [bɪld]
**Bauer/Bäuerin** farmer [ˈfɑːmə]
**Bauernhaus** farmhouse [ˈfɑːmhaʊs]
**Bauernhof** farm [fɑːm]
**Baum** tree [triː]
**beantworten** answer [ˈɑːnsə]
**Becken** *(Schwimmbecken)* pool [puːl]
**bedeuten** mean [miːn]
**Bedeutung** meaning [ˈmiːnɪŋ]
**beeilen: sich beeilen** hurry [ˈhʌri]; hurry up [ˌhʌri‿ˈʌp]
**beeindruckend** grand [grænd]
**beeindruckt** impressed [ɪmˈprest]
**beenden** finish [ˈfɪnɪʃ]; end [end]
**Beförderung** *(Transport)* transport [ˈtrænspɔːt]
**begeistert** *(aufgeregt)* excited [ɪkˈsaɪtɪd]
**Beginn** beginning [bɪˈgɪnɪŋ]
**beginnen (mit)** begin [bɪˈgɪn]; start [stɑːt]
**Begnadigung** amnesty [ˈæmnəsti]
**begreifen** understand [ˌʌndəˈstænd]
**Begründung** *(Grund)* reason [ˈriːzn]
**behaglich** comfortable [ˈkʌmftəbl]
**behalten** keep [kiːp]
**behindert** disabled [dɪsˈeɪbld]
**bei: bei den Shaws zu Hause** at the Shaws' house • **bei der Arbeit** at work • **Englisch bei Mr Kingsley** English with Mr Kingsley
**beide** both [bəʊθ]
**Beifall klatschen** clap [klæp]
**Bein** leg [leg] • **etwas auf die Beine stellen** get sth. off the ground
**Beispiel** example [ɪgˈzɑːmpl] • **zum Beispiel** for example
**Bekanntgabe** announcement [əˈnaʊnsmənt]
**Bekleidungsvorschrift** dress code [ˈdres kəʊd]
**bekommen** get [get] • **ein Baby bekommen** have a baby
**belebt** *(Straße, Ort)* busy [ˈbɪzi]
**beliebig: jede(r, s) beliebige ...** any ... **(irgend)etwas (Beliebiges)** anything [ˈeniθɪŋ]
► S.169 any
**beliebt** popular [ˈpɒpjələ]
**bemerken: nebenbei bemerkt** actually [ˈæktʃuəli]
**benennen** name [kɔːl]
**benötigen** need [niːd]
**benutzen** use [juːz]
**beobachten** watch [wɒtʃ]
**bequem** comfortable [ˈkʌmftəbl]
**Mach es dir bequem. / Machen Sie es sich bequem.** Make yourself comfortable. [ˈkʌmftəbl]
**Bereich** area [ˈeəriə]; section [ˈsekʃn]
**bereit** ready [ˈredi]
**bereits** already [ɔːlˈredi]
**Berg** mountain [ˈmaʊntən]
**Bericht (über)** report (on) [rɪˈpɔːt]
**berichten (über)** tell (about) [tel]
**(jm.) etwas berichten** report sth. (to sb.) [rɪˈpɔːt]
**berichtigen** correct [kəˈrekt]
**beruhigen: sich beruhigen** calm down [ˌkɑːm ˈdaʊn]
**berühmt** famous [ˈfeɪməs]
**berühren** touch [tʌtʃ]
**Bescheid: über etwas Bescheid wissen** know about sth. [nəʊ]
**beschreiben: (jm.) etwas beschreiben** describe sth. (to sb.) [dɪˈskraɪb]
**jm. den Weg beschreiben** tell sb. the way
**Beschreibung** description [dɪˈskrɪpʃn]
**Besichtigungstour** sightseeing trip [ˈsaɪtsiːɪŋ]
**besiegen** beat [biːt]
**besitzen** have [həv, hæv]
**besondere(r, s)** special [ˈspeʃl] • **ein besonderer Tag** a special day
**besorgen** *(holen)* get [get]
**besorgt (wegen, um)** worried about [ˈwʌrid]
**Besprechung** meeting [ˈmiːtɪŋ]
**besser** better [ˈbetə]
**beste: am besten** (the) best [best]
**der/die/das beste ...; die besten ...** the best ... • **Was war das Beste an ...?** What was the best thing about ...?
**bestellen** order [ˈɔːdə]
**Besuch** visit [ˈvɪzɪt]
**besuchen: jn. besuchen** visit sb. [ˈvɪzɪt]; see sb. [siː]
**Besucher/in** visitor [ˈvɪzɪtə]
**Betonung** stress [stres]
**betreten** enter [ˈentə]
**betrunken** drunk [drʌŋk]
**Bett** bed [bed] • **ins Bett gehen** go to bed
**betteln (um)** beg for [beg]
**beunruhigt (wegen, um)** worried about [ˈwʌrid]
**beurteilen (nach)** judge (by) [dʒʌdʒ]
**Beutel** bag [bæg]
**Bevölkerung** population [ˌpɒpjuˈleɪʃn]
**bevor** before [bɪˈfɔː]
**bewegen: sich bewegen** move [muːv]
**Bewegung** movement [ˈmuːvmənt]; *(körperlich, als Training)* exercise *(no pl)*
**Beweis(e)** proof *(no pl)* [pruːf]
**bewölkt** cloudy [ˈklaʊdi]
**bezahlen: etwas bezahlen** pay for sth. [peɪ]
**Beziehungen** relations *(pl)* [rɪˈleɪʃnz]
**Bibliothek** library [ˈlaɪbrəri]
**Bild** picture [ˈpɪktʃə] • **auf dem Bild** in the picture
**Bildergeschichte** picture story
**Bildschirm** monitor [ˈmɒnɪtə]; screen [skriːn]
**billig** cheap [tʃiːp]
**Bindewort** linking word [ˈlɪŋkɪŋ wɜːd]

**Biologie** biology [baɪ'ɒlədʒi]
**bis** *(zeitlich)* until [ən'tɪl]; till [tɪl]
**Bis bald.** See you. ['si: ju:] • **bis (spätestens) zehn Uhr** by ten o'clock • **von Montag bis Freitag** from Mondays to Fridays
**bisschen: ein bisschen** a bit [bɪt]
**bitte 1.** *(in Fragen und Aufforderungen)* please [pli:z]
**2. Bitte sehr. / Hier bitte.** Here you are.
**3. Bitte, gern geschehen.** You're welcome. ['welkəm]
**4. Wie bitte?** Sorry? ['sɒri]
**bitten: (eindringlich) bitten (um)** beg for [beg]
**blau** blue [blu:]
**bleiben** stay [steɪ] • **in Verbindung bleiben** keep in touch [ˌki:p‿ɪn 'tʌtʃ]
**Bleistift** pencil ['pensl]
**Bleistiftanspitzer** pencil sharpener ['pensl ʃɑ:pnə]
**Blick** *(Aussicht)* view [vju:] • **einen Blick werfen auf etwas** have a look at sth. [lʊk]
**Blitz** *(Lichtblitz)* flash [flæʃ]
**Block** *(Häuser-, Wohnblock)* block [blɒk]
**Blockflöte** recorder [rɪ'kɔ:də]
**blöd** stupid ['stju:pɪd]
**Blog** *(Kurz für Weblog: auf einer Website geführtes und damit öffentliches Tagebuch)* blog [blɒg]
**blond** blond [blɒnd]
**bloß** just [dʒʌst]; only ['əʊnli]
**Boden** *(Erdboden)* ground [graʊnd]
**Bohne** bean [bi:n]
**Bohrinsel** *(Ölbohrinsel)* oil rig ['ɔɪl rɪg]
**Boot** boat [bəʊt]
**böse sein (auf jn.)** be cross (with sb.) [krɒs]; be angry (with sb.) ['æŋgri] • **böse sein (über etwas)** be angry (about sth.)
**Boss** boss [bɒs]
**Brand** fire ['faɪə]
**Brandfall: Verhalten im Brandfall** fire safety ['faiə seɪfti]
**brainstormen** *(so viele Ideen wie möglich sammeln)* brainstorm ['breɪnstɔ:m]
**brauchen** need [ni:d]; *(Zeit brauchen, dauern)* take [teɪk] • **nicht zu tun brauchen** needn't do ['ni:dnt]
**braun** brown [braʊn]
**brav** good [gʊd]
**Brief (an)** letter (to) ['letə]
**Briefmarke** stamp [stæmp]
**Brille: (eine) Brille** glasses *(pl)* ['glɑ:sɪz]
**bringen: (mit-, her)bringen** bring [brɪŋ] • **(weg-, hin)bringen** take [teɪk] • **alles in Unordnung bringen** make a mess • **etwas auf den Weg bringen** get sth. off the ground
**britisch; Brite, Britin** British ['brɪtɪʃ]
**Broschüre** brochure ['brəʊʃə]
**Brot** bread *(no pl)* [bred]
**Brötchen** roll [rəʊl]
**Brotdose** sandwich box ['sænwɪtʃ bɒks]
**Brücke** bridge [brɪdʒ]
**Bruder** brother ['brʌðə]
**Buch** book [bʊk]
**Bücherei** library ['laɪbrəri]
**Buchstabe** letter ['letə]
**buchstabieren** spell [spel]
**Bühne** stage [steɪdʒ]
**bunt an-, ausmalen** colour ['kʌlə]
**Burg** castle ['kɑ:sl]
**Burger** burger ['bɜ:gə]
**Bürger/in** citizen ['sɪtɪzn]
**Bürgersteig** pavement ['peɪvmənt] *(BE)*; sidewalk ['saɪdwɔ:k] *(AE)*
**Bus** bus [bʌs]
**Bushaltestelle** bus stop ['bʌs stɒp]
**Butter** butter ['bʌtə]

## C

**Café** café ['kæfeɪ]
**Cafeteria** cafeteria [ˌkæfə'tɪəriə]
**Camp** camp [kæmp]
**Cartoon** cartoon [kɑ:'tu:n]
**CD** CD [ˌsi:'di:] • **CD-Spieler** CD player [ˌsi:'di: ˌpleɪə]
**Celsius (C)** Celsius ['selsiəs]
**Cent** cent (c) [sent]
**Charakter** character ['kærəktə]
**Chatroom** chat room ['tʃæt ru:m]
**chatten** chat [tʃæt]
**Chef/in** boss [bɒs]
**Chor** choir ['kwaɪə]
**clever** clever ['klevə]; smart [smɑ:t]
**Clique** crowd *(infml)* [kraʊd]
**Clown/in** clown [klaʊn]
**Cola** cola ['kəʊlə]
**Comic-Heft** comic ['kɒmɪk]
**Computer** computer [kəm'pju:tə]
**cool** cool [ku:l]
**Cornflakes** cornflakes ['kɔ:nfleɪks]
**Cousin, Cousine** cousin ['kʌzn]
**Creme** cream [kri:m]
**Curry(gericht)** curry ['kʌri]

## D

**da, dahin** *(dort, dorthin)* there [ðeə]
**da drüben** over there [ˌəʊvə 'ðeə]
**Schön, dass du wieder da bist.** Good to have you back.
**daheim** at home [ət 'həʊm]
**daher** so [səʊ]
**dämlich** stupid ['stju:pɪd]
**Dancefloor** dance floor ['dɑ:ns flɔ:]
**danach** *(zeitlich)* after that [ˌɑ:ftə 'ðæt]
**dankbar** thankful ['θæŋkfl]; *(froh)* glad [glæd]
**Danke.** Thank you. ['θæŋk ju:]; Thanks. • **Danke sehr!** Thanks very much! • **Vielen Dank!** Thanks a lot!
**dann** then [ðen]
**darstellende Kunst** drama ['drɑ:mə]
**das 1.** *(Artikel)* the [ðə, ði]
**2.** *(Relativpronomen)* **das Mädchen, das ...** the girl who ... / the girl that ... • **das Auto, das ...** the car that ... / the car which ...
**das (dort)** *(Singular)* that [ðət, ðæt]; *(Plural)* those [ðəʊz] • **Das bin ich.** That's me.
**dass** that [ðət, ðæt]
**dasselbe** the same [seɪm]
**Datum** date [deɪt]
**dauern** *(Zeit brauchen)* take [teɪk]
**davonmachen: sich davonmachen** take off *(infml)*
**decken: den Tisch decken** lay the table [ˌleɪ ðə 'teɪbl]
**dein(e) ...** your ... [jɔ:]
**deiner, deine, deins** yours [jɔ:z]
**denken** think [θɪŋk] • **denken an** think of • **Was denkst du über ...?** What do you think about/of ...?
**der 1.** *(Artikel)* the [ðə, ði]
**2.** *(Relativpronomen)* **der Mann, der ...** the man who ... / the man that ... • **der Laden, der ...** the shop that ... / the shop which ...
**derselbe** the same [seɪm]
**deshalb** so [səʊ]
**Detail** detail ['di:teɪl]
**Detektiv/in** detective [dɪ'tektɪv]
**deuten (auf etwas)** *(zeigen)* point (at/to sth.) [pɔɪnt]
**deutlich** clear [klɪə]
**Deutsch; deutsch; Deutsche(r)** German ['dʒɜ:mən]
**Deutschland** Germany ['dʒɜ:məni]
**Dezember** December [dɪ'sembə]
**Dialog** dialogue ['daɪəlɒg]
**dich** you [ju:] • **dich (selbst)** *(Reflexivpronomen)* yourself [jə'self, jɔ:'self]
**die 1.** *(Artikel)* the [ðə, ði]
**2.** *(Relativpronomen)* **die Frau, die ...** the woman who ... / the woman that ... • **die Jacke, die ...** the jacket that ... / the jacket which ...
**die (dort)** *(Singular)* that [ðət, ðæt]; *(Plural)* those [ðəʊz] • **die (hier)** *(Singular)* this [ðɪs]; *(Plural)* these [ði:z]

**Dieb/in** thief [θi:f], *pl* thieves [θi:vz]
**Diele** hall [hɔ:l]
**Dienstag** Tuesday ['tju:zdeɪ, 'tju:zdi] *(siehe auch unter „Freitag")*
**Dienstmädchen** maid [meɪd]
**dies (hier); diese(r, s)** *(Singular)* this [ðɪs]; *(Plural)* these [ði:z]
**dieselbe(n)** the same [seɪm]
**Ding** thing [θɪŋ]
**dir** you [ju:]
**Diskjockey** DJ ['di:dʒeɪ]
**Disko** disco ['dɪskəʊ]
**Diskussion** discussion [dɪ'skʌʃn]
**Dokumentarfilm** documentary [ˌdɒkju'mentri]
**Dokumentation** documentary [ˌdɒkju'mentri]
**Doktor** doctor ['dɒktə]
**Dollar** dollar ['dɒlə]
**Dom** cathedral [kə'θi:drəl]
**Donnerstag** Thursday ['θɜ:zdeɪ, 'θɜ:zdi] *(siehe auch unter „Freitag")*
**doppelt, Doppel-** double ['dʌbl]
**Dorf** village ['vɪlɪdʒ]
**dort, dorthin** there [ðeə] • **dort drüben** over there [ˌəʊvə 'ðeə] **dort unten** down there
**Dossier** dossier ['dɒsieɪ]
**downloaden** *(runterladen)* download [ˌdaʊn'ləʊd]
**Drachen** kite [kaɪt]
**dran: Ich bin dran.** It's my turn. [tɜ:n]
**draußen** outside [ˌaʊt'saɪd]; out [aʊt] **nach draußen** outside
**dreimal** three times
**drinnen** inside [ˌɪn'saɪd] • **hier drinnen** in here [ˌɪn 'hɪə] • **nach drinnen** inside
**dritte(r, s)** third [θɜ:d]
**Drogerie** chemist ['kemɪst]
**Droge** drug [drʌg] • **Drogen nehmen** be on drugs [drʌgz]
**drüben: da/dort drüben** over there [ˌəʊvə 'ðeə]
**drücken** push [pʊʃ]; *(pressen)* press [pres]
**du** you [ju:]
**dumm** *(albern)* silly ['sɪli]
**dunkel** dark [dɑ:k]
**durch** through [θru:]; *(in...umher)* around [ə'raʊnd] • **durch die Stadt** around the town
**durcheinander: alles durcheinanderbringen** make a mess [ˌmeɪk‿ə 'mes]
**durchführen: ein Projekt durchführen** do a project
**Durchsage** *(Ansage)* announcement [ə'naʊnsmənt]
**Durchschnitt** average ['ævərɪdʒ]
**Durchschnitts-, durchschnittlich** average ['ævərɪdʒ]
► S.173 US school grades

**dürfen** can [kən, kæn]; may [meɪ]; be allowed to [ə'laʊd] • **nicht dürfen** mustn't ['mʌsnt]
**Dusche** shower ['ʃaʊə]
**duschen; sich duschen** have a shower ['ʃaʊə]
**DVD** DVD [ˌdi: vi:' di:]

## E

**echt** real [rɪəl]
**Ecke** corner ['kɔ:nə] • **Green Street, Ecke London Road** on the corner of Green Street and London Road
**egal: aber egal** anyway ['eniweɪ] • **Es ist mir egal.** I don't care. [keə]
**Ehefrau** wife [waɪf], *pl* wives [waɪvz]
**Ehemann** husband ['hʌzbənd]
**Ei** egg [eg]
**Eichhörnchen** squirrel ['skwɪrəl]
**Eifersucht** jealousy ['dʒeləsi]
**eifersüchtig (auf)** jealous (of) ['dʒeləs]
**eigene(r, s): unser eigenes Schwimmbad** our own pool [əʊn]
**eigentlich** *(in Wirklichkeit)* actually ['æktʃuəli]
**Eile: in Eile sein** be in a hurry ['hʌri]
**eilen** *(sich beeilen)* hurry ['hʌri]
**eilig: es eilig haben** be in a hurry ['hʌri]
**ein(e)** a, an [ə, ən]; one [wʌn] • **ein(e) andere(r, s) ...** another ... [ə'nʌðə] **eine Menge** a lot (of) [lɒt]; lots (of) [lɒts] • **ein neuer / eine neue / ein neues** a new one [wʌn] • **ein paar** some [səm, sʌm] • **eines Tages** one day
**einander** *(sich gegenseitig)* each other [i:tʃ‿'ʌðə]
**eindrucksvoll** grand [grænd]
**einfach** *(nicht schwierig)* easy ['i:zi] **einfach nur** just [dʒʌst] • **einfache Fahrkarte** *(nur Hinfahrt)* single (ticket) ['sɪŋgl]
**Einfall** *(Idee)* idea [aɪ'dɪə]
**Einführung (in)** introduction (to) [ˌɪntrə'dʌkʃn]
**eingeschaltet sein** *(Licht usw.)* be on
**einige** some [səm, sʌm]; *(einige wenige)* a few [fju:]
**einigen: sich einigen (auf)** agree (on) [ə'gri:]
**einkaufen** shop [ʃɒp] • **einkaufen gehen** go shopping; shop
**Einkaufen** shopping ['ʃɒpɪŋ]
**Einkaufsliste** shopping list
**Einkaufspassage** (shopping) mall ['ʃɒpɪŋ ˌmɔ:l]
**Einkaufszentrum** *(überdacht)* (shopping) mall ['ʃɒpɪŋ ˌmɔ:l]

**einladen (zu)** invite (to) [ɪn'vaɪt]
**Einladung (zu)** invitation (to) [ˌɪnvɪ'teɪʃn]
**einmal** once [wʌns] • **einmal pro Woche** once a week • **auf einmal** suddenly ['sʌdnli] • **Einmal aussetzen.** Miss a turn. [tɜ:n] • **früher einmal** once
**einpacken** pack [pæk]
**eins, ein, eine** one ['wʌn]
**Einsatzort** location [ləʊ'keɪʃn]
**einschalten** *(Computer usw.)* turn on [ˌtɜ:n‿'ɒn]
**einschüchtern** bully ['bʊli]
**einst** *(früher einmal)* once [wʌns]
**einsteigen (in den Zug/Bus)** get on (the train/bus) [ˌget‿'ɒn]
**Einstellung (zu/gegenüber)** attitude (to/towards) ['ætɪtju:d]
**eintauschen: etwas eintauschen (für etwas/gegen etwas)** swap sth. (for sth.) [swɒp]
**eintreffen** *(ankommen)* arrive [ə'raɪv]
**eintreten (in)** enter ['entə]
**Eintrittskarte** ticket ['tɪkɪt]
**Einwanderer/Einwanderin** immigrant ['ɪmɪgrənt]
**Einwohner(zahl)** population [ˌpɒpju'leɪʃn]
**Einzelheit** detail ['di:teɪl]
**einziehen** *(in Wohnung)* move in [ˌmu:v‿'ɪn]
**einzig: der einzige Gast** the only guest ['əʊnli]
**Eis** ice [aɪs]; *(Speiseeis)* ice cream [ˌaɪs 'kri:m]
**Eisenbahn** railway ['reɪlweɪ]
**Elefant** elephant ['elɪfənt]
**elektrisch** electric [ɪ'lektrɪk]
**Elektro-** electric [ɪ'lektrɪk]
**elektronisch** electronic [ɪˌlek'trɒnɪk]
**Eltern** parents ['peərənts]
**E-Mail (an)** e-mail (to) ['i:meɪl]
**empfangen** receive [rɪ'si:v]
**End-** *(letzte/r/s)* final ['faɪnl]
**Ende** **1.** end [end]; *(einer Geschichte, eines Films usw.)* ending ['endɪŋ] **am Ende (von)** at the end (of) **zu Ende gehen** end [end] • **zu Ende machen** finish ['fɪnɪʃ] • **zu Ende sein** be over ['əʊvə] **2. oberes Ende** *(Spitze)* top [tɒp] **am oberen Ende** at the top **3. unteres Ende** bottom ['bɒtəm] **am unteren Ende** at the bottom ['bɒtəm]
**enden** finish ['fɪnɪʃ]; end [end]
**endlich** at last [ət 'lɑ:st]
**endlos** endless ['endləs]
**Endstand** *(beim Sport)* final score [ˌfaɪnl 'skɔ:]
**eng** tight [taɪt]

**Engel** angel ['eɪndʒl]
**Englisch; englisch** English ['ɪŋglɪʃ]
**Enkel/in** grandchild ['græntʃaɪld], *pl* grandchildren ['græntʃɪldrən]
**entdecken** discover [dɪ'skʌvə]
**Entdecker/in** *(Forscher/in)* explorer [ɪk'splɔ:rə]
**entkommen** escape [ɪ'skeɪp]
**entlang der Straße / die Straße entlang** along the street [ə'lɒŋ]
**entscheiden: Das kannst/musst du (selbst) entscheiden.** That's up to you.
**entschuldigen: sich entschuldigen** say sorry ['sɒri]
**Entschuldigung** 1. *(Tut mir leid.)* I'm sorry. ['sɒri] • **Entschuldigung, dass ich zu spät bin/komme.** Sorry, I'm late.
2. **Entschuldigung, ... / Entschuldigen Sie, ...** *(Darf ich mal stören?)* Excuse me, ... [ɪk'skju:z mi:]
**entspannen; sich entspannen** relax [rɪ'læks]
**entsperren** unlock [ˌʌn'lɒk]
**entwerfen** design [dɪ'zaɪn]
**er** 1. *(männliche Person)* he [hi:]
2. *(Ding, Tier)* it [ɪt]
**Erbse** pea [pi:]
**Erdbeben** earthquake ['ɜ:θkweɪk]
**Erdbeere** strawberry ['strɔ:bəri]
**Erdboden** ground [graʊnd]
**Erde** earth [ɜ:θ]
**Erdkunde** geography [dʒi'ɒgrəfi]
**Ereignis** event [ɪ'vent]
**erfahren: etwas über etwas erfahren** learn sth. about sth. [lɜ:n]
**Erfolg** success [sək'ses]
**erfolgreich** successful [sək'sesfl]
**erforschen** explore [ɪk'splɔ:]
**Erfüllung: in Erfüllung gehen** come true [ˌkʌm 'tru:]
**ergänzen** add (to) [æd]
**Ergebnis** result [rɪ'zʌlt]
**erinnern: sich erinnern (an)** remember [rɪ'membə]
**erkältet sein** have a cold [kəʊld]
**Erkältung** cold [kəʊld] • **eine Erkältung haben** have a cold
**erklären: jm. etwas erklären** explain sth. to sb. [ɪk'spleɪn]
**Erklärung** explanation [ˌeksplə'neɪʃn]
**erkunden** explore [ɪk'splɔ:]
**erlauben: jm. erlauben, etwas zu tun** let sb. do sth. [let]
**erläutern: jm. etwas erläutern** explain sth. to sb. [ɪk'spleɪn]
**ernst** serious ['sɪəriəs]
**ernsthaft** serious ['sɪəriəs]
**erraten** guess [ges]
**erschießen** shoot [ʃu:t]
**erstaunlich** amazing [ə'meɪzɪŋ]; *(überraschend)* surprising [sə'praɪzɪŋ]
**erste(r, s)** first [fɜ:st] • **als Erstes** first • **der erste Tag** the first day
**der/die Erste sein** be first
**erwachsen werden** grow up [ˌgrəʊ_'ʌp]
**Erwachsene(r)** adult ['ædʌlt]
**erwarten** expect [ɪk'spekt] • **ich kann es kaum erwarten, ... zu sehen** I can't wait to see ... [weɪt]
**erwischen** *(fangen)* catch [kætʃ]
**erzählen (von)** tell (about) [tel]
**Erzählung** story ['stɔ:ri]
**erzielen: einen Treffer erzielen** *(ein Tor schießen)* score (a goal) [skɔ:], [gəʊl]
**es** it [ɪt] • **es gibt** *(es ist vorhanden)* there's; *(es sind vorhanden)* there are
**Essen** food [fu:d]; *(Mahlzeit)* meal [mi:l]
**essen** eat [i:t] • **Abendbrot essen** have dinner • **Toast zum Frühstück essen** have toast for breakfast
**Esszimmer** dining room ['daɪnɪŋ ru:m]
**Etagenbett** bunk (bed) [bʌŋk]
**etwas** something ['sʌmθɪŋ]; *(irgendetwas)* anything ['eniθɪŋ]; *(ein bisschen)* a bit [bɪt] • **etwas Käse/Saft** some cheese/juice [səm, sʌm]
**euch** you [ju:] • **euch (selbst)** yourselves [jə'selvz, jɔ:'selvz]
**euer, eure ...** your ... [jɔ:]
**eurer, eure, eures** yours [jɔ:z]
**Euro** euro ['jʊərəʊ]
**Explosion** explosion [ɪk'spləʊʒn]

## F

**Fabrik** factory ['fæktri]
**fähig sein, etwas zu tun** be able to do sth. ['eɪbl]
**Fähre** ferry ['feri]
**fahren** go [gəʊ]; *(ein Auto / mit dem Auto)* drive [draɪv] • **in Urlaub fahren** go on holiday • **mit dem Auto/Zug/Rad/... fahren** go by car/train/bike/... • **Inliner/Skateboard fahren** skate [skeɪt] • **Rad fahren** cycle ['saɪkl]; ride a bike [ˌraɪd_ə 'baɪk]
**Fahrer/in** driver ['draɪvə]
**Fahrkarte** ticket ['tɪkɪt] • **einfache Fahrkarte** *(nur Hinfahrt)* single (ticket) ['sɪŋgl]
**Fahrplan** timetable ['taɪmteɪbl] *(BE)*; schedule [*AE:* 'skedʒu:l, *BE:* 'ʃedju:l] *(AE)*
**Fahrrad** bike [baɪk]
**Fahrstuhl** lift [lɪft] *(BE)*; elevator ['elɪveɪtə] *(AE)*
**Fahrt** journey ['dʒɜ:ni] • **(Auto-)Fahrt** drive [draɪv] • **(Rad-)Fahrt** (bike) ride [raɪd]
**fair** fair [feə]
**Fakt** *(Tatsache)* fact [fækt]
**Fall** *(Kriminalfall)* case [keɪs]
**fallen** fall [fɔ:l]
**fallen lassen** drop [drɒp]
**falls** if [ɪf]
**falsch** wrong [rɒŋ]; false [fɔ:ls] • **in die falsche Richtung** the wrong way
**Familie** family ['fæməli]
**Fan** fan [fæn]; *(Unterstützer/in)* supporter [sə'pɔ:tə]
**fangen** catch [kætʃ]
**fantastisch** fantastic [fæn'tæstɪk]
**Farbe** colour ['kʌlə] • **Welche Farbe hat ...?** What colour is ...?
**färben** *(bunt an-, ausmalen)* colour ['kʌlə]
**farblos** colourless ['kʌlələs]
**Farm** farm [fɑ:m]
**Farmhaus** farmhouse ['fɑ:mhaʊs]
**Fassung: jd. aus der Fassung bringen** upset sb. [ʌp'set]
**Fastfood** fast food [ˌfɑ:st 'fu:d]
**Februar** February ['februəri]
**Federball** badminton ['bædmɪntən]
**Federmäppchen** pencil case ['pensl keɪs]
**fehlen** be missing ['mɪsɪŋ]
**Fehler** mistake [mɪ'steɪk]
**Feiertag** holiday ['hɒlədeɪ]
**Feind/in** enemy ['enəmi]
**Feld** 1. field [fi:ld] • **auf dem Feld** in the field
2. *(bei Brettspielen)* **Geh ein Feld vor.** Move on one space. [speɪs] **Geh ein Feld zurück.** Move back one space.
**Fels, Felsen** rock
**Fenster** window ['wɪndəʊ]
**Ferien** holidays ['hɒlədeɪz] *(BE)*; vacation [və'keɪʃn, *AE:* veɪkeɪʃn] *(AE)*
**Ferienlager** camp [kæmp]
**Ferienwohnung** holiday flat ['hɒlədeɪ flæt]
**Fernbedienung** remote control [rɪˌməʊt kən'trəʊl]
**Fernsehen** television ['telɪvɪʒn]; TV [ti:'vi:] • **im Fernsehen** on TV
**fernsehen** watch TV [ˌwɒtʃ ti:'vi:]
**Fernsehgerät** TV [ˌti:vi:]
**Fernsehkanal** channel ['tʃænl]
**Fernsehprogramm** TV listings *(pl)* ['lɪstɪŋz]
**fertig** *(bereit)* ready ['redi] • **sich fertig machen (für)** *(sich vorbereiten)* get ready (for) • **Dinge fertig machen (für)** *(vorbereiten)* get things ready (for)

**Fest, Festival** festival ['festɪvl]
**Festspiele** festival ['festɪvl]
**fett** fat [fæt]
**Feuer** fire ['faɪə] • **ein Feuer löschen** put out a fire
**Feuerwache** fire station ['faɪə steɪʃn]
**Feuerwehrfrau** firewoman ['faɪəˌwʊmən]; firefighter ['faɪəfaɪtə]
**Feuerwehrmann** fireman ['faɪəmən]; firefighter ['faɪəfaɪtə]
**Fieber haben** have a temperature ['temprətʃə]
**Fiedel** fiddle ['fɪdl] *(infml)* • **Fiedel spielen** play the fiddle
**Film** film [fɪlm]; movie ['mu:vi]
**Filmemacher** film-maker ['fɪlmmeɪkə]
**Filmstar** film star ['fɪlm stɑ:]
**Filzstift** felt tip ['felt tɪp]
**Finale** final ['faɪnl]
**finden** *(entdecken)* find [faɪnd]
**Finder** finder ['faɪndə]
**Finger** finger ['fɪŋgə]
**Firma** company ['kʌmpəni]
**Fisch** fish, *pl* fish [fɪʃ]
**fischen** fish [fɪʃ]
**fit sein** be fit [fɪt]
**Fitness** fitness ['fɪtnəs]
**Fitnesscenter** fitness centre
**Flachbildschirm** flat screen ['flæt skri:n]
**Flasche** bottle ['bɒtl] • **eine Flasche Milch** a bottle of milk
**Fleisch** meat [mi:t]
**Fleischer** butcher ['bʊtʃə] • **beim Fleischer** at the butcher's
**fliegen** fly [flaɪ]
**fliehen (vor jm. / aus etwas)** escape (from sb./sth.) [ɪ'skeɪp]
**Flug** flight [flaɪt] • **ein 14-stündiger Flug, ein 14-Stunden-Flug** a 14-hour flight
**Flügel** wing [wɪŋ]
**Flughafen** airport ['eəpɔ:t]
**Flugsteig** gate [geɪt]
**Flugzeug** plane [pleɪn] • **im Flugzeug** on the plane
**Flur** hall [hɔ:l]
**Fluss** river ['rɪvə]
**Flusspferd** hippo ['hɪpəʊ]
**flüstern** whisper ['wɪspə]
**folgen** follow ['fɒləʊ]
**Folk** folk (music) ['fəʊk ˌmju:zɪk]
**Football** American football [əˌmerɪkən 'fʊtbɔ:l]
**Forscher/in** explorer [ɪk'splɔ:rə]
**fort** away [ə'weɪ]
**Foto** photo ['fəʊtəʊ] • **auf dem Foto** in the photo • **Fotos machen** take photos
**Fotoapparat** camera ['kæmərə]
**Fotograf/in** photographer [fə'tɒgrəfə]
**fotografieren** take photos [teɪk 'fəʊtəʊz]
**Frage** question ['kwestʃn] • **Fragen stellen** ask questions • **Kommt nicht in Frage!** No way!
**fragen** ask [ɑ:sk] • **nach etwas fragen** ask about sth. • **jn. nach dem Weg fragen** ask sb. the way; ask sb. for directions • **sich fragen** wonder ['wʌndə]
**Französisch** French [frentʃ]
**Frau** woman ['wʊmən], *pl* women ['wɪmɪn] • **Frau Brown** Mrs Brown ['mɪsɪz]; Ms Brown [mɪz, məz] • **Frau White** *(unverheiratet)* Miss White [mɪs]
**frei** free [fri:] • **freie Zeit** free time **eine Woche/einen Tag / einen Monat ... frei** a week/day/month ... off
**Freitag** Friday ['fraɪdeɪ, 'fraɪdi] **freitagabends, am Freitagabend** on Friday evening • **freitagnachts, Freitagnacht** on Friday night
**Freiwillige(r)** volunteer [ˌvɒlən'tɪə]
**Freizeit** free time [ˌfri: 'taɪm]
**Freizeitzentrum, -park** leisure centre ['leʒə sentə]
**fremd** *(merkwürdig)* strange [streɪndʒ]
**Fremdenführer/in** guide [gaɪd]
**Fremdenverkehrsamt** tourist information ['tʊərɪst‿ɪnfəˌmeɪʃn]
**Freund/in** friend [frend]; *(Kumpel)* mate [meɪt] *(infml)* • **fester Freund** boyfriend ['bɔɪfrend] / **feste Freundin** girlfriend ['gɜ:lfrend]
**freundlich** friendly ['frendli]
**frieren** be cold [kəʊld]
**Frischkäse** cream cheese [ˌkri:m 'tʃi:z]
**Friseur/Friseurin** hairdresser ['heədresə]
**froh** happy ['hæpi]; glad [glæd]
**Frosch** frog [frɒg]
**Frucht, Früchte** fruit [fru:t]
**früh** early ['ɜ:li]
**früher** *(einst, früher einmal)* once [wʌns]
**Frühling** spring [sprɪŋ]
**Frühstück** breakfast ['brekfəst] **zum Frühstück** for breakfast
**Frühstücksflocken** cereal ['sɪəriəl]
**frühstücken** have breakfast
**Frühstückspension** Bed and Breakfast (B&B) [ˌbed‿ən 'brekfəst]
**Fuchs** fox [fɒks]
**fühlen; sich fühlen** feel [fi:l]
**Führer/in** leader ['li:də]; *(Fremdenführer/in)* guide [gaɪd]
**Füller** pen [pen]
**funktionieren** work [wɜ:k]
**für** for [fə, fɔ:] • **Was für ein Auto ...?** What kind of car ...?
**furchtbar** terrible ['terəbl]; awful ['ɔ:fl]
**fürchterlich aussehen** be a mess [mes]
**Fuß** foot [fʊt], *pl* feet [fi:t]; *(Längenmaß; 1 Fuß = 30,48 cm)* foot
**Fußball** football ['fʊtbɔ:l]; soccer ['sɒkə]
**Fußballplatz** pitch [pɪtʃ]
**Fußballschuhe, -stiefel** football boots ['fʊtbɔ:l bu:ts]
**Fußboden** floor [flɔ:]
**Futter** food [fu:d]
**füttern** feed [fi:d]

## G

**Gabel** fork [fɔ:k]
**gähnen** yawn [jɔ:n]
**ganz: auf der ganzen Welt** all over the world • **aus der ganzen Welt** from all over the world • **den ganzen Tag (lang)** all day • **den ganzen Weg** all the way • **die ganze Zeit** all the time • **Das ist ganz falsch.** This is all wrong.
**ganze(r,s)** whole [həʊl]
**Garage** garage ['gærɑ:ʒ]
**Garten** garden ['gɑ:dn]
**Gasse** lane [leɪn]
**Gast** guest [gest]; *(Besucher/in)* visitor ['vɪzɪtə]
**Gebäude** building ['bɪldɪŋ]
**geben** give [gɪv] • **es gibt** *(es ist vorhanden)* there's; *(es sind vorhanden)* there are • **jm. die Schuld geben (an)** blame sb. (for) [bleɪm]
**Gebiet** *(Zone)* zone [zəʊn]
**geboren sein/werden** be born [bɔ:n]
**gebraucht** *(aus zweiter Hand)* second-hand [ˌsekənd 'hænd]
**gebrochen** *(Arm, Bein)* broken ['brəʊkən]
**Geburtstag** birthday ['bɜ:θdeɪ] **Herzlichen Glückwunsch zum Geburtstag.** Happy birthday. **Ich habe im Mai / am 13. Juni Geburtstag.** My birthday is in May / on 13th June. • **Wann hast du Geburtstag?** When's your birthday?
**Gedicht** poem ['pəʊɪm]
**Gefahr** danger ['deɪndʒə]
**gefährlich** dangerous ['deɪndʒərəs]; *(nicht sicher)* unsafe [ʌn'seɪf]
**Gefängnis** jail [dʒeɪl]
**Geflügel** poultry ['pəʊltri]
**gegen** against [ə'genst] • **gegen sechs** *(um sechs Uhr herum)* around six

**gegenseitig: sich gegenseitig** each other [iːtʃ‿'ʌðə]
**Gegenteil** opposite ['ɒpəzɪt]
**Gegenwart** present ['preznt]
**gehen 1.** go [gəʊ]; *(zu Fuß gehen)* walk [wɔːk]; *(weggehen)* leave [liːv] **Auf geht's!** Let's go. • **einkaufen gehen** go shopping; shop [ʃɒp] **Geh ein Feld vor.** Move on one space. [speɪs] • **Geh ein Feld zurück.** Move back one space. • **in die Sauna gehen** have a sauna **in Erfüllung gehen** come true [ˌkʌm 'truː] • **ins Bett gehen** go to bed • **ins Kino gehen** go to the cinema • **nach Hause gehen** go home • **reiten/schwimmen gehen** go riding/swimming • **spazieren gehen** go for a walk [wɔːk] **2. Es geht mir/ihm gut.** I'm/He's fine. [faɪn] **3. Es geht um Mr Green.** This is about Mr Green. **4. Das geht dich nichts an!** Mind your own business. [ˌmaɪnd jər‿ˌəʊn 'bɪznəs]
**gehören zu** *(passen zu)* go with
**Gehweg** pavement ['peɪvmənt] *(BE)*; sidewalk ['saɪdwɔːk] *(AE)*
**Geige** violin [ˌvaɪə'lɪn]; fiddle *(infml)* ['fɪdl] • **Geige spielen** play the violin
**Geist** *(Gespenst)* ghost [gəʊst]
**gekränkt (wegen)** upset (about) [ˌʌp'set]
**Gelächter** laughter ['lɑːftə]
**gelangen** *(hinkommen)* get [get]
**gelb** yellow ['jeləʊ]
**Geld** money ['mʌni] • **Geld ausgeben (für)** spend money (on) [spend] • **Geld sammeln (für)** raise money (for) [reɪz]
**Geldbörse** purse [pɜːs]
**Gemeindehalle, -saal** community hall [kə'mjuːnəti]
**Gemüse:** *(ein)* **Gemüse** vegetable ['vedʒtəbl]
**genannt werden** *(heißen)* be called [kɔːld]
**genau** exactly [ɪg'zæktli] • **genau in dem Moment** just then • **genau wie du** just like you
**genial** brilliant ['brɪliənt]
**genießen** enjoy [ɪn'dʒɔɪ]
**genug** enough [ɪ'nʌf] • **genug von etwas haben** be tired of sth. ['taɪəd]
**geöffnet** open ['əʊpən]
**Geografie** geography [dʒi'ɒgrəfi]
**gepflegt** neat [niːt]
**gerade** at the moment; *(eben, soeben)* just [dʒʌst] • **gerade dann** *(genau in dem Moment)* just then **jetzt gerade** *(in diesem Moment)* right now [raɪt 'naʊ]
**geradeaus weiter** straight on [streɪt‿'ɒn]
**Geräusch** noise [nɔɪz]
**gerecht** fair [feə]
**Gericht** *(Speise)* dish [dɪʃ]
**gern: Ich hätte gern ... / Ich möchte gern ...** I'd like ... (= I would like ...) **Ich schwimme/tanze/... gern.** I like swimming/dancing/... • **Ich würde gern über ... reden** I'd like to talk about ... • **Gern geschehen.** You're welcome. ['welkəm]
**gernhaben** like [laɪk]
**Geruch** smell
**gesamte(r, s)** whole [həʊl] • **aus dem gesamten Vereinigten Königreich** from all over the UK
**Geschäft** shop [ʃɒp]
**Geschäft(e)** business ['bɪznəs]
**geschehen (mit)** happen (to) ['hæpən]
**Geschenk** present ['preznt]
**Geschichte 1.** story ['stɔːri] **2.** *(vergangene Zeiten)* history ['hɪstri]
**geschieden** divorced [dɪ'vɔːst]
**Geschirrspülmaschine** dishwasher ['dɪʃwɒʃə]
**Geschlecht** sex [seks]
**geschlossen** closed [kləʊzd]
**Gesellschaft** *(Firma)* company ['kʌmpəni]
**Gesetz** law [lɔː]
**gesetzlich** legal ['liːgl]
**Gesicht** face [feɪs]
**Gespenst** *(Geist)* ghost [gəʊst]
**Gespräch** *(Dialog)* dialogue ['daɪəlɒg]
**gestalten** design [dɪ'zaɪn]
**gestern** yesterday ['jestədeɪ, 'jestədi] **gestern Morgen/Nachmittag/Abend** yesterday morning/afternoon/evening • **die Hausaufgaben von gestern** yesterday's homework
**gesund** healthy ['helθi]; well [wel]
**Gesundheit** health [helθ]
**Gesundheitslehre** health [helθ]
**Getränk** drink [drɪŋk] • **alkoholfreies Getränk** soft drink
**Getränkeautomat** soda machine ['səʊdə məʃiːn]
**Getreideflocken** cereal ['sɪəriəl]
**Gewehr** gun [gʌn]
**Gewinn** prize [praɪz]
**gewinnen** win [wɪn]
**Gewinner/in** winner ['wɪnə]
**Gewitter** storm [stɔːm]
**gewöhnlich** usually ['juːʒuəli]
**Giraffe** giraffe [dʒə'rɑːf]
**Gitarre** guitar [gɪ'tɑː] • **Gitarre spielen** play the guitar
**Glas** glass [glɑːs] • **ein Glas Wasser** a glass of water
**glauben** think [θɪŋk] • **glauben an** believe in [bɪ'liːv] • **Das glaube ich nicht. / Ich glaube nicht.** I don't think so. • **Ich glaube (ja).** I think so. • **Glaubst du das wirklich?** Do you really think so?
**gleich sein/aussehen** be/look the same [seɪm]
**Gleis** platform ['plætfɔːm]
**Glocke** bell [bel]
**Glück** happiness ['hæpinəs] • **Glück haben (mit)** be lucky (with) ['lʌki] **Viel Glück (bei/mit ...)!** Good luck (with ...)! [gʊd 'lʌk] • **zum Glück** *(glücklicherweise)* luckily ['lʌkɪli]
**glücklich** happy ['hæpi]
**glücklicherweise** luckily ['lʌkɪli]
**Gokart** go-kart ['gəʊkɑːt]
**Gold** gold [gəʊld]
**goldene(r,s)** golden ['gəʊldən]
**Gott** God [gɒd]
**Grad** degree [dɪ'griː] • **Grad Celsius** degrees Celsius ['selsiəs]
**Grafiker/in** artist ['ɑːtɪst]
**Grammatik** grammar ['græmə]
**Gras** grass [grɑːs]
**grau** grey [greɪ]
**grauenhaft** horrible ['hɒrəbl]
**Grenze** border ['bɔːdə]
**groß** big [bɪg]; large [lɑːdʒ]; *(riesig)* huge [hjuːdʒ]; *(Personen, Körpergröße)* tall [tɔːl]
**großartig** great [greɪt]; awesome ['ɔːsəm] *(AE, infml)*
**Größe** *(Schuhgröße usw.)* size [saɪz]
**Großeltern** grandparents ['grænpeərənts]
**Großmutter** grandmother ['grænmʌðə]
**Großstadt** city ['sɪti]
**Großvater** grandfather ['grænfɑːðə]
**grün** green [griːn]
**Grund** reason ['riːzn] • **aus vielen Gründen** for lots of reasons
**gründen** found [faʊnd]
**Gruppe** group [gruːp]; *(Musikgruppe)* band [bænd]; *(Clique)* crowd *(infml)* [kraʊd]
**gruselig** scary ['skeəri]
**Gruß: Liebe Grüße, ...** *(Briefschluss)* Love ... [lʌv] • **Mit besten Grüßen** *(als Briefschluss)* Best wishes ['wɪʃɪz]
**Grüß Dilip von mir.** Say hi to Dilip for me.
**gucken** look [lʊk]
**gut** good [gʊd]; *(okay)* OK [əʊ'keɪ]; *(in Ordnung)* all right [ɔːl 'raɪt]; *(ge-*

*sundheitlich gut, wohlauf)* well [wel]; fine [faɪn] • **Es geht mir/ihm gut.** I'm/He's fine. • **gute Arbeit leisten** do a good job • **Guten Morgen.** Good morning. • **Guten Tag.** Hello.; *(nachmittags)* Good afternoon. • **gut abschneiden (in)** do well (in) • **gut in etwas sein / etwas gut können** be good at sth. **gut (ver)laufen** *(gutgehen, klappen)* go well • **Das hast du gut gemacht** You did well. • **Alles Gute** *(als Briefschluss)* Best wishes ['wɪʃɪz]
► S.173 US school grades
**gutgehen** *(gut (ver)laufen, klappen)* go well

## H

**Haar, Haare** hair *(no pl)* [heə]
**haarlos** hairless ['heələs]
**haben** have got ['hæv gɒt]; have [həv, hæv] • **Ich habe keinen Stuhl.** I haven't got a chair. • **Ich habe am 13. Juni/im Mai Geburtstag.** My birthday is on 13th June/in May. **Wann hast du Geburtstag?** When's your birthday? • **haben wollen** want [wɒnt] • **Was haben wir als Hausaufgabe auf?** What's for homework?
**Hafen** harbour ['hɑ:bə]
**Hähnchen** chicken ['tʃɪkɪn]
**halb: eine halbe Stunde** half an hour [ˌhɑ:f_ən_'aʊə] • **halb zwölf** half past 11 [hɑ:f] • **dreieinhalb Tage** three and a half days
**Halbfinale** semi-final [ˌsemi'faɪnl]
**Halbzeit** half • **die erste Halbzeit** the first half • **Halbzeit(pause)** half-time [ˌhɑ:f 'taɪm]
**Hälfte** half [hɑ:f], *pl* halves [hɑ:vs]
**Hallo!** Hi! [haɪ]; Hello. [hə'ləʊ]; Hey! [heɪ]
**Hals** throat [θrəʊt]
**Halsschmerzen haben** have a sore throat [sɔ: 'θrəʊt]
**Halt** stop [stɒp]
**halten 1.** hold [həʊld] **2.** *(aufbewahren)* keep [ki:p] **etwas warm/kühl/offen/... halten** keep sth. warm/cool/open/... **3.** *(behalten)* keep • **Kontakt halten** keep in touch [ˌki:p_ɪn 'tʌtʃ] **4. Halt den Mund!** Shut up. [ˌʃʌt_'ʌp] **5. Was hältst du von ...?** What do you think about/of ...?
**Haltung (gegenüber)** attitude (to/towards) ['ætɪtju:d]
**Hamburger** hamburger ['hæmbɜ:gə]
**Hamster** hamster ['hæmstə]
**Hand** hand [hænd] • **aus zweiter Hand** *(gebraucht)* second-hand
**Handball** handball ['hændbɔ:l]
**Handel** *(Geschäfte)* business ['bɪznəs]
**Handy** mobile (phone) ['məʊbaɪl] *(BE)*; cellphone ['selfəʊn] *(AE)*
**hänseln: jn. mit Schimpfwörtern hänseln** call sb. names
**Happyend** happy ending [ˌhæpi_'endɪŋ]
**hart** hard [hɑ:d] • **hart arbeiten** work hard
**hassen** hate [heɪt]
**häufig** often ['ɒfn]
**Haupt-** *(wichtigste(r,s))* main [meɪn]
**Hauptstadt** capital ['kæpɪtl]
**Haus** house [haʊs] • **im Haus der Shaws / bei den Shaws zu Hause** at the Shaws' house • **nach Hause gehen** go home [həʊm] • **nach Hause kommen** come home; get home • **zu Hause** at home
**Hausarrest haben** be grounded ['graʊndɪd]
**Hausaufgabe(n)** homework *(no pl)* ['həʊmwɜ:k] • **die Hausaufgabe(n) machen** do homework • **Was haben wir als Hausaufgabe auf?** What's for homework?
**Häuserblock** block [blɒk]
**Hausmeister/in** caretaker ['keəteɪkə]
**Haustier** pet [pet]
**Haustür** front door [ˌfrʌnt 'dɔ:]
**Haut** skin [skɪn]
**Heim** home [həʊm]
**Heimatstadt** hometown ['həʊmtaʊn]
**Heimweh haben** be homesick ['həʊmsɪk]
**heiraten: (jn.) heiraten** get married (to sb.) ['mærid]
**heiß** hot [hɒt]
**heißen 1.** *(genannt werden)* be called [kɔ:ld] • **Ich heiße ...** My name is ... • **Wie heißt du?** What's your name? **2. Sie heißen dich in ... willkommen** They welcome you to ... ['welkəm]
**helfen** help [help]
**Helikopter** helicopter ['helɪkɒptə]
**hell** *(leuchtend)* bright [braɪt]
**Helm** helmet ['helmɪt]
**Hemd** shirt [ʃɜ:t]
**herauf** up [ʌp]
**heraus** out [aʊt] • **aus ... heraus** out of ... ['aʊt_əv]
**herausarbeiten: etwas herausarbeiten** *(herausfinden)* work sth. out
**herausfinden** find out [ˌfaɪnd_'aʊt]; *(entdecken)* discover [dɪ'skʌvə]
**etwas über etwas herausfinden** learn sth. about sth. [lɜ:n]
**herausnehmen** take out [ˌteɪk_'aʊt]
**Herberge** hostel ['hɒstl]
**herbringen** bring [brɪŋ]
**Herbst** autumn ['ɔ:təm]
**Herd** cooker ['kʊkə]
**hereinkommen** come in [ˌkʌm_'ɪn]
**Herr Brown** Mr Brown ['mɪstə]
**herstellen** produce [prə'dju:s]
**herum: anders herum** the other way round [raʊnd] • **um ... herum** round, around [ə'raʊnd] • **um sechs Uhr herum** *(gegen sechs)* • around six
**herum-: etwas herumgeben** pass sth. round [ˌpɑ:s 'raʊnd] • **herumgehen** walk around [ə'raʊnd] **herumrennen** run around **herumspringen** jump around
**herunter** down [daʊn]
**herunterladbar** downloadable [ˌdaʊn'ləʊdəbl]
**herunterladen: zum Herunterladen** downloadable [ˌdaʊn'ləʊdəbl]
**herunterfallen (von)** fall off [ˌfɔ:l_'ɒf]
**hervorragend** *(ausgezeichnet)* excellent ['eksələnt]
► S.173 US school grades
**Herz** heart [hɑ:t]
**Herzlichen Glückwunsch zum Geburtstag.** Happy birthday. [ˌhæpi 'bɜ:θdeɪ]
**heute** today [tə'deɪ] • **heute Morgen/Nachmittag/Abend** this morning/afternoon/evening **heute Nacht** tonight [tə'naɪt] **das Programm von heute** today's programme
**heutig: das heutige Programm** today's programme
**hier** here [hɪə] • **Hier bitte.** *(Bitte sehr.)* Here you are. • **hier drinnen** in here [ˌɪn 'hɪə] • **hier entlang** this way ['ðɪs weɪ] • **Hier spricht Isabel. / Hier ist Isabel.** *(am Telefon)* This is Isabel. • **Hier steht: ... / Es heißt hier: ...** *(im Text)* It says here: ...
**hierher** here [hɪə]
**Hilfe** help [help]
**Himmel** sky [skaɪ]; *(im religiösen Sinn)* heaven ['hevn] • **am Himmel** in the sky
**hinauf** up [ʌp] • **den Hügel hinauf** up the hill • **auf ... hinauf** onto ['ɒntə, 'ɒntʊ]
**hinaufklettern (auf)** climb [klaɪm]
**hinaus** out [aʊt] • **aus ... hinaus** out of ... ['aʊt_əv]
**hinein: in ... hinein** into ... ['ɪntə, 'ɪntʊ]
**hinfallen** fall [fɔ:l]; fall down
**hinkommen** *(gelangen)* get [get]

**hinsetzen: sich hinsetzen** sit down
**hinstellen: sich hinstellen** stand [stænd]
**hinter** behind [bɪ'haɪnd]
**Hintergrund** background ['bækgraʊnd]
**Hintertür** back door
**hinüber zu/nach ...** over to ... ['əʊvə]
**hinunter** down [daʊn]
**hinzufügen (zu)** add (to) [æd]
**Hirsch** deer, *pl* deer [dɪə]
**Hobby** hobby ['hɒbi], *pl* hobbies
**hoch** high [haɪ]; *(Bäume, Türme usw.)* tall [tɔ:l]
**hochheben: etwas hochheben** pick sth. up [,pɪk_'ʌp]
**hochsehen (von)** look up (from) [,lʊk_'ʌp]
**Hockey** hockey ['hɒki]
**Hockeyplatz, -feld** hockey pitch ['hɒki pɪtʃ]
**Hockeyschuhe** hockey shoes ['hɒki ʃu:z]
**Hof** yard [jɑ:d] • **auf dem Hof** in the yard
**hoffen** hope [həʊp]
**Hoffnung** hope [həʊp]
**holen** *(besorgen)* get [get]
**Hölle** hell [hel]
**hören** hear [hɪə] • **Na hör mal!** Come on. [,kʌm_'ɒn]
**Hose** trousers *(pl)* ['traʊzəz] *(BE)*; pants *(pl)* [pænts] *(AE)*
**Hotel** hotel [həʊ'tel]
**Hotline** hotline ['hɒtlaɪn]
**hübsch** pretty ['prɪti]
**Hubschrauber** helicopter ['helɪkɒptə]
**Hügel** hill [hɪl]
**hügelig** hilly ['hɪli]
**Huhn** chicken ['tʃɪkɪn]
**Hülle** cover ['kʌvə]
**Hund** dog [dɒg]
**hundert** hundred ['hʌndrəd]
**Hunger haben** be hungry ['hʌŋgri]
**hungrig sein** be hungry ['hʌŋgri]
**Hurra!** Hooray! [hu'reɪ]
**Hut** hat [hæt]
**Hütte** cabin ['kæbɪn]

## I

**ich** I [aɪ] • **Ich auch.** Me too. [,mi: 'tu:] • **Das bin ich.** That's me. **Warum ich?** Why me?
**ideal** perfect ['pɜ:fɪkt]
**Idee** idea [aɪ'dɪə] • **Ideen sammeln** brainstorm ['breɪnstɔ:m]
**Igel** hedgehog ['hedʒhɒg]
**igitt** yuck [jʌk]
**ihm** him; *(bei Dingen, Tieren)* it
**ihn** him; *(bei Dingen, Tieren)* it
**ihnen** them [ðəm, ðem]
**Ihnen** *(höfliche Anrede)* you [ju:]
**ihr** *(Plural von „du")* you [ju:] • **ihr zwei** you two [,ju: 'tu:]
**ihr: Hilf ihr.** Help her. [hə, hɜ:]
**ihr(e)** *(besitzanzeigend) (zu „she")* her [hə, hɜ:]; *(zu „they")* their [ðeə]
**Ihr(e)** *(höfliche Anrede)* your [jɔ:]
**ihrer, ihre, ihrs** *(zu „she")* hers [hɜ:z]; *(zu „they")* theirs [ðeəz]
**Ihrer, Ihre, Ihrs** *(höfliche Anrede)* yours [jɔ:z]
**illegal** illegal [ɪ'li:gl]
**im: im Fernsehen** on TV • **im Flugzeug** on the plane • **im Jahre 1837** in 1837 • **im Haus der Shaws** at the Shaws' house • **im Mai** in May • **im Radio** on the radio • **im Zug** on the train
**Imbiss** snack [snæk]
**Imbissstube** café ['kæfeɪ]
**immer** always ['ɔ:lweɪz] • **immer noch** still [stɪl]
**in** in • **in ... (hinein)** into ... ['ɪntə, 'ɪntʊ] • **in den Zug/Bus einsteigen** get on the train/bus • **in der Stadt umher** around the town • **in der ...straße** in ... Street • **in der Hamiltonstraße 7** at 7 Hamilton Street • **in der Nacht** at night **in der Nähe von** near • **in der Pause** *(zwischen Schulstunden)* at break • **in der Schule** at school **in die falsche Richtung** the wrong way • **in die Sauna gehen** have a sauna • **in Eile sein** be in a hurry **ins Bett gehen** go to bed • **ins Kino gehen** go to the cinema • **in Urlaub fahren** go on holiday • **in Verbindung bleiben** keep in touch [,ki:p_ɪn 'tʌtʃ] • **in welche Richtung?** which way? • **in Wirklichkeit** *(eigentlich)* actually ['æktʃuəli]
**Indianer/in** Native American [,neɪtɪv_ə'merɪkən]
**Industrie** industry ['ɪndəstri]
**Industrie-, industriell** industrial [ɪn'dʌstriəl]
**Information(en) (über)** information (about/on) *(no pl)* [,ɪnfə'meɪʃn]
**Ingenieur/in** engineer [,endʒɪ'nɪə]
**Inliner** skates [skeɪts] • **Inliner fahren** skate
**innen (drin)** inside [,ɪn'saɪd]
**Innenstadt** city centre [,sɪti 'sentə]
**Insel** island ['aɪlənd]
**installieren** install [ɪn'stɔ:l]
**Instrument** instrument ['ɪnstrəmənt]
**interessant** interesting ['ɪntrəstɪŋ]
**Interesse** interest ['ɪntrəst]
**interessieren: sich interessieren (für)** be interested (in) ['ɪntrəstɪd]
**interessiert sein (an)** be interested (in) ['ɪntrəstɪd]
**international** international [,ɪntə'næʃnəl]
**Internet** internet ['ɪntənet] • **im Internet surfen** surf the internet [sɜ:f]
**Interview** interview ['ɪntəvju:]
**interviewen** interview ['ɪntəvju:]
**irgendetwas** anything ['eniθɪŋ] **irgendetwas anderes** anything else [els]
► S.169 any ► S.167 ... else
**irgendjemand** anybody ['enibɒdi]; anyone ['eniwʌn] • **irgendjemand anderes** anybody/anyone else
► S.169 any ► S.167 ... else
**irgendwelche** any ['eni]
► S.169 any
**irgendwo(hin)** somewhere ['sʌmweə]; anywhere ['eniweə]
► S.169 any
**irren: sich irren** be wrong [rɒŋ]

## J

**ja** yes [jes]
**Jacke, Jackett** jacket ['dʒækɪt]
**Jagd** hunt [hʌnt]
**jagen** hunt [hʌnt]
**Jahr** year [jɪə] • **im Jahre 1837** in 1837
**Jahrgangsstufe** year [jɪə] *(BE)*; grade [greɪd] *(AE)*
**Jahrhundert** century ['sentʃəri]
**...jährig: ein(e) Sechzehnjährige(r)** a sixteen-year-old • **ein sechzehnjähriges Mädchen** a sixteen-year-old girl
**Januar** January ['dʒænjuəri]
**Jazz** jazz [dʒæz]
**je?** *(jemals?)* ever? ['evə]
**Jeans** jeans *(pl)* [dʒi:nz]
**jede(r, s) ...** *(Begleiter)* **1.** every ... ['evri] **2.** *(jeder einzelne)* each ... [i:tʃ] **3.** *(jeder beliebige)* any ... ['eni]
► S.169 any
**jeder** *(Pronomen)* **1.** everybody ['evribɒdi]; everyone ['evriwʌn] **2.** *(jeder Beliebige)* anybody ['enibɒdi]; anyone ['eniwʌn]
► S.169 any
**jemals?** ever? ['evə]
**jemand** **1.** somebody ['sʌmbədi]; someone ['sʌmwʌn] **2.** *(irgendjemand)* anybody ['enibɒdi]; anyone ['eniwʌn]
► S.169 any
**jene(r, s)** *(Singular)* that [ðət, ðæt]; *(Plural)* those [ðəʊz]
**jetzt** now [naʊ] • **jetzt gerade, jetzt sofort** right now

**Job** job [dʒɒb]
**jubeln** cheer [tʃɪə]
**Judo** judo ['dʒu:dəʊ] • **Judo machen** do judo
**Jugend** youth [ju:θ]
**Jugendclub** youth club ['ju:θ ˌklʌb]
**Jugend-** junior ['dʒu:niə]; *(Teenager-)* teen [ti:n]
**Jugendgruppe** youth group
**Jugendherberge** youth hostel ['ju:θ ˌhɒstl]
**Jugendliche(r)** kid [kɪd]; teenager ['ti:neɪdʒə]
**Juli** July [dʒu'laɪ]
**jung** young [jʌŋ]
**Junge** boy [bɔɪ]
**Juni** June [dʒu:n]
**Junioren-** junior ['dʒu:niə]

# K

**Kabel** *(auch kurz für Kabelfernsehen)* cable ['keɪbl]
**Kaffee** coffee ['kɒfi] • **Kaffee zum Mitnehmen** coffee to go
**Käfig** cage [keɪdʒ]
**kahl** *(unbehaart)* hairless ['heələs]
**Kai** *(Kaimauer)* quay [ki:]
**Kaimauer** quay [ki:]
**Kalender** calendar ['kælɪndə]
**kalt** cold [kəʊld]
**Kälte** cold [kəʊld]
**Kamel** camel ['kæml]
**Kamera** camera ['kæmərə]
**Kampf** fight [faɪt]
**kämpfen (für, um)** fight (for) [faɪt]
**Kanal** **1.** canal [kə'næl]
**2.** *(Fernsehsender)* channel ['tʃænl]
**Känguru** kangaroo [ˌkæŋgə'ru:]
**Kaninchen** rabbit ['ræbɪt]
**Kantine** canteen [kæn'ti:n]
**Kanu** canoe [kə'nu:] • **Kanu fahren** canoe [kə'nu:]
**Kapitän/in** captain ['kæptɪn]
**Kappe** cap [kæp]
**kaputt** broken ['brəʊkən]
**Karotte** carrot ['kærət]
**Karriere** career [kə'rɪə]
**Karte** *(Post-, Spielkarte)* card [kɑ:d]
**Kartoffel** potato [pə'teɪtəʊ], *pl* -toes
**Kartoffelbrei** mashed potatoes [ˌmæʃd pə'teɪtəʊz]
**Kartoffelchips** crisps *(pl)* [krɪsps] *(BE)*; potato chips *(pl)* [tʃɪps] *(AE)*
**Kartoffelpüree** mashed potatoes [ˌmæʃd pə'teɪtəʊz]
**Käse** cheese [tʃi:z]
**Kästchen, Kasten** box [bɒks]
**Kathedrale** cathedral [kə'θi:drəl]
**Katze** cat [kæt]
**kaufen** buy [baɪ]
**Kaufhaus** department store [dɪ'pɑ:tmənt stɔ:]
**Kehle** throat [θrəʊt]
**kein(e)** no; not a; not (...) any • **Ich habe keinen Stuhl.** I haven't got a chair. • **keine Musik mehr** no more music
**Keks** biscuit ['bɪskɪt] *(BE)*; cookie ['kʊki] *(AE)*
**Kellner** waiter ['weɪtə]
**Kellnerin** waitress ['weɪtrəs]
**kennen** know [nəʊ]
**kennenlernen: jn. kennenlernen** get to know sb.; *(zum ersten Mal treffen)* meet sb. [mi:t] • **Nett, dich/euch/Sie kennenzulernen.** Nice to meet you.
**kennzeichnen** mark up [ˌmɑ:k‿'ʌp]
**Kerl** guy *(infml)* [gaɪ]
**Keyboard** *(elektronisches Tasteninstrument)* keyboard ['ki:bɔ:d]
**Kilogramm, Kilo (kg)** kilogram (kg) ['kɪləgræm], kilo ['kiləʊ] • **ein 150 Kilogramm schwerer Bär** a 150-kilogram bear
**Kilometer (km)** kilometre (km) ['kɪləmi:tə] • **eine Zehn-Kilometer-Wanderung** a ten-kilometre walk
**Kind** child [tʃaɪld], *pl* children ['tʃɪldrən]; kid [kɪd] • **ein Kind bekommen** have a child
**Kindergarten** kindergarten ['kɪndəgɑ:tn]
**Kino** cinema ['sɪnəmə] • **ins Kino gehen** go to the cinema
**Kirche** church [tʃɜ:tʃ]
**Kirsche** cherry ['tʃeri]
**Kiste** box [bɒks]
**Kiwi** kiwi ['ki:wi:]
**Klang** sound [saʊnd]
**klar** **1.** clear [klɪə]
**2.** *(sicher, kein Problem)* sure [ʃʊə, ʃɔ:]
**Klasse** class [klɑ:s]; form [fɔ:m]; grade [greɪd] *(AE)*
**klasse** *(großartig)* awesome ['ɔ:səm] *(AE, infml)*
**Klassenkamerad/in** classmate ['klɑ:smeɪt]
**Klassenlehrer/in** class teacher; form teacher
**Klassenzimmer** classroom ['klɑ:sru:m]
**klassisch** classical ['klæsɪkl]
**klatschen** clap [klæp]
**Klavier** piano [pi'ænəʊ] • **Klavier spielen** play the piano
**kleben: (auf-, ein)kleben** glue [glu:]
**Klebestift** glue stick ['glu: stɪk]
**Klebstoff** glue [glu:]
**Kleid** dress [dres]
**Kleider** *(Kleidungsstücke)* clothes *(pl)* [kləʊðz, kləʊz]
**Kleiderschrank** wardrobe ['wɔ:drəʊb]
**Kleiderordnung** dress code ['dres kəʊd]
**Kleidung(sstücke)** clothes *(pl)* [kləʊðz, kləʊz]
**klein** little ['lɪtl]; small [smɔ:l]; *(Körpergröße)* short [ʃɔ:t]
**Kleingeld** change [tʃeɪndʒ]
► S.178 (to) change – change
**Kleinstadt** town [taʊn]
**klettern** climb [klaɪm] • **Klettere auf einen Baum.** Climb a tree.
**Klingel** bell [bel]
**klingeln** ring [rɪŋ] • **Es klingelte.** The bell rang.
**Klingelton** ringtone ['rɪŋtəʊn]
**klingen** sound [saʊnd]
**Klinik** clinic ['klɪnɪk]
**Klon** clone [kləʊn]
**Klub** club [klʌb]
**klug** clever ['klevə]
**knapp: Das war knapp.** That was close. [kləʊs]
**Kneipe** pub [pʌb]
**Knie** knee [ni:]
**Knieschützer** pad [pæd]
**Knopf** button ['bʌtn]
**Koch** cook [kʊk]
**kochen** cook [kʊk]
**Köchin** cook [kʊk]
**Koffer** suitcase ['su:tkeɪs]
**Koje** *(Etagenbett)* bunk (bed) [bʌŋk]
**kolorieren** colour ['kʌlə]
**komisch** funny ['fʌni]
**Komma: 10,4 (zehn Komma vier)** 10.4 (ten point four)
**kommen** come [kʌm]; *(hinkommen)* get [get] • **Ich komme aus ...** I'm from ... • **Wo kommst du her?** Where are you from? • **nach Hause kommen** come home; get home • **zu spät kommen** be late
**Kommt nicht in Frage!** No way! [ˌnəʊ 'weɪ] • **Ach komm!** Come on. [ˌkʌm‿'ɒn] • **Na los, komm.** Come on.
**Kommentar (zu, über)** comment (on, about) ['kɒment]
**Komödie** comedy ['kɒmədi]
**König** king [kɪŋ]
**Königin** queen [kwi:n]
**Königreich: das Vereinigte Königreich** *(Großbritannien und Nordirland)* the United Kingdom (UK) [ju,naɪtɪd 'kɪŋdəm, ˌju:'keɪ]
**können** can [kən, kæn]; be able to ['eɪbl] • **ich kann nicht ...** I can't ... [kɑ:nt] • **Kann ich Ihnen helfen? / Was kann ich für Sie tun?** *(im Laden)* Can I help you? • **etwas**

**gut/schlecht können** be good/ bad at sth.
**könnte(n): ich/er könnte ...** I/he could ... [kəd, kʊd] • **Sie könnte zu beschäftigt sein.** She might be too busy. [maɪt]
► S.177 möglich – wahrscheinlich – sicherlich
**konnte(n): ich/er konnte ...** I/he could ... [kəd, kʊd]
**Kontakt halten** keep in touch [ˌkiːp‿ɪn ˈtʌtʃ]
**kontrollieren** *(überprüfen)* check [tʃek]
**Konzert** concert [ˈkɒnsət] • **ein Konzert geben** *(einen Auftritt haben)* do a gig *(infml)*
**Kopf** head [hed]
**Kopfschmerzen** headache [ˈhedeɪk]
**Kopie** copy [ˈkɒpi]
**kopieren** copy [ˈkɒpi]
**Korb** basket [ˈbɑːskɪt] • **ein Korb Äpfel** a basket of apples
**Körper** body [ˈbɒdi]
**körperlich: körperliche Bewegung** *(Training)* exercise *(no pl)*
**korrigieren** correct [kəˈrekt]
**kosten** *(Essen probieren)* try [traɪ]
**kosten** *(Geld kosten)* cost [kɒst] • **Er/Sie/Es kostet 1 Pfund.** It's £1. • **Sie kosten 35 Pence.** They are 35 p. **Wie viel kostet/kosten ...?** How much is/are ...?
**kostenlos** free [friː]
**köstlich** delicious [dɪˈlɪʃəs]
**Kram** stuff [stʌf]
**krank** ill [ɪl]
**kränken: jd. kränken** *(aus der Fassung bringen)* upset sb. [ʌpˈset]
**Krankenhaus** hospital [ˈhɒspɪtl]
**Krankenwagen** ambulance [ˈæmbjələns]
**Krankheit** illness [ˈɪlnəs]
**kreischen** scream [skriːm]
**kriegen** get [get]
**Krimi** crime film [ˈkraɪm fɪlm], crime story [ˈkraɪm ˌstɔːri]
**Kriminalität** crime [kraɪm]
**Krimiserie** crime series [ˈkraɪm ˌsɪəriːz]
**Krokodil** crocodile [ˈkrɒkədaɪl]
**Krug** jug [dʒʌg] • **ein Krug Orangensaft** a jug of orange juice
**Küche** kitchen [ˈkɪtʃɪn]
**Kuchen** cake [keɪk]
**Kugelschreiber** pen [pen]
**Kuh** cow [kaʊ]
**kühl** cool [kuːl]
**Kühlschrank** fridge [frɪdʒ]
**Kultur** culture [ˈkʌltʃə]
**Kummer** worry [ˈwʌri]
**kümmern 1. sich um etwas/jn. kümmern** look after sth./sb. [ˌlʊk‿ˈɑːftə] **2. Kümmere dich um deine eigenen Angelegenheiten!** Mind your own business. [ˌmaɪnd jər‿ˌəʊn ˈbɪznəs]
**Kumpel** mate [meɪt]
**Kunde, Kundin** customer [ˈkʌstəmə]
**Kunst** art [ɑːt]
**Künstler/in** artist [ˈɑːtɪst]
**künstlich** artificial [ˌɑːtɪˈfɪʃl]
**Kurs** *(Lehrgang)* course [kɔːs]; *(Unterrichtsstunde)* class [klɑːs]
**kurz** short [ʃɔːt] • **kurze Hose** shorts *(pl)* [ʃɔːts]
**Kuss** kiss [kɪs]
**küssen** kiss [kɪs]
**Küste** coast [kəʊst] • **an der Küste** on the coast

## L

**lächeln** smile [smaɪl]
**Lächeln** smile [smaɪl]
**lachen** laugh [lɑːf]
**Laden** *(Geschäft)* shop [ʃɒp]
**Lage: in der Lage sein, etwas zu tun** be able to do sth. [eɪbl]
**Lager** *(Ferienlager)* camp [kæmp]
**Lamm(fleisch)** lamb [læm]
**Lampe** lamp [læmp]
**Land** *(auch als Gegensatz zur Stadt)* country [ˈkʌntri]; countryside [ˈkʌntrisaɪd]; *(Grund und Boden)* land [lænd] • **auf dem Land** *(im Gegensatz zur Stadt)* in the country; in the countryside; *(nicht auf dem Wasser)* on land
**landen** land [lænd]
**Landkarte** map [mæp]
**Landschaft** *(Natur)* countryside [ˈkʌntrisaɪd]
**Landwirt/in** farmer [ˈfɑːmə]
**Landwirtschaft** farming [ˈfɑːmɪŋ]
**lang** long [lɒŋ] • **drei Tage lang** for three days
**langsam** slow [sləʊ]
**langweilig** boring [ˈbɔːrɪŋ]
**Lärm** noise [nɔɪz]
**lärmend** noisy [ˈnɔɪzi]
**Lasagne** lasagne [ləˈzænjə]
**lassen** let [let] • **Lass uns ... / Lasst uns ...** Let's ... • **Lass das!** Stop that!
**Lastkraftwagen** lorry [ˈlɒri]
**Lauf** run [rʌn]
**laufen** run [rʌn]; *(im Fernsehen gezeigt werden)* be on
**Läufer/in** runner [ˈrʌnə]
**Laufschuhe** running shoes
**laut** loud [laʊd]; *(lärmend)* noisy [ˈnɔɪzi] • **etwas lauter stellen** turn sth. up
**Laut** sound [saʊnd]
**läuten** ring [rɪŋ]
**Lautstärke** volume [ˈvɒljuːm]
**leben** live [lɪv]
**Leben** life [laɪf], *pl* lives [laɪvz] • **am Leben** *(lebendig)* alive [əˈlaɪv]
**lebendig** alive [əˈlaɪv]
**Lebensmittel** food [fuːd]
**Leber** liver [ˈlɪvə]
**lecker** delicious [dɪˈlɪʃəs]
**ledig** single [ˈsɪŋgl]
**leer** empty [ˈempti]
**legal** legal [ˈliːgl]
**legen** *(hin-, ablegen)* put [pʊt]
**lehren** teach [tiːtʃ]
**Lehrer/in** teacher [ˈtiːtʃə]
**Lehrgang** *(Kurs, Seminar)* workshop [ˈwɜːkʃɒp]; course [kɔːs]
**leicht** *(nicht schwierig)* easy [ˈiːzi]
**Leichtathletik** athletics [æθˈletɪks]
**leider** I'm afraid [əˈfreɪd]
**leidtun: Tut mir leid.** I'm sorry. [ˈsɒri]
**leise** quiet [ˈkwaɪət] • **etwas leiser stellen** turn sth. down
**Leiter/in** *(Anführer/in)* leader [ˈliːdə]
**Lektion** *(im Schulbuch)* unit [ˈjuːnɪt]
**lernen** learn [lɜːn]; *(für die Schule arbeiten)* study [ˈstʌdi]
**Lern- und Arbeitstechniken** study skills [ˈstʌdi skɪlz]
**lesen** read [riːd]
**Leser/in** reader [ˈriːdə]
**letzte(r, s)** last [lɑːst]; final [ˈfaɪnl]
**leuchtend** bright [braɪt]
**Leute** people [ˈpiːpl]; guys [gaɪz] *(AE, infml)*
**Licht** light [laɪt]
**Lichtblitz** flash [flæʃ]
**Liebe** love [lʌv]
**Liebe Grüße, ...** *(Briefschluss)* Love ... [lʌv]
**lieben** love [lʌv]
**liebenswert** likeable [ˈlaɪkəbl]
**Lieber Jay, ...** Dear Jay ... [dɪə]
**lieber: etwas lieber mögen** like sth. better
**Liebesgeschichte** love story
**Liebling** dear [dɪə]; sweetheart [ˈswiːthɑːt]
**Lieblings-: meine Lieblingsfarbe** my favourite colour [ˈfeɪvərɪt]
**liebsten: etwas am liebsten mögen** like sth. best
**Lied** song [sɒŋ]
**liegen: Das liegt bei dir.** *(Das kannst/musst du (selbst) entscheiden.)* That's up to you.
**lila** purple [ˈpɜːpl]

**Limonade** lemonade [ˌleməˈneɪd] *(BE)*; soda [ˈsəʊdə] *(AE)*
**Lineal** ruler [ˈruːlə]
**Linie: (U-Bahn-)Linie** line [laɪn]
**linke(r, s)** left [left] • **links, auf der linken Seite** on the left • **(nach) links abbiegen** turn left • **nach links schauen** look left
**Liste** list [lɪst]
**Livemusik** live music [laɪv]
**Löffel** spoon [spuːn]
**Lokal** *(Kneipe)* pub [pʌb]
**löschen: ein Feuer löschen** put out a fire
**Löwe** lion [ˈlaɪən]

## M

**machen** do [duː]; make [meɪk] • **die Hausaufgabe(n) machen** do homework • **einen Ausflug machen** go on a trip • **einen Spaziergang machen** go for a walk • **eine Übung machen** do an exercise **ein Picknick machen** have a picnic **Fotos machen** take photos • **jm. Vorwürfe machen (wegen)** blame sb. (for) • **Judo machen** do judo **sich aus dem Staub machen** take off *(infml)* • **sich Notizen machen** take notes • **sich Sorgen machen (um, wegen)** worry (about) [ˈwʌri] **(Zauber-)Kunststücke machen** do tricks • **Mach es dir bequem. / Machen Sie es sich bequem** Make yourself comfortable. [ˈkʌmftəbl] **Reiten macht Spaß.** Riding is fun.
**Mädchen** girl [gɜːl]
**Magazin** *(Zeitschrift)* magazine [ˌmægəˈziːn]
**Magen** stomach [ˈstʌmək]
**Magenschmerzen** stomach ache [ˈstʌmək‿eɪk]
**mager** skinny [ˈskɪni]
**Magst du ...?** Do you like ...? [laɪk] *(siehe auch unter „mögen")*
**mähen: (Rasen) mähen** cut the grass
**Mahlzeit** meal [miːl]
**Mai** May [meɪ]
**mailen: jm. etwas mailen** mail sb. sth. [meɪl]
**Make-up** make-up [ˈmeɪkʌp]
**Mal(e); -mal** time(s) [taɪm(z)]
**malen** paint [peɪnt]
**Maler/in** painter [ˈpeɪntə]
**Mama** mum [mʌm] *(BE)*; mom [mɒm, *AE:* mɑːm] *(AE)*
**manchmal** sometimes [ˈsʌmtaɪmz]
**Mann** man [mæn], *pl* men [men]
**männlich** male [meɪl]
**Mannschaft** team [tiːm]
**Mappe** *(des Sprachenportfolios)* dossier [ˈdɒsieɪ]
**markieren** mark up [ˌmɑːk‿ˈʌp]
**Markt** market [ˈmɑːkɪt]
**Marmelade** *(Orangenmarmelade)* marmalade [ˈmɑːməleɪd]
**März** March [mɑːtʃ]
**Maschine** machine [məˈʃiːn]
**Masse** *(Menschenmasse)* crowd [kraʊd]
**Mathematik** maths [mæθs]
**Matrose** sailor [ˈseɪlə]
**Mauer** wall [wɔːl]
**Maulwurf** mole [məʊl]
**Maus** mouse [maʊs], *pl* mice [maɪs]
**Medaille** medal [ˈmedl]
**Mediation** *(Sprachmittlung)* mediation [ˌmiːdiˈeɪʃn]
**Medien** media *(pl)* [ˈmiːdiə]
**Medikament** drug [drʌg]
**Medikamente nehmen** be on drugs [drʌgz]
**Meer** sea [siː]
**Meerschweinchen** guinea pig [ˈgɪni pɪg]
**mehr** more [mɔː] • **mehr als** more than • **mehr als ich** more than me • **nicht mehr** not ... any more **viel mehr** lots more • **keine Musik mehr** no more music
**Mehrheit** majority [məˈdʒɒrəti]
**Meile** *(= ca. 1,6 km)* mile [maɪl]
**meilenweit** for miles [maɪlz]
**mein(e) ...** my ... [maɪ] • **meine neuen** my new ones [wʌnz]
**meinen** think [θɪŋk]; *(sagen wollen)* mean [miːn] • **Meinst du wirklich?** Do you really think so?
**meiner, meine, meins** mine [maɪn]
**Meinung** opinion [əˈpɪnjən] • **meiner Meinung nach** in my opinion
**meist: (der/die/das) meiste ...; am meisten** most [məʊst] • **die meisten Leute** most people
**meistens** usually [ˈjuːʒuəli]
**Meister/in** *(Champion)* champion [ˈtʃæmpiən]
**Meisterschaft** championship [ˈtʃæmpiənʃɪp]
**Menge** *(Menschenmenge)* crowd [kraʊd]
**Menschen** people [ˈpiːpl]
**Menschenmasse** crowd [kraʊd]
**Menschenmenge** crowd [kraʊd]
**merken: sich etwas merken** remember sth. [rɪˈmembə]
**merkwürdig** strange [streɪndʒ]
**Messer** knife [naɪf], *pl* knives [naɪvz]
**Meter** metre [ˈmiːtə]
**Metzger** butcher [ˈbʊtʃə] • **beim Metzger** at the butcher's
**mich** me [miː] • **mich (selbst)** myself [maɪˈself]
**Mikrofon** microphone [ˈmaɪkrəfəʊn]
**Milch** milk [mɪlk]
**mild** mild [maɪld]
**Million** million [ˈmɪljən]
**Minderheit** minority [maɪˈnɒrəti]
**Mindmap** mind map [ˈmaɪnd mæp]
**minus** minus [ˈmaɪnəs]
**Minute** minute [ˈmɪnɪt]
**mir** me [miː]
**mischen** mix [mɪks]
**Mischung** mix [mɪks]; mixture [ˈmɪkstʃə]
**mit** with [wɪð] • **mit dem Auto/Zug/Rad/... fahren** go by car/train/bike/...
**mitbringen** bring [brɪŋ]
**Mitbringsel** souvenir [ˌsuːvəˈnɪə]
**Mitglied** member [ˈmembə]
**mitmachen: bei etwas/jm. mitmachen** join sth./sb. [dʒɔɪn]
**mitnehmen: Kaffee zum Mitnehmen** coffee to go
**Mitschüler/in** classmate [ˈklɑːsmeɪt]
**Mittagessen** lunch [lʌntʃ] • **zum Mittagessen** for lunch
**Mittagspause** lunch break [ˈlʌntʃ breɪk]
**Mitte** centre [ˈsentə]; middle (of) [ˈmɪdl]
**Mitteilung** *(Notiz)* note [nəʊt]
**Mittel-** *(Zentral-)* central [ˈsentrəl]
**mittel(groß)** medium [ˈmiːdiəm]
**Mittelteil** middle [ˈmɪdl]
**Mittwoch** Wednesday [ˈwenzdeɪ, ˈwenzdi] *(siehe auch unter „Freitag")*
**Mix** mix [mɪks]
**mixen** mix [mɪks]
**Mobiltelefon** mobile (phone) [ˌməʊbaɪl ˈfəʊn] *(BE)*; cellphone [ˈselfəʊn] *(AE)*
**möchte: Ich möchte gern ... (haben)** I'd like ... (= I would like ...) • **Ich möchte über ... reden** I'd like to talk about ... • **Möchtest du etwas (Saft) / ein paar (Kekse)?** Would you like some (juice/biscuits)?
**Mode** fashion [ˈfæʃn]
**Modell***(-auto, -schiff; Fotomodell)* model [ˈmɒdl]
**Moderator/in** presenter [prɪˈzentə]
**modern** modern [ˈmɒdən]
**modisch** *(schick, im Trend)* trendy [ˈtrendi]
**mögen** like [laɪk]; *(sehr mögen)* love [lʌv] • **etwas lieber mögen** like sth. better • **etwas am liebsten/wenigsten mögen** like sth. best/least
**möglich** possible [ˈpɒsəbl]
**Möhre** carrot [ˈkærət]

**Moment** moment ['məʊmənt] **genau in dem Moment** just then • **Moment mal!** Wait a minute. ['mɪnɪt]
**Monat** month [mʌnθ]
**Mond** moon [mu:n]
**Monitor** monitor ['mɒnɪtə]
**Monster** monster ['mɒnstə]
**Montag** Monday ['mʌndeɪ, 'mʌndi] *(siehe auch unter „Freitag")*
**morgen** tomorrow [tə'mɒrəʊ] • **das Wetter von morgen** tomorrow's weather
**Morgen** morning ['mɔ:nɪŋ] • **am Morgen, morgens** in the morning **Guten Morgen.** Good morning. **Montagmorgen** Monday morning
**Motel** motel [məʊ'tel]
**Motor** engine ['endʒɪn]
**MP3-Spieler** MP3 player [ˌempi:'θri: ˌpleɪə]
**müde** tired ['taɪəd]
**Müll** rubbish ['rʌbɪʃ] *(BE)*; garbage ['gɑ:bɪdʒ] *(AE)*
**Mülltonne** bin [bɪn]; dustbin ['dʌstbɪn]
**Multiple-Choice** multiple choice [ˌmʌltɪpl 'tʃɔɪs]
**Mund** mouth [maʊθ] • **Halt den Mund!** Shut up. [ˌʃʌt_'ʌp]
**murren** grumble ['grʌmbl]
**Museum** museum [mju'zi:əm]
**Musical** musical ['mju:zɪkl]
**Musik** music ['mju:zɪk]
**Müsli** muesli ['mju:zli]
**Muss** must [mʌst]
**müssen** have to; must [mʌst] **nicht müssen** needn't ['ni:dnt] ► S.177 möglich – wahrscheinlich – sicherlich
**müssten: Meine Eltern müssten eigentlich jetzt zu Hause sein.** My parents should be at home now. ► S.177 möglich – wahrscheinlich – sicherlich
**mutig** brave [breɪv]
**Mutter** mother ['mʌðə]
**Mutti** mum [mʌm] *(BE)*; mom [mɒm, *AE:* mɑ:m] *(AE)*
**Mütze** cap [kæp]

# N

**Na ja ... / Na gut ...** Oh well ... [əʊ 'wel]
**Na und?** So? [səʊ]
**nach 1.** *(örtlich)* to [tə, tu] • **nach draußen** outside • **nach drinnen** inside • **nach Hause gehen** go home • **nach Hause kommen** come home; get home • **nach oben** up; *(im Haus)* upstairs [ˌʌp'steəz] • **nach unten** down; *(im Haus)* downstairs [ˌdaʊn'steəz] **2.** *(zeitlich)* after ['ɑ:ftə] • **Viertel nach 11** quarter past 11 [pɑ:st] **3. nach etwas fragen** ask about sth. [ə'baʊt]
**Nachbar/in** neighbour ['neɪbə]
**nachdem** after ['ɑ:ftə]
**nachdenken über** think about [θɪŋk]
**Nachforschungen (zu, über)** research (on) *(no pl)* [rɪ'sɜ:tʃ, 'ri:sɜ:tʃ]
**Nachmittag** afternoon [ˌɑ:ftə'nu:n] **am Nachmittag, nachmittags** in the afternoon
**Nachricht** message ['mesɪdʒ] **Nachrichten** *(im Fernsehen, Radio; Neuigkeiten)* news *(no pl)* [nju:z] **Das sind gute Nachrichten.** That's good news.
**nachrufen: jm. Schimpfwörter nachrufen** call sb. names
**nachschlagen: etwas nachschlagen** look sth. up [ˌlʊk_'ʌp]
**nächste(r, s): am nächsten Tag** the next day [nekst] • **der Nächste sein** be next • **Was haben wir als Nächstes?** What have we got next?
**Nacht** night [naɪt] • **heute Nacht** tonight [tə'naɪt] • **in der Nacht, nachts** at night
**Nachteil** disadvantage [ˌdɪsəd'vɑ:ntɪdʒ]
**nahe (bei)** near [nɪə]; close (to) [kləʊs]
**Nähe: in der Nähe von** near [nɪə]
**Name** name [neɪm]
**Nase** nose [nəʊz] • **die Nase voll haben (von etwas)** be fed up (with sth.) [ˌfed_'ʌp]
**Nashorn** rhino ['raɪnəʊ]
**nass** wet [wet]
**Nation** nation ['neɪʃn]
**national** national ['næʃnəl]
**Nationalpark** national park [ˌnæʃnəl 'pɑ:k]
**Natur** nature ['neɪtʃə]; *(Landschaft)* countryside ['kʌntrisaɪd]
**natürlich** of course [əv 'kɔ:s]
**Naturwissenschaft** science ['saɪəns]
**Nebel** fog [fɒg]
**neben** next to ['nekst tə]
**nebenbei bemerkt** actually ['æktʃuəli]
**neblig** foggy ['fɒgi]
**Neffe** nephew ['nefju:]
**nehmen** take [teɪk] • *(bei einer Bestellung im Restaurant etc.)* • **Ich nehme ...** I'll have ... • **Wir nehmen es.** *(beim Einkaufen)* We'll take it. • **ein Taxi nehmen** get a cab
**neidisch (auf)** jealous (of) ['dʒeləs]
**nein** no [nəʊ]
**nennen** *(rufen, bezeichnen)* call [kɔ:l]; *(benennen)* name [neɪm]
**nervös** nervous ['nɜ:vəs]
**Nervosität** nervousness ['nɜ:vəsnəs]
**nett** nice [naɪs]; *(liebenswert, sympathisch)* likeable ['laɪkəbl]
**neu** new [nju:]
**neueste(r, s)** latest ['leɪtɪst]
**Neuigkeiten** news [nju:z]
**nicht** not [nɒt] • **nicht mehr** not (...) any more • **Du brauchst eine Schultasche, nicht wahr?** You need a school bag, right? [raɪt] • **Ich weiß es nicht.** I don't know. [ˌdəʊnt 'nəʊ] • **noch nicht** not (...) yet [jet]
**nichts** nothing ['nʌθɪŋ]; not (...) anything ['eniθɪŋ] • **Nichts zu danken.** You're welcome. ['welkəm]
**Nichte** niece [ni:s]
**nicken (mit)** nod [nɒd]
**nie, niemals** never ['nevə]
**niemand** nobody ['nəʊbədi]; not (...) anybody ['enibɒdi]; no one ['nəʊ wʌn]
**Niere** kidney ['kɪdni]
**nirgendwo(hin)** not (...) anywhere ['eniweə]
**noch: noch ein(e) ...** another ... [ə'nʌðə] • **noch 45 Pence** another 45 p • **noch einmal** again [ə'gen] **noch nicht** not (...) yet [jet] • **(immer) noch** still [stɪl] • **Was (sonst) noch?** What else? • **Wen (sonst) noch?** Who else? ► S.167 ... else
**Norden** north [nɔ:θ] • **nach Norden** north
**nördlich** north [nɔ:θ]
**Nordosten** north-east [ˌnɔ:θ'i:st] **nach Nordosten** north-east
**nordöstlich** north-east [ˌnɔ:θ'i:st]
**Nordwesten** north-west [ˌnɔ:θ'west] **nach Nordwesten** north-west
**nordwestlich** north-west [ˌnɔ:θ'west]
**nörgeln** grumble ['grʌmbl]
**normal** *(Größenangabe bei Getränken und Fastfood)* regular ['regjələ]
**normalerweise** usually ['ju:ʒuəli]
**Note** *(Schulnote)* grade [greɪd]; *(BE auch:)* mark [mɑ:k]
**Notiz** note [nəʊt] • **sich Notizen machen** take notes
**November** November [nəʊ'vembə]
**Nudeln** *(Pasta)* pasta *(no pl)* ['pæstə]
**null** o [əʊ]; zero ['zɪərəʊ]; *(beim Sport)* nil [nɪl]
**Nummer** number ['nʌmbə]
**Nummernschild** number plate ['nʌmbə pleɪt] *(BE)*; license plate ['laɪsns pleɪt] *(AE)*
**nun** now [naʊ] • **Nun, ...** Well, ... [wel]

**nur** only ['əʊnli]; just [dʒʌst] • **nur zum Spaß** just for fun
**Nuss** nut [nʌt]
**nützlich** useful ['ju:sfəl]
**nutzlos** useless ['ju:sləs]

## O

**ob** if [ɪf]
**obdachlos** homeless ['həʊmləs]
**oben** above [ə'bʌv]; *(an der Spitze)* at the top (of) [tɒp]; *(im Haus)* upstairs [ˌʌp'steəz] • **dort oben** up there **nach oben** up; *(im Haus)* upstairs
**Oberbegriff** group word ['gru:p wɜ:d]
**oberhalb von** over ['əʊvə]; above [ə'bʌv]
**Oberteil** top [tɒp]
**Obst** fruit [fru:t]
**Obstkuchen** pie [paɪ]
**Obstsalat** fruit salad ['fru:t ˌsæləd]
**oder** or [ɔ:] • **Das ist nicht dein Ernst, oder?** You're joking, aren't you?
**offen** open ['əʊpən]
**öffentlich** public ['pʌblɪk]
**Öffentlichkeit** public ['pʌblɪk]
**öffnen** open ['əʊpən]
**oft** often ['ɒfn]
**ohne** without [wɪ'ðaʊt]
**Ohr** ear [ɪə]
**Ohrenschmerzen** earache ['ɪəreɪk]
**Ohrring** earring ['ɪərɪŋ]
**Oje!** Oh dear! [əʊ 'dɪə]
**okay** OK [əʊ'keɪ]; okay [əʊ'keɪ]
**Oktober** October [ɒk'təʊbə]
**Öl** oil [ɔɪl]
**Ölbohrinsel** oil rig ['ɔɪl rɪg]
**Oma** grandma ['grænmɑ:]; granny ['græni]
**Onkel** uncle ['ʌŋkl]
**online, Online-** online [ˌɒn'laɪn]
**Opa** grandpa ['grænpɑ:]
**Operation (an)** operation (on) [ˌɒpə'reɪʃn]
**Opfer** victim ['vɪktɪm]
**Orange** orange ['ɒrɪndʒ]
**orange(farben)** orange ['ɒrɪndʒ]
**Orangenmarmelade** marmalade ['mɑ:məleɪd]
**Orangensaft** orange juice ['ɒrɪndʒ dʒu:s]
**ordentlich** tidy ['taɪdi]
**Ordnung: in Ordnung** all right [ɔ:l 'raɪt]; fine [faɪn]
**organisieren** organize ['ɔ:gənaɪz]
**Ort** place [pleɪs]; *(Veranstaltungs-, Wohnort)* location [ləʊ'keɪʃn]
**Orts-, örtlich** local ['ləʊkl]
**Osten** east [i:st] • **nach Osten** east
**Ostern** Easter ['i:stə]
**östlich** east [i:st]
**Outfit** *(Kleidung; Ausrüstung)* outfit ['aʊtfɪt]

## P

**paar: ein paar** some [səm, sʌm]; *(einige wenige)* a few [fju:]
**Paar: ein Paar** a pair (of) [peə]
**Päckchen** packet ['pækɪt] • **ein Päckchen Pfefferminzbonbons** a packet of mints
**packen** pack [pæk]
**Packung** packet ['pækɪt] • **eine Packung Pfefferminzbonbons** a packet of mints
**Paddel** paddle ['pædl]
**paddeln** paddle ['pædl]; canoe [kə'nu:]
**Paket** parcel ['pɑ:sl]
**Palast** palace ['pæləs]
**pantomimisch darstellen** mime [maɪm]
**Papa** dad [dæd]
**Papagei** parrot ['pærət]
**Papier** paper ['peɪpə]
**Paralympische Spiele** *(Olympische Spiele für Sportler/innen mit körperlicher Behinderung)* Paralympics [ˌpærə'lɪmpɪks]
**Park** park [pɑ:k]
**Parkplatz** *(für viele Autos)* car park ['kɑ: pɑ:k]
**Parlament** parliament ['pɑ:ləmənt]
**Partner/in** partner ['pɑ:tnə]
**Party** party ['pɑ:ti]
**passen** fit [fɪt] • **passen zu** go with
**passieren (mit)** happen (to) ['hæpən] **Mir/Dir/Ihr/...wird nichts passieren.** I'll/You'll/She'll/ ... be OK.
**Pasta** pasta *(no pl)* ['pæstə]
**Pause** break [breɪk] • **eine Pause machen** take a break • **in der Pause** *(zwischen Schulstunden)* at break
**peinlich** embarrassing [ɪm'bærəsɪŋ] **Das ist mir peinlich.** I'm embarrassed. [ɪm'bærəst]
**Pence** pence (p) [pens]
**perfekt** perfect ['pɜ:fɪkt]
**Person** person ['pɜ:sn]
**persönliche(r, s)** personal ['pɜ:sənl]
**Pfad** path [pɑ:θ]
**Pfefferminzbonbons** mints [mɪnts]
**pfeifen** whistle ['wɪsl]
**Pferd** horse [hɔ:s]
**Pfund** *(britische Währung)* pound (£) [paʊnd] • **Es kostet 1 Pfund.** It's £1.
**Piano** piano [pi'ænəʊ]
**Picknick** picnic ['pɪknɪk] • **ein Picknick machen** have a picnic
**piepsen** bleep [bli:p]
**Piepton** bleep [bli:p]
**Piercing** piercing ['pɪəsɪŋ]
**Pilz** mushroom ['mʌʃrʊm, -ru:m]
**pink(farben)** pink [pɪŋk]
**Pirat/in** pirate ['paɪrət]
**Pizza** pizza ['pi:tsə]
**Plan** plan [plæn]
**planen** plan [plæn]
**Planet** planet ['plænɪt]
**Platz** *(Ort, Stelle)* place [pleɪs]; *(in der Stadt)* square [skweə]; *(runder Platz in der Stadt)* circus ['sɜ:kəs]; *(Einsatzort)* location [ləʊ'keɪʃn]
**Plätzchen** biscuit ['bɪskɪt]
**plaudern** chat [tʃæt]
**plötzlich** suddenly ['sʌdnli]
**plus** plus [plʌs]
**Pokal** cup [kʌp]
**Polizei** police *(pl)* [pə'li:s]
**Polizeiwache, Polizeirevier** police station [pə'li:s steɪʃn]
**Polizist/in** policeman [pə'li:smən] / policewoman [pə'li:swʊmən]
**Poltergeist** poltergeist ['pəʊltəgaɪst]
**Pommes frites** chips *(pl)* [tʃɪps] *(BE)*; French fries *(pl)* [fraɪz] *(AE)*
**Popcorn** popcorn ['pɒpkɔ:n]
**Pop(musik)** pop (music) [pɒp]
**populär (bei)** popular ['pɒpjələ]
**Porträt** *(Steckbrief)* profile ['prəʊfaɪl]
**Postamt** post office ['pəʊst‿ɒfɪs]
**Poster** poster ['pəʊstə]
**Postkarte** postcard ['pəʊstkɑ:d]
**Präsentation** presentation [ˌprezn'teɪʃn]
**Präsident/in** president ['prezɪdənt]
**Preis** *(Kaufpreis)* price [praɪs]; *(Gewinn)* prize [praɪz]
**pro** per [pɜ:, pə] • **einmal pro Woche** once a week / once per week
**Probe** *(am Theater)* rehearsal [rɪ'hɜ:sl]
**proben** *(am Theater)* rehearse [rɪ'hɜ:s]
**probieren** try [traɪ]
**Problem** problem ['prɒbləm] • **kein Problem** sure [ʃʊə, ʃɔ:]
**Produkt** product ['prɒdʌkt]
**produzieren** produce [prə'dju:s]
**Programm** programme ['prəʊgræm]
**Projekt (über, zu)** project (on, about) ['prɒdʒekt] • **ein Projekt machen, durchführen** do a project
**Prospekt** brochure ['brəʊʃə]
**Prozent** per cent (%) [pə'sent]
**prüfen** *(überprüfen)* check [tʃek]
**Prüfung** test [test]
**PS** *(Nachschrift unter Briefen)* PS [ˌpi:‿'es] (postscript ['pəʊstskrɪpt])
**Publikum** audience ['ɔ:dɪəns]

**Pullover** pullover ['pʊləʊvə]
**Punkt** *(bei Test, Quiz)* point [pɔɪnt]
**Punktestand** *(Spielstand)* score [skɔː]
**Pute/Puter** turkey ['tɜːki]
**putzen** clean [kliːn] • **Ich putze mir die Zähne.** I clean my teeth.
**Putzfrau, -mann** cleaner ['kliːnə]

## Q

**Querflöte** flute [fluːt]
**Quiz** quiz [kwɪz], *pl* quizzes ['kwɪzɪz]

## R

**Rad** **1.** wheel ['wiːl]
**2.** *(Fahrrad)* bike [baɪk]
**Rad fahren** cycle ['saɪkl]; ride a bike [ˌraɪd_ə 'baɪk]
**Radfahrt** bike ride ['baɪk raɪd]
**Radiergummi** rubber ['rʌbə] *(BE)*; eraser [ɪ'reɪzə, *AE:* ɪ'reɪsər] *(AE)*
**Radio** radio ['reɪdiəʊ] • **im Radio** on the radio
**Radiokanal** channel ['tʃænl]
**Radioprogramm** channel ['tʃænl]
**Radweg** cycle path ['saɪkl pɑːθ]
**Rafting** rafting ['rɑːftɪŋ]
**Rap** rap [ræp]
**Rapper/in** rapper ['ræpə]
**Rasen** grass [grɑːs] • **Rasen mähen** cut the grass
**Rat** advice *(no pl)* [əd'vaɪs]
**raten** *(erraten, schätzen)* guess [ges]
**Ratespiel** quiz [kwɪz], *pl* quizzes ['kwɪzɪz]
**Ratschläge** advice *(no pl)* [əd'vaɪs]
**Rauch** smoke [sməʊk]
**rauchen** smoke [sməʊk] • **Rauchen verboten.** No smoking.
**Raum** room [ruːm, rʊm]
**Rauschgift** *(Droge)* drug [drʌg]
**Rauschgift nehmen** be on drugs
**realistisch** realistic [ˌriːə'lɪstɪk]
**Realität** reality [ri'æləti]
**Recherche (zu, über)** research (on) *(no pl)* [rɪ'sɜːtʃ, 'riːsɜːtʃ]
**recherchieren** do research [rɪ'sɜːtʃ, 'riːsɜːtʃ]
**Rechnung** bill [bɪl]
**Recht** right [raɪt] • **Recht haben** be right
**rechte(r, s)** right [raɪt] • **rechts, auf der rechten Seite** on the right • **(nach) rechts abbiegen** turn right • **nach rechts schauen** look right
**Rechtschreibung** spelling ['spelɪŋ]
**rechtzeitig** in time [ɪn 'taɪm]
**recycelt** recycled [ˌriː'saɪkld]
**Recycling** recycling [ˌriː'saɪklɪŋ]
**Redakteur/in** editor ['edɪtə]
**Rede** speech [spiːtʃ] • **eine Rede halten** make a speech
**reden (mit, über)** talk (to, about) [tɔːk]; speak (to, about) [spiːk]
**Wovon redest du?** What are you talking about?
**Refrain** chorus ['kɔːrəs]
**Regal(brett)** shelf [ʃelf], *pl* shelves [ʃelvz]
**Regel** *(Vorschrift)* rule [ruːl]
**Regen** rain [reɪn]
**Reggae** reggae [re'geɪ]
**regnen** rain [reɪn]
**regnerisch** rainy ['reɪni]
**Reh** deer, *pl* deer [dɪə]
**reich** rich [rɪtʃ]
**reichen** *(weitergeben)* pass [pɑːs]
**Reihe** **1.** *(wartende Menschen)* queue [kjuː] *(BE)*; line [laɪn] *(AE)*
**2.** *(Sendereihe, Serie)* series, *pl* series ['sɪəriːz]
**3. Du bist an der Reihe.** It's your turn. [tɜːn] • **Wer ist an der Reihe?** Whose turn is it? [huːz]
**Reis** rice [raɪs]
**Reise** trip [trɪp]; *(Fahrt)* journey ['dʒɜːni] • **eine Reise unterbrechen** break a journey
**Reiseführer** guidebook ['gaɪdbʊk]
**reisen** travel ['trævl]
**Reiseleiter/in** guide [gaɪd]
**reiten** ride [raɪd] • **reiten gehen** go riding
**Religion** *(Religionsunterricht)* RE [ˌɑːr_'iː], Religious Education [rɪˌlɪdʒəs_edʒu'keɪʃn]
**rennen** run [rʌn]
**Reportage (über)** report (on) [rɪ'pɔːt]
**Reporter/in** reporter [rɪ'pɔːtə]
**repräsentieren** represent [ˌreprɪ'zent]
**resignieren** give up [ˌgɪv_'ʌp]
**Rest** rest [rest]
**Restaurant** restaurant ['restrɒnt]; *(Imbissstube, Café)* café ['kæfeɪ]
**Resultat** result [rɪ'zʌlt]
**retten** save [seɪv]
**Rettungshubschrauber** rescue helicopter ['reskjuː ˌhelɪkɒptə]
**richtig** right [raɪt]
**Richtung** way [weɪ] • **in diese Richtung** this way • **in die falsche Richtung** the wrong way • **in welche Richtung?** which way?
**riechen** smell [smel]
**Riesenrad** big wheel [ˌbɪg 'wiːl]
**riesig** huge [hjuːdʒ]
**Rindfleisch** beef [biːf]
**Ring** ring [rɪŋ]
**Rock** skirt [skɜːt]
**Rolle** role [rəʊl]
**Rollenspiel** role play ['rəʊl pleɪ]
**Rollerblades** rollerblades ['rəʊləbleɪdz]
**Rollerskaten** rollerskating ['rəʊləskeɪtɪŋ]
**Rollstuhl** wheelchair ['wiːltʃeə]
**römisch; Römer, Römerin** Roman ['rəʊmən]
**rosa** pink [pɪŋk]
**rot** red [red]
**Route** route [ruːt]
**Rückfahrkarte** return ticket [rɪ'tɜːn ˌtɪkɪt]
**Rückkehr** return [rɪ'tɜːn]
**Rucksack** rucksack ['rʌksæk] *(BE)*; backpack ['bækpæk] *(AE)*
**rufen** call [kɔːl]; shout [ʃaʊt] • **die Polizei rufen** call the police
**ruhig** quiet ['kwaɪət]
**rumhängen (mit Freunden/Freundinnen)** *(abhängen)* hang out (with friends) [ˌhæŋ_'aʊt]
**rund** round [raʊnd]
**Rundgang (durch das Haus)** tour (of the house) [tʊə]
**runterladen** *(downloaden)* download [ˌdaʊn'ləʊd]

## S

**Sache** thing [θɪŋ]
**Saft** juice [dʒuːs]
**sagen** say [seɪ] • **Sagt mir eure Namen.** Tell me your names. [tel]
**Sahne** cream [kriːm]
**Salat** **1.** *(Kopfsalat)* lettuce ['letɪs]
**2.** *(Gericht, Beilage)* salad ['sæləd]
**sammeln** collect [kə'lekt] • **Geld sammeln (für)** raise money (for) [reɪz] • **Ideen sammeln** brainstorm ['breɪnstɔːm]
**Sammler/in** collector [kə'lektə]
**Samstag** Saturday ['sætədeɪ, 'sætədi]
*(siehe auch unter „Freitag")*
**Sandwich** sandwich ['sænwɪtʃ, '-wɪdʒ]
**Sänger/in** singer ['sɪŋə]
**Sanitäter/in** paramedic [ˌpærə'medɪk]
**Satellit** satellite ['sætəlaɪt]
**satt: etwas satt haben** be tired of sth. ['taɪəd]
**Sattel** saddle ['sædl]
**Satz** sentence ['sentəns]
**sauber** clean [kliːn] • **sauber machen** clean
**sauer sein (auf)** be cross (with) [krɒs]
**Sauna** sauna ['sɔːnə] • **in die Sauna gehen** have a sauna
**Saxophon** saxophone ['sæksəfəʊn]
**Schachtel** packet ['pækɪt]; box [bɒks]
**Schaf** sheep, *pl* sheep [ʃiːp]

**Schal** scarf [skɑ:f], *pl* scarves [skɑ:vz]
**Schale** bowl [bəʊl] • **eine Schale Cornflakes** a bowl of cornflakes
**scharf** *(würzig)* spicy ['spaɪsi]
**Schatz** dear [dɪə]; sweetheart ['swi:thɑ:t]
**schätzen** *(raten, erraten)* guess [ges]
**schauen** look [lʊk] • **nach links/rechts schauen** look left/right
**Schaufenster** shop window [ˌʃɒp 'wɪndəʊ]
**Schauspiel** drama ['drɑ:mə]
**Schauspieler/in** actor ['æktə]
**scheinen** 1. *(Sonne)* shine [ʃaɪn] 2. **zu sein/zu tun scheinen** seem to be/to do [si:m]
**scherzen** joke [dʒəʊk]
**scheu** shy [ʃaɪ]
**scheußlich** horrible ['hɒrəbl]
**Schicht** *(bei der Arbeit)* shift [ʃɪft] **in meiner Schicht** on my shift
**schick** *(modisch, im Trend)* trendy ['trendi]
**schicken (an)** *(Post, E-Mail)* send (to) [send]; mail (to) [meɪl] • **jm. eine SMS schicken** text sb. [tekst]
**schieben** push [pʊʃ]
**schießen** shoot [ʃu:t]; *(ein Tor schießen)* score (a goal) [skɔ:], [gəʊl]
**Schiff** boat [bəʊt]; ship [ʃɪp]
**Schild** sign [saɪn]
**Schildkröte** tortoise ['tɔ:təs]
**Schimpfwort: jn. mit Schimpfwörtern hänseln, jm. Schimpfwörter nachrufen** call sb. names
**Schinkenspeck** bacon ['beɪkən]
**Schlaf** sleep [sli:p]
**Schlafanzug** pyjamas *(pl)* [pə'dʒɑ:məz]
**schlafen** sleep [sli:p]; *(nicht wach sein)* be asleep [ə'sli:p]
**schlaflos** sleepless ['sli:pləs]
**Schlafparty** sleepover ['sli:pəʊvə]
**Schlafzimmer** bedroom ['bedru:m]
**schlagen** hit [hɪt]; *(besiegen)* beat [bi:t]
**Schlägerei** fight [faɪt]
**Schlagzeile** headline ['hedlaɪn]
**Schlagzeug** drums *(pl)* [drʌmz] **Schlagzeug spielen** play the drums
**Schlange** snake [sneɪk]; *(wartende Menschen)* queue [kju:] *(BE)*, line [laɪn] *(AE)*
**schlau** clever ['klevə]; smart [smɑ:t]
**schlecht** bad [bæd] • **schlechter** worse [wɜ:s] • **am schlechtesten; der/die/das schlechteste** (the) worst [wɜ:st] • **schlecht abschneiden (in)** do badly (in) • **schlecht in etwas sein / etwas schlecht können** be bad at sth. • **schlechtes Timing** bad timing • **Mir ist schlecht.** I feel sick. [sɪk]
**Schleuse** lock [lɒk]
**schließen** *(zumachen)* close [kləʊz]
**schließlich** at last [ət 'lɑ:st]; *(zum Schluss)* in the end
**schlimm** bad [bæd] • **schlimmer** worse [wɜ:s] • **am schlimmsten; der/die/das schlimmste** (the) worst [wɜ:st]
**Schlitten** sledge [sledʒ]
**Schlittschuhbahn** ice rink ['aɪs rɪŋk]
**Schloss** castle ['kɑ:sl]; *(Palast)* palace ['pæləs]
**Schlucht** canyon ['kænjən]
**Schluss** 1. end [end] • **zum Schluss** in the end 2. *(einer Geschichte, eines Films usw.)* ending ['endɪŋ] 3. *(Schlussfolgerung)* conclusion [kən'klu:ʒn] • **Schlüsse ziehen** draw conclusions [ˌdrɔ: kən'klu:ʒnz]
**Schlüssel** key [ki:]
**Schlüsselring** key ring ['ki: rɪŋ]
**Schlüsselwort** key word ['ki: wɜ:d]
**schlussfolgern** draw conclusions [ˌdrɔ: kən'klu:ʒnz]
**Schlussverkauf** sale ['seɪl]
**Schmuck** jewellery ['dʒu:əlri]
**schmutzig** dirty ['dɜ:ti]
**schnappen: sich etwas schnappen** grab sth. [græb]
**Schnee** snow [snəʊ]
**Schneeball** snowball ['snəʊbɔ:l]
**Schneeschuh** snowshoe ['snəʊʃu:]
**Schneeschuhwandern** snowshoeing ['snəʊʃu:ɪŋ]
**schneiden** cut [kʌt]
**schnell** quick [kwɪk]; fast [fɑ:st]
**schockiert** shocked [ʃɒkt]
**Schokolade** chocolate ['tʃɒklət]
**schon** already [ɔ:l'redi] • **schon?** yet? [jet] • **schon mal?** ever? ['evə]
**schön** beautiful ['bju:tɪfl]; *(nett)* nice [naɪs]; *(gut, in Ordnung)* fine [faɪn] **schön ordentlich** neat and tidy **Schön, dass du wieder da bist.** Good to have you back.
**Schönheit** beauty ['bju:ti]
**Schrank** cupboard ['kʌbəd]; *(Kleiderschrank)* wardrobe ['wɔ:drəʊb]
**schrecklich** terrible ['terəbl]; awful ['ɔ:fl]
**schreiben (an)** write (to) [raɪt]
**Schreiber/in** writer ['raɪtə]
**Schreibtisch** desk [desk]
**Schreibung** *(Rechtschreibung, Schreibweise)* spelling ['spelɪŋ]
**schreien** shout [ʃaʊt]; scream [skri:m]
**Schriftsteller/in** writer ['raɪtə]
**Schritt** step [step]
**schüchtern** shy [ʃaɪ]
**Schuh** shoe [ʃu:]
**Schuld: Das ist nicht meine Schuld.** It's not my fault. [fɔ:lt] • **jm. die Schuld geben (an)** blame sb. (for) [bleɪm]
**schuldig** guilty ['gɪlti]
**Schule** school [sku:l] • **in der Schule** at school
**Schüler/in** student ['stju:dənt]
**Schulfach** (school) subject ['sʌbdʒɪkt]
**Schulheft** exercise book ['eksəsaɪz bʊk]
**Schulleiter/in** head teacher [ˌhed 'ti:tʃə]
**Schulmensa** canteen [kæn'ti:n] *(BE)*; cafeteria [ˌkæfə'tɪəriə] *(AE)*
**Schulnote** grade [greɪd]; *(BE auch:)* mark [mɑ:k] ► S.173 US school grade
**Schulstunde** lesson ['lesn] *(BE)*; period ['pɪəriəd] *(AE)*
**Schultasche** school bag ['sku:l bæg]
**Schulter** shoulder ['ʃəʊldə]
**Schulterpolster** *(beim American Football)* pad [pæd]
**Schüssel** bowl [bəʊl]
**Schusswaffe** gun [gʌn]
**schützen** protect [prə'tekt]
**Schützer** *(Knieschützer usw. für Inlineskater)* pad [pæd]
**schwach** weak [wi:k]
**Schwäche** weakness ['wi:knəs]
**schwarz** black [blæk] • **schwarzes Brett** *(Anschlagtafel)* notice board ['nəʊtɪs bɔ:d] *(BE)*; bulletin board ['bʊlətɪn bɔ:d] *(AE)*
**Schwein** pig [pɪg]
**Schweinefleisch** pork [pɔ:k]
**schwer** 1. *(Gewicht)* heavy ['hevi] **ein 150 Kilogramm schwerer Bär** a 150-kilogram bear 2. *(schwierig)* difficult ['dɪfɪkəlt]; hard [hɑ:d] 3. *(anstrengend)* hard [hɑ:d]
**Schwester** sister ['sɪstə]
**schwierig** difficult ['dɪfɪkəlt]; hard [hɑ:d]
**Schwierigkeiten** trouble ['trʌbl] • **in Schwierigkeiten sein** be in trouble
**Schwimmbad, -becken** swimming pool ['swɪmɪŋ pu:l]
**schwimmen** swim [swɪm] **schwimmen gehen** go swimming
**Schwimmer/in** swimmer ['swɪmə]
**See** 1. *(Binnensee)* lake [leɪk] 2. *(die See, das Meer)* sea [si:]
**Seemann** sailor ['seɪlə]
**sehen** see [si:] • **Siehst du?** See?
**Sehenswürdigkeiten** sights *(pl)* [saɪts]

**sehr** very ['veri] • **Danke sehr!** Thanks very much! • **Er mag sie sehr.** He likes her a lot. [ə 'lɒt] **etwas sehr mögen / sehr lieben** like/love sth. very much
**Seife** soap [səʊp]
**sein** *(Verb)* be [bi:]
**sein(e)** *(besitzanzeigend) (zu „he")* his; *(zu „it")* its
**seiner, seine, seins** his [hɪz]
**seit 1.** *(mit Zeitraum)* **seit 20 Minuten** for 20 minutes
**2.** *(mit Zeitpunkt)* **seit dem 4. April** since April 4th [sɪns]
**Seit wann ...?** How long ...?
► S.177 German 'seit'
**Seite 1.** side [saɪd] • **auf der linken/rechten Seite** on the left/right
**2.** *(Buch-, Heftseite)* page [peɪdʒ] **Auf welcher Seite sind wir?** What page are we on?
**selbstverständlich** of course [əv 'kɔ:s]
**seltsam** strange [streɪndʒ]
**Semester** *(Schulhalbjahr in den USA)* semester [sɪ'mestə]
**senden (an)** *(Post, E-Mail)* send (to) [send]; mail (to) [meɪl]
**Sendereihe** series, *pl* series ['sɪəri:z]
**Sendung** *(Fernsehsendung)* programme ['prəʊgræm]
**September** September [sep'tembə]
**Serie** *(Sendereihe)* series, *pl* series ['sɪəri:z]
**Sessel** armchair ['ɑ:mtʃeə]
**Setup** setup ['setʌp]
**setzen: sich setzen** sit [sɪt] • **Setz dich / Setzt euch zu mir.** Sit with me.
**Shorts** shorts *(pl)* [ʃɔ:ts]
**Show** show [ʃəʊ]
**sich (selbst) 1.** *(zu „she")* herself [hə'self, hɜ:'self]
**2.** *(zu „he")* himself [hɪm'self]
**3.** *(zu „it")* itself [ɪt'self]
**4.** *(zu „they")* themselves [ðəm'selvz]
**5. sich (gegenseitig)** *(einander)* each other [i:tʃ_'ʌðə]; one another [wʌn_ə'nʌðə]
**sicher 1.** *(in Sicherheit)* safe (from) [seɪf] • **nicht sicher** unsafe [ʌn'seɪf]
**2. sicher sein** *(nicht zweifeln)* be sure [ʃʊə, ʃɔ:]
**3.** *(kein Problem, klar)* sure [ʃʊə, ʃɔ:]
**Sicherheit** safety ['seɪfti] • **in Sicherheit (vor)** safe (from) [seɪf]
**sie 1.** *(weibliche Person)* she [ʃi:] **Frag sie.** Ask her. [hə, hɜ:]
**2.** *(Ding, Tier)* it [ɪt]
**3.** *(Plural)* they [ðeɪ] • **Frag sie.** Ask them. [ðəm, ðem]
**Sie** *(höfliche Anrede)* you [ju:]
**Sieg** win [wɪn]
**Sieger/in** winner ['wɪnə]
**Silbe** syllable ['sɪləbl]
**singen** sing [sɪŋ]
**Single** single ['sɪŋgl]
**sitzen** sit [sɪt]
**Skateboard** skateboard ['skeɪtbɔ:d] **Skateboard fahren** skate [skeɪt]
**skaten** skate [skeɪt]
**Sketch** sketch [sketʃ]
**Ski** ski [ski:] • **Ski fahren/laufen** ski [ski:]
**Sklave, Sklavin** slave [sleɪv]
**SMS** text message ['tekst ˌmesɪdʒ] **jm. eine SMS schicken** text sb. [tekst]
**Snack** snack [snæk]
**so 1.** so weit/gut/schlecht/... that far/good/bad/... • **so süß** so sweet [səʊ]
**2. so alt/groß wie** as old/big as
**Soap** soap [səʊp]
**Soapopera** soap opera ['səʊp_ɒprə]
**Socke** sock [sɒk]
**soeben** just [dʒʌst]
**Sofa** sofa ['səʊfə]
**Software** software ['sɒftweə]
**sogar** even ['i:vn]
**Sohn** son [sʌn]
**Soldat/in** soldier ['səʊldʒə]
**sollten: wir sollten ...** we should ... [ʃəd, ʃʊd] • **Meine Eltern sollten eigentlich jetzt zu Hause sein.** My parents should be at home now.
► S.177 möglich – wahrscheinlich – sicherlich
**Sommer** summer ['sʌmə]
**sonderbar** strange [streɪndʒ]
**sondern** but
**Song** song [sɒŋ]
**Sonnabend** Saturday ['sætədeɪ, 'sætədi] *(siehe auch unter „Freitag")*
**Sonne** sun [sʌn]
**Sonnenbrille: (eine) Sonnenbrille** sunglasses *(pl)* ['sʌnglɑ:sɪz]
**sonnig** sunny ['sʌni]
**Sonntag** Sunday ['sʌndeɪ, 'sʌndi] *(siehe auch unter „Freitag")*
**sonst: Was sonst noch?** What else? [els] • **Wen sonst noch?** Who else? [els]
► S.167 ... else
**Sorge** worry ['wʌri] • **sich Sorgen machen (wegen, um)** worry (about) • **Mach dir keine Sorgen.** Don't worry.
**sorgfältig** careful ['keəfl]
**Sorte** sort [sɔ:t]
**Soundfile** sound file ['saund faɪl]
**Souvenir** souvenir [ˌsu:və'nɪə]
**sowieso** anyway ['eniweɪ]
**sozial** social ['səʊʃl]
**Sozial-** social ['səʊʃl]
**Spaghetti** spaghetti [spə'geti]
**spannend** exciting [ɪk'saɪtɪŋ]
**sparen** save [seɪv]
**Spaß** fun [fʌn] • **Spaß haben** have fun • **nur zum Spaß** just for fun **Reiten macht Spaß.** Riding is fun. **Viel Spaß!** Have fun! / Enjoy yourself.
**spät** late [leɪt] • **Wie spät ist es?** What's the time? • **zu spät sein/kommen** be late
**später** later ['leɪtə]
**spätestens: bis spätestens 10 (Uhr)** by ten (o'clock)
**spazieren gehen** go for a walk [wɔ:k]
**Spaziergang** walk [wɔ:k] • **einen Spaziergang machen** go for a walk
**Specht** woodpecker ['wʊdpekə]
**Speise** dish [dɪʃ]
**Speisekarte** menu ['menju:]
**sperren** lock [lɒk]
**Spiegel** mirror ['mɪrə]
**Spiel** game [geɪm]; *(Wettkampf)* match [mætʃ]
**spielen** play [pleɪ]; *(Szene, Dialog)* act [ækt] • **Fußball spielen** play football • **Gitarre/Klavier spielen** play the guitar/the piano
**Spieler/in** player ['pleɪə]
**Spielfilm** *(im Fernsehen)* drama ['drɑ:mə]
**Spielstand** *(Punktestand)* score [skɔ:]
**Spion/in** spy [spaɪ]
**Spitze** *(oberes Ende)* top [tɒp] • **an der Spitze (von)** at the top (of)
**Sport; Sportart** sport [spɔ:t] • **Sport treiben** do sport
**Sporthalle** gym [dʒɪm]
**Sportler** sportsman ['spɔ:tsmən]
**Sportlerin** sportswoman ['spɔ:tswʊmən]
**sportlich** sporty ['spɔ:ti]
**Sportunterricht** PE [ˌpi:_'i:], Physical Education [ˌfɪzɪkəl_edʒu'keɪʃn]
**Sportzentrum** sports centre ['spɔ:ts ˌsentə]
**Spotlight** spotlight ['spɒtlaɪt]
**Sprache** language ['læŋgwɪdʒ]
**Sprachmittlung** *(Mediation)* mediation [ˌmi:di'eɪʃn]
**sprechen (mit)** speak (to) [spi:k] **Hier spricht Isabel.** *(am Telefon)* This is Isabel.
**springen** jump [dʒʌmp]
**Spülbecken, Spüle** sink [sɪŋk]
**Staat** state [steɪt] • **die Vereinigten Staaten (von Amerika)** the United States (US) [ju,naɪtɪd 'steɪts], [ˌju:_'es]
**Staatsangehörige(r)** citizen ['sɪtɪzn]
**Staatsbürger/in** citizen ['sɪtɪzn]
**Stadion** stadium ['steɪdiəm]

**Stadt** *(Großstadt)* city ['sɪti]; *(Kleinstadt)* town [taʊn]
**Stadtbezirk** borough ['bʌrə, *AE:* 'bɜːrəʊ]
► S.166 New York: the five boroughs
**Stadtplan** map [mæp]
**Stadtzentrum** city centre [ˌsɪti 'sentə] *(BE)*; downtown [ˌdaʊn'taʊn] *(AE)* **der Bus in Richtung Stadtzentrum** the downtown bus *(AE)* • **im/in das Stadtzentrum** downtown *(AE)*
**Stahl** steel [stiːl]
**Stall** *(für Kaninchen)* hutch [hʌtʃ]
**Stammbaum** family tree ['fæməli triː]
**Standort** location [ləʊ'keɪʃn]
**Star** *(Film-, Popstar)* star [stɑː]
**stark** strong [strɒŋ]
**starten** start [stɑːt]
**stattfinden** take place [ˌteɪk 'pleɪs]
**Statue** statue ['stætʃuː]
**Staub: sich aus dem Staub machen** take off *(infml)*
**Steak** steak [steɪk]
**Steckbrief** *(Beschreibung)* profile ['prəʊfaɪl]
**Stecker** plug [plʌg]
**Steeldrum** steel drum [ˌstiːl 'drʌm]
**stehen** stand [stænd] • **Hier steht: ...** *(im Text)* It says here: ... • **Wie steht es?** *(beim Sport)* What's the score?
**stehlen** steal [stiːl]
**Steigerung** comparison [kəm'pærɪsn]
**Stein** stone [stəʊn]
**stellen** *(hin-, abstellen)* put [pʊt] **Fragen stellen** ask questions **etwas leiser/lauter stellen** turn sth. down/up • **sich (hin)stellen** stand [stænd]
**sterben (an)** die (of) [daɪ]
**Stereoanlage** stereo ['steriəʊ]
**Stern** star [stɑː]
**Stichwort** *(Schlüsselwort)* key word ['kiː wɜːd]
**Stiefel** boot [buːt]
**still** quiet ['kwaɪət]
**stimmen: Das stimmt.** That's right. [raɪt] • **Du brauchst ein Lineal, stimmt's?** You need a ruler, right?
**Stockwerk** floor [flɔː]
**stolz (auf jn./etwas)** proud (of sb./sth.) [praʊd]
**stoßen** push [pʊʃ]
**Straferlass** amnesty ['æmnəsti]
**Strand** beach [biːtʃ] • **am Strand** on the beach
**Straße** road [rəʊd]; street [striːt]
**Straßenbahn** tram [træm]
**Strecke** *(Route)* route [ruːt]
**Streich** trick [trɪk]
**Streik** strike [straɪk] • **in den Streik treten** go on strike • **sich im Streik befinden** be on strike
**streiken 1.** *(sich im Streik befinden)* be on strike [straɪk]
**2.** *(in den Streik treten)* go on strike
**Streit** argument ['ɑːgjumənt]
**streiten; sich streiten** argue ['ɑːgjuː]
**streng** strict [strɪkt]
**strukturieren** structure ['strʌktʃə]
**Strumpf** sock [sɒk]
**Stück** piece [piːs] • **ein Stück Papier** a piece of paper
**Student/in** student ['stjuːdənt]
**studieren** study ['stʌdi]
**Stuhl** chair [tʃeə]
**stumm: „stummer" Buchstabe** *(nicht gesprochener Buchstabe)* silent letter [ˌsaɪlənt 'letə]
**Stunde** hour ['aʊə]; *(Schulstunde)* lesson ['lesn] *(BE)*; period ['pɪəriəd] *(AE)* • **eine halbe Stunde** half an hour [ˌhɑːf‿ən‿'aʊə] • **ein 14-Stunden-Flug** a 14-hour flight • **ein Supermarkt, der 24 Stunden geöffnet ist** a 24-hour supermarket
**Stundenplan** timetable ['taɪmteɪbl] *(BE)*; schedule [*AE:* 'skedʒuːl, *BE:* 'ʃedjuːl] *(AE)*
**...stündig: ein 14-stündiger Flug** a 14-hour flight
**Sturm** storm [stɔːm]
**stürmisch** stormy ['stɔːmi]
**stürzen** *(hinfallen)* fall [fɔːl]
**suchen** look for ['lʊk fɔː]
**Süden** south [saʊθ] • **nach Süden**
**südlich** south [saʊθ]
**Südosten** south-east [ˌsaʊθ'iːst] **nach Südosten** south-east
**südöstlich** south-east [ˌsaʊθ'iːst]
**Südwesten** south-west [ˌsaʊθ'west] **nach Südwesten** south-west
**südwestlich** south-west [ˌsaʊθ'west]
**super** super ['suːpə]
**Supermarkt** supermarket ['suːpəmɑːkɪt]
**Suppe** soup [suːp]
**Surfbrett** surfboard ['sɜːfbɔːd]
**surfen** surf [sɜːf] • **im Internet surfen** surf the internet [sɜːf]
**süß** sweet [swiːt]
**Süßigkeiten** sweets *(pl)* [swiːts]
**Sweatshirt** sweatshirt ['swetʃɜːt]
**sympathisch** likeable ['laɪkəbl]
**System** system ['sɪstəm]
**Szene** scene [siːn]

## T

**Tabak** tobacco [tə'bækəʊ]
**Tafel** *(Wandtafel)* board [bɔːd] • **an der/die Tafel** on the board
**Tag** day [deɪ] • **drei Tage (lang)** for three days • **eines Tages** one day **Guten Tag.** Hello.; *(nachmittags)* Good afternoon. [gʊd‿ˌɑːftə'nuːn]
**Tagebuch** diary ['daɪəri]
**Tagesausflug** day trip ['deɪ trɪp]
**Tagesfahrkarte** all-day ticket; *(der Londoner Verkehrsbetriebe)* Travelcard ['trævlkɑːd]
**Tal** valley ['væli]
**Tante** aunt [ɑːnt]; auntie ['ɑːnti]
**Tanz** dance [dɑːns]
**tanzen** dance [dɑːns]
**Tanzen** dancing ['dɑːnsɪŋ]
**Tänzer/in** dancer ['dɑːnsə]
**Tanzfläche** dance floor ['dɑːns flɔː]
**Tanzstunden, Tanzunterricht** dancing lessons ['dɑːnsɪŋ ˌlesnz]
**Tasche** *(Tragetasche, Beutel)* bag [bæg]; *(Hosentasche, Jackentasche)* pocket ['pɒkɪt]
**Taschengeld** pocket money ['pɒkɪt mʌni]
**Tasse** cup [kʌp] • **eine Tasse Tee** a cup of tea
**Tätigkeit** activity [æk'tɪvəti]
**Tatsache** fact [fækt]
**tauschen: etwas tauschen (für etwas/gegen etwas)** swap sth. (for sth.) [swɒp]
**tausend** thousand ['θaʊznd]
**Taxi** taxi ['tæksi]; cab [kæb] • **ein Taxi nehmen** get a taxi / get a cab
**Team** team [tiːm]
**Teddy** teddy ['tedi]
**Tee** tea [tiː]
**Teelöffel** teaspoon ['tiːspuːn]
**Teenager** teenager ['tiːneɪdʒə]
**Teenager-** *(Jugend-)* teen [tiːn]
**Teil** part [pɑːt]; *(Abschnitt)* section ['sekʃn]
**teilen: sich etwas teilen (mit jm.)** share sth. (with sb.) [ʃeə]
**Telefon** (tele)phone ['telɪfəʊn] • **am Telefon** on the phone
**telefonieren** phone [fəʊn]
**Telefonnummer** (tele)phone number ['telɪfəʊn ˌnʌmbə]
**Teller** plate [pleɪt] • **ein Teller Pommes frites** a plate of chips
**Temperatur** temperature ['temprətʃə]
**Tennis** tennis ['tenɪs]
**Termin** appointment [ə'pɔɪntmənt]
**Terminkalender** diary ['daɪəri]
**Test** test [test]
**teuer** expensive [ɪk'spensɪv]
**Text** text [tekst]

**Theater** theatre ['θɪətə]
**Theaterstück** play [pleɪ]
**Thema, Themenbereich** topic ['tɒpɪk]
**Thermometer** thermometer [θə'mɒmɪtə]
**Tier** animal ['ænɪml]; *(Haustier)* pet [pet]
**Tierhandlung** pet shop ['pet ʃɒp]
**Tiger** tiger ['taɪgə]
**Timing** timing ['taɪmɪŋ]
**Tipp** tip [tɪp]
**Tisch** table ['teɪbl]
**Tischtennis** table tennis ['teɪbl tenɪs]
**Tischtennisschläger** table tennis bat [bæt]
**Titel** title ['taɪtl]
**Toast(brot)** toast [təʊst]
**Tochter** daughter ['dɔːtə]
**Tod** death [deθ]
**Toilette** toilet ['tɔɪlət]
**toll** fantastic [fæn'tæstɪk]; great [greɪt]; brilliant ['brɪliənt]
**tollpatschig** clumsy ['klʌmzi]
**Tomate** tomato [tə'mɑːtəʊ], *pl* tomatoes
**Tondatei** sound file ['saund faɪl]
**Top** *(Oberteil)* top [tɒp]
**Tor** gate [geɪt]; *(im Sport)* goal [gəʊl] **ein Tor schießen** score (a goal) [skɔː]
**Torfrau, Torwart** goalkeeper ['gəʊlkiːpə]
**torlos** scoreless ['skɔːləs]
**Tornado** tornado [tɔː'neɪdəʊ]
**Torte** cake [keɪk]
**tot** dead [ded]
**töten** kill [kɪl]
**Tour (durch das Haus)** tour (of the house) [tʊə]
**Tourist/in** tourist ['tʊərɪst]
**Tradition** tradition [trə'dɪʃn]
**tragen** *(Kleidung)* wear [weə]
**Trainer/in** coach [kəʊtʃ]
**trainieren** practise ['præktɪs]; train [treɪn]
**Training** *(körperliche Bewegung)* exercise *(no pl)*
**Trainingsstunde, -einheit** training session ['seʃn]
**Transport** *(Beförderung)* transport ['trænspɔːt]
**Traum** dream [driːm]
**träumen (von)** dream (of,about ) [driːm]
**Traumhaus** dream house
**traurig** sad [sæd]
**treffen; sich treffen** meet [miːt]
**Treffer: einen Treffer erzielen** score (a goal) [skɔː], [gəʊl]
**Treppe(nstufen)** stairs *(pl)* [steəz]
**treten** kick [kɪk]
**Trick** *(Zauberkunststück)* trick [trɪk]
**Trimester** term [tɜːm]
**trinken** drink [drɪŋk] • **Milch zum Frühstück trinken** have milk for breakfast
**Trommel** drum [drʌm]
**Trompete** trumpet ['trʌmpɪt]
**trotzdem** anyway ['eniweɪ]
**Truthahn** turkey ['tɜːki]
**Tschüs.** Bye. [baɪ]; See you. ['siː juː]
**T-Shirt** T-shirt ['tiːʃɜːt]
**Tsunami** tsunami [tsuː'nɑːmi]
**tun** do [duː] • **Tue, was ich tue.** Do what I do. • **tun müssen** have to do • **tun wollen** want to do [wɒnt] **Tut mir leid.** I'm sorry. ['sɒri]
**Tunnel** tunnel ['tʌnl]
**Tür** door [dɔː]
**Türklingel** doorbell ['dɔːbel]
**Turm** tower ['taʊə]
**Turnen** *(Sportunterricht)* PE [ˌpiː‿'iː], Physical Education [ˌfɪzɪkəl‿edʒu'keɪʃn]
**Turnhalle** gym [dʒɪm]
**Turnschuhe** trainers *(pl)* ['treɪnəz]
**Tut mir leid.** I'm sorry. ['sɒri]
**Tüte** bag [bæg]
**Typ** type [taɪp] *(infml)*; *(Kerl)* guy [gaɪ] *(infml)*
**Tyrann** *(Schultyrann)* bully ['bʊli]
**tyrannisieren** bully ['bʊli]

## U

**U-Bahn: die U-Bahn** the underground ['ʌndəgraʊnd] *(BE)*; the subway ['sʌbweɪ] *(AE)*; *(in London)* the Tube *(no pl)* [tjuːb]
**U-Bahnlinie** line [laɪn]
**üben** practise ['præktɪs]
**über 1.** about [ə'baʊt] • **über dich selbst** about yourself **2.** *(räumlich)* over ['əʊvə]; *(quer über)* across [ə'krɒs]; *(oberhalb von)* above [ə'bʌv]
**überarbeiten** revise [rɪ'vaɪz]
**übereinstimmen: mit jm./etwas übereinstimmen** agree with sb./sth. [ə'griː]
**überfliegen: einen Text überfliegen** *(um den Inhalt grob zu erfassen)* skim a text [skɪm]
**überleben** survive [sə'vaɪv]
**übernachten** *(über Nacht bleiben)* stay [steɪ]
**überprüfen** check [tʃek]
**überqueren** cross [krɒs]
**überraschend** surprising [sə'praɪzɪŋ]
**überrascht (über etwas)** surprised (at sth.) [sə'praɪzd]
**Überraschung** surprise [sə'praɪz]
**Überschrift** title ['taɪtl]
**übersetzen (aus ... ins)** translate (from ... into) [træns'leɪt]
**Übersetzung** translation [træns'leɪʃn]
**übrigens** *(nebenbei bemerkt)* by the way [ˌbaɪ ðə 'weɪ]; actually ['æktʃuəli]
**Übung** *(im Schulbuch)* exercise ['eksəsaɪz] • **eine Übung machen** do an exercise
**Übungsheft** exercise book ['eksəsaɪz bʊk]
**Uhr 1.** *(Armbanduhr)* watch [wɒtʃ]; *(Wand-, Stand-, Turmuhr)* clock [klɒk] **2. elf Uhr** eleven o'clock • **7 Uhr morgens/vormittags** 7 am [ˌeɪ‿'em] **7 Uhr nachmittags/abends** 7 pm [ˌpiː‿'em] • **um 8 Uhr 45** at 8.45
**Uhrzeit** time [taɪm]
**um 1.** *(örtlich)* **um ... (herum)** round [raʊnd]; around [ə'raʊnd] • **um den See (herum)** around the lake **ganz um die Burg herum** all around the castle **2.** *(zeitlich)* **um 8.45** at 8.45 • **um sechs herum** *(gegen sechs)* around six **3. Es geht um Mr Green.** This is about Mr Green. **4. um zu** to
**umdrehen: sich umdrehen** turn [tɜːn]
**Umfrage (über)** survey (on) ['sɜːveɪ]
**umher: in ... umher** round [raʊnd]; around [ə'raʊnd] • **in der Stadt umher** around the town
**umher-: umhergehen; umherspazieren** walk around • **umherrennen** run around • **umherspringen** jump around
**umschalten** *(Fernsehprogramm)* change channels ► S.178 (to) change – change
**umschreiben** *(anders ausdrücken)* paraphrase ['pærəfreɪz]
**umsehen: sich umsehen** look round [ˌlʊk 'raʊnd]
**umsteigen** change [tʃeɪndʒ] ► S.178 (to) change – change
**umziehen 1. sich umziehen** change [tʃeɪndʒ] **2. umziehen (nach, in)** *(die Wohnung wechseln)* move (to) [muːv] ► S.178 (to) change – change
**unangenehm** *(unbequem, unbehaglich)* uncomfortable [ʌn'kʌmftəbl]
**unbehaart** hairless ['heələs]
**unbehaglich** uncomfortable [ʌn'kʌmftəbl]
**unbequem** uncomfortable [ʌn'kʌmftəbl]
**uncool** uncool [ˌʌn'kuːl] *(infml)*
**und** and [ənd, ænd] • **Und? / Na und?** So? [səʊ]

**unfair** unfair [ˌʌn'feə]
**Unfall** accident ['æksɪdənt]
**unfreundlich** unfriendly [ʌn'frendli]
**ungefähr** about [ə'baʊt]
**Ungeheuer** monster ['mɒnstə]
**ungenügend** *(bei Schulnoten)* failure *(n)* ['feɪljə]
► S.173 US school grades
**ungerecht** unfair [ˌʌn'feə]
**ungeschickt** clumsy ['klʌmzi]
**ungesetzlich** illegal [ɪ'li:gl]
**ungesund** unhealthy [ʌn'helθi]
**unglaublich** unbelievable [ˌʌnbɪ'li:vəbl]; *(sehr erstaunlich)* amazing [ə'meɪzɪŋ]
**unglücklich** unhappy [ʌn'hæpi]
**unheimlich** scary ['skeəri]
**unhöflich** rude [ru:d]
**Uniform** uniform ['ju:nɪfɔ:m]
**unleserlich** unreadable [ʌn'ri:dəbl]
**unmöglich** impossible [ɪm'pɒsəbl]
**unordentlich** untidy [ʌn'taɪdi] • **sehr unordentlich sein** *(Zimmer)* be a mess [mes]
**Unordnung: alles in Unordnung bringen** make a mess [ˌmeɪk‿ə 'mes]
**unrealistisch** unrealistic [ˌʌnrɪə'lɪstɪk]
**Unrecht haben** be wrong [rɒŋ]
**uns** us [əs, ʌs] • **uns (selbst)** ourselves [aʊə'selvz]
**unser(e) ...** our ... ['aʊə] • **unser eigenes Schwimmbad** our own pool [əʊn]
**unserer, unsere, unseres** ours ['aʊəz]
**unten** below [bɪ'ləʊ]; *(im Haus)* downstairs [ˌdaʊn'steəz] • **am unteren Ende (von)** at the bottom (of) ['bɒtəm] • **dort unten** down there • **nach unten** down [daʊn]; *(im Haus)* downstairs
**unter** under ['ʌndə]; *(unterhalb von)* below [bɪ'ləʊ]
**unterbrechen: eine Reise unterbrechen** break a journey [ˌbreɪk‿ə 'dʒɜ:ni]
**unterhalb (von)** below [bɪ'ləʊ]
**unterhalten: sich unterhalten (mit, über)** talk (to, about) [tɔ:k]
**Unterricht** lessons *(pl)* ['lesnz] • **im Unterricht** in class
**unterrichten** teach [ti:tʃ]
**Unterrichtsstunde** lesson *(BE)* ['lesn]; period ['pɪərɪəd] *(AE)*
**Unterschied** difference ['dɪfrəns]
**unterschiedlich** different ['dɪfrənt]
**Untersuchung (über)** *(Umfrage)* survey (on) ['sɜ:veɪ]
**Unterwäsche** underwear ['ʌndəweə]
**unverschämt** rude [ru:d]
**unzählbar** uncountable [ʌn'kaʊntəbl]
**unzerbrechlich** unbreakable [ʌn'breɪkəbl]
**Ureinwohner/in Amerikas** Native American [ˌneɪtɪv‿ə'merɪkən]
**Urlaub** holiday ['hɒlədeɪ] *(BE);* vacation [və'keɪʃn, *AE:* veɪ'keɪʃn] *(AE)* • **in Urlaub fahren** go on holiday • **in Urlaub sein** be on holiday • **ein zweiwöchiger Urlaub** a two-week holiday

# V

**Vater** father ['fɑ:ðə]
**Vati** dad [dæd]
**Vegetarier/in** vegetarian [ˌvedʒə'teəriən]
**vegetarisch** vegetarian [ˌvedʒə'teəriən]
**Verabredung** appointment [ə'pɔɪntmənt]
**verabschieden: sich verabschieden** say goodbye [ˌseɪ gʊd'baɪ]
**verändern: (sich) verändern** change [tʃeɪndʒ]
► S.178 (to) change – change
**Veränderung** change [tʃeɪndʒ]
► S.178 (to) change – change
**verängstigt** scared [skeəd]
**Veranstaltung** event [ɪ'vent]
**Veranstaltungsort** location [ləʊ'keɪʃn]
**verbinden** *(einander zuordnen)* link [lɪŋk]
**Verbindung** *(Verknüfung)* link [lɪnk] • **in Verbindung bleiben** keep in touch [ˌki:p‿ɪn 'tʌtʃ]
**verboten: Rauchen verboten.** No smoking.
**Verbrechen** crime [kraɪm]
**verbringen: Zeit verbringen (mit)** spend time (on) [spend]
**verdienen** earn [ɜ:n]
**Verein** club [klʌb]
**vereinigt: das Vereinigte Königreich** *(Großbritannien und Nordirland)* the United Kingdom (UK) [juˌnaɪtɪd 'kɪŋdəm], [ˌju:'keɪ] • **die Vereinigten Staaten (von Amerika)** the United States (US) [juˌnaɪtɪd 'steɪts], [ju:‿'es]
**verfolgen** follow ['fɒləʊ]
**vergeben** *(verzeihen)* forgive [fə'gɪv]
**vergessen** forget [fə'get]
**Vergleich** comparison [kəm'pærɪsn]
**Verhalten im Brandfall** fire safety ['faɪə seɪfti]
**verheiratet (mit)** married (to) ['mærɪd]
**Verkauf** sale [seɪl] • **zum Verkauf** for sale
**verkaufen** sell [sel]
**Verkäufer/in** *(im Geschäft)* shop assistant ['ʃɒp‿əˌsɪstənt]
**Verkehr** traffic ['træfɪk]
**Verkehrsmittel** transport *(no pl)* ['trænspɔ:t]
**verkehrsreich** *(Straße)* busy ['bɪzi]
**verkehrt** *(falsch)* wrong [rɒŋ]
**verknüpfen** *(einander zuordnen)* link [lɪŋk]
**Verknüpfung** link [lɪnk]
**verlassen** leave [li:v]
**verletzen** hurt [hɜ:t]
**verletzt** hurt [hɜ:t]
**verlieben: sich verlieben (in jn.)** fall in love (with sb.)
**verlieren** lose [lu:z]
**vermissen** miss [mɪs]
**Vermittlung** *(Sprachmittlung, Mediation)* mediation [ˌmi:di'eɪʃn]
**veröffentlichen** publish ['pʌblɪʃ]
**verrückt** mad [mæd] • **verrückt nach/auf etwas sein** be mad about sth.
**Verrücktheit** madness ['mædnəs]
**Versammlung** meeting ['mi:tɪŋ]; *(morgendliche Schulversammlung, oft mit Andacht)* Assembly [ə'sembli]
**verschieden** *(anders)* different ['dɪfrənt]
**verschwinden** disappear [ˌdɪsə'pɪə]
**versprechen** promise ['prɒmɪs]
**verstecken; sich verstecken** hide [haɪd]
**verstehen** understand [ˌʌndə'stænd]
**versuchen** try [traɪ] • **versuchen zu tun** try and do / try to do
**vertreten** *(repräsentieren)* represent [ˌreprɪ'zent]
**verwenden** use [ju:z]
**verwirrt** puzzled ['pʌzld]
**verzeihen** forgive [fə'gɪv]
**Video** video ['vɪdiəʊ]
**viel** a lot (of) [lɒt]; lots (of) [lɒts]; much [mʌtʃ] • **viele** a lot (of) [lɒt]; lots (of) [lɒts]; many ['meni] • **Viel Glück (bei/mit ...)!** Good luck (with ...)! • **viel mehr** lots more **Viel Spaß!** Have fun! / Enjoy yourself. • **wie viel?** how much? **wie viele?** how many? • **Vielen Dank!** Thanks a lot!
**vielleicht** maybe ['meɪbi] • **Vielleicht ist sie zu beschäftigt.** She might be too busy. [maɪt]
► S.177 möglich – wahrscheinlich – sicherlich
**Viertel: Viertel nach 11** quarter past 11 ['kwɔ:tə] • **Viertel vor 12** quarter to 12
**violett** purple ['pɜ:pl]
**Violine** violin [ˌvaɪə'lɪn]
**Vogel** bird [bɜ:d]
**Vogelkäfig** birdcage ['bɜ:dkeɪdʒ]

**Vokabelverzeichnis** vocabulary [və'kæbjələri]
**voll** full [fʊl] • **die Nase voll haben (von etwas)** be fed up (with sth.) [ˌfed_'ʌp]
**Volleyball** volleyball ['vɒlibɔ:l]
**vollkommen** perfect ['pɜ:fɪkt]
**Vollkorn-** whole-grain ['həʊlgreɪn]
**von** of [əv, ɒv]; from [frəm, frɒm] **ein Aufsatz von ...** an essay by ... [baɪ] • **von Montag bis Freitag** from Mondays to Fridays
**vor 1.** *(räumlich)* in front of [ɪn 'frʌnt_əv] **2.** *(zeitlich)* **vor dem Abendessen** before dinner [bɪ'fɔ:] • **vor einer Minute** a minute ago [ə'gəʊ] **Viertel vor 12** quarter to 12
**vorankommen: Wie komme ich voran?** *(Wie sind meine Fortschritte?)* How am I doing?
**vorbei (an)** *(vorüber)* past [pɑ:st]
**vorbei sein** be over ['əʊvə]
**vorbereiten** prepare [prɪ'peə] • **sich vorbereiten (auf)** prepare (for); get ready (for) ['redi] • **Dinge vorbereiten** get things ready
**Vordergrund** foreground ['fɔ:graʊnd]
**Voreingenommenheit (gegen)** prejudice (against) ['predʒudɪs]
**Vormittag** morning ['mɔ:nɪŋ]
**Vorschrift** *(Regel)* rule [ru:l]
**Vorschule** *(in den USA für 5- bis 6-Jährige)* kindergarten ['kɪndəgɑ:tn]
**vorsichtig** careful ['keəfl]
**vorspielen** *(pantomimisch darstellen)* mime [maɪm]
**vorstellen: sich etwas vorstellen** imagine sth. [ɪ'mædʒɪn]
**Vorstellung** *(Präsentation)* presentation [ˌprezn'teɪʃn]; *(Show)* show [ʃəʊ]
**Vorteil** advantage [əd'vɑ:ntɪdʒ]
**vorüber (an)** *(vorbei)* past [pɑ:st]
**Vorurteil (gegenüber)** prejudice (against) ['predʒudɪs]
**Vorwürfe: jm. Vorwürfe machen machen (wegen)** blame sb. (for) [bleɪm]

## W

**Wahl** *(von Kandidaten bei einer Abstimmung)* election [ɪ'lekʃn]
**wählen 1.** *(auswählen)* choose [tʃu:z] **2. jn. zu etwas wählen** elect sb. sth. [ɪ'lekt]
**wahr** true [tru:] • **wahr werden** come true [ˌkʌm 'tru:]
**während 1.** *(vor Nomen)* during ['djʊərɪŋ] • **während des Spiels** during the match **2.** *(vor Nebensatz)* as [əz, æz]; while [waɪl] • **während wir zuschauten** as/while we were watching
**wahrscheinlich** probably ['prɒbəbli]
**Wald** forest ['fɒrɪst]
**walisisch; Walisisch** Welsh [welʃ]
**Wand** wall [wɔ:l]
**wandern** hike [haɪk] • **wandern gehen** go on a hike
**Wanderung** hike [haɪk]
**wann** when [wen] • **seit wann?** how long?
**warm** warm [wɔ:m]
**warten (auf)** wait (for) [weɪt] **Warte mal!** Wait a minute. ['mɪnɪt] **Wart's ab!** Wait and see!
**Wartezimmer** waiting room
**warum** why [waɪ] • **Warum ich?** Why me?
**was** what [wɒt] • **Was für ein Auto ...?** What kind of car ...? **Was haben wir als Hausaufgabe auf?** What's for homework? **Was haben wir als Nächstes?** What have we got next? • **Was ist los? / Was ist denn?** What's the matter? ['mætə] • **Was ist mit ...?** What about ...? • **Was kostet/kosten ...?** How much is/are ...? **Was (sonst) noch?** What else? [els] **Was war das Beste an ...?** What was the best thing about ...? ► S.167 ... else
**waschen** wash [wɒʃ] • **Ich wasche mir das Gesicht.** I wash my face.
**Waschmaschine** washing machine ['wɒʃɪŋ məˌʃi:n]
**Wasser** water ['wɔ:tə]
**Webcam** webcam ['webkæm]
**Website** website ['websaɪt]
**Wechsel** *((Ver-)Änderung)* change [tʃeɪndʒ] ► S.178 (to) change – change
**Wechselgeld** change [tʃeɪndʒ] ► S.178 (to) change – change
**wechseln** change [tʃeɪndʒ] ► S.178 (to) change – change
**weg** away [ə'weɪ]
**Weg** way [weɪ]; *(Pfad)* path [pɑ:θ]; *(Gasse)* lane [leɪn] • **auf dem Weg (zu/nach)** on the way (to) • **den ganzen Weg** all the way • **jm. den Weg beschreiben** tell sb. the way / give sb. directions • **jn. nach dem Weg fragen** ask sb. the way / ask sb. for directions • **etwas auf den Weg bringen** get sth. off the ground
**Wegbeschreibung** directions *(pl)* [də'rekʃnz] • **jd. um eine Wegbeschreibung bitten** ask sb. for directions
**wegdrehen: sich wegdrehen** turn away [tɜ:n_ə'weɪ]
**weggehen** leave [li:v]
**wehtun** hurt [hɜ:t]
**weiblich** female ['fi:meɪl]
**weich** soft [sɒft]
**Weide** field [fi:ld]
**Weihnachten** Christmas ['krɪsməs]
**weil** because [bɪ'kɒz]
**Wein** wine [waɪn]
**weinen** cry [kraɪ]
**Weintraube** grape [greɪp]
**Weise** *(Art und Weise)* way [weɪ]
**weiß** white [waɪt]
**weit 1.** *(entfernt)* far [fɑ:] **2.** *(geschnitten)* baggy ['bægi]
**weiter: geradeaus weiter** straight on [streɪt_'ɒn]
**weitere(r, s): weitere 45 Pence** another 45 p [ə'nʌðə]
**weiter-: weitergeben** pass [pɑ:s] **weitermachen** go on • **weiterreden** go on
**welche(r, s)** which [wɪtʃ] • **Auf welcher Seite sind wir?** What page are we on? [wɒt] • **Welche Farbe hat ...?** What colour is ...?
**wellenreiten gehen** go surfing ['sɜ:fɪŋ]
**Wellensittich** budgie ['bʌdʒi]
**Welt** world [wɜ:ld] • **auf der ganzen Welt** all over the world • **aus der ganzen Welt** from all over the world
**wem?** who? [hu:] • **Wem gehören diese?** Whose are these? [hu:z]
**wen?** who? [hu:] • **Wen (sonst) noch?** Who else? [els] ► S.167 ... else
**wenden: sich an jn. wenden** turn to sb. [tɜ:n]
**wenig 1.** *(mit nicht zählbaren Nomen)* **wenig Zeit/Wasser** little time/water ['lɪtl] • **ein wenig** *(ein bisschen)* a little • **weniger** less [les] • **am wenigsten** least [li:st] **2.** *(mit zählbaren Nomen im Plural)* **wenige Stunden/Flaschen** few hours/bottles [fju:]; *(ein paar)* a few hours/bottles • **weniger** fewer ['fju:ə] • **am wenigsten** fewest ['fju:ɪst] ► S.174 little – less – least
**wenigstens** at least [ət 'li:st]
**wenn 1.** *(zeitlich)* when [wen] **2.** *(falls)* if [ɪf]
**wer?** who? [hu:] • **Wer ist dran / an der Reihe?** Whose turn is it? [hu:z]
**werden** become [bɪ'kʌm] • **wütend/heiß/... werden** get angry/hot/...

**du wirst frieren; ihr werdet frieren** you'll be cold (= you will be cold) [wɪl] • **du wirst nicht frieren; ihr werdet nicht frieren** you won't be cold (= you will not be cold) [wəʊnt]
**werfen** throw [θrəʊ] • **einen Blick werfen auf etwas** have a look at sth. [lʊk]
**Wesen** *(Charakter)* character ['kærəktə]
**wessen?** whose? [hu:z]
**West-** western ['westən]
**Westen** west [west] • **nach Westen** west
**westlich** *(westlich von)* west [west]; *(Gebiet)* western ['westən]
**Wettbewerb** *(Wettkampf)* competition [ˌkɒmpə'tɪʃn]
**wetten** bet [bet]
**Wetter** weather ['weðə]
**Wettkampf** match [mætʃ]; competition [ˌkɒmpə'tɪʃn]
**Whisky** whisky ['wɪski]
**wichtig** important [ɪm'pɔ:tnt]
**wichtigste(r,s)** main [meɪn]
**wie 1.** *(Fragewort)* how [haʊ] • **Wie bitte?** Sorry? ['sɒri] • **Wie geht es dir/Ihnen/euch?** How are you? [ˌhaʊ_'ɑ: jʊ] • **Wie heißt du?** What's your name? • **Wie komme ich voran?** *(Wie sind meine Fortschritte?)* How am I doing? • **Wie spät ist es?** What's the time? • **Wie steht es jetzt?** *(beim Sport)* What's the score? • **wie viel?** how much? **wie viele?** how many? • **Wie war ...?** How was ...? **Wie war das Wetter?** What was the weather like? • **Wie wär's mit ...?** What about ...?
**2. so alt/groß wie** as old/big as
**3. wie ein Filmstar** like a film star [laɪk]
**4. wie auch immer/wie dem auch sei** anyway ['eniweɪ]
**wieder** again [ə'gen] • **Schön, dass du wieder da bist.** Good to have you back.
**wiederholen** *(Lernstoff)* revise [rɪ'vaɪz]
**Wiederholung** *(des Lernstoffs)* revision [rɪ'vɪʒn]
**Wiedersehen: Auf Wiedersehen.** Goodbye. [ˌgʊd'baɪ]
**wiederverwendet/-verwertet** recycled [ˌri:'saɪkld]
**Wiederverwertung** recycling [ˌri:'saɪklɪŋ]
**wild** wild [waɪld]
**willkommen: Willkommen (in Bristol).** Welcome (to Bristol). ['welkəm]
**Sie heißen dich in ... willkommen** They welcome you to ...
**Wind** wind [wɪnd]
**windig** windy ['wɪndi]
**Windjacke** anorak ['ænəræk]
**Windsurfen** windsurfing ['wɪndsɜ:fɪŋ]
**winken** wave [weɪv]
**Winter** winter ['wɪntə]
**wir** we [wi:]
**Wirbelsturm** tornado [tɔ:'neɪdəʊ]
**wirklich 1.** *(tatsächlich)* really ['rɪəli]
**Meinst du wirklich? / Glaubst du das wirklich?** Do you really think so?
**2.** *(echt)* real [rɪəl]
**Wirklichkeit** reality [ri'æləti]
**wirklichkeitsnah** realistic [ˌri:ə'lɪstɪk]
**wissen** know [nəʊ] • **wissen wollen** wonder ['wʌndə] • **Ich weiß es nicht.** I don't know. • **von etwas wissen; über etwas Bescheid wissen** know about sth. • **..., wissen Sie. / ..., weißt du.** ..., you know. **Weißt du was, Sophie?** You know what, Sophie? • **Woher weißt du ...?** How do you know ...?
**Witz** joke [dʒəʊk] • **Witze machen** joke
**witzig** funny ['fʌni]
**wo** where [weə] • **Wo kommst du her?** Where are you from?
**Woche** week [wi:k]
**Wochenende** weekend [ˌwi:k'end]
**am Wochenende** at the weekend
**Wochentage** days of the week
**...wöchig: ein zweiwöchiger Urlaub** a two-week holiday
**Wofür?** What for? [ˌwɒt 'fɔ:]
**Woher weißt du ...?** How do you know ...? [nəʊ]
**wohin** where [weə]; *(in welche Richtung)* which way
**wohlauf** *(gesund)* well [wel]
**Wohltätigkeitsbasar** jumble sale ['dʒʌmbl seɪl]
**Wohnblock** block [blɒk]
**wohnen** live [lɪv]
**Wohnheim** hostel ['hɒstl]
**Wohnort** location [ləʊ'keɪʃn]
**Wohnung** flat [flæt] *(BE)*; apartment [ə'pɑ:tmənt] *(AE)*
**Wohnungstür** front door [ˌfrʌnt 'dɔ:]
**Wohnwagen** caravan ['kærəvæn]
**Wohnzimmer** living room ['lɪvɪŋ ru:m]
**Wolf** wolf, *pl* wolves [wʊlf, wʊlvz]
**Wolke** cloud [klaʊd]
**Wolkenkratzer** skyscraper ['skaɪskreɪpə]
**wolkenlos** cloudless ['klaʊdləs]
**wollen** *(haben wollen)* want [wɒnt]
**tun wollen** want to do
**Workshop** workshop ['wɜ:kʃɒp]
**Wort** word [wɜ:d]
**Wortbildung** word building ['wɜ:d ˌbɪldɪŋ]
**Wörterbuch** dictionary ['dɪkʃənri]
**Wörterverzeichnis** vocabulary [və'kæbjələri]; *(alphabetisches)* dictionary ['dɪkʃənri]
**Wovon redest du?** What are you talking about?
**würden: ich würde ... / du würdest ...** I would ... / you would ... [wəd, wʊd]
**Würfel** dice, *pl* dice [daɪs]
**Wurst, Würstchen** sausage ['sɒsɪdʒ]
**würzig** *(scharf gewürzt)* spicy ['spaɪsi]
**wütend (über etwas/auf jn.)** angry (about sth./with sb.) ['æŋgri]

## Y

**Yoga** yoga ['jəʊgə]

## Z

**Zahl** number ['nʌmbə]
**zählbar** countable ['kaʊntəbl]
**zählen** count [kaʊnt]
**Zahn** tooth [tu:θ], *pl* teeth [ti:θ] • **Ich putze mir die Zähne.** I clean my teeth.
**Zahnarzt, -ärztin** dentist ['dentɪst]
**Zahnschmerzen** toothache ['tu:θeɪk]
**zanken; sich zanken** argue ['ɑ:gju:]
**Zauberkunststück** trick [trɪk]
**Zauberkunststücke machen** do tricks
**Zebra** zebra ['zebrə]
**Zeh** toe [təʊ]
**Zeichen** *(Schild)* sign [saɪn]
**zeichnen** draw [drɔ:]
**Zeichnung** drawing ['drɔ:ɪŋ]
**zeigen** show [ʃəʊ] • **auf etwas zeigen** point at/to sth. [pɔɪnt] • **gezeigt werden** *(im Fernsehen/Kino)* to be on
**Zeile** line [laɪn]
**Zeit** time [taɪm] • **Zeit verbringen (mit)** spend time (on) [spend]
**Zeitschrift** magazine [ˌmægə'zi:n]
**Zeitung** newspaper ['nju:speɪpə]; paper ['peɪpə]
**Zeitungsartikel** article ['ɑ:tɪkl]
**Zelt** tent [tent]
**zelten** camp [kæmp]
**Zensur** *(Schulnote)* grade [greɪd]; *(BE auch:)* mark [mɑ:k]
► S.173 US school grades

**Zentimeter** centimetre (cm) ['sentɪmiːtə]
**Zentral-** *(Mittel-)* central ['sentrəl]
**Zentrum** centre ['sentə]
**zerbrochen** broken ['brəʊkən]
**Zeug** *(Kram)* stuff [stʌf]
**ziehen** pull [pʊl]
**ziemlich gut** pretty good ['prɪti]; quite good [kwaɪt]
**Ziffer** number ['nʌmbə]
**Zimmer** room [ruːm, rʊm]
**Zone** *(Gebiet)* zone [zəʊn]
**Zoo** zoo [zuː]
**zu** **1.** *(örtlich)* to [tə, tu] • **zu Jenny** to Jenny's • **zu Hause** at home **zum Arzt** to the doctor's • **Setz dich zu mir.** Sit with me. • **auf jn./etwas zu** towards sb./sth. [tə'wɔːdz]
**2. zum Beispiel** for example [ˌfər‿ɪg'zɑːmpl] • **zum Frühstück/Mittagessen/Abendbrot** for breakfast/lunch/dinner [fə, fɔː]
**zum Schluss** in the end
**3. zu viel** too much [tuː] • **zu spät sein/kommen** be late
**4. versuchen zu tun** try and do / try to do
**5.** *(geschlossen)* closed [kləʊzd]
**zubereiten** *(kochen)* cook [kʊk]
**Zucker** sugar ['ʃʊgə]
**zuerst** *(als Erstes)* first [fɜːst]; *(zu Beginn)* at first
**Zug** train [treɪn] • **im Zug** on the train
**Zuhause** home [həʊm]
**zuhören** listen (to) ['lɪsn]
**Zuhörer/in** listener ['lɪsnə] • **Zuhörer/innen** *(Publikum)* audience ['ɔːdiəns]
**zum** *siehe „zu"*
**zumachen** close [kləʊz]
**zumindest** at least [ət 'liːst]
**zurück (nach)** back (to) [bæk]
**zurückkehren** return [rɪ'tɜːn]
**zurücklassen** leave [liːv]
**zusammen** together [tə'geðə] • **mit jm. zusammen sein** to be with sb.
**zusammenfassen: etwas zusammenfassen** summarize sth. ['sʌməraɪz]
**Zusammenfassung** summary ['sʌməri]
**zusammenpassen, -gehören** go together
**zusätzlich** extra ['ekstrə]
**Zuschauer/in** viewer ['vjuːə]
**Zuschauer/innen** *(Publikum)* audience ['ɔːdiəns]
**zusehen** watch [wɒtʃ]
**zustimmen: jm./etwas zustimmen** agree with sb./sth. [ə'griː]
**zuwenden: sich jm. zuwenden** turn to sb. [tɜːn]
**zweimal** twice [twaɪs]
**zweite(r, s)** second ['sekənd]
**Zwiebel** onion ['ʌnjən]
**Zwillinge** twins *(pl)* [twɪnz]
**Zwillingsbruder** twin brother ['twɪn ˌbrʌðə]
**zwischen** between [bɪ'twiːn]

## The United States of America

| | |
|---|---|
| **Alabama (AL)** | [ˌælə'bæmə] |
| **Alaska (AK)** | [ə'læskə] |
| **Arizona (AZ)** | [ˌærɪ'zəʊnə] |
| **Arkansas (AR)** | ['ɑːkənsɔː] |
| **California (CA)** | [ˌkælə'fɔːniə] |
| **Colorado (CO)** | [ˌkɒlə'rɑːdəʊ] |
| **Connecticut (CT)** | [kə'netɪkət] |
| **Delaware (DE)** | ['deləweə] |
| **Florida (FL)** | ['flɒrɪdə] |
| **Georgia (GA)** | ['dʒɔːdʒə] |
| **Hawaii (HI)** | [hə'waɪi] |
| **Idaho (ID)** | ['aɪdəhəʊ] |
| **Illinois (IL)** | [ˌɪlə'nɔɪ] |
| **Indiana (IN)** | [ˌɪndi'ænə] |
| **Iowa (IA)** | ['aɪəwə] |
| **Kansas (KS)** | ['kænzəs] |
| **Kentucky (KY)** | [ken'tʌki] |
| **Louisiana (LA)** | [luˌiːzi'ænə] |
| **Maine (ME)** | [meɪn] |
| **Maryland (MD)** | ['meərilənd] |
| **Massachusetts (MA)** | [ˌmæsə'tʃuːsɪts] |
| **Michigan (MI)** | ['mɪʃɪgən] |
| **Minnesota (MN)** | [ˌmɪnɪ'səʊtə] |
| **Mississippi (MS)** | [ˌmɪsɪ'sɪpi] |
| **Missouri (MO)** | [mɪ'zʊəri] |
| **Montana (MT)** | [mɒn'tænə] |
| **Nebraska (NE)** | [nə'bræskə] |
| **Nevada (NV)** | [nə'vɑːdə] |
| **New Hampshire (NH)** | [ˌnjuː 'hæmpʃə] |
| **New Jersey (NJ)** | [ˌnjuː 'dʒɜːzi] |
| **New Mexico (NM)** | [ˌnjuː 'meksɪkəʊ] |
| **New York (NY)** | [ˌnjuː 'jɔːk] |
| **North Carolina (NC)** | [ˌnɔːθ kærə'laɪnə] |
| **North Dakota (ND)** | [ˌnɔːθ də'kəʊtə] |
| **Ohio (OH)** | [əʊ'haɪəʊ] |
| **Oklahoma (OK)** | [ˌəʊklə'həʊmə] |
| **Oregon (OR)** | ['ɒrɪgən] |
| **Pennsylvania (PA)** | [ˌpensl'veɪniə] |
| **Rhode Island (RI)** | [ˌrəʊd‿'aɪlənd] |
| **South Carolina (SC)** | [ˌsaʊθ kærə'laɪnə] |
| **South Dakota (SD)** | [ˌsaʊθ də'kəʊtə] |
| **Tennessee (TN)** | [ˌtenə'siː] |
| **Texas (TX)** | ['teksəs] |
| **Utah (UT)** | ['juːtɑː] |
| **Vermont (VT)** | [və'mɒnt] |
| **Virginia (VA)** | [və'dʒɪniə] |
| **Washington (WA)** | ['wɒʃɪŋtən] |
| **West Virginia (WV)** | [ˌwest və'dʒɪniə] |
| **Wisconsin (WI)** | [wɪs'kɒnsɪn] |
| **Wyoming (WY)** | [waɪ'əʊmɪŋ] |

| Country/Continent | Adjective | Person | People |
|---|---|---|---|
| **Africa** ['æfrɪkə] *Afrika* | African ['æfrɪkən] | an African | the Africans |
| **America** [ə'merɪkə] *Amerika* | American [ə'merɪkən] | an American | the Americans |
| **Asia** ['eɪʃə, 'eɪʒə] *Asien* | Asian ['eɪʃn, 'eɪʒn] | an Asian | the Asians |
| **Australia** [ɒ'streɪliə] *Australien* | Australian [ɒ'streɪliən] | an Australian | the Australians |
| **Austria** ['ɒstriə] *Österreich* | Austrian ['ɒstriən] | an Austrian | the Austrians |
| **Belgium** ['beldʒəm] *Belgien* | Belgian ['beldʒən] | a Belgian | the Belgians |
| **Canada** ['kænədə] *Kanada* | Canadian [kə'neɪdiən] | a Canadian | the Canadians |
| **China** ['tʃaɪnə] *China* | Chinese [ˌtʃaɪ'ni:z] | a Chinese | the Chinese |
| **Croatia** [krəʊ'eɪʃə] *Kroatien* | Croatian [krəʊ'eɪʃn] | a Croatian | the Croatians |
| **the Czech Republic** [ˌtʃek rɪ'pʌblɪk] *Tschechien, die Tschechische Republik* | Czech [tʃek] | a Czech | the Czechs |
| **Denmark** ['denmɑ:k] *Dänemark* | Danish ['deɪnɪʃ] | a Dane [deɪn] | the Danes |
| **England** ['ɪŋglənd] *England* | English ['ɪŋglɪʃ] | an Englishman/-woman | the English |
| **Europe** ['jʊərəp] *Europa* | European [ˌjʊərə'pi:ən] | a European | the Europeans |
| **Finland** ['fɪnlənd] *Finnland* | Finnish ['fɪnɪʃ] | a Finn [fɪn] | the Finns |
| **France** [frɑ:ns] *Frankreich* | French [frentʃ] | a Frenchman/-woman | the French |
| **Georgia** ['dʒɔ:dʒə] *Georgien* | Georgian ['dʒɔ:dʒən] | a Georgian | the Georgians |
| **Germany** ['dʒɜ:məni] *Deutschland* | German ['dʒɜ:mən] | a German | the Germans |
| **(Great) Britain** ['brɪtn] *Großbritannien* | British ['brɪtɪʃ] | a Briton ['brɪtn] | the British |
| **Greece** [gri:s] *Griechenland* | Greek [gri:k] | a Greek | the Greeks |
| **Holland** ['hɒlənd] *Holland, die Niederlande* | Dutch [dʌtʃ] | a Dutchman/-woman | the Dutch |
| **Hungary** ['hʌŋgəri] *Ungarn* | Hungarian [hʌŋ'geəriən] | a Hungarian | the Hungarians |
| **India** ['ɪndiə] *Indien* | Indian ['ɪndiən] | an Indian | the Indians |
| **Ireland** ['aɪələnd] *Irland* | Irish ['aɪrɪʃ] | an Irishman/-woman | the Irish |
| **Italy** ['ɪtəli] *Italien* | Italian [ɪ'tæliən] | an Italian | the Italians |
| **Japan** [dʒə'pæn] *Japan* | Japanese [ˌdʒæpə'ni:z] | a Japanese | the Japanese |
| **Korea** [kə'riə] *Korea* | Korean [kə'riən] | a Korean | the Koreans |
| **the Netherlands** ['neðələndz] *die Niederlande, Holland* | Dutch [dʌtʃ] | a Dutchman/-woman | the Dutch |
| **New Zealand** [ˌnju: 'zi:lənd] *Neuseeland* | New Zealand [ˌnju: 'zi:lənd] | a New Zealander | the New Zealanders |
| **Norway** ['nɔ:weɪ] *Norwegen* | Norwegian [nɔ:'wi:dʒən] | a Norwegian | the Norwegians |
| **Pakistan** [ˌpækɪ'stæn, ˌpɑ:kɪ'stɑ:n] *Pakistan* | Pakistani [ˌpækɪ'stæni, ˌpɑ:kɪ'stɑ:ni] | a Pakistani | the Pakistanis |
| **the Philippines** ['fɪlɪpi:nz] *die Philippinen* | Philippine ['fɪlɪpi:n] | a Filipino [ˌfɪlɪ'pi:nəʊ]/ Filipina [ˌfɪlɪ'pi:nə] | the Filipinos/ Filipinas |
| **Poland** ['pəʊlənd] *Polen* | Polish ['pəʊlɪʃ] | a Pole [pəʊl] | the Poles |
| **Portugal** ['pɔ:tʃʊgl] *Portugal* | Portuguese [ˌpɔ:tʃu'gi:z] | a Portuguese | the Portuguese |
| **Puerto Rico** [ˌpwɜ:təʊ 'ri:kəʊ] *Puerto Rico* | Puerto Rican [ˌpwɜ:təʊ 'ri:kən] | a Puerto Rican | the Puerto Ricans |
| **Russia** ['rʌʃə] *Russland* | Russian ['rʌʃn] | a Russian | the Russians |
| **Scotland** ['skɒtlənd] *Schottland* | Scottish ['skɒtɪʃ] | a Scotsman/-woman, a Scot [skɒt] | the Scots, the Scottish |
| **Slovakia** [sləʊ'vɑ:kiə, sləʊ'vækiə] *die Slowakei* | Slovak ['sləʊvæk] | a Slovak | the Slovaks |
| **Slovenia** [sləʊ'vi:niə] *Slowenien* | Slovenian [sləʊ'vi:niən], Slovene ['sləʊvi:n] | a Slovene, a Slovenian | the Slovenes, the Slovenians |
| **Spain** [speɪn] *Spanien* | Spanish ['spænɪʃ] | a Spaniard ['spænɪəd] | the Spaniards |
| **Sweden** ['swi:dn] *Schweden* | Swedish ['swi:dɪʃ] | a Swede [swi:d] | the Swedes |
| **Switzerland** ['swɪtsələnd] *die Schweiz* | Swiss [swɪs] | a Swiss | the Swiss |
| **Turkey** ['tɜ:ki] *die Türkei* | Turkish ['tɜ:kɪʃ] | a Turk [tɜ:k] | the Turks |
| **the United Kingdom (the UK)** [juˌnaɪtɪd 'kɪŋdəm, ˌju:'keɪ] *das Vereinigte Königreich (Großbritannien und Nordirland)* | British ['brɪtɪʃ] | a Briton ['brɪtn] | the British |
| **the United States of America (the USA)** [juˌnaɪtɪd ˌsteɪts_əv_ə'merɪkə, ˌju:_es_'eɪ] *die Vereinigten Staaten von Amerika* | American [ə'merɪkən] | an American | the Americans |
| **Wales** [weɪlz] *Wales* | Welsh [welʃ] | a Welshman/-woman | the Welsh |

## First names (Vornamen)

**Aaron** ['eərən]
**Abraham** ['eɪbrəhæm]
**Adriana** [ˌeɪdri'ɑ:nə]
**Alicia** [ə'lɪʃə, ə'lɪʃiə]
**Angus** ['æŋgəs]
**Annie** ['æni]
**Anthony** ['æntəni, 'ænθəni]
**Aretha** [ə'ri:θə]
**Bart** [bɑ:t]
**Bessy** ['besi]
**Beyoncé** [bi'jɒnseɪ]
**Brad** [bræd]
**Bruce** [bru:s]
**Buddy** ['bʌdi]
**Caitlin** ['keɪtlɪn, 'kætlɪn]
**Carrie** ['keri, 'kæri]
**Chris** [krɪs]
**Chuck** [tʃʌk]
**Cindy** ['sɪndi]
**Coretta** [kə'retə]
**Cruz** [kru:z]
**David** ['deɪvɪd]
**Diego** [di'eɪgəʊ]
**Domino** ['dɒmɪnəʊ]
**Donna** ['dɒnə]
**Erykah** ['erɪkə]
**George** [dʒɔ:dʒ]
**Jake** [dʒeɪk]
**James** [dʒeɪmz]
**Jelly** ['dʒeli]
**Jim** [dʒɪm]
**Johnny** ['dʒɒni]
**Josephine** ['dʒəʊzəfi:n, 'dʒəʊsəfi:n]
**Josh** [dʒɒʃ]
**Kelly** ['keli]
**Langston** ['læŋstən]
**Lara** ['lɑ:rə]
**Lauryn** ['lɒrən]
**Levi** ['li:vai, 'leɪvi]
**Louie** ['lu:i]
**Louis** ['lu:ɪs, 'lu:i]
**Luis** [lu:'i:s, 'lu:ɪs]
**Luke** [lu:k]
**Madison** ['mædɪsn]
**Marcia** ['mɑ:siə, 'mɑ:ʃə]
**Margaret** ['mɑ:grət]
**Marge** [mɑ:dʒ]
**Maria** [mə'ri:ə]
**Martin** ['mɑ:tɪn]
**Melba** ['melbə]
**Melissa** [mə'lɪsə]
**Morton** ['mɔ:tən]
**Muriel** ['mjʊəriəl]
**Myron** ['maɪrən]
**Ray** [reɪ]
**Ricardo** [rɪ'kɑ:dəʊ]
**Richard** ['rɪtʃəd]
**Rick** [rɪk]
**Robert** ['rɒbət]
**Ruth** [ru:θ]
**Ryan** ['raɪən]
**Shirley** ['ʃɜ:li]
**Simon** ['saɪmən]
**Theodore** ['θi:ədɔ:]
**Thomas** ['tɒməs]
**Todd** [tɒd, tɑ:d]

## Family names (Familiennamen)

**Alvarez** ['ælvərez]
**Armstrong** ['ɑ:mstrɒŋ]
**Badu** [bə'du:]
**Beals** [bi:lz]
**Berry** ['beri]
**Bertanelli** [ˌbɜ:tə'neli]
**Bethune** [be'θu:n]
**Bolden** ['bəʊldən]
**Callahan** ['kæləhən]
**Carter** ['kɑ:tə]
**Charles** [tʃɑ:lz]
**Collier** ['kɒliə]
**Clinton** ['klɪntən]
**Columbus** [kə'lʌmbəs]
**Cooke** [kʊk]
**Crutcher** ['krʌtʃə]
**D'Agostino** [ˌdægə'sti:nəʊ]
**Diddley** ['dɪdli]
**Ebb** [eb]
**Franklin** ['fræŋklɪn]
**Goode** [gʊd]
**Hawley** ['hɔ:li]
**Hughes** [hju:z]
**Ignatow** [ɪg'nɑ:təʊ]
**Jefferson** ['dʒefəsn]
**Johnson** ['dʒɒnsn]
**Kennedy** ['kenədi]
**Kruger** ['kru:gə]
**Langer** ['læŋgə]
**Lawrence** ['lɒrəns]
**Lee** [li:]
**Lefevre** [lə'fi:və]
**Levoy** ['li:vɔɪ]
**Lincoln** ['lɪŋkən]
**Luther** ['lu:θə]
**Marshall** ['mɑ:ʃl]
**McCourt** [mə'kɔ:t]
**Meerbusch** ['mɪəbʊʃ]
**Mitchell** ['mɪtʃəl]
**Moore** [mɔ:]
**Morales** [mə'rɑ:lez, mə'ræləs]
**Muir** [mjʊə]
**Nielson** ['ni:lsən]
**Pattillo** [pə'tɪləʊ]
**Pitt** [pɪt]
**Rainey** ['reɪni]
**Roll** [rəʊl]
**Roosevelt** ['rəʊzəvelt]
**Salgado** [sæl'gɑ:dəʊ]
**Sanford** ['sænfəd]
**Scott** [skɒt]
**Sheckler** ['ʃeklə]
**Simpson** ['sɪmpsən]
**Smith** [smɪθ]
**Springsteen** ['sprɪŋsti:n]
**Strauss** [straʊs]
**Viotti** [vi'ɒti]
**Washington** ['wɒʃɪŋtən]
**Wilkins** ['wɪlkɪnz]

## Place names (Ortsnamen)

(*siehe auch S. 230:* The United States of America)

**Atlanta** [ət'læntə]
**Battery Place** ['bætri, bætəri pleɪs]
**Broadway** ['brɔ:dweɪ]
**Bronx** [brɒŋks]
**Brooklyn** ['brʊklɪn]
**Brownsville** ['braʊnsvɪl]
**Castor River** [ˌkɑ:stə 'rɪvə]
**Chicago** [ʃɪ'kɑ:gəʊ]
**Coloma** [kə'ləʊmə]
**Coney Island** [ˌkəʊni_'aɪlənd]
**Dahlonega** [də'lɒnəgə]
**Ellis Island** [ˌelɪs_'aɪlənd]
**Empire State Building** [ˌempaɪə 'steɪt ˌbɪldɪŋ]
**Eureka** [ju'ri:kə]
**Gateway Arch** [ˌgeɪtweɪ_'ɑ:tʃ]
**Grand Canyon** [ˌgrænd 'kænjən]
**Hayden Street** ['heɪdn stri:t]
**Herald Square** [ˌherəld 'skweə]
**Hermann** ['hɜ:mən]
**Hermannthal Winery** [ˌhɜ:məntɑ:l 'waɪnəri]
**Hollywood** ['hɒliwʊd]
**Inglewood** ['ɪŋglwʊd]
**Jamestown** ['dʒeɪmztaʊn]
**Las Vegas** [læs 'veɪgəs]
**Lenox** ['lenəks]
**Los Angeles** [lɒs_'ændʒəli:z]
**Macy's** ['meɪsiz]
**Malibu** ['mælɪbu:]
**Mission Viejo** [ˌmɪʃn vi'eɪhəʊ]
**Montgomery** [mənt'gʌmri]
**Manhattan** [mæn'hætn]
**Nathan's** ['neɪθnz]
**New Echota** [ˌnju:_ɪ'kəʊtə]
**New York** [ˌnju: 'jɔ:k]
**Paris** ['pærɪs]
**Queens** [kwi:nz]
The **Ramble** ['ræmbl]
**Rhineland** ['raɪnlənd]
**Rome** [rəʊm]
**Sacramento** [ˌsækrə'mentəʊ]
**San Clemente** [ˌsæn klə'menti]
**San Diego** [ˌsæn di'eɪgəʊ]
**San Francisco** [ˌsæn frən'sɪskəʊ]
**Santa Monica** [ˌsæntə 'mɒnɪkə]
**Santa Rosa** [ˌsæntə 'rəʊzə]
**Savannah** [sə'vænə]
**Sequoia National Park** [sɪˌkwɔɪə ˌnæʃnəl 'pɑ:k]
**Shorecliffs Middle School** ['ʃɔ:klɪfs]
**Sicily** ['sɪsəli]
**Silicon Valley** [ˌsɪlɪkən 'væli]
**Sinaloa** [ˌsɪnə'ləʊə]
**Staten Island** [ˌstætn_'aɪlənd]
**St. Louis** [sənt 'lu:ɪs]
**Tucumcari** [ˌtu:kəm'keəri]
**Tulsa** ['tʌlsə]
**Washington** ['wɒʃɪŋtən]
**Watsonville** ['wɒtsnvɪl]
**World Trade Center** [ˌwɜ:ld 'treɪd ˌsentə]
**Yankee Stadium** [ˌjæŋki 'steɪdiəm]
**Yosemite** [jəʊ'seməti]

## Other names (Andere Namen)

**Bearcats** ['beəkæts]
**Bellagio** [bə'lɑ:dʒɪəʊ]
**Cherokees** ['tʃerəki:z]
**Colorado** [ˌkɒlə'rɑ:dəʊ]
**Harlem Globetrotters** [ˌhɑ:ləm 'gləʊbˌtrɒtəz]
**Kool** [kʊl]
**LeToya** [lə'tɔɪə]
The **Mets** [mets]
**Mississippi** [ˌmɪsɪ'sɪpi]
**Ne-Yo** ['ni:əʊ]
**Oscar** ['ɒskə]
**Outkast** ['aʊtkɑ:st]
**Rhine** [raɪn]
**Rushmore** ['rʌʃmɔ:]
**Sledge** [sledʒ]
**Usher** ['ʌʃə]
**Yankees** ['jæŋkiz]

## 7 Questions and answers ▸ Unit 5 (p. 98)

*If you are a* ***suspect****, you have to answer some questions.*

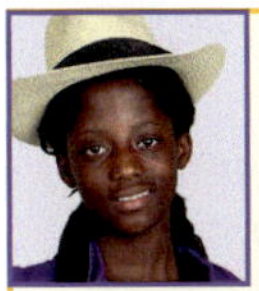

### Role card **SCENE 1**, Sam

**Why do you think Sam got a good grade on the test?**

**You:** Why I did get a good grade? Well, I really didn't need to study for the test. My grandmother told me all about Martin Luther King. She met him once. I have a photo of her with Dr King. This was an easy test for me.

**Did you want to win Jacko's MP3 player?**

**You:** No, I've already got one.

### Role card **SCENE 1**, Nat

**Why do you think Sam got a good grade on the test?**

**You:** I don't know. That was a big surprise. She never gets good grades. But I don't want to say anything. Ask Sam.

**Did you want to win Jacko's MP3 player?**

**You:** No, I've already got one. Try someone else.

### Role card **SCENE 1**, Jacko

**Why do you think Sam got a good grade on the test?**

**You:** Well, it was a surprise, but how should I know why she was so good? Ask Sam.

**Did you want to win Jacko's MP3 player?**

**You:** I'm Jacko. It was my MP3 player. Ask the others.

### Role card **SCENE 1**, Scott

**Why do you think Sam got a good grade on the test?**

**You:** I think Sam was very interested in Martin Luther King's story. Cindy says that there's a photo of Sam's grandmother and Dr King.

**Did you want to win Jacko's MP3 player?**

**You:** No. I've already got an MP3 player.

### Role card **SCENE 1**, Flash

**Why do you think Sam got a good grade on the test?**

**You:** I don't know. She's not one of my friends. I don't really know her. Ask Sam.

**Did you want to win Jacko's MP3 player?**

**You:** No. My MP3 player is much better. It cost a lot of money.

### Role card **SCENE 1**, Cindy

**Why do you think Sam got a good grade on the test?**

**You:** She showed me a photo of her grandmother and Martin Luther King. I think that she knows a lot about him.

**Did you want to win Jacko's MP3 player?**

**You:** No, I've already got one and I hate Jacko's music. It's so loud and fast! Only CJ likes the same music as Jacko!

### Role card **SCENE 1**, CJ

**Why do you think Sam got a good grade on the test?**

**You:** I'm new to this class. I don't know. Ask Sam.

**Did you want to win Jacko's MP3 player?**

**You:** Well, I've already got an MP3 player. But Jacko's got a great playlist on his MP3. So the true answer is yes, I did want to win it ... but I didn't cheat!

### Role card **SCENE 1**, Mr Bell

**Why do you think Sam got a good grade on the test?**

**You:** She showed me a photo of Martin Luther King and her grandmother. Her grandmother told her a lot about him.

**Did you want to win Jacko's MP3 player?**

**You:** No, of course not. I'm the teacher. Ask the students.

## 10 Questions and answers ▸ Unit 5 (p. 101)

*If you are a **suspect**, you have to answer some questions.*

### Role card **SCENE 2**, Sam

**Do you want to take the test again?**

**You:** No! I got an A! My first A! I don't think I can do that again.

**Who do you think did it?**

**You:** I don't know. Maybe it was Mr Bell. I think he's worried about what the principal will say.

### Role card **SCENE 2**, Nat

**Do you want to take the test again?**

**You:** No! I hate tests. I get so stressed! I don't want to do it again!

**Who do you think did it?**

**You:** I don't know. I don't think it was Mr Bell. He's not like that. It must be one of the students.

### Role card **SCENE 2**, Jacko

**Do you want to take the test again?**

**You:** No! I worked hard to get the best grade. I wanted to keep my MP3 player. I don't want to take the test again.

**Who do you think did it?**

**You:** I don't know. Maybe it was Mr Bell. That would be so funny!

### Role card **SCENE 2**, Scott

**Do you want to take the test again?**

**You:** Well, I got a B. Maybe I'd get an A if I took it again. But I don't have time to study. No, I don't want to take the test again.

**Who do you think did it?**

**You:** It must be Flash. He's trying to get me into trouble.

### Role card **SCENE 2**, Flash

**Do you want to take the test again?**

**You:** No, not really. But I don't really care. Tests are not important to me.

**Who do you think did it?**

**You:** Scott. I'm sure it was him ... well, I hope it was him!

### Role card **SCENE 2**, Cindy

**Do you want to take the test again?**

**You:** No, not really. I'm happy with my grade. And I think Scott is happy too. No, we don't want to take the test again.

**Who do you think did it?**

**You:** I don't know. Maybe it was Flash. He isn't very nice to Scott.

### Role card **SCENE 2**, CJ

**Do you want to take the test again?**

**You:** No. What a boring idea!

**Who do you think did it?**

**You:** I don't know. Maybe Cindy or Scott cheated! They are so perfect. That would be so funny! Or Mr Bell. That would be funny too.

### Role card **SCENE 2**, Mr Bell

**Do you want to take the test again?**

**You:** Well, most of the students got really bad grades. Maybe it's not such a bad idea! But it would be a lot of work for me. So, the answer is NO!

**Who do you think did it?**

**You:** I really don't know.

Key to the self-assessment tests

## Unit 1 ▸ p. 29

1 C boroughs
2 E Manhattan
3 B south
4 B the World Trade Center
5 D a book
6 B Ellis Island
7 B (American English **French fries** – British English **potato chips**)
8 a) lift
b) holiday(s)
c) underground
9 B awful
10 C put out
11 D deli
12 C Hiking
13 C I'm good at swimming.
14 C A bagel to go, please.
15 B Egg and tomato, please.

## Unit 2 ▸ p. 51

1 A the Golden State
2 C Silicon Valley
3 D Spanish
4 D border
5 C the Golden Gate Bridge
6 C (nicht) Wort für Wort lesen.
7 B bestimmten Informationen.
8 B immigrants
9 A prejudice
10 B industrial
11 D grown
12 A mountain
13 C are made
14 A was found
15 B by
16 C Someone stole my camera.

## Unit 3 ▸ p. 69

1 A middle
2 Germany
3 C river
4 elementary school
5 grade
6 extracurricular activities/extracurriculars
7 A (excellent)
8 possible answers:
elementary school, kindergarten, grade, semester, lesson/period, timetable/schedule, school subjects (...), bulletin board/notice board, classroom, desk, ...
4 points
9 poultry: chicken
10 exercise
11 per cent
12 one point eight
13 falsch: C
14 a) Can I have **a** glass of milk, please?
– Of course, there's **some** milk in the fridge. 2 points
b) Would you like **some** fruit with your sandwich?
– Yes, **an** apple would be nice.
2 points
c) Dad, can I have **some** money for school lunch?
15 B had lost
16 C when

## Key to the self-assessment tests

### Unit 4

► p. 91

1 C Georgia
2 B to get the same rights for all people
3 A the White House
4 a) series
   b) comedy show
   c) documentary
   d) viewer
5 D books
6 C the TV listings
7 D waiter
8 C remote control
9 C Wenn du eine Recherche im Internet machst, ist es besser, wenn du mehr als eine Website nutzt.
10 C Es ist nicht unbedingt nötig, dass du alle Informationen auf einer Webseite liest.
11 C Informationen im Internet sind nicht immer richtig.
12 C Fakten, die mit der Frage zu tun haben.
13 B have lived
14 C My parents **have been** married for 15 years.
15 a) **since** yesterday
   b) **for** an hour
   c) **for** two days
   d) **since** Monday

## Illustrationen

**Silke Bachmann**, Hamburg (30; 48–49; 66–68; 77-78); **Roland Beier**, Berlin (25; 29; 40; 46; 51; 54; 56; 62; 64; 69; 85 (u. 115); 86; 91; 94-95; 97; 100-104; 127;136–179); **Dr. Volkhard Binder**, Berlin (S. 125); **Carlos Borrell**, Berlin (vordere u. hintere Umschlaginnenseite; 8-11; 13; 14; 20 oben (u. 103); 40; 52; 53; 52-53 (Hintergrund); 58; 59 oben; 116; 117; 119;127; 134); **Stéphane Gamain/NB Illustration**, London (20 Mitte, unten; 22 (u. 106); 26-28; 38; 45 (u. 104); 47); **Jörn Hennig**, Berlin (130–131)

## Bildquellen

**Michelle Abesamis**, New York (S. 23 zoo); **Alamy**, Abingdon (Inhaltsverz. Caitlin (u. 8 oben li.): Geoff du Feu (RF); Luis (u. 9 u. 109 li.): David R. Frazier Photolibrary, Inc., skyline (M) (u. 12/13): JUPITERIMAGES/ Thinkstock (RF), surfers (M) (u. 34): Juice Images Limited (RF); S. 9 Mitte school bus: Directphoto.org; S. 9 Mitte pool: Radius Images; S. 10 Route 66 logo: wendy connett, condor: John Cancalosi; S. 12 Bild A: Jon Arnold Images Ltd., Bild B: Tetra Images; S. 13 Bild F: Jochen Tack; S. 14 oben girls (M): Andrew Rubtsov, Bild 1: Dieter Melhorn, Bild 2: Stockbyte(RF), Bild 3: Kitt Cooper-Smith (RF), Bild 4: fStop (RF), Bild 6: John Taylor; S. 15 oben: Picture Partners, Mitte: eStock Photo/Gg; S. 17 oben: Sandra Baker, unten li.: Arcaid/G Jackson, unten re.: PCL; S. 18 unten li.: Mary Evans Picture Library; S. 19 oben re.: John Davidson; S. 21 shop assistant (u. 106): John Sturrock, hairdresser (u. 106): Tetra Images (RF), paramedic (u. 106): Blend Images (RF); S. 22 oben: dbimages/Derek Brown; S. 23 Mitte: Harry van Gorkum (RF); S. 34 Bild A (M) beach: Stephen Saks Photography, Bild C (M) sign: Frank Vetere, highway 101: Stock Connection Blue; S. 35 Bild F: Richard Broadwell; S. 36 strawberries: Tony Hertz, vineyard: Fabian Gonzales, Google HQ: Rodolfo Arpia, Magic Mountain: LHB Photo; S. 39 oben li.: North Wind Picture Archives, oben re.: ABN Stock Images, Mitte: Russ Bishop, unten li.: Pick and Mix Images, unten re.: Horizon International Images Limited; S. 42 re. (u. 108): Maximiliam Weinzierl; S. 47 Bild 4 (u. 110): Pick and Mix Images; S. 52 Bild A: Danita Delimont; S. 54: Richard G. Bingham II; S. 55 Bild A: Devinder Sangha, Bild B: dmac, Bild D: Red Foxx; S. 56: Bill Bachmann; S. 59 unten: Don Smetzer; S. 60 re. (u. 120): Chuck Eckert; S. 74 Bild B, Bild C: Andre Jenny, Bild D: PCL, Bild E: Digital Vision (RF), Bild F: Jim West, Bild G: Adrian Sherratt; S. 80 oben li.: North wind Picture Archives; S. 83 unten: Helene Rogers; S. 84: VStock (RF); S. 109 re.: Formcourt (Form Advertising) (RF); S. 114 oben li.: Picture Partners, oben Mitte: Oote Boe, oben re.: Adrian Sherratt, unten: Tony Roddam; S. 116 unten re.: Deco; S. 117 slave ship: The Print Collector, unten: North Wind Pictures Archives; S. 119 Mitte li.: Chris A Crumley; S. 120 oben re.: LOOK Die Bildagentur der Fotografen GmbH/Konrad Wothe; S. 121 Mitte: Gavin Gough; S. 122: Gail Mooney-Kelly; S. 128 observation room: Andre Jenny, park: Rich Iwasaki; S. 132 oben re.: Content Mine International, Mitte re.: Factoryhill, unten re: Pictorial Press; S. 133 oben li.: Pictorial Press, unten: Scott London, oben Mitte: Allstar Picture Library; **Animal Planet**, München (S. 78 Animal Planet logo); **Arteaga Photos** LTD., St. Louis (S. 129 Bild 1 u. 3); **Associated Press**, Frankfurt/Main (S. 35 Bild G: PAUL SAKUMA, S. 87 oben re., S. 88 Mitte li., S. 90: Danny Johnston, S. 124: Amy Sancetta); **Dave Briccetti**, Lafayette (S. 43 unten); **Bridgeman**, Berlin (S. 117 ships: Private Collection/ Look and Learn/ BridgemanArt. de); **Jan Burwick**, Hamburg (S. 125); **Cable News Network. A Time Warner Company**, Atlanta (S. 78 CNN logo); **CBS Broadcasting Inc.**, Los Angeles (S. 78 CBS logo: Use of logo from CBS Eye Logos - Courtesy of CBS Broadcasting Inc., Los Angeles); **Cinetext**, Frankfurt/Main (S. 47 Bild 3 (u. 110): Cinetext Bildarchiv; S. 45 Bild B (u. 74): Cinetext Bildarchiv; S. 83 oben (u. 115): 20th Century Fox); **The Coca-Cola Company**, Atlanta (S. 80 unten re.); **Corbis**, Düsseldorf (S. 7 (u. 140): Reuters/Jeff Topping; S. 18: Bettmann; S. 81 oben: Franz-Marc Frei; S. 87 Mitte li., unten li.: Bettmann; S. 88 oben re., Mitte unten: Bettmann; S. 123: Bo Bridges; S. 126 unten li.: Lloyd Cluff, unten re.: Grant Smith; S. 129 Bild 2, Bild 4: Bettmann; S. 135: Bettmann/William Horace Smith; S. 133 oben re.: Tim Mosenfelder, Mitte: Laura Levine); **Angel & Wilma Delgadillo's Route 66 Gift Shop & Visitor's Center**, Seligman (S. 10 license plate); **Denver Public Library**, Denver (S. 58 unten: Colorado Historical Society & Denver Art Museum); **FDNY/NYC & Company**, New York (S. 25 FDNY logos: All New York City logos and marks depicted herein are the property of the City of New York and may not be used without prior written consent); **First National Bank of Atlanta**, Atlanta (Inhaltsverz. (u. 80 (M)): Atlanta burning photo: Taken from "Atlanta Rusurgens". Written and published by the First National Bank of Atlanta. November 1971, Atlanta. Photo: Metro-Goldwyn-Mayer); **FOX Broadcasting Company**, Los Angeles (S. 78 FOX logo: FOX is the trademark of FOX Broadcasting Company and is used with permission of FOX Broadcasting Company); **Fricke Studio**, Hermann (Inhaltsverz. Jake (u. 10 oben); S. 52 Bild B, Bild D, Bild E; S. 53 Bild F, Bild G, Bild H; S. 55 oben li.; S. 57; 60 li. (u. 120); S. 61; S. 62); **Getty Images**, München (S. 6, S. 11 skywalk: David McNew; S. 8 oben: Richard Price, unten li.: Michael Clark; S. 15 unten: Aurora/Ian Shive; S. 21 firefighter (u.106): Getty Images News/Gilles Mingasson; S. 32: AFP/Stan Honda; S. 38: Getty Images News/ Chip Somodevilla; S. 41 oben li.: Photographer's Choice/Grant Faint; S. 43 oben: Justin Sullivan; S. 59 Mitte: The Bridgeman Art Library/Charles Marion Russell; S. 64: Justin Sullivan; S. 71: Image Source (RF); S. 74 Bild A Martin Luther King (M) (u. 81): Time & Life Pictures; S. 79 oben: München: Popperfoto/Rolls Press; S. 80 oben re.: Currier and Ives; S. 81 unten re.: WireImage; S. 87 oben li.: Hulton Archive/William Lovelace; S. 93 unten Martin Luther King (M): Hulton Archive/Agence France Presse; S. 120 li.: Mitchell Funk, unten re.: Mario Tama; S. 123: Peter Kramer; S. 126 oben: Cindy Karp; S. 132 oben li.: FPG, Mitte: Michael Ochs Archives); **www.Gleis4.de** (S. 65 unten); **Grand Canyon NP Museum Collection**, Grand Canyon (S. 21 ranger (u. 106)); **Howard Architectural Models, Inc.**, Toldedo (S. 121 oben li.); **iStockphoto**, Calgary (S. 45 Bild A: Greg Nicholas; S. 73 Bild 4, Bild 7: Sergia Kishan, Bild 8: Lisa Fletcher); **Chris Junker**, Portland (S. 129 Arch skin); **jupiterimages**, Ottobrunn/München (Inhaltsverz. Madison (u. 11, 82): Polka Dot Images (RF)); **Adam Kuban**, New York (S. 121 oben re.); **Elliot Larson**, Walnut Creek (S. 16 oben); **Major League Baseball Properties, Inc.** (S. 122 oben: Major League Baseball trademarks and copyrights are used with permission of Major League Baseball Properties, Inc.); **mauritius images**, Mittenwald (S. 11 mule train: Jeff O'Brien; S. 13 Bild G: age; S. 14 oben street (M): age); **MTV Networks Germany GmbH**, Berlin (S. 78 MTV logo); **National Park Service**, Washington (S. 9 unten li.); **Peter Newcomb Photography**, St. Louis (Inhaltsverz.: Hermann (u. 52); **The New York Public Library**, New York (S. 19 oben li.); **Barack Obama Office**, Washington D.C. (S. 79 unten re.); **Thomas Parker**, Vienna, Missouri, USA (S. 53 Bild F); **Photolibrary**, London (Atlanta (M) Inhaltsverz. (u. S. 81): Jon Arnold Travel/Walter Bibikow; **Picture-Alliance**, Frankfurt/Main (S. 9 unten: dpa/Jörg Schmitt; S. 10 unten re.: MAXPPP/Marianna Day Massey; S. 25 unten li.: dpa-Report/PA Magdalena Mayo; S. 47 Bild 6 (u. 110): dpa-Fotoreport/epa afp Scott Nelson; S. 74 Bild A (M) Outkast, Black Eyed Peas, Fergie: dpa; S. 80 unten li.: akg-images; S. 83 unten li. (u. 139): Sven Simon; S. 103 unten: HB-Verlag/Martin Sasse; S. 110 (u. 47): dpa-Fotoreport/epa afp Scott Nelson; S. 144: HB-Verlag/Martin Sasse); **Marion Schönenberger**, Berlin (Inhaltsverz. Teenagers (u. 95); S. 92–102); **Redferns**, London (S. 132 unten li.: Deltahaze Corporation); **Ohad Shahar/PhotoStock-Israel**: www.photographersdirect.com (S. 128 tram); **Shutterstock**, New York (Inhaltsverz. Statue of Liberty (M) (u. 12): gary718, homeless (M) (u. 34): Nikita Rogul, fire (M) (u. 80/81): David Lee; S. 10 book (M): Martina I. Meyer, T-shirt: R. Gino Santa Maria, bag: zolwiks, key ring: Tina Rencelj; S. 11 Bellagio: Andy Z.; S. 12 Bild C: Marcin Wasilewski; S. 13 Bild E: Sandy Maya Matzen; S. 14 Bild 5: emin kuliyev; S. 16 Mitte: Hannamariah, unten: Scott Rothstein; S. 23 unten Mitte: Bill Kennedy; S. 24 (u. 107): Vladimir Korostyshevskiy; S. 33 Bild 1: Ali Mazraie Shadi, Bild 2: erikdegraaf fotografie; Bild 3: Jason Kasumovic, Bild 5: Jostein Hauge, Bild 6: cardiae, Bild 8: Jostein Hauge; S. 34 Bild A sign (M): Michael Ledray, Bild D: Michal G Smith; S. 35 Bild E: Chee-Onn Leong; S. 36 strawberries: Norman Chan; S. 37: MANDYGIDBEHEAR; S. 40/41: Brandon Holmes; S. 40 oben: Albo; S. 41 oben li.: Rena Schild, Mitte: Byron W.Moore, unten li.: David Alexander Liu, Oscar: Oliver Johannes Uhrig; S. 46 Bild 1 notepad: luminouslens, pen: EuToch, Bild 2: amfoto, Bild 3 camera: terekhov igor, tripod: design56, Bild 4 costume: Margo Harrison, clipboard: Natalia Siverina, powder: Sean O. S. Barley, Bild 5: Bjorn Heller, Bild 6 teacher: Adam Borkowski, chalk: Kuzma, books: pixelman, Bild 7 duster: Mark Stout Photography, vacuum cleaner: angelo gilardelli, Bild 8 money: Morgan Lane Photography, gun: vadim kozlovsky; S. 42 li. (u. 108): ilker canikligil; S. 45 Bild D: stocksnapp, Bild C: Ivan Stevanovic; S. 55 Bild C: Michael Chamberlin; S 47 Bild 1 (u. 110): Feverpitched, Bild 2 (u. 110): Stas Volik; Bild 5 (u. 110): crystalfoto; S. 60 unten re.: ARTEKI, unten li.: Beth Van Trees; S. 63 steak: shadow216, pasta: Elena Elisseeva, muesli: Rohit Seth, apples: Marc Dietrich; S. 65 oben: Ron Hilton; S. 73 Bild 1: Maxim Petrichuk, Bild 2: Palto, Bild 3: Jose Marines; Bild 5: B. Speckart, Bild 6: Olga Chernetskaya, Bild 9: Glenda M. Powers; S. 74 screen: digitalife, Bild A bedroom (M): Rafa Irusta, frames: Mario Bruno, three girls: Karen Struthers, elderly couple: Monkey Business Images; S. 78 oben: Monkey Business Images; S. 82 unten li.: Kutlazev Dmitry, unten Mitte: Andryej Petelski, unten re.: Lee Torrens; S. 86 unten re. (u. 117): Condor 36; S. 93 oben re.: Remus; S. 103 oben: Ilja Mašik; S. 105: iofoto; S. 116 oben li.: Goxy, oben re.: Mario Bruno, unten li.: ifoto; S. 117 oben re.: Oralleff; S. 119 unten li.: Chee-Onn Leong, unten re.: Tomasz Szymanski); **Stone Hill Winery**, Hermann (S. 58 oben); **Topeka Room, Topeka & Shawnee County Public Library**, Topeka (S. 87 Mitte re.); **ullstein bild**, Berlin (S. 19 unten: Hohlfeld; S. 40 unten: Peter Arnold Inc.; S. 81 unten Mitte: dpa; S. 78 NBC logo: Keith (used by permission of NBC Universal, Inc., New York); S.117 trail of tears: Granger Collection; S. 118 oben, Mitte, unten: Granger Collection; S. 121 unten: CARO/ Muhs; S. 127: Still Pictures; S. 132 unten Mitte: Carl Van Vechten); **U.S. Department of the Interior, National Park Service** (S. 128/129 Gateway Arch (Artist: David Leech); S. 128 Gateway Arch triangle detail (Artist David Leech); S. 129 construction progress (Artist: David Leech))

## Titelbild

**Corbis**, Düsseldorf (yellow cab (M): image100 (RF), Times Square (M): Jose Fuste Raga);
**Corel Library**: (US Flag Hintergrund (M))

## Textquellen

S. 26–27: *You can tell me.* Adapted from "Kelly'n Me" by Myron Levoy. Published by iUniverse.com, Inc. Lincoln. All Rights Reserved © 1992, 2000 by Myron Levoy. Reprinted by arrangement with the author and Writers House LLC, acting as agent for the author; S. 66–67: *Angus Bethune's moment.* Adapted from „Telephone Man" from "Athletic Shorts" © 1989, 1991 by Chris Crutcher. Printed with permission from Greenwillow Books, an imprint of HarperCollins Publishers; S. 88–89: *Melba's story.* Adaptation based on an online interview with Melba Patillo Beals from Scholastic.com. Copyright © 1988 Scholastic Inc. Reprinted by Permission; S. 120: *The City* by David Ignatow. Reprinted with permission from the March 17, 1969 issue of "The Nation". For subscription information, call 1-800-333-8563. Portions of each week's Nation magazine can be accessed at http://www.thenation.com; S. 120: *Skyscraper* by Dennis Lee. From "Alligator Pie" (Macmillan of Canada, 1974; Key Porter Books, 2001). Copyright © 1974 Dennis Lee. With permission of the author; S. 120: *Subway rush hour* © 1994 by the Estate of Langston Hughes; S. 121: *To the visitor.* © 2003 Frank McCourt; S. 124: *Child labour on the US-Mexican border.* Abridged and adapted from "Illegal child labor in Mexico puts food on tables of Americans" by Chris Hawley. The Arizona Republic, May 9, 2008; S. 138: Auszug von S. 582 aus „English G 2000 Wörterbuch - Das Wörterbuch zum Lehrwerk". Herausgegeben von der Langenscheidt-Redaktion Wörterbücher und der Cornelsen-Redaktion Englisch. © 2002 Cornelsen Verlag GmbH & Co. OHG, Berlin und Langenscheidt KG, Berlin und München.

## Liedquellen

S. 17: *A heart in New York*: K+T: Gallagher, Benny/Lyle, Graham. © Good Single Ltd./Imagem Songs Ltd. Tj musicservice GmbH, Hamburg. Imagem Music GmbH, Hamburg; S. 121: *New York, New York*: K+T: Ebb, Fred. © by EMI Unart Catalog Inc. D/A/CH/Osteuropäische Länder: EMI Partnership Musikverlag GmbH, Hamburg

| Infinitive | Simple past form | Past participle | |
|---|---|---|---|
| (to) **be** | **was/were** | **been** | sein |
| (to) **beat** | **beat** | **beaten** | schlagen; besiegen |
| (to) **become** | **became** | **become** | werden |
| (to) **begin** | **began** | **begun** | beginnen, anfangen (mit) |
| (to) **bet** | **bet** | **bet** | wetten |
| (to) **break** a journey | **broke** | **broken** | eine Reise unterbrechen |
| (to) **bring** | **brought** | **brought** | (mit-, her)bringen |
| (to) **build** | **built** | **built** | bauen |
| (to) **buy** | **bought** | **bought** | kaufen |
| (to) **catch** | **caught** | **caught** | fangen; erwischen |
| (to) **choose** [uː] | **chose** [əʊ] | **chosen** [əʊ] | (aus)wählen; (sich) aussuchen |
| (to) **come** | **came** | **come** | kommen |
| (to) **cost** | **cost** | **cost** | kosten |
| (to) **cut** | **cut** | **cut** | schneiden |
| (to) **do** | **did** | **done** [ʌ] | tun, machen |
| (to) **draw** | **drew** | **drawn** | zeichnen |
| (to) **drink** | **drank** | **drunk** | trinken |
| (to) **drive** [aɪ] | **drove** | **driven** [ɪ] | *(ein Auto)* fahren |
| (to) **eat** | **ate** [et, eɪt] | **eaten** | essen |
| (to) **fall** | **fell** | **fallen** | (hin)fallen, stürzen |
| (to) **feed** | **fed** | **fed** | füttern |
| (to) **feel** | **felt** | **felt** | (sich) fühlen; sich anfühlen |
| (to) **fight** | **fought** | **fought** | kämpfen |
| (to) **find** | **found** | **found** | finden |
| (to) **fly** | **flew** | **flown** | fliegen |
| (to) **forget** | **forgot** | **forgotten** | vergessen |
| (to) **forgive** | **forgave** | **forgiven** | vergeben, verzeihen |
| (to) **get** | **got** | **got** | bekommen; holen; werden; (hin)kommen |
| (to) **give** | **gave** | **given** | geben |
| (to) **go** | **went** | **gone** [ɒ] | gehen, fahren |
| (to) **grow** | **grew** | **grown** | wachsen; anbauen, anpflanzen |
| (to) **hang out** *(infml)* | **hung out** | **hung out** | rumhängen, abhängen |
| (to) **have (have got)** | **had** | **had** | haben, besitzen |
| (to) **hear** [ɪə] | **heard** [ɜː] | **heard** [ɜː] | hören |
| (to) **hide** [aɪ] | **hid** [ɪ] | **hidden** [ɪ] | (sich) verstecken |
| (to) **hit** | **hit** | **hit** | schlagen |
| (to) **hold** | **held** | **held** | halten |
| (to) **hurt** | **hurt** | **hurt** | wehtun; verletzen |
| (to) **keep** | **kept** | **kept** | (be)halten |
| (to) **know** [nəʊ] | **knew** [njuː] | **known** [nəʊn] | wissen; kennen |
| (to) **lay** the table | **laid** | **laid** | den Tisch decken |

| Infinitive | Simple past form | Past participle | |
|---|---|---|---|
| (to) **leave** | **left** | **left** | (weg)gehen; abfahren; verlassen; zurücklassen |
| (to) **let** | **let** | **let** | lassen |
| (to) **lose** [uː] | **lost** [ɒ] | **lost** [ɒ] | verlieren |
| (to) **make** | **made** | **made** | machen; bauen; bilden |
| (to) **mean** [iː] | **meant** [e] | **meant** [e] | bedeuten; meinen |
| (to) **meet** | **met** | **met** | (sich) treffen |
| (to) **pay** | **paid** | **paid** | bezahlen |
| (to) **put** | **put** | **put** | legen, stellen, *(wohin)* tun |
| (to) **read** [iː] | **read** [e] | **read** [e] | lesen |
| (to) **ride** [aɪ] | **rode** | **ridden** [ɪ] | reiten; *(Rad)* fahren |
| (to) **ring** | **rang** | **rung** | klingeln, läuten |
| (to) **run** | **ran** | **run** | rennen, laufen |
| (to) **say** [eɪ] | **said** [e] | **said** [e] | sagen |
| (to) **see** | **saw** | **seen** | sehen; besuchen, aufsuchen |
| (to) **sell** | **sold** | **sold** | verkaufen |
| (to) **send** | **sent** | **sent** | schicken, senden |
| (to) **shine** | **shone** [ɒ] | **shone** [ɒ] | scheinen *(Sonne)* |
| (to) **shoot** [uː] | **shot** [ɒ] | **shot** [ɒ] | schießen, erschießen |
| (to) **show** | **showed** | **shown** | zeigen |
| (to) **shut up** | **shut** | **shut** | den Mund halten |
| (to) **sing** | **sang** | **sung** | singen |
| (to) **sit** | **sat** | **sat** | sitzen; sich setzen |
| (to) **sleep** | **slept** | **slept** | schlafen |
| (to) **speak** | **spoke** | **spoken** | sprechen |
| (to) **spend** | **spent** | **spent** | *(Zeit)* verbringen; *(Geld)* ausgeben |
| (to) **stand** | **stood** | **stood** | stehen; sich (hin)stellen |
| (to) **steal** | **stole** | **stolen** | stehlen |
| (to) **swim** | **swam** | **swum** | schwimmen |
| (to) **take** | **took** | **taken** | nehmen; (weg-, hin)bringen; dauern, *(Zeit)* brauchen |
| (to) **teach** | **taught** | **taught** | unterrichten, lehren |
| (to) **tell** | **told** | **told** | erzählen, berichten |
| (to) **think** | **thought** | **thought** | denken, glauben, meinen |
| (to) **throw** | **threw** | **thrown** | werfen |
| (to) **understand** | **understood** | **understood** | verstehen |
| (to) **upset** | **upset** | **upset** | ärgern, kränken, aus der Fassung bringen |
| (to) **wake** up | **woke** | **woken** | aufwachen; wecken |
| (to) **wear** [eə] | **wore** [ɔː] | **worn** [ɔː] | tragen *(Kleidung)* |
| (to) **win** | **won** [ʌ] | **won** [ʌ] | gewinnen |
| (to) **write** | **wrote** | **written** | schreiben |

# Classroom English

| Was *du* im Klassenzimmer sagen kannst | What *you* can say in the classroom |
|---|---|
| **Du brauchst Hilfe** | **You need help** |
| Können Sie mir bitte helfen? | **Can you help me, please?** |
| Auf welcher Seite sind wir, bitte? | **What page are we on, please?** |
| Was heißt ... auf Englisch/Deutsch? | **What's ... in English/German?** |
| Wie spricht man das erste Wort in Zeile 2 aus? | **How do you say the first word in line 2?** |
| Können Sie bitte ... buchstabieren? | **Can you spell ..., please?** |
| Können Sie es bitte an die Tafel schreiben? | **Can you write it on the board, please?** |
| Kann ich es auf Deutsch sagen? | **Can I say it in German?** |
| Können Sie/Kannst du bitte lauter sprechen? | **Can you speak louder, please?** |
| Können Sie/Kannst du das bitte noch mal sagen? | **Can you say that again, please?** |
| **Über Texte und Themen sprechen** | **Talking about texts and topics** |
| Ich finde die Geschichte ... | **I think the story is ...** |
| schön/interessant/langweilig/schrecklich/.... | **nice/interesting/boring/terrible/...** |
| Es war lustig/gruselig/langweilig/..., als ... | **It was funny/scary/boring/... when ...** |
| Ich fand es gut/nicht gut, als ... | **I liked it/didn't like it when ...** |
| Ich finde, Tom hat recht/nicht recht, weil ... | **I think Tom is right/wrong because ...** |
| Ich bin mir nicht sicher. Vielleicht ... | **I'm not sure. Maybe ...** |
| Was meinst du? | **What do you think?** |
| Ich stimme ... zu/nicht zu, weil ... | **I agree/disagree (with ...) because ...** |
| **Hausaufgaben und Übungen** | **Homework and exercises** |
| Tut mir leid, ich habe mein Schulheft nicht dabei, Herr ... | **Sorry, I haven't got my exercise book, Mr ...** |
| Ich habe meine Hausaufgaben vergessen, Frau ... | **I've forgotten my homework, Mrs/Ms/Miss ...** |
| Ich kann Nummer 3 nicht lösen. | **I can't do number 3.** |
| Entschuldigung, ich bin noch nicht fertig. | **Sorry, I haven't finished yet.** |
| Ich habe ... Ist das auch richtig? | **I've got ... Is that right too?** |
| Tut mir leid, das weiß ich nicht. | **Sorry, I don't know.** |
| Was haben wir (als Hausaufgabe) auf? | **What's for homework?** |
| **Bei der Partnerarbeit** | **Work with a partner** |
| Kann ich mit Julian arbeiten? | **Can I work with Julian?** |
| Wer ist dran? - Du bist dran. | **Whose turn is it? - It's your turn.** |
| Ich finde, wir sollten/könnten ... | **I think we should/could ...** |
| Was machen wir zuerst? | **What are we going to do first?** |
| **What your teacher says** | **Was dein/e Lehrer/in sagt** |
| **Open your books at page 24, please.** | Schlagt bitte Seite 24 auf. |
| **Look at the picture/line 8/... on page 24.** | Seht euch das Bild/Zeile 8/... auf Seite 24 an. |
| **Copy/Complete the chart/network/...** | Übertragt/Vervollständigt die Tabelle/das Wörternetz/... |
| **Correct the mistakes.** | Verbessert die Fehler. |
| **Take notes.** | Macht euch Notizen. |
| **Do exercise 3 for homework, please.** | Macht bitte Übung 3 als Hausaufgabe. |
| **Have you finished?** | Seid ihr fertig? / Bist du fertig? |
| **Switch off your mobile phones.** | Schaltet eure Handys aus. |
| **Walk around the class and ask other students.** | Geht durch die Klasse und fragt andere Schüler/innen. |
| **Discuss ... with ...** | Diskutiere/Diskutiert ... mit ... |
| **Give a presentation about ...** | Halte/Haltet einen Vortrag über ... |
| **Report to the class.** | Berichte/Berichtet der Klasse. |